Voting Rights in America

Voting Rights in America

Primary Documents in Context

Bridgett A. King, Editor

ABC-CLIO®

An Imprint of ABC-CLIO, LLC
Santa Barbara, California • Denver, Colorado

Library of Congress Cataloging-in-Publication Data

Names: King, Bridgett A., editor.
Title: Voting rights in America : primary documents in context / Bridgett A. King, editor.
Description: First edition. | Santa Barbara, California : ABC-CLIO, [2020] | Includes bibliographical references and index.
Identifiers: LCCN 2019026665 (print) | LCCN 2019026666 (ebook) | ISBN 9781440871542 (hardcover) | ISBN 9781440871559 (ebook)
Subjects: LCSH: Suffrage—United States—History—Sources.
Classification: LCC KF4891 .V68 2020 (print) | LCC KF4891 (ebook) | DDC 342.73/072—dc23
LC record available at https://lccn.loc.gov/2019026665
LC ebook record available at https://lccn.loc.gov/2019026666

ISBN: 978-1-4408-7154-2 (print)
978-1-4408-7155-9 (ebook)

24 23 22 21 20 1 2 3 4 5

This book is also available as an eBook.

ABC-CLIO
An Imprint of ABC-CLIO, LLC

ABC-CLIO, LLC
147 Castilian Drive
Santa Barbara, California 93117
www.abc-clio.com

This book is printed on acid-free paper ∞

Manufactured in the United States of America

Contents

CHAPTER 6 Open Partisan Warfare over Voting Rights: 2016 to Present

Introduction

> If there is one sacred feature of the American democracy, it is the right to vote.
>
> —*Twiley W. Barker Jr. and Lucious J. Barker (1987)*

Historically, the United States has excluded certain segments of the population from the voting process: women, racial and ethnic minorities, non-property owners, the poor, citizens with felony convictions, and members of certain faiths. Over the course of many decades, however, the franchise was extended to most of these groups, albeit only after years of struggle. As access expanded and the administrative structure surrounding the right to vote evolved, consideration was given to the procedures that structure voting and registration and how they might limit participation for groups, including the poor, racial and ethnic minorities, military, citizens who live overseas, the homeless, and those with disabilities. For each of these groups, securing the right to vote was won through the collective action of citizen groups who often turned to the Federal Courts and Congress to secure voting rights. Although great strides have been made, and we often think of the fight for the right to vote as a settled part of history in the United States, controversies, challenges, and barriers still remain to ensure that all eligible citizens have access to the franchise and are able to vote freely and fairly.

At the founding of the nation, the founding fathers were very much aware of the power of the vote and the way it could be used by citizens to shape governance. The decision to exclude certain groups—notably people of African descent (both free and slave), women, and the poor—from the franchise was rooted in the idea that there should be requisite qualifications for voting. Many of these stipulations were established by the colonies and through British tradition. Although there were those who believed that by founding the new nation there was an opportunity to create a more inclusive republic that did not limit voting to white men who owned property, arguments for the exclusion of blacks, women, and the poor persisted. In a 1776 correspondence with James Sullivan, John Adams (who would go on to become the nation's second president) explained his reasons for supporting the exclusion of women and the poor for the franchise:

> It is certain in Theory, that the only moral Foundation of Government is the Consent of the People. But to what an Extent Shall We carry this Principle? Shall We Say, that every Individual of the Community, old and young, male and female, as well as rich and poor, must consent, expressly to every Act of Legislation? No, you

> will Say. This is impossible. How then does the Right arise in the Majority to govern the Minority, against their Will? Whence arises the Right of the Men to govern Women, without their Consent? Whence the Right of the old to bind the Young, without theirs . . .
>
> But why exclude Women? You will Say, because their Delicacy renders them unfit for Practice and Experience, in the great Business of Life, and the hardy Enterprizes of War, as well as the arduous Cares of State. Besides, their attention is So much engaged with the necessary Nurture of their Children, that Nature has made them fittest for domestic Cares. And Children have not Judgment or Will of their own . . .
>
> Depend upon it, sir, it is dangerous to open So fruitfull a Source of Controversy and Altercation, as would be opened by attempting to alter the Qualifications of Voters. There will be no End of it. New Claims will arise. Women will demand a Vote. Lads from 12 to 21 will think their Rights not enough attended to, and every Man, who has not a Farthing, will demand an equal Voice with any other in all Acts of State. (Letter to James Sullivan from John Adams, 1776)

At the ratification of the Constitution, the founders left the right to establish the time, place, and manner of holding elections to the states. This decision laid the foundation for a political landscape where the right to vote and the way that citizens exercise the right to vote varies state by state across the United States.

As an example, as the country expanded westward, states that were applying for admission to the Union established voting rights for women. Before the Nineteenth Amendment was passed in 1920, women had full suffrage rights in twenty states, partial suffrage rights in nine states, and the right to vote in school elections in five states. Women had no suffrage rights in Alabama, Georgia, Maryland, North Carolina, South Carolina, Virginia, and West Virginia.

Although black Americans were granted citizenship by the Fourteenth Amendment in 1868, and the Fifteenth Amendment (adopted two years later) prohibits denying the right to vote on the basis of race or previous condition of servitude, it would be almost one hundred years after those two amendments were ratified before African Americans had a guarantee to the right to vote that could not be infringed upon by the administrative procedures created by the states. Following the ratification of the above-mentioned "Reconstruction amendments," several states, most notably those in the South, began to adopt and implement policies (poll taxes, literacy tests, grandfather clauses, etc.) with the express intention of limiting the suffrage rights of black Americans.

In 1965, Dr. Martin Luther King Jr., one of the most prominent figures in the American civil rights movement, asserted,

> If Negroes could vote . . . there would be no more oppressive poverty directed against Negroes. Our children would not be crippled by segregated schools, and the whole community might live together in harmony.

Dr. King, like the founding fathers before him, recognized the power of the right to vote. King recognized and believed that access to the ballot box was a fundamental tool that could be used to alleviate many of the injustices and disparities that blacks had endured for so long. And although his assertion that those discriminatory injustices would disappear altogether with the power of enfranchisement proved overly optimistic, increased voting by black citizens and participation in government has helped reduce these problems in American society.

At the time the Voting Rights Act (VRA) was passed in 1965, there were large registration gaps between black and white Americans. The gap was more than 60 percent in Mississippi, 50 percent in South Carolina, and almost 50 percent in both Alabama and Louisiana. A little more than two decades after the passage of the VRA, the gap in most states had dropped to less than 10 percent, and in Louisiana the state had a higher percentage of registered black voters (77.1%) than white voters (75.1%).

The use of poll taxes was not exclusive to the southern states. Many states adopted poll taxes as a way to generate revenue, including California, Connecticut, Maine, Texas, and Ohio. The consequence of such action, however, was that citizens who were poor were unable to participate, a consequence that disproportionally affected racial/ethnic minorities. Some states outside of the South, like Massachusetts, also required voters to demonstrate that they could read or pass a literacy test prior to being eligible to vote. The Voting Rights Act (1965), coupled with federal legislation, and decisions by the Supreme Court of the United States nullified the use of these and other practices as qualifications to vote. The actions of the federal government also provided for the expansion of voting rights in the twentieth century to include American Indians; Asian Americans; and other racial, ethnic, and religious groups.

In addition to the participatory challenges that citizens faced in the United States, citizens who were deployed or living abroad faced hurdles when trying to exercise the right to vote. While today we consider absentee voting to be a standard feature of the election landscape in the United States, the ability of citizens to vote absentee was borne out of necessity as the United States was engaged in wars, both domestic and international, that required citizens to be away from their permanent residences for extended periods of time.

During the election of 1864, which occurred during the bloody final months of the Civil War, voting rights for soldiers were expanded in many states with the express purpose of providing soldiers with an avenue for voting to ensure Lincoln's re-election (Martin, 1945). Eleven of the twenty-five Union states passed bills with the purpose of allowing soldiers to vote through the creation of a state commission that would gather votes in the field or for absentee voting, and a few states allowed soldiers to vote by proxy. In three states, provisions for soldier voting were defeated. Although it is unclear if the soldier vote had a substantial effect on the outcome of the election, Lincoln won 77.5 percent of the soldier votes cast (Martin, 1945). Although there were efforts in Congress to create a federal agency that would oversee the soldier and sailor vote and to permit military personnel to vote for president, vice president, and other offices while deployed, neither was adopted. By the early 1900s, soldiers who cast ballots did so primarily through state provisions that allowed absentee voting for certain military personnel, as there was no federal organization or agency tasked with ensuring military personnel could vote. Prior to federal intervention, the enfranchisement status of military personnel, like those of other groups in the history of the United States, was dependent upon individual state laws.

Federal laws were also adopted during the second half of the twentieth century to ensure that citizens with disabilities are able to participate in democratic governance. In spite of these provisions, access challenges still remain, not only as they relate to the physical accessibility of polling places but also in terms of access to digital information and voting services and ensuring that voters with disabilities are able to vote freely and independently. As election offices have increasingly come to rely on technology to improve election administration processes and identify new ways to better serve all voters, ensuring these innovations are accessible for citizens with disabilities remains a priority for disability advocates and election administrators alike.

In recent years, laws limiting voting rights for citizens with felony convictions have come under scrutiny, as the population of prisons in the United States has continued to grow, and awareness has risen of the disproportionate effect of felony disenfranchisement on racial and ethnic minorities, most notably African Americans (Wacquant, 2010). Estimates by the Sentencing Project suggest that one in thirteen African Americans of voting age is disenfranchised, a rate more than four times greater than that of non-African Americans, and over 7.4 percent of the adult African American population is disenfranchised compared to 1.8 percent of the non-African American population (Uggen, Larson, and Shannon, 2016).

Comparatively, the United States is the only democratic country that systematically disenfranchises large numbers of non-incarcerated citizens with felony convictions (those on probation or parole) (Ewald, 2004; Manza and Uggen, 2004). In France, for example, courts can impose restrictions on voting rights, but these restrictions are a part of the original sentence and do not apply to ex-felons. In Germany, courts have the power to remove voting rights for up to five years after the completion of a sentence (Manza and Uggen, 2004). However, the use of this sanction is very rare (Demleitner, 2000). Additionally, the German legal system not only allows incarcerated felons to vote but also requires that officials assist with and encourage the voter participation of the incarcerated (Fellner and Mauer, 1998).

Similar to other groups, arguments for excluding citizens with felony convictions from the right to vote rest on notions of requisite qualifications for participation—and concerns expressed by opponents that those with felony convictions may use the franchise to corrupt existing institutions. In 1967, in *Green v. Board of Elections*, Circuit Judge Henry Friendly wrote,

> It can scarcely be deemed unreasonable for a state to decide that perpetrators of serious crimes shall not take part in electing the legislators who make the laws, the executives who enforce these, the prosecutors who must try them for future violations, or the judges who are to consider their cases. This is especially so when account is taken for the heavy incidence of recidivism and the prevalence of organized crime. A contention that the equal protection clause requires New York to allow convicted mafiosi to vote for district attorney or judges would not only be without merit but as obviously so many things can be. (*Green v. Board of Elections,* 380, F. 2d 445 (2nd ca. 1976))

Others, however, asserted that citizens with felony convictions who had completed their sentences deserved to have their voting rights restored. As Thurgood Marshall stated in his dissent of *Richardson v. Ramirez* (418 U.S. at 78),

> [Citizens with felony convictions] are persons who have fully paid their debt to society. They are as much affected by the actions of government as any other citizen, and have as much of a right to participate in governmental decision-making. The denial of a right to vote to such persons is a hindrance to the efforts of society to rehabilitate former felons and convert them into law-abiding and productive citizens.

Although voting rights were expanded to include those aged eighteen to twenty in the 1960s, concerns remain about the engagement of young voters. One scholar suggests that the best place to challenge the nonparticipation of the young is in high school. He finds that in high schools,

> Most students leave school without registering to vote or obtaining even rudimentary information about how to vote in their community and the powers of the range of offices they can elect; those who do get registered tend to reflect the socioeconomic advantages of their parents . . . Most [registration and voting] efforts toward young eligible voters are targeted at college students, which skews the electorate toward better-educated and wealthier citizens. Young people who are not in college, who are of color, or who live in a rural area are often ignored. (Richie, 2007, 41)

Although school-based interventions have been shown to effectively develop civic responsibility, many education experts believe that civic education in the United States has been on the decline for more than thirty years.

During the 1996 meeting of the American Political Science Association, scholar Elinor Ostrom pointed out the need to address "deep concerns about the viability of democracy in America . . . [and the] decline in civic engagement, political efficacy, and in the capacity of citizens to organize themselves" (quoted in Dudley and Gitelson, 2002). Although Ostrom was primarily focused on citizen participation, the viability of democracy in recent elections has been challenged by administrative irregularities, questions about voting and registration procedures, claims of voter fraud and international interference. Citizen perceptions about election integrity and outcome accuracy have emerged as new challenges at the forefront of elections and election administration. As noted by scholar Jordan Stringer (2008),

> A political system should not confuse its ability to conduct elections with politically legitimate authority. Rather, a legitimate political institution must also be able to meet the reasonable expectations of diverse constituents who consent to the institution's authority. Legitimacy thus requires the government communicates election laws and procedures to its stakeholders and apply them consistently across different voting precincts.
>
> In other words, the voting system becomes corrupted not only when the laws are repeatedly broken but also when voters *perceive* that they are being victimized by a voting system that is vulnerable to coercive and discriminatory effects.

In order for democracy to survive, citizens must participate, trust the system, and accept the outcomes of elections. Democracy not only encompasses the idea of each individual citizen having the right to vote but also having the opportunity, the knowledge, and the skill to effectively use that right to ensure that political outcomes best reflect the preferences of the electorate. Scholar Costas Panagopoulos also suggests that "after universal suffrage, the next aim for democracy must be universal or near-universal use of the right to vote" (Panagopoulos, 2008, 11). As it stands, democracy in the United States is far from encompassing these ideals; however, if as a nation we the people truly value voting as one of our most sacred rights, our ultimate goals should include guaranteeing access to the franchise for all citizens and providing them with the educational foundation necessary to effectively utilize their vote.

Political participation in the United States has been contested since the founding of the nation. Over time, access to the franchise has gone through distinct periods of expansion and contraction. While we often center the expansion of the voting rights around African Americans, women, and individuals aged eighteen to twenty, many of the nuances of the history of voting in the United States—and controversies, claims, and counterclaims about voting suppression, voter fraud, and political representation that have dominated headlines during the Obama and Trump years—have been lost, inadequately understood, or twisted for partisan benefit. What follows is a collection of primary documents that speak to the political, administrative, and social environment surrounding voting and elections over six distinct time periods in the United States. The benefit of studying these resources is that it allows the reader to put their hands on the documents and consider the motivation and perspective of the author(s) first hand, and the context in which those documents—which range from political speeches to Supreme Court decisions to passages from some of the country's most famous champions of expanding the franchise—were created. Taken together, they provide essential and illuminating insights into the history of voting rights in the United States of America.

SOURCES

Barker Jr., Twiley W., and Lucious Barker. (1987). "The Courts, Section 5 of the Voting Rights Act, and the Future of Black Politics." In M. B. Preston, L. J. Henderson, and P. L. Puryear (Eds.), *The New Black Politics: The Search for Political Power.* 2nd ed. White Plains, NY: Longman, pp. 59–75.

Carnegie Corporation of New York and CIRCLE: The Center for Information and Research on Civic Learning and Engagement. (2003). "The Civic Mission of Schools." Retrieved from http://www.civicmissionofschools.org/site/campaign/documents/CivicMissionofSchools.pdf.

Demleitner, Nora. (2000). "Continuing Payment on One's Debt to Society: The German Model of Felon Disenfranchisement as an Alternative." *Minnesota Law Review, 84* (4), 753–804.

Dudley, Robert, and Alan Gitelson. (2002). "Political Literacy, Civic Education and Civic Engagement: A Return to Political Socialization?" *Applied Developmental Science, 6*, 175–182.

Ewald, Alec C. (2004). "An 'Agenda for the Demolition': The Fallacy of and the Danger of the Subversive Voting' Argument for Felony Disenfranchisement." *Columbia Human Rights Law Review, 36*, 109–143.

Fellner, Jamie, and Marc Mauer. (1998). "Losing the Vote: The Impact of Felony Disenfranchisement Laws in the United States." Retrieved from https://www.sentencingproject.org/wp-content/uploads/2016/01/Losing-the-Vote-The-Impact-of-Felony-Disenfranchisement-Laws-in-the-United-States.pdf.

Galston, William A. (2004). "Civic Education and Political Participation." *PS: Political Science and Politics, 37*, 263–266.

Harvard Law Review. (2007). "Notes: The Case for Compulsory Voting in the United States." *Harvard Law Review, 121* (2), 591–612.

Manza, Jeff, and Christopher Uggen. (2004). "Punishment and Democracy: Disenfranchisement of Nonincarcerated Felons in the United States." *Perspectives on Politics, 2* (3), 491–505.

Martin, Boyd A. (1945). "American Government and Politics: The Service Vote in the Elections of 1944." *American Political Science Review, 39*, 720–732.

Panagopoulos, Costas. (2008). "The Calculus of Compulsory Voting Systems." *Political Behavior, 30*, 455–467.

Rhine, Staci. (1995). "Registration Reform and Turnout Change in the American States." *American Politics Quarterly, 23* (4), 409–426.

Richie, Rob. (2007). Leave No Voter Behind: Seeking 100 Percent Voter Registration and Effective Civic Education. *National Civic Review*, Fall, 39–45.

Sherrod, Lonnie, Constance Flanagan, and James Youniss. (2002). "Dimensions of Citizenship and Opportunities of Youth Development: The What, Why, When, Where and Who of Citizenship Development." *Applied Developmental Science, 6*, 264–272.

Stringer, Jordon. (2008). "Criminalizing Voter Suppression: The Necessity of Restoring Legitimacy in Federal Elections and Reversing Disillusionment in Minority Communities." *Emory Law Review, 57* (4), 1011–1048.

Timeline and Map of Woman Suffrage Legislation State by State 1838–1919. University of Washington. Retrieved from http://depts.washington.edu/moves/WomanSuffrage_map.shtml.

Uggen, Christopher, Ryan Larson, and Sarah Shannon. (2016, October 6). "6 Million Lost Voters: State-level Estimates of Felony Disenfranchisement." Retrieved from https://www.sentencingproject.org/publications/6-million-lost-voters-state-level-estimates-felony-disenfranchisement-2016/.

Wacquant, Loc. (2010). "Class, Race & Hyperincarceration in Revanchist America." *Daedalus, 139* (3), 74–90.

1

On the Outside of the Voting Booth Looking In: Early America to 1850

As the United States formed a union and began to expand geographically, policies were needed to determine how those who lived in the new areas would be integrated into American political, cultural, and social life. For these groups, achieving integration would be hard fought through collective action and require acts on the part of Congress, the Supreme Court, and state legislatures.

When we think about the right to vote in the United States, we often begin with the generalization that all white men who owned property were able to vote and all others were excluded. In reality, however, the right to vote—or exclusion from the right to vote—was much more nuanced in the nation's formative years. In addition to race, gender, and socioeconomic status, exclusion from the franchise also extended to certain ethnic groups and individuals who were affiliated with various religious faiths. These exclusions were not consistent across the colonies and territories that would eventually become states. Before the ratification of the constitution, territories used their charters to determine who had rights and what those rights would be. They included not only voting but also who was eligible to serve on juries, run for office, and so on. Once the federal constitution was ratified in 1788, the federalist structure of the United States provided the states that were formerly colonies or territories with the authority to make determinations regarding who was eligible to vote and how they voted. Most explicitly, the Tenth Amendment of the constitution provides states with the authority to make rules that were not explicitly identified in the constitution as being under the sole authority of the federal government.

VOTING REGULATIONS IN COLONIAL CHARTERS

As an example of the way charters were utilized to determine who had the authority to vote, the Massachusetts Bay Company Charter (1629) and the Orders of Connecticut (1639) stated that the right to vote was explicitly for puritans (or puritan men in the case of the Orders of Connecticut). Led by John Winthrop, the

Massachusetts Bay Colony was founded by Puritans in 1628 under the conditions of the Massachusetts Bay Company charter. According to the charter, only freedmen (or stockholders) were permitted to vote. As they desired to create a more formal government, the approximately twelve individuals who arrived in the colony during the first voyage elected a governor, deputy governor, and seven assistants to enact the colony's laws. Those who were elected as assistants also served as the colony's judges and highest court of appeals. The nine elected officers, who were also stakeholders in the company, essentially became the colony's government, known as the General Court. During the first meeting of the General Court, the officers expanded the number of eligible voters by declaring all white men who were present to be freemen. In subsequent meetings of the court, adult males were invited to apply for "freemanship." When the court met the following year, there were more than one hundred men who took the oath to become freemen. These individuals were subsequently eligible to vote. As the franchise expanded, the court voted to pass a law limiting future freedmanship and restricting the right to vote to members of the Congregational (Puritan) Church. These restrictions were imposed to guarantee a more "godly" government. While ineligible to vote, individuals who were not members of the church could petition the government and participate in town meetings. After 1647, they were also eligible to vote for town officers but remained ineligible to vote for members of the General Court. The inclusion of puritans and exclusion of others is just one of many examples in colonial America of decisions made to exclude individuals because it was believed that certain individuals did not have the requisite qualifications to fully participate in governance.

In 1776, the colonies entered into open rebellion against the British Crown after years of escalating tensions. That year, the Declaration of Independence was adopted by the Second Continental Congress and the American Revolution began. In the midst of the war, a variety of perspectives emerged relative to what representation should look like. While many advocated for a strong central government that used qualifications to insulate elected officials from the tyranny of the majority, others advocated for a government that allowed individuals to more freely govern themselves. Harry Cushing was one such voice. In a pamphlet titled *The People the Best Governors,* Cushing advocated for a single legislative body and argued that citizens should have the right to vote or hold office and govern without qualification. He also advocated for a delegate form of government in which the role of the executive branch was to carry out the will of the people. For him, the ideal government was one in which the people determined their taxes, assembled the local militia, operated their churches and schools, and regulated the local economy in town meetings. For Cushing, the role of the central government was one of coordination. The ideals of Cushing, similar to those of John Adams, were later prevalent and integrated into the constitutions of many commonwealths and states that were later admitted into the union.

VOTING IN A NEW NATION

Following the American Revolution, the nation was governed under the Articles of Confederation. While the articles addressed the relationship between the central government and the states, they did not address the admission of new states. Before the Northwest Ordinance, there was considerable conflict about ownership of the land west of the Appalachians to the Mississippi River (known as the Old Northwest). Seven of the states argued that their boundaries should be expanded to include the new land. The other six states, however, believed that expanding the boundaries would throw off the balance of power and importance among the states. As a resolution, Jefferson put forth a plan (the Northwest Ordinance of 1784) that would divide the new territory into ten states that would be admitted to the union with the same status of the other states already in existence. The ordinance also included a provision that would ban slavery. Although the ordinance passed, the ban on slavery failed. There were no states admitted under the 1784 ordinance, and, in 1787, the Confederation Congress again addressed the Northwest Territory. Using Jefferson's plan, the Congress chartered a government for the Northwest. The Northwest Ordinance of 1787 not only addressed the admission of new states but also established the foundation for their governance and suffrage rights. The ordinance required the territory to be divided into at least three but no more than five states, laid out the three-stage admission process, provided suffrage rights for any man who owned fifty acres of property, and forbade slavery and involuntary servitude in the territory, making the Ohio River a natural geographic dividing line between the slave and free states.

As suffrage rights and the rules for participating in government were expanded for citizens in the newly admitted states following the passage of the Northwest Ordinance, federal law was passed to define and limit what it meant to be a citizen of the United States. The Naturalization Act of 1790 was the first piece of legislation that codified naturalization law. The Naturalization Act of 1790 defined the criteria for naturalization to include two years of residency, proof of good moral character, and an oath to the Constitution. To ensure that the United States would be a nation separate and apart from Great Britain, one of the requirements for naturalization was for individuals to "absolutely and entirely renounce and abjure all allegiance and fidelity to every foreign Prince, Potentate, State or Sovereignty." Although the Naturalization Act extended citizenship to all children of citizens, it limited the population of individuals who could naturalize to "any alien, being a free white person." This effectively limited the ability of indentured servants, slaves, and some women to become naturalized citizens. The statute, however, said nothing about the citizenship status of nonwhite individuals who were born in the United States.

As the Naturalization Act of 1790 underscored, women were regularly excluded from access to the full rights of suffrage. Many writings by the women of the era conveyed the marks of their social, economic, and cultural subordination. One such writing is *The Female Advocate*. Although published anonymously or more specifically by "Written by a Lady," it is often attributed to British feminist Mary Anne Radcliffe. In the piece, the author asserts that men who fill women's occupations limit their job prospects and make it hard for them to earn a living.

Just as women were not afforded the full rights of citizenship and participation in American life or government, exclusions also continued for individuals who professed non-Protestant faiths. The exclusion of those who professed the Jewish faith in Maryland is one such example. The immigration pattern of Jews in Maryland was not a single influx, as had been the case in other places. To the contrary, the immigration of Jews to Maryland is perhaps best likened to a slow and steady stream of individuals who resolved to engage in a quiet exercise of their faith, rather than an open profession, in their new homeland. As a Crown Colony, Maryland associated citizenship with membership in the Protestant church, a state of affairs that broadly disenfranchised Jews. Although the charter of Annapolis and some other cities and towns provided for the suffrage rights of anyone possessing a freehold or an estate worth a certain amount, Jews were still prohibited from holding office. Potential officeholders were also required to take the oath of abjuration, which included the words, "upon the true Christian faith." Beyond this, the profession of faith in Judaism was deemed by Maryland lawmakers to be an offense punishable by death. In 1723, Maryland adopted an act to punish blasphemers, swearers, and drunkards and Sabbath breakers that included the following passage: "If any person shall hereafter within this province . . . deny our Saviour Jesus Christ to be the Son of God, or shall deny the Holy Trinity," he shall for the first offense be fined and have his tongue bored; for the second, have his head burned; for the third, be put to death.

Given this deep intolerance for anyone who did not adhere to Christian dogma, it is little wonder that the Jewish community struggled to get the legislature to allow Jews to hold office following the adoption of the Maryland Constitution in 1776. In 1825—a full half century after Maryland passed its first constitution—the legislature finally passed "an Act to extend to the sect of people professing the Jewish religion, the same rights and privileges enjoyed by Christians." With the passage of the act, members of the Jewish faith were required to swear on "the doctrine of reward and punishment" rather than profess a belief in Christianity in order to secure the aforementioned rights and privileges. Maryland was the last state in the United States to remove a prohibition on Jews holding office.

EXPANDED VOTING RIGHTS CONTINUE TO EXCLUDE WOMEN

Women also organized to fight for their social, civil, and religious rights during the first half of the nineteenth century. The Seneca Falls Convention, held in 1848, was the first convention for women's rights and for many marked the launch of the first wave of feminism in the United States. The convention began with a speech by Elizabeth Cady Stanton during which she asserted the goals and purpose of the convention: "to protest against a form of government, existing without the consent of the governed—to declare our right to be free as man is free."

The nation continued to expand west and acquire new territory as it had with the Northwest Ordinance. The Treaty of Guadalupe Hidalgo was signed by the United States and Mexico in February 1848. The treaty ended the Mexican-American War and expanded the boundaries of the United States by over 525,000 square miles and included what would eventually become California, Texas, Nevada, Utah, most of New Mexico and Arizona, and parts of Colorado and

Wyoming. The treaty provided a path to citizenship for Mexicans who remained in the newly acquired territory but required them to choose if they wanted to remain Mexican citizens or become citizens of the United States within a year. Those who chose United States citizenship were guaranteed the full rights of citizenship including "free enjoyment of their liberty and property, and secured free exercise of their religion without restriction." Constitutions ratified in newly minted western states like California, meanwhile, did away with property ownership requirements and other wealth-related provisions that had kept poor voters from exercising the franchise. However, even in these states, English-language requirements and violent intimidation by whites in some communities against citizens of Mexican descent limited access to voting rights.

SOURCES

Alder, Cyrus, and J. H. Hollander. "Maryland." Jewish Encyclopedia. Accessed January 20, 2019. http://www.jewishencyclopedia.com/articles/10455-maryland.

American Jewish Historical Society. "Publications of the American Jewish Historical Society." Papers presented at the First Scientific Meeting, Held at Philadelphia, December 15, 1892.

Constitutional Rights Foundation. "Bill of Rights in Action: Puritan Massachusetts: Theocracy or Democracy?" Last modified fall 2013. http://www.crf-usa.org/images/pdf/gates/puritans-of-mass.pdf.

Eitches, Edward. "Maryland's 'Jew Bill.'" *American Jewish Historical Quarterly*, 60, no. 1–4 (1971): 258–278.

Gibbs, Samantha. "'All this seemed vastly like a novel!': Writing the Life of Mary Anne Radcliffe in *The Fate of Velina de Guidova* and *Manfroné; or, the One-Handed Monk.*" Corvey Project at Sheffield Hallman University. Accessed January 26, 2019. https://extra.shu.ac.uk/corvey/corinne/essay%20gibbs.html#.

Imai, Shiho. "Naturalization Act of 1790." Densho Encyclopedia. Accessed January 15, 2019. http://encyclopedia.densho.org/Naturalization_Act_of_1790/#cite_note-ftnt_ref2-2.

"Massachusetts Facts." Accessed January 26, 2019. http://www.sec.state.ma.us/cis/cismaf/mf2.htm#introduction.

"Northwest Ordinance 1787." Accessed January 2, 2019. https://www.ourdocuments.gov/doc.php?flash=false&doc=8.

Oliver, Pamela. "What the Treaty of Guadalupe Hidalgo Actually Says." *Race, Politics, and Justice* (blog). July 12, 2017. https://www.ssc.wisc.edu/soc/racepoliticsjustice/2017/07/12/what-the-treaty-of-guadalupe-actually-says/.

PRIMARY DOCUMENTS

Fundamental Orders of Connecticut, 1639

As the first English colonies sprouted across the Atlantic seaboard in the early seventeenth century, one of their first orders of business was to establish and implement rules of government, including the process by which officials and administrators would be selected. The election rules that were established in these early settlements varied from colony to colony in different respects, but all limited voting rights—and eligibility for office—to various classes of freemen. One of the earliest such documents of this type, the Fundamental Orders of Connecticut, *was adopted by the Connecticut Colony Council on January 14, 1639. Among other things, it established voting eligibility requirements pertaining to residency, limited the franchise to freemen, laid out procedures for filling the governor and magistrate positions, and emphasized that the colony's "civil affairs" should be guided by "the Gospel of our Lord Jesus."*

January 14, 1639

For as much as it hath pleased Almighty God by the wise disposition of his divine providence so to order and dispose of things that we the Inhabitants and Residents of Windsor, Hartford and Wethersfield are now cohabiting and dwelling in and upon the River of Connectecotte and the lands thereunto adjoining; and well knowing where a people are gathered together the word of God requires that to maintain the peace and union of such a people there should be an orderly and decent Government established according to God, to order and dispose of the affairs of the people at all seasons as occasion shall require; do therefore associate and conjoin ourselves to be as one Public State or Commonwealth; and do for ourselves and our successors and such as shall be adjoined to us at any time hereafter, enter into Combination and Confederation together, to maintain and preserve the liberty and purity of the Gospel of our Lord Jesus which we now profess, as also, the discipline of the Churches, which according to the truth of the said Gospel is now practiced amongst us; as also in our civil affairs to be guided and governed according to such Laws, Rules, Orders and Decrees as shall be made, ordered, and decreed as followeth:

1. It is Ordered, sentenced, and decreed, that there shall be yearly two General Assemblies or Courts, the one the second Thursday in April, the other the second Thursday in September following; the first shall be called the Court of Election, wherein shall be yearly chosen from time to time, so many Magistrates and other public Officers as shall be found requisite: Whereof one to be chosen Governor for the year ensuing and until another be chosen, and no other Magistrate to be chosen for more than one year: provided always there be six chosen besides the Governor, which being chosen and sworn according to an Oath recorded for that purpose, shall have the power to administer justice according to the Laws here established, and for want thereof, according to the Rule of the Word

of God; which choice shall be made by all that are admitted freemen and have taken the Oath of Fidelity, and do cohabit within this Jurisdiction having been admitted Inhabitants by the major part of the Town wherein they live or the major part of such as shall be then present.

2. It is Ordered, sentenced, and decreed, that the election of the aforesaid Magistrates shall be in this manner: every person present and qualified for choice shall bring in (to the person deputed to receive them) one single paper with the name of him written in it whom he desires to have Governor, and that he that hath the greatest number of papers shall be Governor for that year. And the rest of the Magistrates or public officers to be chosen in this manner: the Secretary for the time being shall first read the names of all that are to be put to choice and then shall severally nominate them distinctly, and every one that would have the person nominated to be chosen shall bring in one single paper written upon, and he that would not have him chosen shall bring in a blank; and every one that hath more written papers than blanks shall be a Magistrate for that year; which papers shall be received and told by one or more that shall be then chosen by the court and sworn to be faithful therein; but in case there should not be six chosen as aforesaid, besides the Governor, out of those which are nominated, than he or they which have the most writen papers shall be a Magistrate or Magistrates for the ensuing year, to make up the aforesaid number.
3. It is Ordered, sentenced, and decreed, that the Secretary shall not nominate any person, nor shall any person be chosen newly into the Magistracy which was not propounded in some General Court before, to be nominated the next election; and to that end it shall be lawful for each of the Towns aforesaid by their deputies to nominate any two whom they conceive fit to be put to election; and the Court may add so many more as they judge requisite. . . .

Source: Thorpe, Francis Newton. *The Federal and State Constitutions, Colonial Charters, and Other Organic Laws of the States, Territories, and Colonies Now or Heretofore Forming the United States of America.* Vol. 1. Washington, DC: Government Printing Office, 1909.

Pennsylvania Passes Legislation to "Regulate the Elections," 1700

In 1700, eighteen years after William Penn and other leaders formally passed the first working constitution for the colony, the general assembly passed a law laying out additional specifications for holding elections in Pennsylvania. This law, passed on November 27, laid out eligibility rules for voting that were similar in most general respects to those passed into law by other colonies in the same era. The statute specified that to qualify as a voter in Pennsylvania, men—and they were all men—had to be at least twenty-one years of age, be a native born or naturalized subject of the colony or of England, be a resident of the colony for at least two years, and pass certain property ownership stipulations.

An Act to Ascertain the Number of Members of Assembly and to Regulate the Elections

For the prevention of all dispute and uncertainty for the future, what persons shall be accounted freemen of this Province and Territories and have right of electing or being elected members of Assembly. Be it Enacted by the Proprietary and Governor and by and with the advice and consent of the freemen of this Province and Territories in General Assembly me and by the authority of the same . . .

And that no inhabitant of this Province and Territories shall have the right of electing or being elected as aforesaid unless he or they be natural or native born subject or subjects of England or be naturalized in England or in this Province and Territories and unless said person or persons as aforesaid be of the age of twenty-one years or upward and be a free-holder or free-holders of this Province or Territories and have fifty acres of land or more well seated and twelve acres thereof or more cleared and improved or be otherwise worth fifty pounds lawful money of this Government, clear estate and have been resident therein for the space of two years before said elections. And to the end that elections on which the good of the Government so much depends may not be corruptly managed or obtained. It is Enacted by the authority aforesaid that all elections of the said Representatives shall be free and voluntary and that the elector that shall receive any reward or gift for his vote shall forfeit his right of electing for that year and be fined in the sum of five pounds to the use of the Proprietary and Governor. And that all and every person and persons that shall give, offer or promise any reward to be elected or that shall offer to serve for nothing or less allowance than the law prescribes shall be fined in the like sum of five pounds for the use of aforesaid and be incapable of serving for that year and the Representatives so chosen as above directed shall yield their attendance accordingly and being in Assembly shall be the sole judges of the regularity or irregularity of the elections of the respective members according to this Act.

Source: Law 1700, Chapter 28. Amended to William Penn's Charter of Privileges, as passed by the Pennsylvania Assembly November 27, 1700. Pennsylvania Assembly. "An Act to Ascertain the Number of Members of Assembly and to Regulate the Elections." November 27, 1700.

The People the Best Governors, 1776

As colonial governments expanded and became more complex in response to growing populations, landholdings, and economic activity—and as dissatisfaction with living under the authority of the English Crown spread and intensified—American towns and cities were flooded with pamphlets, broadsides, and essays championing arguments about the best forms of independent government, the appropriate roles and responsibilities of officials, lawmakers, and magistrates, and the extent to which citizens should be able to choose the men to lead them. The following is an example of one such pamphlet. Published anonymously (as many works of its type were at the time), the author freely declares that he is a "friend to the popular government"—one in which lawmakers and administrators owe their place and authority to the people. The author (who some historians believe to have been a colonist named Harry Cushing) also emphasizes his conviction that holding public office should not be the exclusive province of the wealthy: "Let it not be said in future generations that money was made by the founders of the American states, an essential qualification in the rulers of a free people."

It seems there is another objection [to electing some public officials] started by some: That the common people are not under so good advantages to choose judges, sheriffs, and other executives as their representatives are. This is a mere delusion, which many have taken in, and, if I may be allowed a vulgar expression, the objectors in this instance put the cart before the horse. For they say, that the people have wisdom and knowledge enough to appoint proper persons through a state to make laws, but not to execute them. It is much easier to execute, than to make and regulate the system of laws, and upon this single consideration the force of the objection falls: The more simple, and the more immediate dependent . . . the authority is upon the people the better, because it must be granted that they themselves are the best guardians of their own liberties. . . .

We will next lay open the nature and right of jurisdiction more clearly, in examining the best standard, by which representation may be regulated. In the first place, it is asserted by some, that representation ought to be enlarged or diminished, in proportion to the amount of taxes in the different parts of a state; but such a procedure would be very unreasonable. For taxation only respects property without regard to the liberties of a person: And, if representation should be wholly limited by that, the man, who owns six times as much as another, would consequently have six times the power, through their natural right to freedom is the same; Nature itself abhors such a system of civil government, for it will make an inequality among the people, and set up a number of lords over the rest. . . .

That this short treatise may not be left imperfect, I will only propose, for the consideration of the people, a concise plan, founded on the principles that have been laid down.

It is observed then, in the first place, that the freemen of each incorporated town . . . shall choose by ballot, at an annual meeting, one person respectively, whom they shall think suitable to represent them in a general assembly.

2dly, That, if the metropolis, and some particular large places, may require an additional number of representatives, it may be granted them by the general assembly as the latter shall think proper.

3dly, That the general assembly should meet at certain times, twice every year; and, if the state is extensive, there may be two seats of government, in which case, the said assembly are to convene at them, once in their turns.

4thly, That the people choose annually by ballot in their town meetings, a council, consisting of twelve persons, through the government at large, whose business shall be to help in preparing matters for the consideration of the assembly, to assist them with their advice; And lastly, it shall be their duty to inquire into . . . the regulations of government, and to give the people reasonable notice, in a public way, with their opinion respecting the matter.

5thly, That they likewise choose annually a first executive officer, without any concern in the legislature; but it shall be his duty to transact such occasional business, as the assembly may devolve upon him; And that he be the general commander of the militia, and in these capacities the people, if they please, may style him a governor . . .

6thly, The said governor, with advice of any three of the council, may, at any time, call a special assembly on extraordinary business.

7thly, That the freemen vote annually, in their town meetings respectively, for the judges of the superior court, at large through the government.

8thly, That the judges of the inferior court, attorney's general, probate judges, registers, &c . be chosen, in manner before mentioned, by the inhabitants of each respective county: And, that the justices of the people be also chosen by the people of each respective town, in proportion to the representatives.

9th, That there be one general proxy day agreed upon for the people through the government, to vote for the officers as aforesaid and that the representatives, likewise, fix upon one day of election, to be annual at which time the votes are to be brought in from the different towns and examined; and the persons for governors, a council, judges, registers, sheriffs, &c. are to be then published through the state.

10thly, That all the resolves of every assembly be conveyed from time to time, by the representatives to each respective town, and there enrolled for the inhabitants to see, in order to instruct their said representatives.

11thly, That no person shall hold two public offices in a state, at the same time.

12thly, That no person shall be capable of holding any public office, except he professes a belief of one only invisible God, that governs all things; and that the bible is his revealed word; and that he be also an honest moral man. . . .

16thly, That any orderly free male of ordinary capacity, and more than 21 years of age, having resided one year in a town, may be a legal voters, during his continuance; but, if he should be absent afterwards steadily more than a year that he should be divested then, of the privilege of voting in said town as if he never had resided there: Provided, has not a real estate in the aforesaid town of at least one hundred pounds value lawful money.

17thly, That any legal voters shall be capable of holding any office, unless something that has been said to the contrary.

Source: Anonymous. *The People the Best Governors; Or a Plan of Government Founded on the Just Principles of Natural Freedom.* [Boston], 1776, pp. 6–7, 10–12.

The Northwest Ordinance, 1787

The 1787 legislation commonly known as the Northwest Ordinance—but officially called An Ordinance for the Government of the Territory of the United States, North-West of the River Ohio—established the framework by which a vast territory encompassing all or part of the later states of Illinois, Indiana, Michigan, Minnesota, Ohio, and Wisconsin would be governed. Since the region was established as a single federally controlled district rather than dispersed in parcels to existing states that were empowered to make their own voting rules, it fell on the U.S. Congress to establish voting rules and regulations within the territory. The following excerpt from the ordinance, however, shows that Congress did not stray too far from the general state model of that time in establishing voting guidelines and practices for the territory (the ordinance also established laws for the acquisition of land, eligibility rules to hold elected office, the process by which portions of the district could seek statehood, and numerous other matters). According to the terms of the ordinance, which was first passed by the Confederation Congress on July 13, 1787, then passed two years later by the first U.S. Congress, voting rights in the territory were limited to men who had previously been a citizen of an existing state in the confederation, had lived in the territory for at least two years, and owned at least fifty acres of property within the Northwest Territory boundaries. Following are excerpts from the ordinance pertaining to the establishment of a government (including selection of representatives to the general assembly) and eligibility for voting (Section 9).

Sec. 3. Be it ordained by the authority aforesaid, That there shall be appointed from time to time by Congress, a governor, whose commission shall continue in force for the term of three years, unless sooner revoked by Congress; he shall reside in the district, and have a freehold estate therein in 1,000 acres of land, while in the exercise of his office.

Sec. 4. There shall be appointed from time to time by Congress, a secretary, whose commission shall continue in force for four years unless sooner revoked; he shall reside in the district, and have a freehold estate therein in 500 acres of land, while in the exercise of his office. It shall be his duty to keep and preserve the acts and laws passed by the legislature, and the public records of the district, and the proceedings of the governor in his executive department, and transmit authentic copies of such acts and proceedings, every six months, to the Secretary of Congress: There shall also be appointed a court to consist of three judges, any two of whom to form a court, who shall have a common law jurisdiction, and reside in the district, and have each therein a freehold estate in 500 acres of land while in the exercise of their offices; and their commissions shall continue in force during good behavior.

Sec. 5. The governor and judges, or a majority of them, shall adopt and publish in the district such laws of the original States, criminal and civil, as may be necessary and best suited to the circumstances of the district, and report them to Congress from time to time: which laws shall be in force in the district until the organization of the General Assembly therein, unless disapproved of by Congress; but afterwards the Legislature shall have authority to alter them as they shall think fit.

Sec. 6. The governor, for the time being, shall be commander-in-chief of the militia, appoint and commission all officers in the same below the rank of general officers; all general officers shall be appointed and commissioned by Congress.

Sec. 7. Previous to the organization of the general assembly, the governor shall appoint such magistrates and other civil officers in each county or township, as he shall find necessary for the preservation of the peace and good order in the same: After the general assembly shall be organized, the powers and duties of the magistrates and other civil officers shall be regulated and defined by the said assembly; but all magistrates and other civil officers not herein otherwise directed, shall, during the continuance of this temporary government, be appointed by the governor.

Sec. 8. For the prevention of crimes and injuries, the laws to be adopted or made shall have force in all parts of the district, and for the execution of process, criminal and civil, the governor shall make proper divisions thereof; and he shall proceed from time to time as circumstances may require, to lay out the parts of the district in which the Indian titles shall have been extinguished, into counties and townships, subject however to such alterations as may thereafter be made by the legislature.

Sec. 9. So soon as there shall be five thousand free male inhabitants of full age in the district, upon giving proof thereof to the governor, they shall receive authority, with time and place, to elect representatives from their counties or townships to represent them in the general assembly: Provided, That, for every five hundred free male inhabitants, there shall be one representative, and so on progressively with the number of free male inhabitants shall the right of representation increase, until the number of representatives shall amount to twenty-five; after which, the number and proportion of representatives shall be regulated by the legislature: Provided, That no person be eligible or qualified to act as a representative unless he shall have been a citizen of one of the United States three years, and be a resident in the district, or unless he shall have resided in the district three years; and, in either case, shall likewise hold in his own right, in fee simple, two hundred acres of land within the same; Provided, also, That a freehold in fifty acres of land in the district, having been a citizen of one of the states, and being resident in the district, or the like freehold and two years residence in the district, shall be necessary to qualify a man as an elector of a representative.

Sec. 10. The representatives thus elected, shall serve for the term of two years; and, in case of the death of a representative, or removal from office, the governor shall issue a writ to the county or township for which he was a member, to elect another in his stead, to serve for the residue of the term.

Sec. 11. The general assembly or legislature shall consist of the governor, legislative council, and a house of representatives. The Legislative Council shall consist of five members, to continue in office five years, unless sooner removed by Congress; any three of whom to be a quorum: and the members of the Council shall be nominated and appointed in the following manner, to wit: As soon as representatives shall be elected, the Governor shall appoint a time and place for them to meet together; and, when met, they shall nominate ten persons, residents in the district, and each possessed of a freehold in five hundred acres of land, and return their names to Congress; five of whom Congress shall appoint and commission to serve as aforesaid; and, whenever a vacancy shall happen in the council, by death or removal from office, the house of representatives shall nominate two persons, qualified as aforesaid, for each vacancy, and return their names to Congress; one of whom congress shall appoint and commission for the residue of the term. And every five years, four months at least before the expiration of the time of service of the members of council, the said house shall nominate ten persons, qualified as aforesaid, and return their names to Congress; five of whom Congress shall appoint and commission to serve as members of the council five years, unless sooner removed. And the governor, legislative council, and house of representatives, shall have authority to make laws in all cases, for the good government of the district, not repugnant to the principles and articles in this ordinance established and declared. And all bills, having passed by a majority in the house, and by a majority in the council, shall be referred to the governor for his assent; but no bill, or legislative act whatever, shall be of any force without his assent. The governor shall have power to convene, prorogue, and dissolve the general assembly, when, in his opinion, it shall be expedient.

Sec. 12. The governor, judges, legislative council, secretary, and such other officers as Congress shall appoint in the district, shall take an oath or affirmation of fidelity and of office; the governor before the president of congress, and all other officers before the Governor. As soon as a legislature shall be formed in the district, the council and house assembled in one room, shall have authority, by joint ballot, to elect a delegate to Congress, who shall have a seat in Congress, with a right of debating but not voting during this temporary government.

Sec. 13. And, for extending the fundamental principles of civil and religious liberty, which form the basis whereon these republics, their laws and constitutions are erected; to fix and establish those principles as the basis of all laws, constitutions, and governments, which forever hereafter shall be formed in the said territory: to provide also for the establishment of States, and permanent government therein, and for their admission to a share in the federal councils on an equal footing with the original States, at as early periods as may be consistent with the general interest.

Source: U.S. Congress. *An Ordinance for the Government of the Territory of the United States, North-West of the River Ohio [The Northwest Ordinance].* 1787. In Thorpe, Francis Newton, ed. *The Federal and State Constitutions, Colonial Charters, and Other Organic Laws.* Washington, DC: Government Printing Office, 1909.

Federal Naturalization Laws, 1790 and 1795

On March 26, 1790, the U.S. Congress passed a landmark law that laid down the requirements for becoming a citizen of the young American nation—a necessity for any man hoping to cast a vote in U.S. elections. Under this 1790 law, citizenship was reserved for free white persons who had lived in the United States for at least two years and pledged loyalty to the United States "and the children of people so naturalized." This act lasted for only five years before it was replaced with a new naturalization law. The 1795 legislation left many of the stipulations and conditions contained in the original law intact, but it increased the residency requirement for naturalization from two to five years.

"An act to establish an Uniform Rule of Naturalization"— March 26, 1790

Be it enacted by the Senate and House of Representatives of the United States of America, in Congress assembled, That any Alien being a free white person, who shall have resided within the limits and under the jurisdiction of the United States for the term of two years, may be admitted to become a citizen thereof on application to any common law Court of record in any one of the States wherein he shall have resided for the term of one year at least, and making proof to the satisfaction of such Court that he is a person of good character, and taking the oath or affirmation prescribed by law to support the Constitution of the United States, which Oath or Affirmation such Court shall administer, and the Clerk of such Court shall record such Application, and the proceedings thereon; and thereupon such person shall be considered as a Citizen of the United States. And the children of such person so naturalized, dwelling within the United States, being under the age of twenty one years at the time of such naturalization, shall also be considered as citizens of the United States. And the children of citizens of the United States that may be born beyond Sea, or out of the limits of the United States, shall be considered as natural born Citizens: Provided, that the right of citizenship shall not descend to persons whose fathers have never been resident in the United States: Provided also, that no person heretofore proscribed by any States, shall be admitted a citizen as aforesaid, except by an Act of the Legislature of the State in which such person was proscribed.

"An act to establish an uniform rule of Naturalization; and to repeal the act heretofore passed on that subject"—January 29, 1795

For carrying into complete effect the power given by the constitution, to establish an uniform rule of naturalization throughout the United States:

SEC.1. Be it enacted by the Senate and House of Representatives of the United States of America, in Congress assembled, That any alien, being a free white person, may be admitted to become a citizen of the United States, or any of them, on the following conditions, and not otherwise: —

First. He shall have declared, on oath or affirmation, before the supreme, superior, district, or circuit court of some one of the states, or of the territories northwest or south of the river Ohio, or a circuit or district court of the United States, three years, at least, before his admission, that it was bona fide, his intention to become a citizen of the United States, and to renounce forever all allegiance and fidelity to any foreign prince, potentate, state, or sovereignty whatever, and particularly, by name, the prince, potentate, state or sovereignty whereof such alien may, at that time, be a citizen or subject.

Secondly. He shall, at the time of his application to be admitted, declare on oath or affirmation before some one of the courts aforesaid, that he has resided within the United States, five years at least, and within the state or territory, where such court is at the time held, one year at least; that he will support the constitution of the United States; and that he does absolutely and entirely renounce and abjure all allegiance and fidelity to any foreign prince, potentate, state, or sovereignty whatever, and particularly by name, the prince, potentate, state, or sovereignty, whereof he was before a citizen or subject; which proceedings shall be recorded by the clerk of the court.

Thirdly. The court admitting such alien shall be satisfied that he has resided within the limits and under the jurisdiction of the United States five years; and it shall further appear to their satisfaction, that during that time, he has behaved as a man of a good moral character, attached to the principles of the constitution of the United States, and well disposed to the good order and happiness of the same.

Fourthly. In case the alien applying to be admitted to citizenship shall have borne any hereditary title, or been of any of the orders of nobility, in the kingdom or state from which he came, he shall, in addition to the above requisites, make an express renunciation of his title or order of nobility, in the court to which his application shall be made; which renunciation shall be recorded in the said court.

SEC. 2. Provided always, and be it further enacted, That any alien now residing within the limits and under the jurisdiction of the United States may be admitted to become a citizen on his declaring, on oath or affirmation, in some one of the courts aforesaid, that he has resided two years, at least, within and under the jurisdiction of the same, and one year, at least, within the state or territory where such court is at the time held; that he will support the constitution of the United States; and that he does absolutely and entirely renounce and abjure all allegiance and fidelity to any foreign prince, potentate, state, or sovereignty whatever, and particularly by name the prince, potentate, state, or sovereignty, whereof he was before a citizen or subject; and moreover, on its appearing to the satisfaction of the court, that during the said term of two years, he has behaved as a man of good moral character, attached to the constitution of the United States, and well disposed to the good order and happiness of the same; and when the alien applying for admission to citizenship, shall have borne any hereditary title, or been of any of the orders of nobility in the kingdom or state from which he came, on his moreover making in the court an express renunciation of his title or order of nobility, before he shall be entitled to such admission; all of which proceedings, required in this proviso to be performed in the court, shall be recorded by the clerk thereof.

SEC. 3. And be it further enacted, that the children of persons duly naturalized, dwelling within the United States, and being under the age of twenty-one years, at the time of such naturalization, and the children of citizens of the United States, born out of the limits and jurisdiction of the United States, shall be considered as citizens of the United States: Provided, That the right of citizenship shall not descend to persons, whose fathers have never been resident of the United States: Provided also, That no person heretofore proscribed by any state, or who has been legally convicted of having joined the army of Great Britain during the late war, shall be admitted a citizen as foresaid, without the consent of the legislature of the state, in which such person was proscribed.

SEC. 4. And be it further enacted, That the Act intituled, "An act to establish an uniform rule of naturalization," passed the twenty-sixth day of March, one thousand seven hundred and ninety, be, and the same is hereby repealed.

Source: "An Act to Establish an Uniform Rule of Naturalization." Annals of Congress, House of Representatives, 1st Congress, 2nd Session: Rule of Naturalization." 1790. From the *Library of Congress: A Century of Lawmaking for a New*

Nation: U.S. Congressional Documents and Debates, 1774–1875. Accessed December 20, 2018. http://memory.loc.gov/cgi-bin/ampage?collId=llac&fileName=001/llac001.db&recNum=574; *An Act to Establish an Uniform Rule of Naturalization; and to Repeal the Act heretofore passed on that subject.* U. S. Laws, Statutes Etc. . . . *Philadelphia: Printed by Francis Childs.* Philadelphia, 1795. Pdf. Accessed December 20, 2018. https://www.loc.gov/item/rbpe.2220020e/.

A "Lady" Asserts That American Principles of Freedom "Embrace Only Half Mankind," 1800

In the early years of the American republic, a small but important number of women began to speak out against their inferior status in the nation's legal, business, and political worlds. Though their words were published anonymously so as to spare the authors from public condemnation and ostracization, they nonetheless spoke to a deep dissatisfaction with the many ways in which they were kept powerless, from severely circumscribed educational opportunities to their disenfranchisement. The following is an excerpt from an 1800 publication "written by a lady" that excoriates the men of America for not recognizing the contributions that women could make to the nation—and for failing to live up to their stated ideals of liberty. The pamphlet only obliquely references the right to vote, but its author (believed by many scholars to be early British feminist Mary Anne Radcliffe) suggests that the "rights of sufferages" should be extended to women as well as immigrant men whose potential contributions are more widely recognized, and that women like suffrage activist Mary Wollstonecraft have proven their mettle despite the monumental societal barriers to their gender. More broadly, she claims that the continued subjugation of "our daughters" is no different an "abuse of power" than found in systems of monarchy and slavery, and that keeping women and girls subordinate and without means of self-determination is a waste of human capital.

One of the causes, which induced the American people to depose their tyrant [Britain's King George III], was his neglect of the duties of PUBLIC HOSPITALITY; which was manifested by his obstruction of the naturalization of foreigners. . . . Well might the tyrant oppose the naturalization of foreigners, who like birds that have been entangled in a net, will shun the steps of the destroyer, and infuse the same shyness into all their associates. And well did the Americans to abolish a government which so artfully counteracted every cause, which prevented the assassination of their liberty. The people well knew, that except the Indians, the inhabitants of America were *all foreigners* . . .

Well might public hospitality be expected from such a people. They felt also that public hospitality was public utility. The inhabitants of a *new* country, cannot possibly derive such immediate profits from their land as those of older districts: they have forests to clear, rocks to remove, roads to open, bridges to construct, court houses, meeting and school houses to erect, and a hundred other things to do. . .

We have besides a chance for getting a good neighbor, and in our thinly people country, we have room enough for them and for us. They divide with us our taxes, they lighten our labor on the public roads, and if they increase our stock of knowledge; if we have learned the use of the saw mill from the Hollenders; if the Russians should further instruct us in its improvement, by the application of the circular saw, without a retrograde motion. If the Polanders have taught us to make starch; if the Germans have taught us to refine sugar, to make stone ware and above all, to reclaim our exhausted soil by the application of Plaister of Paris; if Italy has given us some idea of the nurture of the silk-worm, and will farther teach us the culture of the Olive and the Vine; if China will bring its lathes, and India its looms: if England has thrown away its philosophic Priestly: and will throw its Arkwrights, its Brindleys, its Bakewells, its Boultons, its Wilkinsons, its Wedgewoods, its Whitebreads, its Walkers, and its Watts: must we partake of their blindness and trample under foot the pearls which they reject? Forbid it patriotism! Forbid it common sense! Let the men who have enlightened Europe, enlighten us; and our sole return let us give them a full asylum! Let them share with us, after a short probation, the rights of citizenships, the rights of sufferages: rights inestimable to them, *"and formidable to tyrants only."*

CITIZENS. —You who love liberty, will love it *everywhere*—you would have it thaw the frozen souls of Greenlanders, and cheer the fainting Ethiop under the fervid rays of an ever vertical sun; you would bid that sun in his course shine on freemen only. You must therefore, constantly have it in your eye: its name must forever vibrate from your tongue; you must teach men their rights, even men the most ignorant and oppressed; those who know their road, may animate and cheer each other, it is the bewildered traveler alone that needs guide.

You must teach your children the principles of this day, and by the best education in your power to bestow, teach them to understand them. You must plant, and water, and prune, and weed the infant mind: you must fence and dress the ardent growth of youth: you must preside over and assist at securing the harvest of maturity.

But citizens, in this, as in all other things, if you do not being well, you will never end well. Those principles of freedom, which embrace only half mankind, are only *half systems,* and will not more support the burden of humanity, than the perpetual section of an arch will support a column. Our daughters are the same relations to us as our sons; we owe them the same duties, they have the same science, and are equally competent to their attainments. The contrary idea originated in the same abuse of power, as monarchy and slavery, and owes its little remaining support to the idle sophistry.

Indeed the first moulding of the human mind, falls so naturally upon the sex, that the voice of nature would have induced us to fit them for the task, if the voice of nature had not been drowned in the clamour of other prejudices. How shall our children learn fortitude from mothers who scream at the appearance of a spider? How shall they learn that they are formed for their country and mankind, from mothers who know nothing of the history of either? . . .

Had we no examples of women breaking down the barriers of the tyrant man, and storming the temple of fame, if we but reflected that the effects of [their] degradation recoiled upon ourselves, our own sense would induce us to rescue them from *tambour* and *fillagree,* and in the endless concerns of the *toilet,* and raise them to nature and philosophy. But to confound our presumption, and forever to destroy our cobweb theories, the history of women is forever obtruding on our unwilling eyes, bold and ardent spirits, who no tyrant could tame, no prejudice enslave. Besides the heroic daughters of antiquity, our own age has been blessed with the deep classic erudition of a Dacier: the flowery meanderings of a Rowe: the comic wit of Centliver [Centlivre]: the laborious patience and republican energy of a Macauly: the dramatic genius of Moore, of Lee, and of Inchbald: the melody and piety of Barbauld: the untaught towerings of Yeastly and Wheatly: the sprightly sallies of Piozzi: the magic pencil of Kaufman: the animated chisel of Damer: the unconquerable heroism of Roland, and the invulnerable reason of Mary Wolstoncraft [Wollstonecraft]!

FEMALE CITIZENS, follow examples so glorious; accept the station nature intended for you, and double the knowledge and happiness of mankind.

Source: *An Oration Delivered on the Fourth Day of July 1800, By a Citizen of the United States. Written by a Lady.* Springfield: Henry Brewer, 1808, pp. 9–13.

Maryland Passes an Act Allowing Jews to Hold Public Office, 1826

In the first years after the American colonies declared their independence from British rule, several of the state constitutions that were passed into law contained provisions that limited the political rights and actions of non-Protestants. States like Delaware, Georgia, and South Carolina all included measures in their founding constitutions that either prevented Jews, Catholics, Muslims, Quakers, and other non-Protestants from voting or from holding elected office. Most of these provisions were gradually repealed due to the fact that they clearly clashed with sentiments of religious freedom expressed in the U.S. Constitution, but the prejudice against non-Protestants remained strong in many parts of the country. As late as 1825, in fact, Maryland did not permit Jews to hold public office. That year, however, legislation that had long been thwarted by anti-Semitic constituencies was finally passed to address this blatant religious discrimination. The legislation still required citizens to formally declare their belief in a heavenly afterlife to be eligible for public office or other public trust (reflecting a widespread but mistaken belief that Jews and Judaism reject such a possibility). But this language nonetheless reflected a considerable loosening of state law, which had previously explicitly required all public officeholders to profess belief in the "Christian religion." From this point forward, Jews in Maryland could seek and secure public office. Following is the text of what was commonly known as "The Jew Bill," which received final passage on January 5, 1826.

An Act to extend to the sect of people professing the Jewish religion, the same rights and privileges enjoyed by Christians

Section 1: Be it enacted by the General Assembly of Maryland, that every citizen of this state professing the Jewish Religion, and who shall hereafter be appointed to any office or public trust under the State of Maryland, shall in addition to the oaths required to be taken by the constitution and laws of the United States, make and subscribe to a declaration of his belief in a future state of rewards and punishments, instead of the declaration now required by the constitution and form of government of this state.

Section 2: Be it enacted, that the several clauses and sections of the declaration of rights, constitution and form of government, and every part of any law of this state contrary to the provisions of this act, so far as respects the sect of people aforesaid, shall be, and the same is hereby declared to be repealed and annulled on the confirmation hereof.

Source: *Votes and Proceedings of the House of Delegates of Maryland, 1824 Session*. Annapolis: John Green, 1825, p. 162.

Elizabeth Cady Stanton Calls for Women's Suffrage at Seneca Falls, 1848

In 1848, Elizabeth Cady Stanton and a small group of fellow women's rights activists organized what turned out to be a landmark convention for women's rights at Wesleyan Chapel in Seneca Falls, New York, on July 19 and 20. This convention is often cited as the event that turned sentiment for women's suffrage from an abstraction into an actual crusade—one that finally ended in success more than seventy years later, with the ratification of the Nineteenth Amendment giving women the right to vote. Following are excerpts from the famous keynote address that Stanton delivered to the assembled activists at Seneca Falls on the opening day of the convention.

I should feel exceedingly diffident to appear before you wholly unused as I am to public speaking, were I not nerved by a sense of right and duty—did I not feel that the time had fully come for the question of woman's wrongs to be laid before the public—did I not believe that woman herself must do this work—for woman alone can understand the height and the depth, the length and the breadth of her own degradation and woe. Man cannot speak for us—because he has been educated to believe that we differ from him so materially, that he cannot judge of our thoughts, feelings and opinions by his own. Moral beings can only judge of others by themselves—the moment they give a different nature to any of their own kind they utterly fail. The drunkard was hopelessly lost until it was discovered that he was governed by the same laws of mind as the sober man. Then with what magic power, by kindness and love, was he raised from the slough of despond and placed rejoicing on high land. Let a man once settle the question that woman does not think and feel like himself and he may as well undertake to judge of the amount of intellect and sensation of any of the animal creation as of woman's nature. He can know but little with certainty, and that but by observation.

Among the many important questions which have been brought before the public, there is none that more vitally affects the whole human family than that which is technically termed Woman's rights. Every allusion to the degraded and inferior position occupied by woman all over the world, has ever been met by scorn and abuse. From the man of highest mental cultivation, to the most degraded wretch who staggers in the streets do we hear ridicule and coarse jests, freely bestowed upon those who dare assert that woman stands by the side of man—his equal, placed here by her God to enjoy with him the beautiful earth, which is her home as it is his—having the same sense of right and wrong and looking to the same Being for guidance and support. So long has man exercised a tyranny over her injurious to himself and benumbing to *her* faculties, that but few can nerve themselves against the storm, and so long has the chain been about her that however galling it may be she knows not there is a remedy.

The present social, civil and religious condition of women is a subject too vast to be brought within the limits of one short lecture. Suffice it to say for the present, that wherever we turn the history of woman is sad and drear and dark, without any alleviating circumstances, nothing from which we can draw consolation. As the nations of the earth emerge from a state of barbarism, the sphere of woman gradually becomes wider but not even under what is thought to be the full blaze of the sun of civilization is it what God designed it to be. In every country and clime does man assume the responsibility of marking out the path for her to tread,—in every country does he regard her as a being inferior to himself and one whom he is to guide and control. From the Arabian Kerek whose wife is obliged to steal from her Husband to supply the necessities of life,—from the Mahometan who forbids pigs, dogs, women, and other impure animals to enter a mosque, and does not allow a fool, madman or women to proclaim the hour of prayer,—from the German who complacently smokes his meerschaum while his wife, yoked with the ox draws the plough through its furrow,—from the delectable gentleman who thinks an inferior style of conversation adapted to women—to the legislator who considers her incapable of saying what laws shall govern her, is this same feeling manifested. In all eastern countries she is a mere slave bought and sold at pleasure. There are many differences in habits, manners, and customs, among the heathen nations of the old world, but there is little change for the better in woman's lot—she is either the drudge of man to perform all the hard labour of the field and the menial duties of the hut, tent, or house, or she is the idol of his lust the mere creature of his ever varying whims and will . . .

We, the women of this state have met in convention within the last few months both in Rochester and Seneca Falls to discuss our rights and wrongs. We did not as some have supposed assemble to go into the detail of social life alone, we did not propose to petition the legislature to make our Husbands just, generous and courteous, to seat every man at the head of a cradle and to clothe every woman in male attire, no none of these points however important they may be considered by humble minds, were touched upon in the convention. As to their costume the gentlemen need feel no fear of our imitating that for we think it in violation of every principle of beauty taste and dignity and notwithstanding all the contempt and abuse cast upon our loose flowing garments we still admire their easy graceful folds, and consider our costume as an object of taste much more beautiful than theirs. Many of the nobler sex seem to agree with us in this opinion for all the Bishops, Priests, Judges, Barristers, and Lord Mayors of the first nation on the globe and the Pope of Rome too, when officiating in their highest offices, they all wear the loose flowing robes, thus tacitly acknowledging that the ordinary male attire is neither dignified nor imposing. No! we shall not molest you in your philosophical experiments with stocks, pants, high heeled boots and Russian belt. Yours be the glory to discover by personal experience how long the knee pan can resist the terrible strapping down which you impose—in how short time the well developed muscles of the throat can be reduced to mere threads by the constant pressure of the stock, how high the heel of the boot must be to make a short man tall and how tight the Russian belt may be drawn and yet have wind enough to sustain life. Our ambition leads us neither to discovery or martyrdom of this sort.

But we did assemble to protest against a form of government existing without the consent of the governed, to declare our right to be free as man is free—to be represented in the government which we are taxed to support—to have such disgraceful laws as give to man the right to chastise and imprison his wife—to take the wages which she earns,—the property which she inherits and in case of separation the children of her love—laws which make her the mere dependent on his bounty—it was to protest against such unjust laws as these and to have them if possible forever erased from our statute books, deeming them a standing shame and disgrace to a professedly republican, christian people in the nineteenth century. We met

To uplift woman's fallen divinity
Upon an even pedestal with man

And strange as it may seem to many we then and there declared our right to vote according to the Declaration of the government under which we live. This right no one pretends to deny. We need not prove ourselves equal to Daniel Webster to enjoy this privilege for the most ignorant Irishman in the ditch has all the civil rights he has, we need not prove our muscular power equal to this same Irishman to enjoy this privilege for the most tiny, weak, ill shaped, imbecile stripling of 21 has all the civil rights of the Irishman. We have no objection to discuss the question of equality, for we feel that the weight of argument lies wholly with us, but we wish the question of equality kept distinct from the question of rights, for the proof of the one does not determine the truth of the other. All men in this country have the same rights however they may differ in mind, body, or estate. The right is ours. The question now is, how shall we get possession of what rightfully belongs to us. We should not feel so sorely grieved if no man who had not attained the full stature of a Webster, Van Buren, Clay or Gerrit Smith could claim the right of the elective franchise, but to have the rights of drunkards, idiots, horse-racing, rum selling rowdies, ignorant foreigners, and silly boys fully recognised, whilst we ourselves are thrust out from all the rights that belong to citizens—it is too grossly insulting to the dignity of woman to be longer quietly submitted to. The right is ours, have it we must—use it we will. The pens, the tongues, the fortunes, the indomitable wills of many women are already pledged to secure this right. The great truth that no just government can be formed without the consent of the governed, we shall echo and re-echo in the ears of the unjust judge until by continual coming we shall weary him.

But say some would you have woman vote? What refined delicate woman at the polls, mingling in such scenes of violence and vulgarity—most certainly—where there is so much to be feared for the pure, the innocent, the noble, the mother surely should be there to watch and guard her sons, who must encounter such stormy dangerous scenes at the tender age of 21. Much is said of woman's influence, might not her presence do much towards softening down this violence—refining this vulgarity? Depend upon it that places that by their impure atmosphere are rendered unfit for woman cannot but be dangerous to her sires and sons. But if woman claims all the rights of a citizen will she buckle on her armour and fight in defence of her country? Has not woman already often shown herself as courageous in the field as wise and patriotic in counsel as man? But for myself—I think all war sinful. I believe in Christ—I believe that command Resist not evil to be divine. Vengeance is mine and I will repay saith the Lord—Let frail man, who cannot foresee the consequences of an action walk humbly with his God—loving his enemies, blessing those who curse him and always returning good for evil. This is the highest kind of courage that mortal man can attain to and this moral warfare with ones own bad passions requires no physical power to achieve. I would not have man go to war. I can see no glory in fighting with such weapons as guns and swords whilst man has in his possession the infinitely superior and more effective ones of righteousness and truth.

But what would you gain by voting. Man must know the advantages of voting for they all seem very tenacious about the right. Think you if woman had a voice in this government, that all those laws affecting her interests would so entirely violate every principle of right and justice? Had we a vote to give might not the office holders and seekers propose some change in woman's condition? Might not "woman's rights" come to be as great a question as "free soil"? But are you not already sufficiently represented by your Fathers, Husbands, Brothers and Sons. Let your statute books answer the question. We have had enough of such representation. In nothing is woman's true happiness consulted, men like to call her an angel—to feed her with what they think sweet food nourishing her vanity, to induce her to believe her organization is so much finer more delicate than theirs, that she is not fitted to struggle with the tempests of public life but needs their care and protection. Care and protection? such as the wolf gives the lamb—such as the eagle the hare he carries to his eyrie. Most cunningly he entraps her and then takes from her all those rights which are dearer to him than life itself, rights which have been baptized in blood and the maintenance of which is even now rocking to their foundations the kingdoms of the old world. The most discouraging, the most lamentable aspect our cause wears is the indifference indeed the contempt with which women themselves regard our movement. When the subject is introduced among our young ladies among those even who claim to be intelligent and educated it is met by the scornful curl of the lip and by expressions of disgust and ridicule. But we shall hope better things of them when they are enlighted in regard to their present position, to the laws under which they live—they will not then publish their degradation by declaring themselves satisfied nor their ignorance by declaring they have all the rights they want . . .

Now is the time, now emphatically, for the women of this country to buckle on the armour that can best resist the weapons of the enemy, ridicule and holy horror. "Voices" were the visitors and advisers of Joan of Arc, "voices" have come to us, oftimes from the depths of sorrow degradation and despair,—they have been too long unheeded. The same religious enthusiasm that nerved her to what she deemed her work now nerves us to ours, her work was prophesied of, ours too is the fulfilling of what has long since been foretold. In the better days your sons and your daughters shall prophesy. Her struggle and triumph were alike short, our struggle shall be hard and long but our triumph shall be complete and forever. We do not expect that our path will be strewn with the flowers of popular favour—that our banner which we have flung to the wind will be fanned by the breath of popular applause, no we know that over the nettles of prejudice and bigotry will be our way, that upon our banner will beat the dark stormcloud of opposition from those who have entrenched themselves behind the strong bulwark of might, of force and who have fortified their position by every means holy and unholy, but we steadfastly abide the result. Unmoved we will bear it aloft—undaunted we will unfurl it to the gale,—we know the storm cannot rend from it a shred, that the electric flash will but more clearly show to us the glorious words inscribed upon it, "Equality of rights" and the rolling thunder will be sweet music in our ears, telling us of the light [*rest of line torn away*] of the purer clearer atmosphere [*rest of line torn away*] . . . .

Source: Address of Mrs. Elizabeth Cady Stanton delivered at Seneca Falls and Rochester, New York, July 19 and August 2d, 1848. National American Woman Suffrage Association Collection, Library of Congress.

California Eliminates Property and Wealth Requirements to Vote, 1849

In the fall of 1849, delegates to California's constitutional convention approved provisions that gave voting rights to a higher percentage of men than was typical for the era. It eliminated a variety of financial-based eligibility requirements that were commonplace in the nation's eastern states, such as property ownership stipulations and poll taxes that kept poor white men from the ballot box. But when California became a state the following year (after first ratifying the proposed constitution on November 13, 1849), the franchise was still only available to men, and the constitution established a separate enfranchisement approval process for the newly minted state's Native American population.

ARTICLE II.

Right of Suffrage.

Sec. 1. Every white male citizen of the United States, and every white male citizen of Mexico, who shall have elected to become a citizen of the United States, under the treaty of peace exchanged and ratified at Queretaro, on the 30th day of May, 1848 of the age of twenty-one years, who shall have been a resident of the State six months next preceding the election, and the county or district in which he claims his vote thirty days, shall be entitled to vote at all elections which are now or hereafter may authorized by law: Provided, nothing herein contained, shall be construed to prevent the Legislature, by a two-thirds concurrent vote, from admitting to the right of suffrage, Indians or the descendants of Indians, in such special cases as such proportion of the legislative body may deem just and proper.

Sec. 2. Electors shall, in all cases except treason, felony, or breach of the peace, be privileged from arrest on the days of the election, during their attendance at such election, going to and returning therefrom.

Sec. 3. No elector shall be obliged to perform militia duty on the day of election, except in time of war or public danger.

Sec. 4. For the purpose of voting, no person shall be deemed to have gained or lost a residence by reason of his presence or absence while employed in the service of the United States; nor while engaged in the navigation of the waters of this State, or of the United States, or of the high seas; nor while a student of any seminary of learning; nor while kept at any almshouse, or other asylum, at public expense; nor while confined in any public prison.

Sec. 5. No idiot or insane person, or person convicted of any infamous crime, shall be entitled to the privilege of an elector.

Sec. 6. All elections by the people shall be by ballot.

Source: Constitutional Convention of California, 1849. Records of the Constitutional Convention of 1849. California State Archives. Accessed December 21, 2018. https://www.sos.ca.gov/archives/collections/constitutions/1849/.

2

Demanding, Getting, and Losing the Vote: 1850–1925

The expansion of the right to vote though Congressional and judicial action was integral during this period. Although all groups did not have the same level of success across federal institutions, efforts to expand voting rights for African Americans and women and expand the definion of personhood were in many ways successful.

In the years leading up to and following the Civil War, the struggle for racial and gender equality in voting and many other aspects of American life continued to intensify. One landmark in this quest was the Second National Women's Rights Convention in Worcester, Massachusetts, in 1851. During this event, Ernestine Rose delivered a famous speech known as the "Tender Ivy Plant" speech, which likened the condition of women to the conditions of slavery. Neither women nor slaves could vote or participate in political discussions. Rose concluded her speech with a depiction of women as an ivy plant that wraps around men depicted as a fallen oak: "She, like the tender ivy plant bent yet unbroken by the storms of life, not only upholds her own hopeful courage, but clings around the tempest-fallen oak, to speak hope to his faltering spirit, and shelter him from the returning blast of the storm."

At the same time, abolitionist crusaders like former slave Fredrick Douglass lobbied tirelessly to extend the franchise to blacks. In April 1865, for example, he delivered a speech at the Massachusetts Anti-Slavery Society demanding that the government secure land, voting rights, and civil equality for blacks only just emerging from the shackles of slavery.

THE FRANCHISE IN POST–CIVIL WAR AMERICA

At the conclusion of the Civil War, slavery was abolished with the passage of the Thirteenth Amendment in 1865. The nation, however, still had to determine the process for readmitting the former Confederate states to the Union. The Reconstruction Acts of 1867 laid out the process of readmission to the Union for the Southern states. The First Reconstruction Act, which was passed over the veto of President Andrew Johnson, divided the former Confederate South into five military districts. The military districts were under the control of a federal general who was to protect life and property. The act also required new state constitutions and delegates, ratification of the Fourteenth Amendment (which addresses citizenship and the equal application of laws), and provisions of equal rights for all citizens (except ex-Confederates). The Second Reconstruction Act supplemented the first and cleared up confusion associated with the language in the first regarding whose responsibility it was to enforce the First Reconstruction Act. The Second Reconstruction Act specified that the military commanders were responsible for registering voters and holding elections in their districts. The act also required that every voter recite the registration oath and pledge their support to the Constitution and their obedience to the law.

In spite of the clarifications provided the by second act, the implementation was not without challenges. Congress did not send enough troops to the South to register voters and hold elections; the act only provided for the suffrage of blacks in the South and not those in the North, and the federal government did not provide a bureaucratic structure to help the newly freed men truly achieve equality. The Third Reconstitution Act gave ultimate power to the federal authorities who were overseeing the Reconstruction in the South. The generals had the power to suspend or remove from office any person—elected or appointed—if they believed the individual was interfering with the Reconstruction. Although the Reconstruction Acts were intended to improve relations between the North and South and improve the condition for blacks in the South, many Southern whites believed that the acts were yet another attempt of the North to impose their will on the South. Many of them responded by forming domestic terrorist organizations like the Ku Klux Klan and the White League and pushing for the adoption of Jim Crow laws that essentially stripped blacks of their economic, legal, and political rights, including the right to vote.

Whereas the Reconstruction Acts provided suffrage solely for blacks in the South, the passage of the Fifteenth Amendment (ratified in 1870) provided suffrage for black male citizens across the nation. The amendment, which prohibits denial of the right to vote on account of race, color, or previous condition of servitude, also enfranchised citizens from other racial and ethnic groups (this does not include American Indians who were not granted citizenship rights until the passage of the Indian Citizenship or Snyder Act in 1924). As a reaction to the adoption of the Fifteenth Amendment, many states adopted statutes and practices that either overtly or covertly disenfranchised black Americans. These included literacy tests, poll taxes, and "grandfather clauses." White lawmakers in the state of Mississippi, for example, passed several such measures, collectively known as the "Mississippi Plan," that were copied by other states across the South.

RISE OF THE WOMEN'S SUFFRAGE MOVEMENT

Women continued to fight for full suffrage rights. Some focused on the passage of a constitutional amendment, while others concentrated on winning the right to vote state by state. Some suffragists even turned to the courts, arguing that the Fourteenth Amendment of the Constitution guaranteed women the right to vote. Although the arrest and subsequent trial of Susan B. Anthony for voting in 1872 became a widely recognized milestone in the crusade for women's enfranchisement, an 1874 Supreme Court decision in the case of *Minor v. Happersett* had a longer-lasting impact.

In 1872, Virginia Minor, a resident of Missouri, tried to register to vote but was rejected by the registrar, Reese Happersett, because she was a woman. She subsequently filed a suit (albeit through her husband, as women were not permitted to sue in Missouri) against the registrar for failing to allow her to register. The Minor case was, in effect, a test of the ability of women to gain full suffrage rights utilizing a judicial strategy. After the Minors lost their case in the lower court, they appealed to the Missouri Supreme Court. In 1873, the Missouri Supreme Court ruled that the purpose of the Fourteenth Amendment was to extend the right to vote to newly freed slaves, giving African Americans the right to vote. The court also asserted, "There could have been no intention [in the amendment] to abridge the power of the States to limit the right of suffrage to the male inhabitants." When the Minors subsequently appealed to the Supreme Court of the United States, the Court ruled unanimously that "the Constitution of the United States does not confer the right of suffrage upon anyone," effectively disassociating citizenship and voting rights. This 1874 decision not only gave additional authority to individual states to conduct elections as they saw fit, it also was a disheartening rebuke to suffragists who had hoped to win the vote through legal challenges.

American Indians who had been forcibly exiled from their land in Nebraska and relocated to reservations in Oklahoma also turned to the Fourteenth Amendment to establish their personhood. The Ponca Tribe was removed from their native and rich lands in Nebraska to the plains of Oklahoma which were infested with malaria. Upon trying to return to Nebraska to bury his son, Standing Bear and the other Ponca people he was traveling with were arrested and imprisoned at Fort Omaha by General Crook for leaving the reservation. Standing Bear argued that the confinement of American Indians by the United States Army violated the Due Process Clause of the Fourteenth Amendment. While some argued that Indians could not sue the government because they did not have rights, the Supreme Court upheld Standing Bear's claim and ordered the Poncas who were being detained by the United States Army be released from custody. The ruling is significant because it established in U.S. legal jurisprudence that Indians are persons.

A women's suffrage amendment was introduced in Congress in 1878. The language of the amendment was the same language that would eventually become enshrined in the Nineteenth Amendment to the United States Constitution. In 1892, the proposed amendment was still being debated by the House Committee of the Judiciary. During the debate, women who had been prominent in the fight for suffrage provided testimony to support the passage of the amendment and champion the idea that women, who were after all citizens of the United States, should have the same rights as male citizens. One year later, the World's Congress of Representative Women was held in Chicago, Illinois, during the World's

Columbian Exposition. The congress was a weeklong meeting held for voicing concerns regarding the condition of women around the world. Approximately 150,000 people attended the congress and listened to speeches given by almost five hundred women from twenty-seven countries.

DIVERGENCE OF FRANCHISE FORTUNES FOR BLACKS AND WOMEN

As the nineteenth century gave way to the twentieth century, frustration at the racial inequities being perpetrated by Jim Crow in the South led some northerners to call for more robust enforcement of the Fourteenth and Fifteenth Amendments in the former slaveholding states. One prominent critic was Representative Edward de Veaux Morrell of Pennsylvania. He declared that "I can not agree with those who advance the argument that the South should be left to solve the negro problem, for the reason that when States enact legislation affecting the political status of large numbers of its citizens of voting age the result of such legislation is national in its effect, and, therefore, must at once become the object of concern to all sections of the country." But every time legislation was crafted to give black men the voting rights guaranteed to them by the Fourteenth and Fifteenth Amendments, it crumbled in the face of a united southern political opposition.

While the merits of African American enfranchisement continued to be debated in the halls of Congress and state legislatures, women continued to pressure the nation and states to provide for women's suffrage. They advanced arguments that not only highlighted the ways in which rights for women in the United States lagged behind the rights of women in other countries but also the ways in which women, once enfranchised, could contribute to the democratic functioning of the nation and the public good. Although many of the faces of women's suffrage are those of white women, black suffragists also worked for women's suffrage in their own groups and organizations (e.g., National Federation of Afro-American Women and the National League of Colored Women) and with white suffragists. As the twentieth century progressed, an increasing number of black women organized for suffrage rights. Some notable African American women in the suffrage movement include Sojourner Truth, Charlotte Vandine Forten Sr., Sarah Remond, Mary Ann Shadd Cary, Ida B. Wells, Anna J. Cooper, and Nannie Helen Burroughs. Burroughs founded the Woman's Convention of the National Baptist Convention, a woman's church organization that became one of the most important and nationally powerful organizations of African American women.

Suffragists continued to compel Congress to adopt women's suffrage across the nation. In 1917, for example, Carrie Chapman Catt argued that women's suffrage was inevitable in an address before Congress. Although women's suffrage had yet to become adopted by the nation, states had independently adopted full suffrage rights for women beginning with Wyoming in 1869. In states where the right to vote was secure, women flexed their political muscle by running for political office. In 1914, eligible voters in Montana voted to adopt full suffrage rights for women. Two years later, eligible men and women voted together to elect Jeannette Rankin to the United States House of Representatives. And, in 1920, the Nineteenth Amendment to the United States Constitution was ratified, finally providing full suffrage rights for all women. The Nineteenth Amendment did not end the fight for women's political and social equality, however, as women continued to strive for freedom in occupational choice and economic independence.

Until the passage of the Indian Citizenship Act in 1924, many American Indians were not citizens (although some gained citizenship through marriage, military service, special treaties, or special status). While other groups actively fought to secure the rights of citizenship, the expansion of citizenship rights to American Indians was an act on the part of the federal government to assimilate them into white American society and life.

SOURCES

Blackmon, Douglas A. *Slavery by Another Name: The Re-Enslavement of Black Americans from the Civil War to World War II.* New York: Doubleday, 2008.

Kratz, Jessie. "Jeannett Rankin: The Women Who Voted to Give Women the Right to Vote." National Archive: Pieces of History. Last modified January 26, 2017. https://prologue.blogs.archives.gov/2017/01/26/jeannette-rankin-the-woman-who-voted-to-give-women-the-right-to-vote/.

Lane, Charles. *The Day Freedom Died: The Colfax Massacre, the Supreme Court, and the Betrayal of Reconstruction.* New York: Macmillan, 2008.

Lange, Allison. "The Legal Case of *Minor v. Happersett.*" National Women's History Museum. Accessed January 13, 2019. http://www.crusadeforthevote.org/minor/.

Library of Congress. "Voting Rights for Native Americans." Accessed January 13, 2019. https://www.loc.gov/teachers/classroommaterials/presentationsandactivities/presentations/elections/voting-rights-native-americans.html.

Mayo, Edith. "African American Women Leaders in the Suffrage Movement." Turning Point Suffragist Memorial website. Accessed January 25, 2019. https://suffragistmemorial.org/african-american-women-leaders-in-the-suffrage-movement/.

National Park Service. "1924 Indian Citizenship Act." Accessed January 20, 2019. https://www.nps.gov/jame/learn/historyculture/upload/Native-American-Citizenship-2.pdf.

National Park Service. "*Standing Bear v. The United States.*" Accessed January 13, 2019. https://www.nps.gov/mnrr/learn/historyculture/upload/Standing%20Bear.pdf.

National Park Service. "Virginia Minor and Women's Right to Vote." Accessed January 13, 2019. https://www.nps.gov/jeff/learn/historyculture/the-virginia-minor-case.htm.

Stanton, Elizabeth Cady, Susan B. Anthony, and Matilda Joslyn Gage, eds. *History of Woman Suffrage.* New Hampshire: Fowler and Wells, 1881.

Wormser, Richard. *The Rise and Fall of Jim Crow.* New York: St. Martin's Press, 2014.

PRIMARY DOCUMENTS

Ernestine Rose Demands Universal Suffrage, 1851

On October 15, 1851, women's suffrage activists gathered in Worcester, Massachusetts, for the second-ever national convention for women's rights in the United States. One of the highlights of the convention was a stem-winding speech by veteran feminist activist Ernestine Rose in which she urged the women in attendance to accept nothing less than full political, economic, and social equality with men. Rose's address, which became known in subsequent years as the "Tender Ivy Plant" speech, also emphasized that similar struggles for suffrage and economic equality were being waged in Europe by feminist "sisters" like Jeanne Deroin and Pauline Roland, two French suffrage activists who had been imprisoned in retribution for their protest actions. Following are excerpts from Rose's 1851 speech in Worcester.

My Friends: —The observing and reflecting mind that casts his vision far beyond the panoramic scenes of every-day life, must perceive that our present age is fast ripening for the most important changes in the affairs of man. The desire for Freedom has shaken Europe to its very centre. The love of Liberty has convulsed the nations like the mighty throes of an earthquake. The oppressed are struggling against the oppressors. Kings and priests are called upon to give an account of their stewardship, for man no longer believes in the divine right of force and fraud.

Yet great as these signs of the times are, they are not new. From the time of absolute despotism to the present hour of comparative freedom, the weak had ever to struggle against the strong, right against might. But a new sign has appeared in our social zodiac, prophetic of the most important changes, pregnant with the most beneficial results that have ever taken place in the annals of human history. And to him that can trace the various epochs in human life, it is as cheering as it is interesting to mark the onward movement of the race towards higher state of human progression—that while nations strive against nations, people against people to attain the same amount of freedom already possessed in this country, Woman is rising in the full dignity of her being to claim the recognition of her rights. And though the first public demonstration has been here, already has the voice of Woman in behalf of her sex been carried as it were on the wings of lightning to all parts of Europe, whose echo has brought back the warmest and most heartfelt responses from our sisters there.

Among the many encouraging letters received at the recent Woman's Convention at Worcester, there was one exceeding all the rest in the soul-stirring interest it created. It spoke, through the dungeon walls, the cheering and encouraging words of sympathy from two incarcerated women of Paris, to the hearts of their sisters in America. The cause of their imprisonment was their practically claiming the fulfillment of that glorious motto, "Liberty, Equality, and Fraternity," destined to shake the thrones, break the scepires and bow down the mitres of Europe. One of them presented herself as candidate for Mayor of an Arrondissement, the other (to the honor of the genuine Republicans of Paris, be it said,) was nominated by the Industrial Union, consisting of two hundred and twenty Societies, as a member of the Assembly. For these offences they were cast into prison. Oh! France, where is the glory of thy revolutions? Is the blood thy children poured out on the altar of freedom so effaced, that thy daughters dare not lift their voices in behalf of their rights? But a long as might constitutes right, every good cause must have its martyrs. Why then, should woman not be a martyr to her cause?

But how can we wonder that France, governed as side is by Russian and Austrian despotism, does not recognize the higher laws of humanity in the recognition of the rights of woman, when even here, in this far-famed land of freedom and of knowledge, under a republic that has inscribed on its banner the great truth that all men are created free and equal and are endowed with inalienable rights to life, liberty, and the pursuit of happiness—a Declaration wafted like the voice of Hope on the breezes of heaven to the remotest parts of earth, to whisper freedom and equality to the oppressed and down-trodden children of men—a Declaration that lies at the very foundation of human freedom and happiness, yet in the very face of that eternal truth, woman, the mockingly so-called "better half of man," has yet to plead for her rights, nay, for her life; for what is life without liberty? and what is liberty without equality of rights; and as for the pursuit of happiness, she is not allowed to pursue any line of life that might promote it; she has only thankfully to accept what man, in the plenitude of his wisdom and generosity, decides as proper for her to do, and that is, what he does not choose to do himself.

Is woman then not included in that Declaration? Answer, ye wise men of the nation, and answer truly; add not hypocrisy to your other sins. Say she is not created free and equal, and therefore, (for the sequence follows on the premises) she is not entitled to life, liberty, and the pursuit of happiness. But you dare not answer this simple question. With all the audacity arising from an assumed superiority, you cannot so libel and insult humanity as to say she is not; and if she is, then what right has man, except that of might, to deprive her of the same rights and privileges he claims for himself? And why, in the name of reason and justice, I ask, why should she not have the same rights as man? Because she is woman? Humanity recognizes no sex; mind recognizes no sex; virtue recognizes no sex; life and death, pleasure and pain, happiness and misery recognize no sex. Like him she comes involuntarily into existence; like him she possesses physical, mental, and moral powers, on the proper cultivation of which depends her happiness; like him she is subject to all the vicissitudes of life; like him she has to pay the penalty for disobeying nature's laws, and far greater penalties has she to suffer from ignorance of her far more complicated nature than he; like him she enjoys or suffers with her country. Yet she is not recognized as his equal. In the laws of the land she has no rights; in government she has no voice, and in spite of another principle recognize in this republic, namely, that taxation without representation is tyranny, woman is taxed without being represented; her property may be consumed by heavy taxes, to defray the expenses of that unholy and unrighteous thing called war, yet she cannot give her veto against it. From the cradle to the grave, she is subject to the power and control of man, father, guardian and husband. One conveys her like some piece of merchandise over to the other. . . .

We can hardly have an adequate idea how all-powerful law is in forming public opinion, in giving tone and character to the mass of society. To illustrate this point, look at that inhuman, detestable law, written in human blood, signed and sealed with life and liberty, that eternal stain on the statute books of this country, the Fugitive Slave Law. Think you, that before its passage you could have found any in the free States, except a few politicians in the market, base enough to desire such a law? No, no! Even those that took no interest in the subject, would have shrunk from so barbarous a thing; but no sooner is it passed, than the ignorant mass, the rabble of the self-styled Union Safety Committee, found out we were a law-loving and law-abiding people. Such is the magic power of law; hence the necessity to guard against bad ones, hence also the reason why we call on the nation to remove the legal shackles from woman.

Set her politically and civilly free, and it will have a more beneficial effect on that still greater tyrant she has to contend with, public opinion. Carry out the Republican principle of universal suffrage, or strike it from your banner, and substitute freedom and power to one half of society, and submission and slavery to the other. Give women then the elective franchise. Let married women have the same right to property that man has; for whatever the difference in their respective occupations, the duties of the wife are as indispensable and far more arduous than the husband's. Why, then, should the wife at the death of her husband, not be his heir to the same extent that he is to her?

In this legal inequality there is involved another wrong. When the wife dies, the husband is left in the undisturbed possession of all, and the children are left with him. No change is made, no stranger intrudes on his home and his affliction; but when the husband dies, not only is she, as is too often the case, deprived of all, or at best receives but a mere pittance, but strangers assume authority denied to the wife and mother. The sanctuary of affliction must be desecrated by executors, every thing must be ransacked and assessed, lest she should steal something out of her own house, and to cap the climax, the children are taken from her and placed under guardians. When he dies poor, no guardian is required, the children are left with the mother to care and toil for them as best she may; but when any thing is left for the maintenance and education of the children, then it must be placed in the hands of strangers for safe keeping, lest the mother might defraud them. The whole care and bringing up of the children are left with the mother, and safe they are in her hands; but a few hundred or thousand dollars cannot be entrusted with her.

But it will be said, that in case of a second marriage, the children must be protected in their possession. Does that reason not hold as good in his case? Oh! no!- When he marries again, he still retains his identity and power to act, but she becomes merged once more into a mere nonentity, and therefore the first husband must rob her to prevent the second from doing it. But we say, make the laws regulating marriage, if any are required at all, equal for both, and all these difficulties would be obviated. According to a late act, the wife has a right to the property she brings at marriage, or received in any way after marriage. Here is some provision for the favored few, but for the laboring many there is none. The mass of the people commence life with no other capital than the head, heart, and hand. To the result of this best of all capital, the wife has no right. If they are unsuccessful in married life, who suffers more the bitter consequences of poverty than the wife? But if successful, she cannot call a dollar her own. He may will away every dollar (of his personal property) and leave her destitute and penniless, and she has no redress by law; and even when real estate is left, she receives but a life interest in a third part of it, and at her death she cannot leave it to any of her relations; it falls back even to the remotest of his relations.

This is law, but where is the justice of it? Well might we say, that laws were made to prevent, but not promote the ends of justice. Or, in case of separation, why should the children be taken from the protecting care of the mother? Who has a better right to them than she? How much do fathers generally do towards the bringing them up? When he comes home from business, and the child is in good humor and handsome trim, he takes the little darling on his knee and plays with it; but when the wife, with the care of the whole household on her shoulders, with little or no help, was not able to put them in the best order and trim, how much does the father do towards it? Oh! no! Father like to have children good-natured, well-behaved, and comfortable; but how to put them in that desirable condition is out of their philosophy. Children always depend more on the tender, watchful care of the mother, that the father. Whether from nature or habit, or both, the mother is more capable of administering to their health and comfort than the father, and therefore she has the best right to them; and where there is property, it ought to be divided equally between them with an additional provision from the father towards the maintenance and education of the children. . . .

It is high time, then, to denounce such gross injustice, to compel man by the might of right to give woman her political, legal, and social rights. Open to her all the avenues of emolument, distinction, and greatness; give her an object for which to cultivate her powers, and a fair chance to do so, and there will be no need to speculate as to her proper sphere. She will find her own sphere in accordance with her capacities, powers, and tastes; and yet she will be woman still. Her rights will not change, but strengthen, develop, and elevate her nature. Away with that folly that her rights would be detrimental to her character—that if she is recognized as the equal to man, she would cease to be woman!—Have his rights as a citizen of a republic, the elective franchise with all its advantages, so changed his nature that he has ceased to be man? Oh! no! But woman could not bare such a degree of power; what has benefited him would injure her; what has strengthened him would weaken her; what prompted him to the performance of his duties would make her neglect hers!

Such is the superficial mode of reasoning, if it deserves that name, that is brought against the subject. It reminds me of two reasons given by a minister of Milton, on the North River. Having heard I had spoken on the rights of woman, he took the subject up the following Sunday, to prove that woman ought not to have equal rights with man, first, because Adam was created before Eve, and secondly, man was compared to the fore wheel, and woman to the hind wheel of a wagon! These reasons are about as philosophical as any that can be brought on the subject. Man forgets, or he never knew, that our duties spring from our rights; and in proportion to the rights we enjoy, are the duties we owe, and he that enjoys the most rights owes in return the most duties; though until now, while man enjoys the rights, he preaches all the duties to woman.

But, say some, in point of principle we grant it is right enough, but would you expose woman to the contact of rough, rude, drinking, swearing, fighting men at the ballot-box? What a humiliating confession lies in this plea for keeping women in the back-ground! Is the brutality of some men, then, a reason why woman should be kept from her rights? If man, in his superior wisdom, cannot devise means to enable woman to deposit her vote without having her finer sensibilities shocked by such disgraceful conduct, then there is an additional reason as well as necessity why she should be there to civilize, refine, and purify him, even at the ballot-box. Yes, in addition to the principle of right, this is one of the reasons why women should participate in all the important duties of life; for, with all due respect to the other sex, she is the true civilizer of man. Without her, he is at best a semi-barbarian. From my very heart do I pity the man who has grown up and lives without the benign influence of woman!

Even now, in spite of being considered the inferior, she has a most beneficial effect on man. Look at your annual festivities where woman is excluded, and you will find more or less drunkenness, disorder, vulgarity, and excess to be the order of the day. Compare them with such, where woman is the equal participant with man, and you will find rational social enjoyment and decorum prevail; and if this is the case now,—and who can deny it?—how much more beneficial would be her influence, if, as the equal to man, she would take her stand by his side, to cheer, counsel, and aid him in the drama of life, in the Legislative Halls, in the Senate Chamber, in the Judge's chair, in the Jury box, on the Forum, in the Laboratory of the Arts and Sciences, and wherever duty would call her for the benefit of herself, her county, her race. In every step she would carry a humanizing influence.

And why, I would ask, should she not occupy all these stations? Why would one half of the race legislate for the other? In this country it is considered wrong for one nation to enact laws and enforce them against another. Does the same wrong not hold good of the sexes?—Is she a being like him? Then she is entitled to the same rights—is she not? Then how can he legislate rightfully against a being whose nature he cannot understand, whose motives he cannot appreciate, and whose feelings he cannot realize? how can he sit in judgment and pronounce a verdict against a being so entirely different? No, there are no reasons for it, but there are deep-rooted, hoary-headed prejudices against her.

The main cause of them is, that pernicious falsehood propagated against her being, viz.:—that she is inferior by her nature. Inferior in what? What has man ever done, that woman, under the same advantages, could not be made to do? In morals, bad as she is, she is generally considered his superior. In intellect, give her a fair chance before you pronounce a verdict against her. Cultivate that portion of the brain as much as that of man's, and she will stand his equal, at least. Even now, where her mind has been called out at all, her intellect is as bright, as capacious, and as powerful as his. Will you tell me, we have no Newtons, Shakespeares, and Byrons? Greater natural powers than even these possessed, have been destroyed in woman for want of proper culture—a just appreciation and reward for merit, as an incentive to exertion and freedom of action, without which, mind becomes cramped and stifled. It cannot expand under bolts and bats; and yet, under all these blighting, crushing circumstances, confined within the narrowest possible limits, trampled upon by prejudice and injustice, from her education and position forced to occupy herself almost exclusively with the most trivial affairs—in spite of all these difficulties, her intellect is as good as man's.

The few bright meteors in man's intellectual horizon could well be matched by woman, were she allowed to occupy the same elevated poison. There is no need of naming the De Staels, the Rolands, the Somervilles, the Wollstonecrafts, the Wrights, the Fullers, the Martineaus, the Hemanses, the Sigourneys, the Jagiellos, and the many more of modern as well as ancient times, to prove her mental powers, her patriotism, her heroism, her self-sacrificing devotion to the cause of humanity—the eloquence that gushes from her pen or from her tongue. These things are too well known to require repetition. And do you ask for fortitude of mind, energy, and perseverance? Then look at woman under suffering, reverse of fortune, and affliction, when the strength and power of man has sunk to the lowest ebb, when his mind is overwhelmed by the dark waters of despair.—She, like the tender plant, bent but not broken by the storms of life, now only upholds her own hopeful courage, but, like the tender shoots of the ivy, clings around the tempest-fallen oak, to bind up the wounds, peak hope to his faltering spirit, and shelter him from the returning blast of the storm.

Source: Rose, Ernestine. Address before the Second National Women's Rights Convention, Worcester, Massachusetts. October 15, 1851. In Stanton, Elizabeth Cady, Susan B. Anthony, and Matilda Joslyn Gage. *History of Woman Suffrage*, Vol 1, 2nd ed. Rochester, NY: Charles Mann, 1889, pp. 237–242.

Frederick Douglass Tells America "What the Black Man Wants," 1865

Frederick Douglass was one of the most prominent African Americans of the nineteenth century. Born into slavery in Maryland, he escaped bondage in the late 1830s as a young man, fleeing for the free North. He eventually settled in Massachusetts, where he raised a family and became an eloquent and influential abolitionist author, newspaper publisher, orator, and activist, as well as a prominent champion of women's suffrage.

Douglass delivered the following address in Boston on January 26, 1865, at the annual convention of the Massachusetts Anti-Slavery Society. In this speech, given two years after President Abraham Lincoln's Emancipation Proclamation took effect, the abolitionist leader emphasized both the societal importance and the moral necessity of giving African American men full voting rights.

I have had but one idea for the last three years to present to the American people, and the phraseology in which I clothe it is the old abolition phraseology. I am for the "immediate, unconditional, and universal" enfranchisement of the black man, in every State in the Union. [Loud applause.]

Without this, his liberty is a mockery; without this, you might as well almost retain the old name of slavery for his condition; for in fact, if he is not the slave of the individual master, he is the slave of society, and holds his liberty as a privilege, not as a right. He is at the mercy of the mob, and has no means of protecting himself.

It may be objected, however, that this pressing of the Negro's right to suffrage is premature. Let us have slavery abolished, it may be said, let us have labor organized, and then, in the natural course of events, the right of suffrage will be extended to the Negro. I do not agree with this. The constitution of the human mind is such, that if it once disregards the conviction forced upon it by a revelation of truth, it requires the exercise of a higher power to produce the same conviction afterwards. The American people are now in tears. The Shenandoah has run blood—the best blood of the North. All around Richmond, the blood of New England and of the North has been shed—of your sons, your brothers and your fathers. We all feel, in the existence of this Rebellion, that judgments terrible, wide-spread, far-reaching, overwhelming, are abroad in the land; and we feel, in view of these judgments, just now, a disposition to learn righteousness. This is the hour. Our streets are in mourning, tears are falling at every fireside, and under the chastisement of this Rebellion we have almost come up to the point of conceding this great, this all-important right of suffrage. I fear that if we fail to do it now, if abolitionists fail to press it now, we may not see, for centuries to come, the same disposition that exists at this moment. [Applause.] Hence, I say, now is the time to prcss this right.

It may be asked, "Why do you want it? Some men have got along very well without it. Women have not this right." Shall we justify one wrong by another? This is a sufficient answer. Shall we at this moment justify the deprivation of the Negro of the right to vote, because some one else is deprived of that privilege? I hold that women, as well as men, have the right to vote [applause.], and my heart and my voice go with the movement to extend suffrage to woman; but that question rests upon another basis than that on which our right rests. We may be asked, I say, why we want it. I will tell you why we want it. We want it because it is our *right*, first of all. No class of men can, without insulting their own nature, be content with any deprivation of their rights. We want it again, as a means for educating our race. Men are so constituted that they derive their conviction of their own possibilities largely from the estimate formed of them by others. If nothing is expected of a people, that people will find it difficult to contradict that expectation. By depriving us of suffrage, you affirm our incapacity to form an intelligent judgment respecting public men and public measures; you declare before the world that we are unfit to exercise the elective franchise, and by this means lead us to undervalue ourselves, to put a low estimate upon ourselves, and to feel that we have no possibilities like other men. Again, I want the elective franchise, for one, as a colored man, because ours is a peculiar government, based upon a peculiar idea, and that idea is universal suffrage. If I were in a monarchial government, or an autocratic or aristocratic government, where the few bore rule and the many were subject, there would be no special stigma resting upon me, because I did not exercise the elective franchise. It would do me no great violence. Mingling with the mass I should partake of the strength of the mass; I should be supported by the mass, and I should have the same incentives to endeavor with the mass of my fellow-men; it would be no particular burden, no particular deprivation; but here where universal suffrage is the rule, where that is the fundamental idea of the Government, to rule us out is to make us an exception, to brand us with the stigma of inferiority, and to invite to our heads the missiles of those about us; therefore, I want the franchise for the black man.

There are, however, other reasons, not derived from any consideration merely of our rights, but arising out of the conditions of the South, and of the country—considerations which have already been referred to by Mr. Phillips—considerations which must arrest the attention of statesmen. I believe that when the tall heads of this Rebellion shall have been swept down, as they will be swept down, when the Davises and Toombses and Stephenses, and others who are leading this Rebellion shall have been blotted out, there will be this rank undergrowth of treason, to which reference has been made, growing up there, and interfering with, and thwarting the quiet operation of the Federal Government in those states. You will see those traitors, handing down, from sire to son, the same malignant spirit which they have manifested, and which they are now exhibiting, with malicious hearts, broad blades, and bloody hands in the field, against our sons and brothers. That spirit will still remain; and whoever sees the Federal Government extended over those Southern States will see that Government in a strange land, and not only in a strange land, but in an enemy's land. A post-master of the United States in the South will find himself surrounded by a hostile spirit; a collector in a Southern port will find himself surrounded by a hostile spirit; a United States marshal or United States judge will be surrounded there by a hostile element. That enmity will not die out in a year, will not die out in an age. . . . Now, where will you find the strength to counterbalance this spirit, if you do not find it in the Negroes of the South? They are your friends, and have always been your friends. They were your friends even when the Government did not regard them as such. They comprehended the genius of this war before you did. It is a significant fact, it is a marvellous fact, it seems almost to imply a direct interposition of Providence, that this war, which began in the interest of slavery on both sides, bids fair to end in the interest of liberty on both sides. [Applause.]

It was begun, I say, in the interest of slavery on both sides. The South was fighting to take slavery out of the Union, and the North fighting to keep it in the Union; the South fighting to get it beyond the limits of the United States Constitution, and the North fighting to retain it within those limits; the South fighting for new guarantees, and the North fighting for the old guarantees;—both despising the Negro, both insulting the Negro. Yet, the Negro, apparently endowed with wisdom from on high, saw more clearly the end from the beginning than we did. When Seward said the status of no man in the country would be changed by the war, the Negro did not believe him. [Applause.]

When our generals sent their underlings in shoulder-straps to hunt the flying Negro back from our lines into the jaws of slavery, from which he had escaped, the Negroes thought that a mistake had been made, and that the intentions of the Government had not been rightly understood by our officers in shoulder-straps, and they continued to come into our lines, threading their way through bogs and fens, over briers and thorns, fording streams, swimming rivers, bringing us tidings as to the safe path to march, and pointing out the dangers that threatened us. They are our only friends in the South, and we should be true to them in this their trial hour, and see to it that they have the elective franchise.

I know that we are inferior to you in some things—virtually inferior. We walk about you like dwarfs among giants. Our heads are scarcely seen above the great sea of humanity. The Germans are superior to us; the Irish are superior to us; the Yankees are superior to us [Laughter]; they can do what we cannot, that is, what we have not hitherto been allowed to do. But while I make this admission, I utterly deny, that we are originally, or naturally, or practically, or in any way, or in any important sense, inferior to anybody on this globe. [Loud applause.] . . .

The story of our inferiority is an old dodge, as I have said; for wherever men oppress their fellows, wherever they enslave them, they will endeavor to find the needed apology for such enslavement and oppression in the character of the people oppressed and enslaved. When we wanted, a few years ago, a slice of Mexico, it was hinted that the Mexicans were an inferior race, that the old Castilian blood had become so weak that it would scarcely run down hill, and that Mexico needed the long, strong and beneficent arm of the Anglo-Saxon care extended over it. We said that it was necessary to its salvation, and a part of the "manifest destiny" of this Republic, to extend our arm over that dilapidated government. So, too, when Russia wanted to take possession of a part of the Ottoman Empire, the Turks were "an inferior race." So, too, when England wants to set the heel of her power more firmly in the quivering heart of old Ireland, the Celts are an "inferior race." So, too, the Negro, when he is to be robbed of any right which is justly his, is an "inferior man." It is said that we are ignorant; I admit it. But if we know enough to be hung, we know enough to vote. If the Negro knows enough to pay taxes to support the government, he knows enough to vote; taxation and representation should go together. If he knows enough to shoulder a musket and fight for the flag, fight for the government, he knows enough to vote. If he knows as much when he is sober as an Irishman knows when drunk, he knows enough to vote, on good American principles. [Laughter and applause.]

But I was saying that you needed a counterpoise in the persons of the slaves to the enmity that would exist at the South after the Rebellion is put down. I hold that the American people are bound, not only in self-defence, to extend this right to the freedmen of the South, but they are bound by their love of country, and by all their regard for the future safety of those Southern States, to do this—to do it as a measure essential to the preservation of peace there. But I will not dwell upon this. I put it to the American sense of honor. The honor of a nation is an important thing. It is said in the Scriptures, "What doth it profit a man if he gain the whole world, and lose his own soul?" It may be said, also, What doth it profit a nation if it gain the whole world, but lose its honor? I hold that the American government has taken upon itself a solemn obligation of honor, to see that this war—let it be long or let it be short, let it cost much or let it cost little—that this war shall not cease until every freedman at the South has the right to vote. [Applause.]

It has bound itself to it. What have you asked the black men of the South, the black men of the whole country, to do? Why, you have asked them to incur the deadly enmity of their masters, in order to befriend you and to befriend this

Government. You have asked us to call down, not only upon ourselves, but upon our children's children, the deadly hate of the entire Southern people. You have called upon us to turn our backs upon our masters, to abandon their cause and espouse yours; to turn against the South and in favor of the North; to shoot down the Confederacy and uphold the flag—the American flag. You have called upon us to expose ourselves to all the subtle machinations of their malignity for all time. And now, what do you propose to do when you come to make peace? To reward your enemies, and trample in the dust your friends? Do you intend to sacrifice the very men who have come to the rescue of your banner in the South, and incurred the lasting displeasure of their masters thereby? Do you intend to sacrifice them and reward your enemies? Do you mean to give your enemies the right to vote, and take it away from your friends? Is that wise policy? Is that honorable?. . .

I ask my friends who are apologizing for not insisting upon this right, where can the black man look, in this country, for the assertion of his right, if he may not look to the Massachusetts Anti-Slavery Society? Where under the whole heavens can he look for sympathy, in asserting this right, if he may not look to this platform? Have you lifted us up to a certain height to see that we are men, and then are any disposed to leave us there, without seeing that we are put in possession of all our rights? We look naturally to this platform for the assertion of all our rights, and for this one especially. I understand the anti-slavery societies of this country to be based on two principles,—first, the freedom of the blacks of this country; and, second, the elevation of them. Let me not be misunderstood here. I am not asking for sympathy at the hands of abolitionists, sympathy at the hands of any. I think the American people are disposed often to be generous rather than just. I look over this country at the present time, and I see Educational Societies, Sanitary Commissions, Freedmen's Associations, and the like,—all very good: but in regard to the colored people there is always more that is benevolent, I perceive, than just, manifested towards us. What I ask for the Negro is not benevolence, not pity, not sympathy, but simply *justice*. [Applause.]

The American people have always been anxious to know what they shall do with us. Gen. Banks was distressed with solicitude as to what he should do with the Negro. Everybody has asked the question, and they learned to ask it early of the abolitionists, "What shall we do with the Negro?" I have had but one answer from the beginning. Do nothing with us! Your doing with us has already played the mischief with us. Do nothing with us! If the apples will not remain on the tree of their own strength, if they are worm-eaten at the core, if they are early ripe and disposed to fall, let them fall! I am not for tying or fastening them on the tree in any way, except by nature's plan, and if they will not stay there, let them fall. And if the Negro cannot stand on his own legs, let him fall also. All I ask is, give him a chance to stand on his own legs! Let him alone! If you see him on his way to school, let him alone, don't disturb him! If you see him going to the dinner-table at a hotel, let him go! If you see him going to the ballot-box, let him alone, don't disturb him! [Applause.]

If you see him going into a work-shop, just let him alone,—your interference is doing him a positive injury. Gen. Banks' "preparation" is of a piece with this attempt to prop up the Negro. Let him fall if he cannot stand alone! If the Negro cannot live by the line of eternal justice, so beautifully pictured to you in the illustration used by Mr. Phillips, the fault will not be yours, it will be his who made the Negro, and established that line for his government. [Applause.]

Let him live or die by that. If you will only untie his hands, and give him a chance, I think he will live. He will work as readily for himself as the white man. A great many delusions have been swept away by this war. One was, that the Negro would not work; he has proved his ability to work. Another was, that the Negro would not fight; that he possessed only the most sheepish attributes of humanity; was a perfect lamb, or an "Uncle Tom;" disposed to take off his coat whenever required, fold his hands, and be whipped by anybody who wanted to whip him. But the war has proved that there is a great deal of human nature in the Negro, and that "he will fight," as Mr. Quincy, our President, said, in earlier days than these, "when there is a reasonable probability of his whipping anybody." [Laughter and applause.]

Source: Douglass, Frederick. "What the Black Man Wants: Speech of Frederick Douglass at the Annual Meeting of the Massachusetts Anti-Slavery Society in Boston." January 1865. In *The Equality of All Men Before the Law.* Boston: Rand and Avery, 1865, pp. 36–39. Accessed December 21, 2018. https://www.loc.gov/resource/mfd.22014/?sp=34.

Congress Passes the Enforcement Acts to Protect African American Voting Rights, 1870, 1871

In the immediate aftermath of the conclusion of the Civil War, several landmark laws were passed to protect the safety and guarantee the civil liberties—including the right to vote—to millions of newly freed slaves. These laws ranged from the Fourteenth and Fifteenth Amendments (which granted U.S. citizenship to former slaves and granted African American men the voting franchise, respectively) to the Reconstruction Acts of 1867. The latter established a program for readmitting the defeated Confederate states back into the Union, including provisions mandating that the states pass new constitutions granting suffrage to all men within their borders and requiring them to ratify the Fourteenth Amendment. To enforce these new amendments and laws, the Republican-controlled U.S. Congress also passed three Civil Rights Acts, also known as Enforcement Acts, in May 1870, February 1871, and April 1871. These laws were intended to reverse the rising tide of violence and intimidation aimed at African Americans in the South, both at the ballot box and in communities at large (these acts were also sometimes referred to as the Ku Klux Klan Acts). But within a few years of the passage of the Enforcement Acts, the Supreme Court issued rulings—in U.S. v. Reese *(1876) and* U.S. v. Cruikshank *(1876)—that nullified the laws, thus empowering the South's white political power base to institute Jim Crow laws that disenfranchised African American voters across the entire region.*

The First Enforcement Act, May 1870

Be it enacted by the Senate and House of Representatives of the United States of America in Congress assembled, That all citizens of the United States who are or shall be otherwise qualified by law to vote at any election . . . shall be entitled and allowed to vote at all such elections, without distinction of race, color, or previous condition of servitude. . . .

SEC. 2. *And be it further enacted,* That it shall be the duty of every person and officer to give to all citizens of the United States the same and equal opportunity to perform [any] prerequisite, and to become qualified to vote without distinction of race, color, or previous condition of servitude; and if any person or officer shall refuse or knowingly omit to give full effect to this section, he shall . . . be deemed guilty of a misdemeanor, and shall, on conviction thereof, be fined not less than five hundred dollars, or be imprisoned not less than one month and not more than one year, or both, at the discretion of the court. . . .

SEC. 6. *And be it further enacted,* That if two or more persons shall band or conspire together, or go in disguise upon the public highway, or upon the premises of another, with intent to violate any provision of this act, or to injure, oppress, threaten, or intimidate any citizen with intent to prevent or hinder his free exercise and enjoyment of any right or privilege granted or secured to him by the Constitution or laws of the United States, or because of his having exercised the same, such persons shall be held guilty of felony, and, on conviction thereof, shall be fined or imprisoned, or both, at the discretion of the court,—the fine not to exceed five thousand dollars, and the imprisonment not to exceed ten years,—and shall, moreover, be thereafter ineligible to, and disabled from holding, any office or place of honor, profit, or trust created by the Constitution or laws of the United States. . . .

SEC. 17. *And be it further enacted,* That any person who, under color of any law, statute, ordinance, regulation, or custom, shall subject, or cause to be subjected, any inhabitant of any State or Territory to the deprivation of any right secured or protected by the last preceding section [giving all persons the same rights as white citizens] of this act, or to different punishment, pains, or penalties on account of such person being an alien, or by reason of his color or race, than is prescribed for the punishment of citizens, shall be deemed guilty of a misdemeanor, and, on conviction, shall be punished by fine not exceeding one thousand dollars, or imprisonment not exceeding one year, or both, in the discretion of the court. . . .

The Second Enforcement Act, February 1871

SEC. 20. *And be it further enacted,* That if, [at] any registration of voters for an election for representative or delegate in the Congress of the United States, any person shall knowingly personate and register, or attempt to register, in the name of any other person, whether living, dead, or fictitious, or fraudulently register, or fraudulently attempt to register, not having a lawful right to do so; or do any unlawful act to secure registration for himself or any other person; or by force, threat, menace, intimidation, bribery, reward, or offer, or promise thereof, or other unlawful means, prevent or hinder any person having a lawful right to register [to vote] from duly exercising such right; or compel or induce, by any of such means, or other unlawful means, any officer of registration to admit to registration any person not legally entitled thereto, or interfere in any manner with any officer of registration in the discharge of his duties, or by any such means, or other unlawful means, induce any officer of registration to violate or refuse to comply with his duty or any law regulating the same; or if any such officer shall knowingly and willfully register as a voter any person not entitled to be registered, or refuse to so register any person entitled to be registered; or if any such officer or other person whose duty it is to perform any duty in relation to such registration or election, or to ascertain, announce, or declare the result thereof, or give or make any certificate, document, or evidence in relation thereto, shall knowingly neglect or refuse to perform any duty required by law, or violate any duty imposed by law, or do any act unauthorized by law relating to or affecting such registration or election, or the result thereof, or any certificate, document, or evidence in relation thereto, or if any person shall add, counsel, procure, or advise any such voter, person, or officer to do any act hereby made a crime, or to omit any act the omission of which is hereby made a crime, every such person shall be deemed guilty of a crime, and shall be liable to prosecution and punishment therefor as provided in section nineteen of said act of May thirty-one, eighteen hundred and seventy [First Enforcement Act], for persons guilty of any of the crimes therein specified. . . .

The Third Enforcement Act, April 1871

SEC. 1. *Be it enacted by the Senate and House of Representatives of the United States of America in Congress assembled,* That any person who, under color of any law, statute, ordinancc, rcgulation, custom, or usage of any State, shall subject, or cause to be subjected any person within the jurisdiction of the United States to the deprivation of any rights, privileges, or immunities secured by the Constitution of the United States, shall, any such law, statute, ordinance, regulation, custom or usage of the State to the contrary notwithstanding, be liable to the party injured in any action at law, suit in equity, or other proper proceeding for redress; such proceeding to be prosecuted in the several district or circuit courts of the United States, with and subject to the same rights of appeal, review upon error, and other remedies provided in like cases in such courts, under the provisions of the [Civil Right Act of 1866], and the other remedial laws of the United States which are in their nature applicable in such cases.

SEC. 2. That if two or more persons within any State or Territory of the United States shall conspire together to overthrow, or to put down, or to destroy by force the government of the United States, or to levy war against the United States, or to oppose by force the authority of the government of the United States, or by force, intimidation, or threat to prevent, hinder, or delay the execution of any law of the United States, or by force to seize, take, or possess any property of the United States contrary to the authority thereof, or by force, intimidation, or threat to prevent any person from accepting or holding any office or trust or place of confidence under the United States, or from discharging the duties thereof, or by force, intimidation, or threat to induce any officer of the United States to leave any State, district, or place where his duties as such officer might lawfully be performed, or to injure him in his person or property on account of his lawful discharge of the duties of his office, or to injure his person while engaged in the lawful discharge of the duties of his office, or to injure his property so as to molest, interrupt, hinder, or impede him in the discharge of his official duty, or by force, intimidation, or threat to deter any party or witness in any court of the United States from attending such court, or from testifying in any matter pending in such court fully, freely, and truthfully, or to injure any such party or witness in his person or property on account of his having so attended or testified, or by force, intimidation, or threat to influence the verdict, presentment, or indictment, of any juror or grand juror in any court of the United States, or to injure such juror in his person or property on account of any verdict, presentment, or indictment lawfully assented to by him, or on account of his being or having been such juror, or shall conspire together, or go in disguise upon the public highway or upon the premises of another for the purpose, either directly or indirectly, of depriving any person or any class of persons of the equal protection of the laws, or of equal privileges or immunities under the laws, or for the purpose of preventing or hindering the constituted authorities of any State from giving or securing to all persons within such State the equal protection of the laws, or shall conspire together for the purpose of in any manner impeding, hindering, obstructing, or defeating the due course of justice in any State or Territory, with intent to deny to any citizen of the United States the due and equal protection of the laws, or to injure any person in his person or his property for lawfully enforcing the right of any person or class of persons to the equal protection of the laws, or by force, intimidation, or threat to prevent any citizen of the United States lawfully entitled to vote from giving his support or advocacy in a lawful manner towards or in favor of the election of any lawfully qualified person as an elector of President or Vice-President of the United States, or as a member of the Congress of the United States, or to injure any such citizen in his person or property on account of such support or advocacy, each and every person so offending shall be deemed guilty of a high crime, and, upon conviction thereof in any district or circuit court of the United States or district or supreme court of any Territory of the United States having jurisdiction of similar offences, shall be punished by a fine not less than five hundred nor more than five thousand dollars, or by imprisonment, with or without hard labor, as the court may determine, for a period of not less than six months nor more than six years, as the court may determine, or by both such fine and imprisonment as the court shall determine.

Source: Enforcement Acts of 1870–1871. U.S. Senate Historical Office. Accessed December 21, 2018. https://www.senate.gov/artandhistory/history/resources/pdf/EnforcementAct_1870.pdf; https://www.senate.gov/artandhistory/history/resources/pdf/EnforcementAct_Feb1871.pdf; https://www.senate.gov/artandhistory/history/resources/pdf/EnforcementAct_Apr1871.pdf.

Announcement of the Ratification of the Fifteenth Amendment Guaranteeing Black Men the Right to Vote, 1870

In early 1869, Congress passed a proposed amendment to the U.S. Constitution guaranteeing the vote to African American men. A year later, on February 3, the Fifteenth Amendment was ratified and passed into law. Following is a formal announcement of ratification released by Hamilton Fish, U.S. Secretary of State, on March 30, 1870.

Know ye, that the Congress of the United States, on or about the twenty-seventh day of February, in the year one thousand eight hundred and sixty-nine, passed a resolution in the words and figures following, to wit:

A Resolution proposing an Amendment to the Constitution of the United States.

Resolved by the Senate and House of Representatives of the United States of America in Congress assembled (two thirds of both Houses concurring), That the following article be proposed to the legislatures of the several States as an amendment to the Constitution of the United States, which, when ratified by three fourths of said legislatures, shall be valid as part of the Constitution, namely:

ARTICLE XV

Section 1. The right of citizens of the United States to vote shall not be denied or abridged by the United States or by any State on account of race, color, or previous condition of servitude.

Section 2. The Congress shall have power to enforce this article by appropriate legislation.

And, further, that it appears from official documents on file in this Department that the amendment to the Constitution of the United States, proposed as aforesaid, has been ratified by the legislatures of the States of North Carolina, West Virginia, Massachusetts, Wisconsin, Maine, Louisiana, Michigan, south Carolina, Pennsylvania, Arkansas, Connecticut, Florida, Illinois, Indiana, New York, New Hampshire, Nevada, Vermont, Virginia, Alabama, Missouri, Mississippi, Ohio, Iowa, Kansas, Minnesota, Rhode Island, Nebraska, and Texas, in all twenty-nine States.

And, further, that the States whose legislatures have so ratified the said proposed amendment constitute three fourths of the whole number of States in the United States.

And further, that it appears from an official document on file in this Department that the legislature of the State of New York has since passed resolutions claiming to withdraw the said ratification of the said amendment which had been made by the legislature of that State, and of which official notice had been filed in this Department.

And, further, that it appears from an official document on file in this Department that the legislature of Georgia has by resolution ratified the said proposed amendment:

Now, therefore, be it known that I, Hamilton Fish, Secretary of State of the United States, by virtue and in pursuance of the second section of the act of congress approved the twentieth day of April, in the year eighteen hundred and eighteen, entitled, "An act to provide for the publication of the laws of the United States and for other purposes," do hereby certify that the amendment aforesaid has become valid to all intents and purposes as part of the Constitution of the United States.

In testimony whereof, I have hereunto set my hand, and caused the seal of the Department of State to be affixed.

Done at the city of Washington, this thirtieth day of March, in the year of our Lord one thousand eight hundred and seventy, and of the Independence of the United States the ninety-fourth.

HAMILTON FISH

Source: Fish, Hamilton. Statement announcing ratification of the Fifteenth Amendment, March 30, 1870. U.S. Statutes at Large, 41st Congress, 1st Session. Boston: Little, Brown, and Company, 1871, p. 1131.

Susan B. Anthony's Stump Speech on Suffrage, 1873

After Susan B. Anthony (and fourteen other women in the state of New York) defiantly voted in the 1872 presidential election despite laws that limited the ballot box to men, her vote was disqualified and she was fined $100 (which she never paid) after a short trial in which—as was the common practice of the day—she was not permitted to speak in her own defense. This experience angered the suffragist so much that she embarked on a speaking tour around the state of New York in 1873 in support of women's suffrage. The following are excerpts from the stump speech she delivered at various stops along the way.

Friends and fellow citizens:

I stand before you to-night, under indictment for the alleged crime of having voted at the last Presidential election, without having a lawful right to vote. It shall be my work this evening to prove to you that in thus voting, I not only committed no crime, but, instead, simply exercised my citizen's right, guaranteed to me and all United States citizens by the National Constitution, beyond the power of any State to deny.

Our democratic-republican government is based on the idea of the natural right of every individual member thereof to a voice and a vote in making and executing the laws. We assert the province of government to be to secure the people in the enjoyment of their unalienable rights. We throw to the winds the old dogma that governments can give rights. Before governments were organized, no one denies that each individual possessed the right to protect his own life. liberty and property. And when 100 or 1,000,000 people enter into a free government, they do not barter away their natural rights; they simply pledge themselves to protect each other in the enjoyment of them, through prescribed judicial and legislative tribunals. They agree to abandon the methods of brute force in the adjustment of their differences, and adopt those of civilization.

Nor can you find a word in any of the grand documents left us by the fathers that assumes for government the power to create or to confer rights. The Declaration of Independence, the United States Constitution, the constitutions of the several states and the organic laws of the territories, all alike propose to protect the people in the exercise of their God-given rights. Not one of them pretends to bestow rights.

"All men are created equal, and endowed by their Creator with certain unalienable rights. Among these are life, liberty and the pursuit of happiness. That to secure these, governments are instituted among men, deriving their just powers from the consent of the governed."

Here is no shadow of government authority over rights, nor exclusion of any from their full and equal enjoyment. Here is pronounced the right of all men, and "consequently," as the Quaker preacher said, "of all women," to a voice in the government. And here, in this very first paragraph of the declaration, is the assertion of the natural right of all to the ballot; for, how can "the consent of the governed" be given, if the right to vote be denied. Again:

"That whenever any form of government becomes destructive of these ends, it is the right of the people to alter or abolish it, and to institute a new government, laying its foundations on such principles, and organizing its powers in such forms as to them shall seem most likely to effect their safety and happiness."

Surely, the right of the whole people to vote is here clearly implied. For however destructive in their happiness this government might become, a disfranchised class could neither alter nor abolish it, nor institute a new one, except by the old brute force method of insurrection and rebellion. One-half of the people of this nation to-day are utterly powerless to blot from the statute books an unjust law, or to write there a new and a just one. The women, dissatisfied as they are with this form of government, that enforces taxation without representation,—that compels them to obey laws to which they have never given their consent,—that imprisons and hangs them without a trial by a jury of their peers, that robs them, in marriage, of the custody of their own persons, wages and children,—are this half of the people left wholly at the mercy of the other half, in direct violation of the spirit and letter of the declarations of the framers of this government, every one of which was based on the immutable principle of equal rights to all. . . .

For any State to make sex a qualification that must ever result in the disfranchisement of one entire half of the people, is to pass a bill of attainder, or an ex post facto law, and is therefore a violation of the supreme law of the land. By it, the blessings of liberty are forever withheld from women and their female posterity. To them, this government has no just powers derived from the consent of the governed. To them this government is not a democracy. It is not a republic. It is an odious aristocracy; a hateful oligarchy of sex. The most hateful aristocracy ever established on the face of the globe. An oligarchy of wealth, where the rich govern the poor; an oligarchy of learning, where the educated govern the ignorant; or even an oligarchy of race, where the Saxon rules the African, might be endured; but this oligarchy of sex, which makes father, brothers, husband, sons, the oligarchs over the mother and sisters, the wife and daughters of every household; which ordains all men sovereigns, all women subjects, carries dissension, discord and rebellion into every home of the nation. And this most odious aristocracy exists, too, in the face of Section 4, of Article 4, which says: "The United States shall guarantee to every State in the Union a republican form of government."

What, I ask you, is the distinctive difference between the inhabitants of a monarchical and those of a republican form of government, save that in the monarchical the people are subjects, helpless, powerless, bound to obey laws made by superiors—while in the republican, the people are citizens, individual sovereigns, all clothed with equal power, to make and unmake both their laws and law makers, and the moment you deprive a person of his right to a voice in the government, you degrade him from the status of a citizen of the republic, to that of a subject, and it matters very little to him whether his monarch be an individual tyrant, as is the Czar of Russia, or a 15,000,000 headed monster, as here in the United States; he is a powerless subject, serf or slave; not a free and independent citizen in any sense.

But is urged, the use of the masculine pronouns he, his and him, in all the constitutions and laws, is proof that only men were meant to be included in their provisions. If you insist on this version of the letter of the law, we shall insist that you be consistent, and accept the other horn of the dilemma, which would compel you to exempt women from taxation for the support of the government, and from penalties for the violation of laws.

A year and a half ago I was at Walla, Walla, Washington Territory. I saw there a theatrical company, called the "Pixley Sisters," playing before crowded houses, every night of the whole week of the territorial fair. The eldest of those three fatherless girls was scarce eighteen. Yet every night a United States officer stretched out his long fingers, and clutched six dollars of the proceeds of the exhibition of those orphan girls, who, but a few years before, were half starvelings in the streets of Olympia, the capital of the far-off northwest territory. So the poor widow, who keeps a boarding house, manufacturers shirts, or sells apples and peanuts on the street corners of our cities, is compelled to pay taxes from her scanty pittance. I would that the women of this republic, at once, resolve, never again to submit of taxation, until their right to vote be recognized. Amen. . . .

So long as any classes of men were denied their right to vote, the government made a show of consistency, by exempting them from taxation. When a property qualification of $250 was required of black men in New York, they were not compelled to pay taxes, so long as they were content to report themselves worth less than that sum; but the moment the black man died, and his property fell to his widow or daughter, the black woman's name would be put on the assessor's list, and she be compelled to pay taxes on the same property exempted to her husband. The same is true of ministers in New York. So long as the minister lives, he is exempted from taxation on $1,500 of property, but the moment the breath goes out of his body, his widow's name will go down on the assessor's list, and she will have to pay taxes on the $1,500. So much for the special legislation in favor of women.

In all the penalties and burdens of the government, (except the military,) women are reckoned as citizens, equally with men. Also, in all privileges and immunities, save those of the jury box and ballot box, the two fundamental privileges on which rest all the others. The United States government not only taxes, fines, imprisons and hangs women, but it allows them to pre-empt lands, register ships, and take out passport and naturalization papers. Not only does the law permit single women and widows to the right of naturalization, but Section 2 says: "A married woman may be naturalized without the concurrence of her husband." (I wonder the fathers were not afraid of creating discord in the families of foreigners); and again: "When an alien, having complied with the law, and declared his intention to become a citizen, dies before he is actually naturalized, his widow and children shall be considered citizens, entitled to all rights and privileges as such, on taking the required oath." If a foreign born woman by becoming a naturalized citizen, is entitled to all the rights and privileges of citizenship, is not a native born woman, by her national citizenship, possessed of equal rights and privileges? . . .

Clearly, then, the national government must not only define the rights of citizens, but it must stretch out its powerful hand and protect them in every state in this Union.

But if you will insist that the fifteenth amendment's emphatic interdiction against robbing United States citizens of their right to vote, "on account of race, color, or previous condition of servitude," is a recognition of the right, either of the United States, or any state, to rob citizens of that right, for any or all other reason, I will prove to you that the class of citizens for which I now plead, and to which I belong, may be, and sure, by all the principles of our government, and many of the laws of the states, included under the term "previous condition of servitude."

First. —The married women and their legal status. What is servitude? "The condition of a slave." What is a slave? "A person who is robbed of the proceeds of his labor; a person who is subject to the will of another."

By the law of Georgia, South Carolina, and all the states of the South, the negro had no right to the custody and control of his person. He belonged to his master. If he was disobedient, the master had the right to use correction. If the negro didn't like the correction, and attempted to run away, the master had a right to use coercion to bring him back.

By the law of every state in this Union to-day, North as well as South, the married woman has no right to the custody and control of her person. The wife belongs to her husband; and if the refuses obedience to his will, he may use moderate correction, and if she doesn't like his moderate correction, and attempts to leave his "bed and board," the husband may use moderate coercion to bring her back. The little word "moderate," you see, is the saving clause for the wife, and would doubtless be overstepped should offended husband administer his correction with the "cat-o'-nine-tails," or accomplish his coercion with blood-hounds.

Again, the slave had no right to the earnings of his hands, they belonged to his master; no right to the custody of his children, they belonged to his master; no right to sue or be sued, or testify in the courts. If he committed a crime, it was the master who must sue or be sued.

In many of the states there has been special legislation, giving to married women the right to property inherited, or received by bequest, or earned by the pursuit of any avocation outside of the home; also, giving her the right to sue and be sued in matters pertaining to such separate property; but not a single state of this Union has eve secured the wife in the enjoyment of her right to the joint ownership of the joint earnings of the marriage copartnership. And since, in the nature of things, the vast majority of married women never earn a dollar, by work outside of their families, nor inherit a dollar from their fathers, it follows that from the day of their marriage to the day of the death of their husbands, not one of them ever has a dollar, except it shall please her husband to let her have it.

In some of the states, also, there have been laws passed giving to the mother a joint right with the father in the guardianship of the children. But twenty years ago, when our woman's rights movement commenced, by the laws of the State of New York, and all the states, the father had the sole custody and control of the children. No matter if he were a brutal, drunken libertine, he had the legal right, without the mother's consent, to apprentice her sons to rum sellers, or her daughters to brothel keepers. He could even will away an unborn child, to some other person than the mother. And in many of the states the law still prevails, and the mothers are still utterly powerless under the common law.

I doubt if there is, to-day, a State in this Union where a married woman can sue or be sued for slander of character, and until quite recently there was not one in which she could sue or be sued for injury of person. However damaging to the wife's reputation any slander may be, she is wholly powerless to institute legal proceedings against her accuser, unless her husband shall join with her; and how often have we heard of the husband conspiring with some outside barbarian to blast the good name of his wife? A married woman cannot testify in courts in cases of joint interest with her husband. A good farmer's wife near Earlville, Ill., who had all the rights she wanted, went to a dentist of the village and had a full set of false teeth, both upper and under. The dentist pronounced them an admirable fit, and the wife declared they gave her fits to wear them; that she could neither chew nor talk with them in her mouth. The dentist sued the husband; his counsel brought the wife as witness; the judge ruled her off the stand; saying "a married woman cannot be a witness in matters of joint interest between herself and her husband." Think of it, ye good wives, the false teeth in your mouths are joint interest with your husbands, about which you are legally incompetent to speak!! If in our frequent and shocking railroad accidents a married woman is injured in her person, in nearly all of the States, it is her husband who must sue the company, and it is to her husband that the damages, if there are any, will be awarded. In Ashfield, Mass., supposed to be the most advanced of any State in the Union in all things, humanitarian as well as intellectual, a married woman was severely injured by a defective sidewalk. Her husband sued the corporation and recovered $13,000 damages. And those $13,000 belong to him bona fide; and whenever that unfortunate wife wishes a dollar of it to supply her needs she must ask her husband for it; and if the man be of a narrow, selfish, niggardly nature, she will have to hear him say, every time, "What have you done, my dear, with the twenty-five cents I gave you yesterday?" Isn't such a position, ask you, humiliating enough to be called "servitude?" That husband, as would any other husband, in nearly every State of this Union, sued and obtained damages for the loss of the services of his wife, precisely as the master, under the old slave regime, would have done, had his slave been thus injured, and precisely as he himself would have done had it been his ox, cow or horse instead of his wife. . . .

Does any lawyer doubt my statement of the legal status of married women? I will remind him of the fact that the old common law of England prevails in every State in this Union, except where the Legislature has enacted special laws annulling it. And I am ashamed that not one State has yet blotted from its statue books the old common law of marriage, by which Blackstone, summed up in the fewest words possible, is made to say, "husband and wife are one, and that one is the husband."

Thus may all married women, wives and widows, by the laws of the several States, be technically included in the fifteenth amendment's specification of "condition of servitude," present or previous. And not only married women, but I will also prove to you that by all the great fundamental principles of our free government, the entire womanhood of the nation is in a "condition of servitude" as surely as were our revolutionary fathers, when they rebelled against old King George. Women are taxed without representation, governed without their consent, tried, convicted and punished without a jury of their peers. And is all this tyranny any less humiliating and degrading to women under our democratic-republican government to-day than it was to men under their aristocratic, monarchical government one hundred years ago? There is not an utterance of old John Adams, John Hancock or Patrick Henry, but finds a living response in the soul of every intelligent, patriotic woman of the nation. Bring to me a common-sense woman property holder, and I will show you one whose soul is fired with all the indignation of 1776 every time the tax-gatherer presents himself at her door. You will not find one such but feels her condition of servitude as galling as did James Otis when he said:

"The very act of taxing exercised over those who are not represented appears to me to be depriving them of one of their most essential rights, and if continued, seems to be in effect an entire disfranchisement of every civil right. For, what one civil right is worth a rush after a man's property is subject to be taken from him at pleasure without his consent? If a man is not his own assessor in person, or by deputy, his liberty is gone, or he is wholly at the mercy of others." . . .

I admit that prior to the rebellion, by common consent, the right to enslave, as well as to disfranchise both native and foreign born citizens, was conceded to the States. But the one grand principle, settled by the war and the reconstruction legislation, is the supremacy of national power to protect the citizens of the United States in their right to freedom and the elective franchise, against any and every interference on the part of the several States. And again and again, have the American people asserted the triumph of this principle, by their overwhelming majorities for Lincoln and Grant.

The one issue of the last two Presidential elections was, whether the fourteenth and fifteenth amendments should be considered the irrevocable will of the people; and the decision was, they shall be—and that it is only the right, but the duty of the National Government to protect all United States citizens in the full enjoyment and free exercise of all their privileges and immunities against any attempt of any State to deny or abridge.

And in this conclusion Republican and Democrats alike agree. . . .

If that means anything, it is that Congress should pass a law to require the States to protect women in their equal political rights, and that the States should enact laws making it the duty of inspectors of elections to receive women's votes on precisely the same conditions they do those of men. . . .

We no longer petition Legislature or Congress to give us the right to vote. We appeal to the women everywhere to exercise their too long neglected "citizen's right to vote." We appeal to the inspectors of election everywhere to receive the votes of all United States citizens as it is their duty to do. We appeal to United States commissioners and marshals to arrest the inspectors who reject the names and votes of United States citizens, as it is their duty to do, and leave those alone who, like our eighth ward inspectors, perform their duties faithfully and well.

We ask the juries to fail to return verdicts of "guilty" against honest, law-abiding, tax-paying United States citizens for offering their votes at our elections. Or against intelligent, worthy young men, inspectors of elections, for receiving and counting such citizens votes.

We ask the judges to render true and unprejudiced opinions of the law, and wherever there is room for a doubt to give its benefit on the side of liberty and equal rights to women, remembering that "the true rule of interpretation under our national constitution, especially since its amendments, is that anything for human rights is constitutional, everything against human right unconstitutional."

And it is on this line that we propose to fight our battle for the ballot—all peaceably, but nevertheless persistently through to complete triumph, when all United States citizens shall be recognized as equals before the law.

Source: Anthony, Susan B. "Women's Rights to the Suffrage," 1873. In *The Life and Work of Susan B. Anthony*, edited by Ida H. Harper, Vol. 2. Indianapolis and Kansas City: The Bowen-Merrill Company, 1898, pp. 977–992.

The Supreme Court Hands Suffragists a Defeat in *Minor v. Happersett*, 1874

In the fall of 1872, Virginia Minor, a Missouri woman who had been born in America, submitted a voter-registration application for the upcoming presidential election. When her application was turned down by Reese Happersett, the registrar of voters, Minor launched a legal campaign to strike down Happersett's decision—and Missouri's wider prohibition against women voting—as a violation of the Fourteenth Amendment's Privileges and Immunities Clause. But when the case finally reached the U.S. Supreme Court, Minor's argument was rejected. Following are excerpts from the majority decision, which was delivered in October 1874. According to Chief Justice Morrison Waite, who authored the decision, voting rights—even for federal elections—were the province of individual states that could extend or withhold the franchise to women as they so chose.

CHIEF JUSTICE WAITE delivered the opinion of the Court.

[O]n the 15th of October, 1872 (one of the days fixed by law for the registration of voters), Mrs. Virginia Minor, a native born, free, white citizen of the United States, and of the State of Missouri, over the age of twenty-one years, wishing to vote for electors for President and Vice-President of the United States, and for a representative in Congress, and for other officers, at the general election held in November, 1872, applied to one Happersett, the registrar of voters, to register her as a lawful voter, which he refused to do, assigning for cause that she was not a "male citizen of the United States," but a woman. She thereupon sued him in one of the inferior State courts of Missouri, for willfully refusing to place her name upon the list of registered voters, by which refusal she was deprived of her right to vote.

. . .The question is presented in this case, whether, since the adoption of the Fourteenth Amendment, a woman, who is a citizen of the United States and of the State of Missouri, is a voter in that State, notwithstanding the provision of the constitution and laws of the State, which confine the right of suffrage to men alone . . .

It is contended that the provisions of the constitution and laws of the State of Missouri which confine the right of suffrage and registration therefore to men, are in violation of the Constitution of the United States, and therefore void. The argument is, that as a woman, born or naturalized in the United States and subject to the jurisdiction thereof, is a citizen of the United States and of the State in which she resides, she has the right of suffrage as one of the privileges and immunities of her citizenship, which the State cannot by its laws or constitution abridge.

There is no doubt that women may be citizens. They are persons, and by the Fourteenth Amendment "all persons born or naturalized in the United States and subject to the jurisdiction thereof" are expressly declared to be "citizens of the United States and of the State wherein they reside." But, in our opinion, it did not need this amendment to give them that position. Before its adoption the Constitution of the United States did not in terms prescribe who should be citizens of the United States or of the several States, yet there were necessarily such citizens without such provision . . .

Other proof of like character might be found, but certainly more cannot be necessary to establish the fact that sex has never been made one of the elements of citizenship in the United States. In this respect men have never had an advantage over women. The same laws precisely apply to both. The Fourteenth Amendment did not affect the citizenship of women any more than it did of men. In this particular, therefore, the rights of Mrs. Minor do not depend upon the [Fourteenth] Amendment. She has always been a citizen from her birth, and entitled to all the privileges and immunities of citizenship. The amendment prohibited the State, of which she is a citizen, from abridging any of her privileges and immunities as a citizen of the United States; but it did not confer citizenship on her. That she had before its adoption.

If the right of suffrage is one of the necessary privileges of a citizen of the United States, then the constitution and laws of Missouri confining it to men are in violation of the Constitution of the United States, as amended, and consequently void. *The direct question is, therefore, presented whether all citizens are necessarily voters.* (emphasis added)

The Constitution does not define the privileges and immunities of citizens. For that definition we must look elsewhere. In this case we need not determine what they are, but only whether suffrage is necessarily one of them.

It certainly is nowhere made so in express terms. The United States has no voters in the States of its own creation. The elective officers of the United States are all elected directly or indirectly by State voters. The times, places, and manner of holding elections for Senators and Representatives are to be prescribed in each

State by the legislature thereof . . . The power of the State in this particular is certainly supreme until Congress acts.

The [Fourteenth] amendment did not add to the privileges and immunities of a citizen. It simply furnished an additional guaranty for the protection of such as he already had. No new voters were necessarily made by it. Indirectly it may have had that effect, because it may have increased the number of citizens entitled to suffrage under the constitution and laws of the States, but it operates for this purpose, if at all, through the States and the State laws, and not directly upon the citizen.

It is clear, therefore, we think, that the Constitution has not added the right of suffrage to the privileges and immunities of citizenship as they existed at the time it was adopted. This makes it proper to inquire whether suffrage was coextensive with the citizenship of the States at the time of its adoption. If it was, then it may with force be argued that suffrage was one of the rights which belonged to citizenship, and in the enjoyment of which every citizen must be protected. But if it was not, the contrary may with propriety be assumed.

When the Federal Constitution was adopted, all the States, with the exception of Rhode Island and Connecticut, had constitutions of their own. These two continued to act under their charters from the Crown. Upon an examination of those constitutions we find that in no State were all citizens permitted to vote. Each State determined for itself who should have that power. . . .

In this condition of the law in respect to suffrage in the several States it cannot for a moment be doubted that if it had been intended to make all citizens of the United States voters, the framers of the Constitution would not have left it to implication. So important a change in the condition of citizenship as it actually existed, if intended, would have been expressly declared . . .

And still again, after the adoption of the Fourteenth Amendment, it was deemed necessary to adopt a Fifteenth, as follows: "The right of citizens of the United States to vote shall not be denied or abridged by the United States, or by any State, on account of race, color, or previous condition of servitude." The Fourteenth Amendment had already provided that no State should make or enforce any law which should abridge the privileges or immunities of citizens of the United States. If suffrage was one of these privileges or immunities, why amend the Constitution to prevent its being denied on account of race, &c.? Nothing is more evident than that the greater must include the less, and if all were already protected why go through with the form of amending the Constitution to protect a part?

It is true that the United States guarantees to every State a republican form of government. It is also true that no State can pass a bill of attainder, and that no person can be deprived of life, liberty, or property without due process of law. All these several provisions of the Constitution must be construed in connection with the other parts of the instrument, and in the light of the surrounding circumstances.

The guaranty is of a republican form of government. No particular government is designated as republican, neither is the exact form to be guaranteed, in any manner especially designated. Here, as in other parts of the instrument, we are compelled to resort elsewhere to ascertain what was intended.

The guaranty necessarily implies a duty on the part of the States themselves to provide such a government. All the States had governments when the Constitution was adopted. In all the people participated to some extent, through their representatives elected in the manner specially provided. These governments the Constitution did not change. They were accepted precisely as they were, and it is, therefore, to be presumed that they were such as it was the duty of the States to provide. Thus we have unmistakable evidence of what was republican in form, within the meaning of that term as employed in the Constitution.

As has been seen, all the citizens of the States were not invested with the right of suffrage. In all, save perhaps New Jersey, this right was only bestowed upon men and not upon all of them. Under these circumstances it is certainly now too late to contend that a government is not republican, within the meaning of this guaranty in the Constitution, because women are not made voters.

The same may be said of the other provisions just quoted. Women were excluded from suffrage in nearly all the States by the express provision of their constitutions and laws. If that had been equivalent to a bill of attainder, certainly its abrogation would not have been left to implication. Nothing less than express language would have been employed to effect so radical a change. So also of the amendment which declares that no person shall be deprived of life, liberty, or property without due process of law, adopted as it was as early as 1791. If suffrage was intended to be included within its obligations, language better adapted to express that intent would most certainly have been employed. The right of suffrage, when granted, will be protected. He who has it can only be deprived of it by due process of law, but in order to claim protection he must first show that he has the right . . .

The Constitution was submitted to the States for adoption in 1787, and was ratified by nine States in 1788, and finally by the thirteen original States in 1790. Vermont was the first new State admitted to the Union, and it came in under a constitution which conferred the right of suffrage only upon men of the full age of twenty-one years, having resided in the State for the space of one whole year next before the election, and who were of quiet and peaceable behavior. This was in 1791. The next year, 1792, Kentucky followed with a constitution confining the right of suffrage to free male citizens of the age of twenty-one years who had resided in the State two years or in the county in which they offered to vote one year next before the election. Then followed Tennessee, in 1796, with voters of freemen of the age of twenty-one years and upwards, possessing a freehold in the county wherein they may vote, and being inhabitants of the State or freemen being inhabitants of any one county in the State six months immediately preceding the day of election. But we need not particularize further. No new State has ever been admitted to the Union which has conferred the right of suffrage upon women, and this has never been considered a valid objection to her admission. On the contrary, as is claimed in the argument, the right of suffrage was withdrawn from women as early as 1807 in the State of New Jersey, without any attempt to obtain the interference of the United States to prevent it. Since then the governments of the insurgent States have been reorganized under a requirement that before their representatives could be admitted to seats in Congress they must have adopted new constitutions, republican in form. In no one of these constitutions was suffrage conferred upon women, and yet the States have all been restored to their original position as States in the Union.

Besides this, citizenship has not in all cases been made a condition precedent to the enjoyment of the right of suffrage. Thus, in Missouri, persons of foreign birth, who have declared their intention to become citizens of the United States, may under certain circumstances vote. The same provision is to be found in the constitutions of Alabama, Arkansas, Florida, Georgia, Indiana, Kansas, Minnesota, and Texas.

Certainly, if the courts can consider any question settled, this is one. For nearly ninety years the people have acted upon the idea that the Constitution, when it conferred citizenship, did not necessarily confer the right of suffrage. If uniform practice long continued can settle the construction of so important an instrument as the Constitution of the United States confessedly is, most certainly it has been done here. Our province is to decide what the law is, not to declare what it should be.

We have given this case the careful consideration its importance demands. If the law is wrong, it ought to be changed; but the power for that is not with us. The arguments addressed to us bearing upon such a view of the subject may perhaps be sufficient to induce those having the power, to make the alteration, but they ought not to be permitted to influence our judgment in determining the present rights of the parties now litigating before us. No argument as to woman's need of suffrage can be considered. We can only act upon her rights as they exist. It is not for us to look at the hardship of withholding. Our duty is at an end if we find it is within the power of a State to withhold.

Being unanimously of the opinion that the Constitution of the United States does not confer the right of suffrage upon any one, and that the constitutions and laws of the several States which commit that important trust to men alone are not necessarily void, we affirm the judgment.

Source: "Opinion of the Court." *Minor v. Happersett,* 88 U.S. (21 Wall.) 162 (1875).

President Ulysses S. Grant Denounces Attacks on Black Voters and Republican Officeholders in Reconstruction-Era Louisiana, 1875

During the Radical Reconstruction era in the American South, President Ulysses S. Grant and his administration took a number of measures to support and defend black voters and Republican officeholders. For instance, Grant was a strong supporter of the Fifteenth Amendment, which guaranteed the franchise to African American men. He described it in a March 1870 message to Congress as "the most important event that has occurred since the nation came into life" and declared that "a measure which makes at once 4,000,000 people voters who were heretofore declared by the highest tribunal in the land not citizens of the United States, nor eligible to become so . . . is indeed a measure of grander importance than any other one act of the kind from the foundation of our free Government to the present day."

By the early 1870s, though, whites in the South had become openly hostile to Republican officials in their midst, and they were furious that former slaves had the franchise. They subsequently flooded to the Democratic Party and joined the ranks of white supremacist paramilitary groups like the White League and the Ku Klux Klan, where they vowed to "reclaim" their states.

One particular flashpoint of tension and violence was Louisiana, especially after a hotly disputed 1872 gubernatorial election in which Grant ultimately sent federal troops to support the Republican candidate, William P. Kellogg. In April 1873, a mob of whites attacked a local courthouse in Colfax, Louisiana, that had been occupied by a group of black militia. The black group surrendered after an exchange of gunfire—then were murdered by firearms or hanging over the course of the next several hours (estimates of the total number of murdered African Americans range from 60 to 150). The "Colfax Massacre," as it came to be known, was perhaps the most notorious incident of racial violence of the entire Reconstruction era.

By early 1875, the incidents of intimidation and violence against black citizens and Republican lawmakers and officials across Louisiana had become so alarming and widespread that Grant was moved to send a special message to Congress. In this message, excerpted below, Grant recounted the deteriorating and increasingly lawless situation in the state and urged Congress to take measures to safeguard black voting rights and defend the rule of law in Louisiana. But he sent this message mere weeks after Democrats had routed Republicans in the 1874 midterms. Those elections results enabled Democrats to reclaim control of the House of Representatives for the first time since before the Civil War and convinced northern Republican senators that their constituents were weary of federal entanglements in the states of the former Confederacy. The new political environment ensured that Grant's plea for congressional intervention in Louisiana would go nowhere.

To the Senate of the United States:

. . .To say that lawlessness, turbulence, and bloodshed have characterized the political affairs of [Louisiana] since its reorganization under the reconstruction acts is only to repeat what has become well known as a part of its unhappy history; but it may be proper here to refer to the election of 1868, by which the Republican vote of the State, through fraud and violence, was reduced to a few thousands, and the bloody riots of 1866 and 1868, to show that the disorders there are not due to any recent causes or to any late action of the Federal authorities.

Preparatory to the election of 1872 a shameful and undisguised conspiracy was formed to carry that election against the Republicans, without regard to law or right, and to that end the most glaring frauds and forgeries were committed in the returns, after many colored citizens had been denied registration and others deterred by fear from casting their ballots.

When the time came for a final canvass of the votes, in view of the foregoing facts William P. Kellogg, the Republican candidate for governor, brought suit upon the equity side of the United States circuit court for Louisiana, and against

Warmoth and others, who had obtained possession of the returns of the election, representing that several thousand voters of the State had been deprived of the elective franchise on account of their color, and praying that steps might be taken to have said votes counted and for general relief. To enable the court to inquire as to the truth of these allegations, a temporary restraining order was issued against the defendants, which was at once wholly disregarded and treated with contempt by those to whom it was directed. These proceedings have been widely denounced as an unwarrantable interference by the Federal judiciary with the election of State officers; but it is to be remembered that by the fifteenth amendment to the Constitution of the United States the political equality of colored citizens is secured, and under the second section of that amendment, providing that Congress shall have power to enforce its provisions by appropriate legislation, an act was passed on the 31st of May, 1870, and amended in 1871, the object of which was to prevent the denial or abridgment of suffrage to citizens on account of race, color, or previous condition of servitude; and it has been held by all the Federal judges before whom the question has arisen, including Justice Strong, of the Supreme Court, that the protection afforded by this amendment and these acts extends to State as well as other elections. That it is the duty of the Federal courts to enforce the provisions of the Constitution of the United States and the laws passed in pursuance thereof is too clear for controversy. . . .

That the courts of the United States have the fight to interfere in various ways with State elections so as to maintain political equality and rights therein, irrespective of race or color, is comparatively a new, and to some seems to be a startling, idea, but it results as clearly from the fifteenth amendment to the Constitution and the acts that have been passed to enforce that amendment as the abrogation of State laws upholding slavery results from the thirteenth amendment to the Constitution. . . .

It has been bitterly and persistently alleged that Kellogg was not elected. Whether he was or not is not altogether certain, nor is it any more certain that his competitor, McEnery, was chosen. The election was a gigantic fraud, and there are no reliable returns of its result. Kellogg obtained possession of the office, and in my opinion has more right to it than his competitor.

On the 20th of February, 1873, the Committee on Privileges and Elections of the Senate made a report in which they say they were satisfied by testimony that the manipulation of the election machinery by Warmoth and others was equivalent to 20,000 votes; and they add that to recognize the McEnery government "would be recognizing a government based upon fraud, in defiance of the wishes and intention of the voters of the State." Assuming the correctness of the statements in this report (and they seem to have been generally accepted by the country), the great crime in Louisiana, about which so much has been said, is that one is holding the office of governor who was cheated out of 20,000 votes, against another whose title to the office is undoubtedly based on fraud and in defiance of the wishes and intentions of the voters of the State.

Misinformed and misjudging as to the nature and extent of this report, the supporters of McEnery proceeded to displace by force in some counties of the State the appointees of Governor Kellogg, and on the 13th of April, in an effort of that kind, a butchery of citizens was committed at Colfax, which in bloodthirstiness and barbarity is hardly surpassed by any acts of savage warfare. . . .

To hold the people of Louisiana generally responsible for these atrocities would not be just, but it is a lamentable fact that insuperable obstructions were thrown in the way of punishing these murderers; and the so-called conservative papers of the State not only justified the massacre, but denounced as Federal tyranny and despotism the attempt of the United States officers to bring them to justice. Fierce denunciations ring through the country about office holding and election matters in Louisiana, while every one of the Colfax miscreants goes unwhipped of justice, and no way can be found in this boasted land of civilization and Christianity to punish the perpetrators of this bloody and monstrous Crime.

Not unlike this was the massacre in August last. Several Northern young men of capital and enterprise had started the little and flourishing town of Coushatta. Some of them were Republicans and officeholders under Kellogg. They were therefore doomed to death. Six of them were seized and carried away from their homes and murdered in cold blood. No one has been punished, and the conservative press of the State denounced all efforts to that end and boldly justified the crime.

. . . To say that the murder of a negro or a white Republican is not considered a crime in Louisiana would probably be unjust to a great part of the people, but it is true that a great number of such murders have been committed and no one has been punished therefor; and manifestly, as to them, the spirit of hatred and violence is stronger than law.

Representations were made to me that the presence of troops in Louisiana was unnecessary and irritating to the people, and that there was no danger of public disturbance if they were taken away. Consequently early in last summer the troops were all withdrawn from the State, with the exception of a small garrison at New Orleans Barracks. It was claimed that a comparative state of quiet had supervened. Political excitement as to Louisiana affairs seemed to be dying out. But the November election was approaching, and it was necessary for party purposes that the flame should be rekindled.

Accordingly, on the 14th of September D. P. Penn, claiming that he was elected lieutenant-governor in 1872, issued an inflammatory proclamation calling upon the militia of the State to arm, assemble, and drive from power the usurpers, as he designated the officers of the State. The White Leagues, armed and ready for the conflict, promptly responded.

On the same day the governor made a formal requisition upon me, pursuant to the act of 1795 and section 4, Article IV, of the Constitution, to aid in suppressing domestic violence. On the next day I issued my proclamation commanding the insurgents to disperse within five days from the date thereof; but before the proclamation was published in New Orleans the organized and armed forces recognizing a usurping governor had taken forcible possession of the statehouse and temporarily subverted the government. Twenty or more people were killed, including a number of the police of the city. The streets of the city were stained with blood. All that was desired in the way of excitement had been accomplished, and, in view of the steps taken to repress it, the revolution is apparently, though it is believed not really, abandoned, and the cry of Federal usurpation and tyranny in Louisiana was renewed with redoubled energy. Troops had been sent to the State under this requisition of the governor, and as other disturbances seemed imminent they were allowed to remain there to render the executive such aid as might become necessary to enforce the laws of the State and repress the continued violence which seemed inevitable the moment Federal support should be withdrawn.

Prior to, and with a view to, the late election in Louisiana white men associated themselves together in armed bodies called "White Leagues," and at the same time threats were made in the Democratic journals of the State that the election should be carried against the Republicans at all hazards, which very naturally greatly alarmed the colored voters. By section 8 of the act of February 28, 1871, it is made the duty of United States marshals and their deputies at polls where votes are cast for Representatives in Congress to keep the peace and prevent any violations of the so-called enforcement acts and other offenses against the laws of the United States; and upon a requisition of the marshal of Louisiana, and in view of said armed organizations and other portentous circumstances, I caused detachments of troops to be stationed in various localities in the State, to aid him in the performance of his official duties. That there was intimidation of Republican voters at the election, notwithstanding these precautions, admits of no doubt. . . .

I am well aware that any military interference by the officers or troops of the United States with the organization of the State legislature or any of its proceedings, or with any civil department of the Government, is repugnant to our ideas of government. I can conceive of no case, not involving rebellion or insurrection, where such interference by authority of the General Government ought to be permitted or can be justified. But there are circumstances connected with the late legislative imbroglio in Louisiana which seem to exempt the military from any intentional wrong in that matter. Knowing that they had been placed in Louisiana to prevent domestic violence and aid in the enforcement of the State laws, the officers and troops of the United States may well have supposed that it was their duty to act when called upon by the governor for that purpose.

Each branch of a legislative assembly is the judge of the election and qualifications of its own members; but if a mob or a body of unauthorized persons seize and hold the legislative hall in a tumultuous and riotous manner, and so prevent any organization by those legally returned as elected, it might become the duty of the State executive to interpose, if requested by a majority of the members elect, to suppress the disturbance and enable the persons elected to organize the house.

Any exercise of this power would only be justifiable under most extraordinary circumstances, and it would then be the duty of the governor to call upon the constabulary or, if necessary, the military force of the State. But with reference to Louisiana, it is to be borne in mind that any attempt by the governor to use the police force of that State at this time would have undoubtedly precipitated a bloody conflict with the White League, as it did on the 14th of September.

There is no doubt but that the presence of the United States troops upon that occasion prevented bloodshed and the loss of life. Both parties appear to have relied upon them as conservators of the public peace.

The first call was made by the Democrats, to remove persons obnoxious to them from the legislative halls; and the second was from the Republicans, to remove persons who had usurped seats in the legislature without legal certificates authorizing them to seats, and in sufficient number to change the majority.

Nobody was disturbed by the military who had a legal right at that time to occupy a seat in the legislature. That the Democratic minority of the house undertook to seize its organization by fraud and violence; that in this attempt they trampled under foot law; that they undertook to make persons not returned as elected members, so as to create a majority; that they acted under a preconcerted plan, and under false pretenses introduced into the hall a body of men to support their pretensions by force if necessary, and that conflict, disorder, and riotous proceedings followed are facts that seem to be well established; and I am credibly informed that these violent proceedings were a part of a premeditated plan to have the house organized in this way, recognize what has been called the McEnery senate, then to depose Governor Kellogg, and so revolutionize the State government.

Whether it was wrong for the governor, at the request of the majority of the members returned as elected to the house, to use such means as were in his power to defeat these lawless and revolutionary proceedings is perhaps a debatable question; but it is quite certain that there would have been no trouble if those who now complain of illegal interference had allowed the house to be organized in a lawful and regular manner. When those who inaugurate disorder and anarchy disavow such proceedings, it will be time enough to condemn those who by such means as they have prevent the success of their lawless and desperate schemes. . . .

It is a deplorable fact that political crimes and murders have been committed in Louisiana which have gone unpunished, and which have been justified or apologized for, which must rest as a reproach upon the State and country long after the present generation has passed away.

I have no desire to have United States troops interfere in the domestic concerns of Louisiana or any other State.

On the 9th of December last Governor Kellogg telegraphed to me his apprehensions that the White League intended to make another attack upon the statehouse, to which, on the same day, I made the following answer, since which no communication has been sent to him:

> Your dispatch of this date just received. It is exceedingly unpalatable to use troops in anticipation of danger. Let the State authorities be right, and then proceed with their duties without apprehension of danger. If they are then molested, the question will be determined whether the United States is able to maintain law and order within its limits or not.

I have deplored the necessity which seemed to make it my duty under the Constitution and laws to direct such interference. I have always refused except where it seemed to be my imperative duty to act in such a manner under the Constitution and laws of the United States. I have repeatedly and earnestly entreated the people of the South to live together in peace and obey the laws; and nothing would give me greater pleasure than to see reconciliation and tranquillity everywhere prevail, and thereby remove all necessity for the presence of troops among them. I regret, however, to say that this state of things does not exist, nor does its existence seem to be desired, in some localities; and as to those it may be proper for me to say that to the extent that Congress has conferred power upon me to prevent it neither Ku Klux Klans, White Leagues, nor any other association using arms and violence to execute their unlawful purposes can be permitted in that way to govern any part of this country; nor can I see with indifference Union men or Republicans ostracized, persecuted, and murdered on account of their opinions, as they now are in some localities.

I have heretofore urged the case of Louisiana upon the attention of Congress, and I can not but think that its inaction has produced great evil.

Source: Richardson, James D. *A Compilation of the Messages and Papers of the Presidents*. Vol. VII. Accessed June 24, 2019. http://www.gutenberg.org/files/13012/13012.txt.

Supreme Court Cripples Black Voting Rights in *U.S. v. Cruikshank*, 1876

One of the key legal decisions paving the way for the advancement of racially discriminatory Jim Crow laws across the post-Reconstruction American South came in 1876 with the U.S. Supreme Court's decision in U.S. v. Cruikshank. *This case concerned William J. Cruikshank and eight other white radicals in Colfax, Louisiana, who had been charged with attacking two black freedmen seeking to exercise their voting rights. They were indicted on charges of violations of both the Enforcement Act of 1870, which made it a crime to interfere with the voting rights of others—including African American voters. Specifically, the defendants were charged with violating the First and Second Amendment rights of the freedmen, and of being in violation of the Due Process and Equal Protection Clauses of the recently passed Fourteenth Amendment. In* Cruikshank, *however, the Supreme Court declared that since voting rights are governed by states, Congress did not have the authority to pass laws dictating how states monitored, administered, or carried out elections. In other words, the court asserted in its opinion (excerpted below) that the Fifteenth Amendment, expressly crafted to give the vote to blacks, was virtually worthless because voting rights were the purview of individual states—including states dedicated to stripping away all political rights of their African American populations.*

Chief Justice Waite delivered the opinion of the Court

This case comes here with a certificate by the judges of the Circuit Court for the District of Louisiana that they were divided in opinion upon a question which occurred at the hearing. It presents for our consideration an indictment containing sixteen counts, divided into two series of eight counts each, based upon sect. 6 of the Enforcement Act of May 31, 1870. That section is as follows:

"That if two or more persons shall band or conspire together, or go in disguise upon the public highway, or upon the premises of another, with intent to violate any provision of this act, or to injure, oppress, threaten, or intimidate any citizen,

with intent to prevent or hinder his free exercise and enjoyment of any right or privilege granted or secured to him by the constitution or laws of the United States, or because of his having exercised the same, such persons shall be held guilty of felony, and, on conviction thereof, shall be fined or imprisoned, or both, at the discretion of the court,—the fine not to exceed $5,000, and the imprisonment not to exceed ten years; and shall, moreover, be thereafter ineligible to, and disabled from holding, any office or place of honor, profit, or trust created by the constitution or laws of the United States." 16 Stat. 141.

The question certified arose upon a motion in arrest of judgment after a verdict of guilty generally upon the whole sixteen counts, and is stated to be, whether "the said sixteen counts of said indictment are severally good and sufficient in law, and contain charges of criminal matter indictable under the laws of the United States." (emphasis added)

The general charge in the first eight counts is that of "banding," and in the second eight, that of "conspiring" together to injure, oppress, threaten, and intimidate Levi Nelson and Alexander Tillman, citizens of the United States, of African descent and persons of color, with the intent thereby to hinder and prevent them in their free exercise and enjoyment of rights and privileges "granted and secured" to them "in common with all other good citizens of the United States by the constitution and laws of the United States."

The offences provided for by the statute in question do not consist in the mere "banding" or "conspiring" of two or more persons together, but in their banding or conspiring with the intent, or for any of the purposes, specified. To bring this case under the operation of the statute, therefore, it must appear that the right, the enjoyment of which the conspirators intended to hinder or prevent, was one granted or secured by the constitution or laws of the United States. If it does not so appear, the criminal matter charged has not been made indictable by any act of Congress.

We have in our political system a government of the United States and a government of each of the several States. Each one of these governments is distinct from the others, and each has citizens of its own who owe it allegiance, and whose rights, within its jurisdiction, it must protect. The same person may be at the same time a citizen of the United States and a citizen of a State, but his rights of citizenship under one of these governments will be different from those he has under the other. *Slaughterhouse Cases* (1873).

Citizens are the members of the political community to which they belong. They are the people who compose the community, and who, in their associated capacity, have established or submitted themselves to the dominion of a government for the promotion of their general welfare and the protection of their individual as well as their collective rights. In the formation of a government, the people may confer upon it such powers as they choose. The government, when so formed, may, and when called upon should, exercise all the powers it has for the protection of the rights of its citizens and the people within its jurisdiction; but it can exercise no other. The duty of a government to afford protection is limited always by the power it possesses for that purpose.

Experience made the fact known to the people of the United States that they required a national government for national purposes. The separate governments of the separate States, bound together by the articles of confederation alone, were not sufficient for the promotion of the general welfare of the people in respect to foreign nations, or for their complete protection as citizens of the confederated States. For this reason, the people of the United States, 'in order to form a more perfect union, establish justice, insure domestic tranquility, provide for [92 U.S. 542, 550] the common defense, promote the general welfare, and secure the blessings of liberty' to themselves and their posterity (Const. Preamble), ordained and established the government of the United States, and defined its powers by a constitution, which they adopted as its fundamental law, and made its rule of action.

The government thus established and defined is to some extent a government of the States in their political capacity. It is also, for certain purposes, a government of the people. Its powers are limited in number, but not in degree. Within the scope of its powers, as enumerated and defined, it is supreme and above the States; but beyond, it has no existence. It was erected for special purposes, and endowed with all the powers necessary for its own preservation and the accomplishment of the ends its people had in view. It can neither grant nor secure to its citizens any right or privilege not expressly or by implication placed under its jurisdiction.

The people of the United States resident within any State are subject to two governments: one State, and the other National; but there need be no conflict between the two. The powers which one possesses, the other does not. They are established for different purposes, and have separate jurisdictions. Together they make one whole, and furnish the people of the United States with a complete government, ample for the protection of all their rights at home and abroad. True, it may sometimes happen that a person is amenable to both jurisdictions for one and the same act. Thus, if a marshal of the United States is unlawfully resisted while executing the process of the courts within a State, and the resistance is accompanied by an assault on the officer, the sovereignty of the United States is violated by the resistance, and that of the State by the breach of peace, in the assault. So, too, if one passes counterfeited coin of the United States within a State, it may be an offence against the United States and the State: the United States, because it discredits the coin; and the State, because of the fraud upon him to whom it is passed. This does not, however, necessarily imply that the two governments possess powers in common, or bring them into conflict with each other. It is the natural consequence of a citizenship [92 U.S. 542, 551] which owes allegiance to two sovereignties, and claims protection from both. The citizen cannot complain, because he has voluntarily submitted himself to such a form of government. He owes allegiance to the two departments, so to speak, and within their respective spheres must pay the penalties which each exacts for disobedience to its laws. In return, he can demand protection from each within its own jurisdiction.

The government of the United States is one of delegated powers alone. Its authority is defined and limited by the Constitution. All powers not granted to it by that instrument are reserved to the States or the people. No rights can be acquired under the Constitution or laws of the United States, except such as the government of the United States has the authority to grant or secure. All that cannot be so granted or secured are left under the protection of the States.

We now proceed to an examination of the indictment, to ascertain whether the several rights, which it is alleged the defendants intended to interfere with, are such as had been in law and in fact granted or secured by the Constitution or laws of the United States. . . .

. . .The sixth and fourteenth counts state the intent of the defendants to have been to hinder and prevent the citizens named, being of African descent, and colored, 'in the free exercise and enjoyment of their several and respective right and privilege to vote at any election to be thereafter by law had and held by the people in and of the said State of Louisiana, or by the people of and in the parish of Grant aforesaid." In *Minor v. Happersett* (1875), we decided that the Constitution of the United States has not conferred the right of suffrage upon any one, and that the United States [has] no voters of their own creation in the States. In *United States v. Reese* (1876) we hold that the Fifteenth Amendment has invested the citizens of the United States with a new constitutional right, which is, exemption from discrimination in the exercise of the elective franchise on account of race, color, or previous condition of servitude. From this it appears that the right of suffrage is not a necessary attribute of national citizenship; but that exemption from discrimination in the exercise of that right on account of race and color is. The right to vote in the States comes from the States; but the right of exemption from the prohibited discrimination comes from the United States. The first has not been granted or secured by the Constitution of the United States; but the last has been.

Inasmuch, therefore, as it does not appear in these counts that the intent of the defendants was to prevent these parties from exercising their right to vote on account of their race and color, it does not appear that it was their intent to interfere with any right granted or secured by the Constitution or laws of the United States. We may suspect that race was the cause of the hostility; but it is not so averred. This is material to a description of the substance of the offence, and cannot be supplied by implication. Every thing essential must be charged positively, and not inferentially. The defect here is not in form, but in substance.

The seventh and fifteenth counts are no better than the sixth and fourteenth. The intent here charged is to put the parties named in great fear of bodily harm, and to injure and oppress them, because, being and having been in all things qualified, they had voted "at an election before that time had and held according to law by the people of the said State of Louisiana, in said State, to wit, on the fourth day of November, 1872, and at divers other elections by the people of the State, also before that time had and held according to law." There is nothing to show that the elections voted at were any other than State elections, or that the conspiracy was formed on account of the race of the parties against whom the conspirators were to act. The charge as made is really of nothing more than a conspiracy to commit a breach of the peace within a State. Certainly it will not be claimed that the United States have the power or are required to do mere police duly in the States. If a State cannot protect itself against domestic violence, the United States may, upon the call of the executive, when the legislature cannot be convened, lend their assistance for that purpose. This is a guaranty of the Constitution (art. 4, sect. 4); but it applies to no case like this.

We are, therefore, of the opinion that the first, second, third, fourth, sixth, seventh, ninth, tenth, eleventh, twelfth, fourteenth, [92 U.S. 542, 557] and fifteenth counts do not contain charges of a criminal nature made indictable under the laws of the United States, and that consequently they are not good and sufficient in law. They do not show that it was the intent of the defendants, by their conspiracy, to hinder or prevent the enjoyment of any right granted or secured by the Constitution. . . .

. . .The order of the Circuit Court arresting the judgment upon the verdict is, therefore, affirmed; and the cause remanded, with instructions to discharge the defendants.

Source: *U.S. v. Cruikshank,* 92 U.S. 542, 1876.

The "Mississippi Plan," 1890

In 1890 white lawmakers in Mississippi approved and instituted a new constitution for the state. This document replaced an 1868 constitution that had been put in place in the wake of the Civil War—one that formally extended the franchise to the state's black citizens. With the close of Reconstruction, though, white Democrats seized control of the state's political system and quickly and methodically moved to keep the ballot from African Americans. Mississippi's new state constitution, which included a slate of racially discriminatory voting rules that came to be known as the "Mississippi Plan," became a model for white legislators in other former Confederate states that were eager to strip blacks of their voting rights. Its various restrictions made it impossible for all but a tiny fraction of Mississippi's black citizens to vote—if they were willing to risk the wrath of the Ku Klux Klan and other violent white supremacist groups roaming freely across much of the country during this time. Following are pertinent excerpts from Mississippi's 1890 constitution.

ARTICLE 12—FRANCHISE

Sec. 240. All elections by the people shall be by ballot.

Sec. 241. Every male inhabitant of this State, except idiots, insane persons and Indians not taxed, who is a citizen of the United States, twenty-one years old and upwards, who has resided in this State two years, and one year in the election district, or in the incorporated city or town, in which he offers to vote, and who is duly registered as provided in this article, and who has never been convicted of bribery, burglary, theft, arson, obtaining money or goods under false pretenses, perjury, forgery, embezzlement or bigamy, and who has paid, on or before the first day of February of the year in which he shall offer to vote, all taxes which may have been legally required of him, and which he has had an opportunity of paying according to law, for the two preceding years, and who shall produce to the officers holding the election satisfactory evidence that he has paid said taxes, is declared to be a qualified elector; but any minister of the gospel in charge of an organized church shall be entitled to vote after six months residence in the election district, if otherwise qualified.

Sec. 242. The legislature shall provide by law for the registration of all persons entitled to vote at any election, and all persons offering to register shall take the following oath or affirmation: "I ________________, do solemnly swear (or affirm) that I am twenty-one years old, (or I will be before the next election in this county) and that I will have resided in this State two years, and ________ election district of ____________ county one year next preceding the ensuing election [or if it be stated in the oath that the person proposing to register is a minister of the gospel in charge of an organized church, then it will be sufficient to aver therein, two years residence in the State and six months in said election district], and am now in good faith a resident of the same, and that I am not disqualified from voting by reason of having been convicted of any crime named in the constitution of this State as a disqualification to be an elector; that I will truly answer all questions propounded to me concerning my antecedents so far as they relate to my right to vote, and also as to my residence before my citizenship in this district; that I will faithfully support the constitution of the United States and of the State of Mississippi, and will bear true faith and allegiance to the same. So help me God." In registering voters in cities and towns, not wholly in one election district, the name of such city or town may be substituted in the oath for the election district. Any willful and corrupt false statements in said affidavit, or in answer to any material question propounded as herein authorized, shall be perjury.

Sec. 243. A uniform poll tax of two dollars, to be used in aid of the common schools, and for no other purpose, is hereby imposed on every male inhabitant of this State between the ages of twenty-one and sixty years, except persons who are deaf and dumb or blind, or who are maimed by loss of hand or foot; said tax to be a lien only upon taxable property. The board of supervisors of any county may, for the purpose of aiding the common schools in that county, increase the poll tax in said county, but in no case shall the entire poll tax exceed in any one year three dollars on each poll. No criminal proceedings shall be allowed to enforce the collection of the poll tax.

Sec. 244. On and after the first day of January, A. D., 1892, every elector shall, in addition to the foregoing qualifications, be able to read any section of the constitution of this State; or he shall be able to understand the same when read to him, or give a reasonable interpretation thereof. A new registration shall be made before the next ensuing election after January the first, A.D., 1892.

Sec. 245. Electors in municipal elections shall possess all the qualifications herein prescribed, and such additional qualifications as may be provided by law.

Sec. 246. Prior to the first day of January, A.D., 1896, the elections by the people in this State shall be regulated by an ordinance of this convention.

Sec. 247. The legislature shall enact laws to secure fairness in party primary elections, conventions or other methods of naming party candidates.

Sec. 248. Suitable remedies by appeal or otherwise shall be provided by law, to correct illegal or improper registration and to secure the elective franchise to those who may be illegally or improperly denied the same.

Sec. 249. No one shall be allowed to vote for members of the legislature or other officers who has not been duly registered under the constitution and laws of this State, by an officer of this State, legally authorized to register the voters thereof. And registration under the constitution and laws of this State by the proper officers of this State is hereby declared to be an essential and necessary qualification to vote at any and all elections.

Sec. 250. All qualified electors and no others shall be eligible to office as otherwise provided in this constitution.

Sec. 251. Electors shall not be registered within four months next before any election at which they may offer to vote; but appeals may be heard and determined and revision take place at any time prior to the election; and no person who, in respect to age and residence, would become entitled to vote, within the said four months, shall be excluded from registration on account of his want of qualification at the time of registration.

Sec. 252. The term of office of all elective officers under this constitution shall be four years, except as otherwise provided herein. A general election for all elective officers shall be held on the Tuesday next after the first Monday of November, A.D., 1895, and every four (4) years thereafter; provided, the legislature may change the day and date of general elections to any day and date in October, November or December.

Sec. 253. The legislature may by a two-thirds vote of both houses, of all members elected, restore the right of suffrage to any person disqualified by reason of crime; but the reasons therefor shall be spread upon the journals, and the vote shall be by yeas and nays.

Source: 1890 Constitution of Mississippi. *Mississippi History Now.* Accessed January 2, 2019. http://mshistorynow.mdah.state.ms.us/articles/103/index.php?s=extra&id=270.

Lucy Stone Addresses Congressional Committee on Women's Suffrage, 1892

Lucy Stone was one of the leading suffragists and abolitionists of the nineteenth century. Though she did not always see eye-to-eye with other women's suffrage luminaries like Elizabeth Cady Stanton or Susan B. Anthony—Stone grudgingly accepted the limitations of the Fourteenth and Fifteenth Amendments, which granted voting rights to black men while leaving women without the franchise, whereas Anthony, Stanton, and other women's rights champions were outraged at being left behind—she nonetheless played an important leadership role in advancing the women's suffrage cause. She was a cofounder, for example, of the American Woman Suffrage Association (AWSA), and wrote and lectured frequently on the issue. In 1892, a mere two years after the AWSA finally merged with Stanton and Anthony's National Women's Suffrage Association (NWSA) to form the National American Women's Suffrage Association (NAWSA), Stone testified at a special congressional hearing on the issue of women's suffrage. Following are excerpts from Stone's remarks (in which she references testimony already given to the committee from Stanton).

Mr. Chairman and gentlemen of the committee, I arrived in town only last night and did not even know of a hearing here to-day, so I have not any speech prepared. Nevertheless I am glad to be here, and I am glad to see this committee, and—I suppose I have the right to say it—I am glad to see you are the kind of looking men I see before me. It is something on our side to have you be the men you seem to be. I come before this committee with the sense which I always feel, that we are handicapped as women in what we try to do for ourselves by the single fact that we have no vote. This cheapens us. You do not care so much for us as if we had votes, so that we come always with that infinite disadvantage.

But the thing I want to say particularly is that we have our immortal Declaration of Independence and the various bills of rights of the different States (and George Washington advised us to recur often to first principles), and in the Declaration of Independence nothing is clearer than the basis of the claim that women should have equal rights with men. It is that those that are to obey the laws should make them. A complete government is a perfectly just government. Now it is easy to say that our fathers announced that principle but did not apply it. Of course they were in no condition to do so, and they could not. In the white heat of the struggle of the war of the Revolution these men declared better things than they could do. They saw the great truth that a complete government must be a just government; but they were too near the throne; they had the idea of the one man power, and so they were unable to carry out the principle of a just government. In my own State of Massachusetts they allowed none but church members to vote. Then property holders alone had the right to vote; and then the Democratic party came in and said that the poor man had as much right to vote as the man of property, and abolished the property qualification. Then the Republicans came and abolished the disfranchisement of the negroes; and to-day every human being in the United States except woman has the right to vote.

Now, what I want particularly to impress upon this committee is the gross and grave injustice of holding forty millions of women absolutely helpless under the Government. The laws touch us at every point. From the time the little girl baby is born until the time the aged woman makes her last will and testament, there is not one of our affairs which the law does not control. It says who shall own property, and what rights the woman shall have, and it settles all her affairs, whether she shall buy or sell or will or deed; it settles all that a woman has to do; and so, except in the single State of Wyoming—how glad I am you have two Senators from Wyoming—women are in a helpless position. Mrs. Stanton has told you about the solitude of the individual, but think what it is to be in the power of others in such a way that in nothing that concerns you have you any voice! If you are a woman and happen to have property and wish to rent it, somebody decides what you shall have for rent, how much you shall pay for taxes, etc., and in not a single solitary thing are you allowed to have a voice for yourself. Persons are elected by men to represent them in Congress and the State legislatures; and here are forty millions of women, with just the same stake in the Government that men have, with a class interest of their own, and with not one solitary word to say or power to help settle one of the things that concern them.

Men must know the value of votes and the value of the possession of power, and I look at them and wonder how it is possible for them to be willing that their own sisters, mothers, wives, and daughters should be debarred from the possession of like power. We have been going to the legislature in Massachusetts—we have been going there longer than Mrs. Stanton has been coming here—and we asked that when a husband and wife made a contract with each other as, for instance, if the wife loan the husband her money, the contract should be considered valid just as it would between any other parties, for now, in case the husband fails in business, she can not get her money, and the legislature very kindly gave us leave to withdraw. Then we asked that when a man dies and the wife is left alone, with no man to help her and she has to bear the whole burden of life on her shoulders, the law might give the widow more than forty days in which to stay in the house without paying rent.

But we could not defeat one of our legislators, and they cared not a cent for our vote and less than a cent for our opinion; and so when we went there and asked this they gave us leave to withdraw. But when some voters wanted about 6 inches of mud out of a river, the legislature passed it unanimously. They respect the wants of the voter, but they care nothing about the wants of those who do not have votes. So, when we asked in Massachusetts for protection for wives beaten by their husbands, that there might be a committee to stand between such wives and their husbands, and that the husband should be made to give a portion of his earnings to support the minor children, again we had leave to withdraw. Of course we have obtained many concessions, and I am happy to say that in the legislatures of the different States the laws have been modified very greatly since the old common law which prevailed everywhere, which took away from the wife everything, even the right to herself, even the right to her children, even the right to her money and her real estate. The daughters of Cassius Clay are here to-day; and in Kentucky this same question is being considered, and they are trying there to get property rights for wives. As Mrs. Stanton says, we believe in the rights of the individual, hence this efforts is being made to secure the right of married women to their property.

Now you see, gentlemen, the helplessness of our position. I can think of nothing so helpless and humiliating as the position of a disfranchised person. I do not know whether I am treading on dangerous toes when I say that after the late war the Government in power wished to punish Jefferson Davis, and it considered that the worst punishment it could inflict upon him was to take away from him the right to vote. Now, the odium which attached to him from his disfranchisement is just the same that attaches to women from their disfranchisement. The only persons who are not allowed to vote in Massachusetts are the lunatics, idiots, and felons, and people who can not read and write. In what a category is that to place women, after one hundred years, and at the close of this nineteenth century! And yet that is history. In Massachusetts we are trying to get a small concession—the right to vote in the cities and towns in which we live in regard to the taxes we have to pay. In 1792, in the town of Newburyport, Mass., it was not thought necessary to give women education. At that time there were no schools for girls; the public money was not used for girl's schools, and when one man said that he had five daughters, and paid his taxes like other men, and his girls were not allowed to attend school, and that they ought to give the girls a chance, another man said, "Take the public money and educate shes? Never!"

Remember, this was one hundred years ago. One of the fathers urged that the girls should be educated in the public schools, and the men—God forgive them!—said this: "We will let the girls go to school in the morning between 6 and 8 o'clock, before the boys want the schoolhouse." Just think of the time those girls would have had to rise in order to get a little education before the boys got there! This plan did not work well, and the teacher was instructed not to teach females any longer. Every descendant of those men in the town now feels ashamed of them; and I think that in one hundred years the children of the men who are now year, pleading for suffrage, will feel ashamed. Men would rather lose anything than their votes; they would fight for their right to vote, and if anybody attempted to deprive them of the suffrage, it would be war to the knife and the knife to the hilt. We come here to carry on this bloodless warfare, year after year, asking and praying that the privilege granted in the foundation of the Government should be applied to women.

What I wish, gentlemen, this winter, is for you to recommend a sixteenth amendment with an educational qualification in it. I believe you should never put obstacles in the way of anybody's right to vote. Everybody should have the right to vote who cares to vote, but anyone who does can learn to read. What I think you should recommend is a sixteenth amendment with an educational qualification. I do not suppose there is a State in the Union that would adopt it, not one; but the fact that you put it forward as a thing which ought to be adopted is a part education of the great public mind. What we look forward to is part of the eternal order. It is not possible that forty millions of women should be held forever as lunatics, fools, and idiots. It is not possible, as the years go on, that each person should not at last have the right to look after his own interests. As the home is at its best when the father and mother consult together in regard to the family interests, so it is with the Government. I do not think it possible for a man to see from a man's point of view all the things that a woman needs, and I do not think a woman from her single point of view sees all the things that a man needs. Now, I think men have brought their best, and also brought their worst, into the Union, and it is all here, but the thing you have not in the Government at all is the qualities that women possess, the feminine qualities. It has been said in regard to this matter that women are more economical and peaceful and law-abiding than men, and all those qualities are lacking in the Government to-day.

How much do we spend for war, and how much should we save if this peace element were only represented in the Government? If the peaceful sex can have their way it will go toward helping peace. It will be the same way in regard to the economy of the Government. The part that a woman does in the family no man can do. When she brings up her children who are to be Senators and Representatives, or farmers or ranchmen, that woman, who has given twenty years to bringing up that family, has rendered a service to the Government that no man can render. She does not get compensation for it in money; there is no compensation in money that can buy such labor, and she does not ask for that. At the same time, women who earn a compensation (and I am sorry to say it is very much less than the wages of men), when they get a dollar do not go and spend it on carriage hire, etc., but they get the things they need, for they have learned economy. If women came into the Government, they would bring with them that economy and those traits which the Government needs.

But whether this would be so or not, it is right that every class should be heard in behalf of its own interests. When the common law was being indited, if there had been one single woman there, and the question had come up as to when a baby was born who should own that baby, would it have been decided that the man should own the baby? Not at all. The woman would have said, "I had an equal share in this child's life, and I have an equal share in its future." Suppose a woman had been there when the question was raised as to when a woman married who should own that woman. Would a law have been passed that the custody of her person shall belong to the husband, who may give her mild correction and use gentle restraint, and that if she breaks her leg and damages are awarded, he shall receive the damages? Not at all. The woman would have said, "My legs are my own, and I shall have the custody of my own person, and if I break my leg and get damages, the money shall be my own."

Now, gentlemen, I hope you will try and make this case your own. It is simple justice and fair play, and it is also a fundamental principle of the Government. Here are we trying to have a complete government, and yet there are forty millions of disfranchised people. I believe, among the great people—and by the people I do not mean men, but men and women, the whole people—that nothing that makes such disrespect for the fundamental principle of our Government as not to apply it. The Government was founded upon the principle that those who obey the laws should make them, and here it shuts out a full half. As long as that is done and continues to be done, it certainly tends to create disrespect for the principle itself. Do you not see it?

What I wish to impress upon you is that you should present a sixteenth amendment, with an educational qualification, and strongly support it, and as far as in you lies, try to get rid of this odious class distinction, this oligarchy of sex which is more hateful than the oligarchy of wealth or the oligarchy of color. This Government gives to a criminal taken from the State's prison and pardoned higher privileges than it grants to Mrs. Stanton, and makes her his political inferior. I have seen a man who was so drunk that he had to be helped to the polls, yet who in the eye of the law the political superior of Miss Anthony. Why not reach out a hand to woman and say, "Come and help us make the laws and see fair play."

I wish I had the power to impress you with the fact that greater than the free coinage of silver, or the tariff, or anything you have before you, is the question whether the people shall have the right to govern themselves, irrespective of whether they are men or women.

Source: Testimony of Lucy Stone. Hearing of the Woman Suffrage Association before the U.S. Committee on the Judiciary, January 18, 1892. Accessed January 2, 2019. https://www.loc.gov/resource/rbnawsa.n9898/?sp=3&st=text.

Black Suffragist Frances E. W. Harper Discusses "Woman's Political Future," 1893

Baltimore native Frances E. W. Harper (1825–1911) was a prominent and active member of both the abolitionist and women's rights movement. A founding member of the National Association of Colored women (in 1896) and stalwart of organizations such as the Women's Christian Temperance Union, the American Woman Suffrage Association, and the Universal Peace Union, Harper was a prolific voice for societal advancement for both African Americans and women. One of her best known public appearances came on May 20, 1893, when she addressed an audience of white women at the World's Columbian Exhibition in Chicago (better known as the Chicago World Fair). In her remarks, she argues that access to the ballot box should hinge on the literacy and character of the would-be voter rather than gender or skin color. This was not an unheard-of argument from supporters of women's suffrage—leaders in the movement ranging from Elizabeth Cady Stanton to Frances Willard expressed similar sentiments at one time or another—but it was notable coming from a black woman, since literacy tests were used so often across the American South to keep African Americans from voting. But Harper believed that if barriers to voting were shifted from sex or race to character and education, both women and blacks would ultimately benefit. Following are Harper's remarks from her appearance at the World Fair.

If before sin had cast its deepest shadows or sorrow had distilled its bitterest tears, it was true that it was not good for man to be alone, it is no less true, since the shadows have deepened and life's sorrows have increased, that the world has need of all the spiritual aid that woman can give for the social advancement and moral development of the human race. The tendency of the present age, with its restlessness, religious upheavals, failures, blunders, and crimes, is toward broader freedom, an increase of knowledge, the emancipation of thought, and a recognition of the brotherhood of man; in this movement woman, as the companion of man, must be a sharer. So close is the bond between man and woman that you can not raise one without lifting the other. The world can not move without woman's sharing in the movement, and to help give a right impetus to that movement is woman's highest privilege.

If the fifteenth century discovered America to the Old World, the nineteenth is discovering woman to herself. Little did Columbus imagine, when the New World broke upon his vision like a lovely gem in the coronet of the universe, the glorious possibilities of a land where the sun should be our engraver, the winged lightning our messenger, and steam our beast of burden. But as mind is more than matter, and the highest ideal always the true real, so to woman comes the opportunity to strive for richer and grander discoveries than ever gladdened the eye of the Genoese mariner.

Not the opportunity of discovering new worlds, but that of filling this old world with fairer and higher aims than the greed of gold and the lust of power, is hers. Through weary, wasting years men have destroyed, dashed in pieces, and overthrown, but today we stand on the threshold of woman's era, and woman's work is grandly constructive. In her hand are possibilities whose use or abuse must tell upon the political life of the nation, and send their influence for good or evil across the track of unborn ages.

As the saffron tints and crimson flushes of morn herald the coming day, so the social and political advancement which woman has already gained bears the promise of the rising of the full-orbed sun of emancipation. The result will be not to make home less happy, but society more holy; yet I do not think the mere extension of the ballot a panacea for all the ills of our national life. What we need today is not simply more voters, but better voters. Today there are red-handed men in our republic, who walk unwhipped of justice, who richly deserve to exchange the ballot of the freeman for the wristlets of the felon; brutal and cowardly men, who torture, burn, and lynch their fellow-men, men whose defenselessness should be their best defense and their weakness an ensign of protection. More than the changing of institutions we need the development of a national conscience, and the upbuilding of national character. Men may boast of the aristocracy of blood, may glory in the aristocracy of talent, and be proud of the aristocracy of wealth, but there is one aristocracy which must ever outrank them all, and that is the aristocracy of character; and it is the women of a country who help to mold its character, and to influence if not determine its destiny; and in the political future of our nation woman will not have done what she could if she does not endeavor to have our republic stand foremost among the nations of the earth, wearing sobriety as a crown and righteousness as a garment and a girdle. In coming into her political estate woman will find a mass of illiteracy to be dispelled. If knowledge is power, ignorance is also power. The power that educates wickedness may manipulate and dash against the pillars of any state when they are undermined and honeycombed by injustice.

I envy neither the heart nor the head of any legislator who has been born to an inheritance of privileges, who has behind him ages of education, dominion, civilization, and Christianity, if he stands opposed to the passage of a national education bill, whose purpose is to secure education to the children of those who were born under the shadow of institutions which made it a crime to read.

Today women hold in their hands influence and opportunity, and with these they have already opened doors which have been closed to others. By opening doors of labor woman has become a rival claimant for at least some of the wealth monopolized by her stronger brother. In the home she is the priestess, in society the queen, in literature she is a power, in legislative halls law-makers have responded to her appeals, and for her sake have humanized and liberalized their laws. The press has felt the impress of her hand. In the pews of the church she constitutes the majority; the pulpit has welcomed her, and in the school she has the blessed privilege of teaching children and youth. To her is apparently coming the added responsibility of political power; and what she now possesses should only be the means of preparing her to use the coming power for the glory of God and the good of mankind; for power without righteousness is one of the most dangerous forces in the world.

Political life in our country has plowed in muddy channels, and needs the infusion of clearer and cleaner waters. I am not sure that women are naturally so much better than men that they will clear the stream by the virtue of their womanhood; it is not through sex but through character that the best influence of women upon the life of the nation must be exerted.

I do not believe in unrestricted and universal suffrage for either men or women. I believe in moral and educational tests. I do not believe that the most ignorant and brutal man is better prepared to add value to the strength and durability of the government than the most cultured, upright, and intelligent woman. I do not think that willful ignorance should swamp earnest intelligence at the ballot-box, nor that educated wickedness, violence, and fraud should cancel the votes of honest men. The unsteady hands of a drunkard can not cast the ballot of a freeman. The hands of lynchers are too red with blood to determine the political character of the government for even four short years. The ballot in the hands of woman means power added to influence. How well she will use that power I can not foretell. Great evils stare us in the face that need to be throttled by the combined power of an upright manhood and an enlightened womanhood; and I know that no nation can gain its full measure of enlightenment and happiness if one-half of it is free and the other half is fettered. China compressed the feet of her women and thereby retarded the steps of her men. The elements of a nation's weakness must ever be found at the hearthstone.

More than the increase of wealth, the power of armies, and the strength of fleets is the need of good homes, of good fathers, and good mothers.

The life of a Roman citizen was in danger in ancient Palestine, and men had bound themselves with a vow that they would eat nothing until they had killed the Apostle Paul. Pagan Rome threw around that imperiled life a bulwark of living clay consisting of four hundred and seventy human hearts, and Paul was saved. Surely the life of the humblest American citizen should be as well protected in America as that of a Roman citizen was in heathen Rome. A wrong done to the weak should be an insult to the strong. Woman coming into her kingdom will find enthroned three great evils, for whose overthrow she should be as strong in a love of justice and humanity as the warrior is in his might. She will find intemperance sending its flood of shame, and death, and sorrow to the homes of men, a fretting leprosy in our politics, and a blighting curse in our social life; the social evil sending to our streets women whose laughter is sadder than their tears, who slide from the paths of sin and shame to the friendly shelter of the grave; and lawlessness enacting in our republic deeds over which angels might weep, if heaven knows sympathy.

How can any woman send petitions to Russia against the horrors of Siberian prisons if, ages after the Inquisition has ceased to devise its tortures, she has not done all she could by influence, tongue, and pen to keep men from making bonfires of the bodies of real or supposed criminals?

O women of America! into your hands God has pressed one of the sublimest opportunities that ever came into the hands of the women of any race or people. It is yours to create a healthy public sentiment; to demand justice, simple justice, as the right of every race; to brand with everlasting infamy the lawless and brutal cowardice that lynches, burns, and tortures your own countrymen.

To grapple with the evils which threaten to undermine the strength of the nation and to lay magazines of powder under the cribs of future generations is no child's play.

Let the hearts of the women of the world respond to the song of the herald angels of peace on earth and good will to men. Let them throb as one heart unified by the grand and holy purpose of uplifting the human race, and humanity will breathe freer, and the world grow brighter. With such a purpose Eden would spring up in our path, and Paradise be around our way.

Source: Harper, Frances. "Women's Political Future." In *World's Congress of Representative Women, 1893 Proceedings*, edited by May Wright Sewall. Chicago: Rand, McNally & Co., 1894, pp. 433–437.

Supreme Court Upholds Jim Crow Literacy Tests in *Williams v. Mississippi*, 1898

On April 25, 1898, the U.S. Supreme Court handed down a decision that effectively sanctioned the purging of black voters from voting rolls in states across the American South—and also created circumstances in which black defendants accused of crimes in those states routinely faced all-white juries. The Court's Williams v. Mississippi *ruling gave state authorities the right—enshrined in the state's 1890 constitution—to unilaterally determine whether black citizens seeking to vote had passed mandated literacy tests (usually they were given failing grades, irrespective of actual performance). It also meant that juries across the South would almost always be entirely white in their makeup, since jurors were selected from pools of registered voters. Remarkably, however, the court rejected claims that such pools showed racially discriminatory intent. The* Williams v. Mississippi *decision further paved the way for the legal disenfranchisement of African Americans by white southern lawmakers until the 1960s. Following are excerpts from the majority opinion, which was delivered by Justice Joseph McKenna.*

The question presented is, are the provisions of the constitution of the state of Mississippi and the laws enacted to enforce the same repugnant to the Fourteenth Amendment of the Constitution of the United States?

. . .[Plaintiff argues the below provisions of the Mississippi constitution as discriminatory against blacks and, therefore, in violation of the Fifteenth Amendment]:

"Section 241 of the [state] constitution of 1890 prescribes the qualifications for electors; that residence in the state for two years, one year in the precinct of the applicant, must be effected; that he is twenty-one years or over of age, having paid all taxes legally due of him for two years prior to 1st day of February of the year he offers to vote, not having been convicted of theft, arson, rape, receiving money or goods under false pretenses, bigamy, embezzlement."

"Section 242 of the constitution provides the mode of registration; that the legislature shall provide by law for registration of all persons entitled to vote at any election, and that all persons offering to register shall take the oath; that they are not disqualified for voting by reason of any of the crimes named in the constitution of this state; that they will truly answer all questions propounded to them concerning their antecedents so far as they relate to the applicant's right to vote, and also as to their residence before their citizenship in the district in which such application for registration is made."

The court readily sees the scheme. If the applicant swears, as he must do, that he is not disqualified by reason of the crimes specified, and that he has effected the required residence, what right has he to answer all questions as to his former residence? Section 244 of the constitution requires that the applicant for registration, after January, 1892, shall be able to read any section of the constitution, or he shall be able to understand the same (being any section of the organic law), or give a reasonable interpretation thereof. Now, we submit that these provisions vest in the administrative officers the full power, under section 242, to ask all sorts of vain, impertinent questions; and it is with that officer to say whether the questions relate to the applicant's right to vote. This officer can reject whomsoever he chooses, and register whomsoever he chooses, for he is vested by the constitution with that power.

Under section 244 it is left with the administrative officer to determine whether the applicant reads, understands, or interprets the section of the constitution designated. The officer is the sole judge of the examination of the applicant, and, even though the applicant be qualified, it is left with the officer to so determine; and the said officer can refuse him registration.

To make the possible dereliction of the officers the dereliction of the constitution and laws, the remarks of the supreme court of the state are quoted by plaintiff as to their intent. The constitution provides for the payment of a poll tax, and by a section of the Code its payment cannot be compelled by a seizure and sale of property. We gather from the brief of counsel that its payment is a condition of the right to vote, and, in a case to test whether its payment was or was not optional (*Ratcliff v. Beal*, 20 South. 865), the supreme court of the state said: "Within the field of permissible action under the limitations imposed by the federal constitution, the convention swept the field of expedients, to obstruct the exercise of suffrage by the negro race." And further the court said, speaking of the negro race: "By reason of its previous condition of servitude and dependencies, this race had acquired or accentuated certain peculiarities of habit, of temperament, and of character, which clearly distinguished it as a race from the whites; a patient, docile people, but careless, landless, migratory within narrow limits, without forethought, and its criminal members given to furtive offenses, rather than the robust crimes of the whites. Restrained by the federal constitution from discriminating against the negro race, the convention discriminates against its characteristics, and the offenses to which its criminal members are prone."

But nothing tangible can be deduced from this. If weakness were to be taken advantage of, it was to be done "within the field of permissible action under the limitations imposed by the federal constitution," and the means of it were the alleged characteristics of the negro race, not the administration of the law by officers of the state. *Besides, the operation of the constitution and laws is not limited by their language or effects to one race.* (emphasis added) They reach weak and vicious white men as well as weak and vicious black men, and whatever is sinister in their intention, if anything, can be prevented by both races by the exertion of that duty which voluntarily pays taxes and refrains from crime.

It cannot be said, therefore, that the denial of the equal protection of the laws arises primarily from the constitution and laws of Mississippi; nor is there any sufficient allegation of an evil and discriminating administration of them. The only allegation is "by granting a discretion to the said officers, as mentioned in the several sections of the constitution of the state, and the statute of the state adopted under the said constitution, the use of which discretion can be and has been used by said officers in the said Washington county to the end here complained of, to wit, the abridgment of the elective franchise of the colored voters of Washington county; that such citizens are denied the right to be selected as jurors to serve in the circuit court of the county; and that this denial to them of the right to equal protection and benefits of the laws of the state of Mississippi on account of their color and race, resulting from the exercise of the discretion partial to the white citizens, is in accordance with the purpose and intent of the framers of the present constitution of said state. . . ."

. . .There is an allegation of the purpose of the convention to disfranchise citizens of the colored race; but with this we have no concern, unless the purpose is executed by the constitution or laws or by those who administer them. If it is done in the latter way, how or by what means should be shown. We gather from the statements of the motion that certain officers are invested with discretion in making up lists of electors, and that this discretion can be and has been exercised against the colored race, and from these lists jurors are selected. The supreme court of Mississippi, however, decided, in a case presenting the same questions as the one at bar, "that jurors are not selected from or with reference to any lists furnished by such election officers." *Dixon v. Mississippi* (Nov. 9, 1896) 20 South. 839.

Source: *Williams v. Mississippi,* 170 U.S. 213, 1898.

A Pennsylvania Congressman Defends the Fourteenth and Fifteenth Amendments, 1904

In the early 1900s, voting rights advocates in Congress became so angry about the systemic disenfranchisement of African American voters in the South that they expressed support for legislative measures that would punish offending states. One such proposal, dubbed the Crumpacker Resolution in a nod to lead sponsor Edgar D. Crumpacker of Indiana, called on the House Census Committee to investigate whether states were unfairly denying or abridging the right of male citizens to vote—and, if so, to reduce their electoral representation in Congress in accordance with Section 2 of the Fourteenth Amendment. Alarmed by this threat to their political power, lawmakers in southern states responded not by reconsidering the Jim Crow laws that they had imposed to disenfranchise black voters but rather by proposing to repeal the Fourteenth and Fifteenth Amendments. These efforts were ridiculed by supporters of enfranchisement such as Edward de Veaux Morrell, a Republican representative from Pennsylvania who served in the U.S. House of Representatives from 1900 to 1907. Following are excerpts from a famous speech that Morrell gave on the House floor in 1904, expressing support for the (ultimately unsuccessful) Crumpacker Resolution—and denouncing southern lawmakers for their disenfranchisement actions.

By the introduction of his resolutions for the repeal of the fourteenth and fifteenth amendments the gentleman from George admits the necessity of some action by Congress concerning these particular parts of the Constitution. The question at once arises, What is this necessity and what would be the effect if these amendments were not repealed? No other answer can be made except that their provisions are in danger of being enforced by Congress. What provision in these amendments is to be feared by the Representatives from certain Southern States who have introduced these resolutions? Surely not that which provides that the right of suffrage shall not be denied on account of race, color, or previous condition of servitude, for the manner in which these States have brought about the abridgment of the suffrage has been twice decided by the Supreme Court of the United States to be matters for State regulation. The only conclusion, therefore, which can be arrived at for the necessity for the repeal of the amendment referred to in the resolutions is the fear that the provisions which require that representation in Congress shall be reduced accordingly might be enforced.

I shall not follow the gentleman in his zig-zag journey through the last half century of American history. . . . I shall frankly admit that most of the Northern States have at one time or another refused the ballot to the negro, and that there are only three or four States in the Union where the suffrage has always been extended to the negro. . . . I also concede that a majority of the statesmen of the North before the rebellion were not in favor of interfering with slavery in the South or of extending negro suffrage in the North. Many of the most conspicuous, fearless, and effective abolitionists that this country ever saw, men in favor of universal emancipation, and effecting it whenever they could, regarding slavery as an unmixed evil, a curse to white and black alike, and to be abolished at the earliest practicable moment, were southern men. I need not mention such names as Washington, Jefferson, Richard Henry Lee, Grimke, Birney, Cassius M. Clay, and if we could call the roll a thousand brave and generous souls would answer. . . .

Many millions of our people assume, without thinking, that negro suffrage was forced upon the South by the fourteenth and fifteenth amendments as an act of hostility and in a spirit of revenge. The exact opposite is true. These amendments were added to the Constitution in the interest of harmony and for the purpose of perfecting the real purpose of the thirteenth amendment. Here is the state of things: Slavery had been abolished. The white of the South could not conceive of the possibility that the free negro would work without physical compulsion. When it became known that President Johnson's purpose was to allow "the States lately in rebellion" to resume their former relations to the Union, with full control of their own affairs, the whites perceived that by municipal laws they could reduce the black race to semislavery, which would keep it industrially and politically in the power of the former masters. Several of the Southern States adopted legislative statutes and civic ordinances for the purpose of carrying out this policy and realizing this reestablished relation of servitude. Louisiana adopted these ordinances:

> Every negro is required to be in the regular service of some white person or former owner, who shall be responsible for the conduct of said negro; but said employer or former owner may permit said negro to hire his own time by special permission in writing, which permit shall not extend over seven days at one time.
>
> No negro shall sell, barter, or exchange any article of merchandise without the special written permission of his employer.

Regulations were also adopted compelling negroes, under penalty, to be in their quarters at certain hours, and others defining the time, places, and methods of their buying and selling. This, of course, established a peonage scarcely less dear than the slavery from which they had escaped. It made their emancipation a mockery. It abolished free labor. It reestablished the overseer system. If these laws continued to exist, slavery was not abolished.

Mr. [Abraham] Lincoln has been quoted as saying that he was not in sympathy with giving the right of franchise to the negro. Let me ask if it is imagined that had Mr. Lincoln lived and realized that practically the only condition which was imposed by the victors of that most terrible of all terrible struggles—namely, the adoption in spirit as well as in fact of the thirteenth amendment—was not being carried out, and therefore the chief result of the war nullified, would he not have sanctioned and put into force the fourteenth and fifteenth amendments with all that dogged earnestness of purpose with which he waged the war for the preservation of the Union, even though it cost him as much or even more sorrow?

In this situation two alternatives presented themselves—indefinite or prolonged military rule by the Federal Army in the Southern States or the endowment of the black race with enough political power to ensure their protection.

In this dilemma the ablest and most distinguished men in both Houses of Congress were gathered about President Johnson, including General Grant, his successor, and an earnest and prolonged conference was held. After much discussion it was decided that permanent military rule was too obnoxious to be seriously considered, and that remedy was rejected.

The majority of the Republican party did not consider the enfranchisement of the negro an ideal solution of the vexing problem. But it seemed the best at hand, and was adopted as a great improvement upon anarchy. . . .

On July 28, 1868, the Secretary of State, in pursuance of a concurrent resolution of Congress passed one week previously, issued a proclamation declaring that the fourteenth amendment had been ratified by three-fourths of the states; and on the 30th day of March, 1870, he issued a similar proclamation, declaring that the fifteenth amendment had been duly ratified by three-fourths of the States. The Supreme Court has decided a great number of cases arising under both these amendments. . . . The validity of the amendments has been sustained in every one of these cases. It is now too late to question their validity or disobey their mandates. Indeed, I do not think their validity was ever question in this House until the 27th of January, 1904, when the gentleman from Georgia consented to illuminate the subject.

It is attempted to apologize for the violation by some of the Southern States of these amendments, or at least to minimize their offense against human rights, by asserting that some Northern States, as Ohio, Kansas, and Minnesota, rejected negro suffrage for themselves during the very year that the fifteenth amendment was adopted, and that no State in the Union except New York had ever explicitly extended to the negro the right to vote. This is indeed true, but it is to be added that since the adoption of the fifteenth amendment they have never denied to him the right to vote on account of color.

Notwithstanding the immense majority in Congress and of States by which these amendments were ratified, the gentleman from Georgia has the assurance to say:

> The fourteenth and fifteenth amendments were adopted, if adopted at all, against the will of a majority of all the people in the Union, by trickery and treachery in the North and by force and violence in the South.

He announces that awful things will happen if the United States shall have the temerity to attempt to enforce these amendments. It will cause a cyclone, a hurricane, possibly an earthquake. The fourteenth amendment provides than when the right to vote for President, Representatives in Congress, or State officers is denied to citizens of the United States "except for participation in rebellion or other crimes, the basis of representation therein shall be reduced in the proportion which the number of such male citizens bears to the whole number of male citizens 21 years of age in said State."

And here the gentleman from Georgia raises his voice and exclaims:

> If Congress should be unwise enough to elect to exercise the discretionary power vested in it by section 5 of Article XIV, it will not only be the most serious strain of the present cordial relations so happily existing between the sections, but it will require a readjustment of the basis of representation that will not start at the Potomac and at Rio Grande, but will stretch from Hatteras to the Golden Gate, from Maine to Florida, and will embrace in its majestic sweep every State and Territory in the Union and even our new islands of the sea.

. . . I admit the contention. That is what it means. He further claims that several of the Northern States do in fact at the present time abridge the franchise of citizens of the United States who are 21 years old by requiring educational or property qualifications, or prepayment of taxes, or a specific religious belief, or nativity in the United States, or the use of the Australian ballot, requiring a certain degree of intelligence; and he insists that the basis of representation shall be reduced accordingly in said States. I shall not enter upon that discussion. It is a question for the Federal courts. If after due consideration they shall deliberately decide and declare that such limitations of the franchise do in fact come within the purport of that amendment, the people of the States which for the promotion of the public welfare have placed such limitations upon the franchise will accept the decision without a murmur and modify their basis of apportionment according thereto.

Of the 9,000,000 so-called negroes in the United States, 8,000,000 are in the fifteen Southern States. Of males 21 years of age the negroes number about 2,000,000 in this nation. The gentleman from Georgia alleges that "of the more than a million and a half negro males of voting age" in the eleven States that once constituted the Southern Confederacy "three-fourths of a million can neither read nor write."

I would ask him if he is proud of this record; if he experiences self-satisfaction in the reflection and the declaration that a majority of the negroes of the South can neither read nor write. He says that the illiteracy of the southern negro has been rapidly reduced since he was made free; that negro illiteracy in those States was 77 percent in 1880, 63 percent in 1890, and 49 per cent in 1900—in other words, that more than one-half the negroes of the South can now read and write, and that the number who can read and write to-day is 50 per cent greater than it was when Lincoln issued his emancipation proclamation.

This would seem to be a marvelously good showing, but it is argued otherwise. It is insisted that while the southern negro is more intelligent, he is more wicked and pernicious. Or, in the language of the gentleman, "During this same period his criminality increased in more rapid ratio than his illiteracy decreased." This he tries to provide adducing the alleged fact that the number of negroes arrested in the South has increased one third-during the last twenty years. On arriving at this datum my friend exclaims: "There you are; there are more prisoners than there used to be; ergo, more crime." He seems to think that settles the question. I want to ask: Does it settle the question? Let us see. In "old slavery times" there were very few negroes arrested in the entire south. If a negro "went bad," he was flogged or subjected to some physical remonstrance, which he appreciated and which was continued until he went good again.

So there were almost no arrests. After the war the negroes became subject to the statute law, but the planter was still to some extent the patriarch and had his own methods of restraining the vicious and lawless. When the ballot was given to the negro by the fifteenth amendment and the reconstruction measures were enforced, it caused tremendous irritation and exasperation between the races. The bitter hostilities then engendered still exist, and, I might suggest, have something to do with the increase in the number of negro prisoners. . . .

The negro must not imagine that simply because he is a negro those who would befriend him among the whites will step in and protect him if he commits a crime. On the other hand, the whites must not impose unjust restrictions, unjust laws, and unjust sentences upon the negro simply because he is a negro. To do so is undemocratic, un-American, and in direct opposition to the principles upon which this government was founded and opposed to the welcome which we have extended to the oppressed of all nations. . . .

I cannot agree with those who advance the argument that the South should be left to solve the negro problem, for the reason that when States enact legislation affecting the political status of large numbers of its citizens of voting age the result of such legislation is national in its effect, and, therefore, must at once become the object of concern of all sections of the country. . . .

It has been urged that some Northern States have restrictions on the suffrage. The object of the Crumpacker resolution is to have a full and fair investigation of the election laws of all the States, for the purpose of ascertaining to what extent manhood citizenship has been disenfranchised. If the result of the investigation should be such as to justify it, the purpose is to urge a reduction of the representation of the disfranchising States in accordance with the requirements of the Constitution.

If, after this investigation, it is discovered that these other States restrict the franchise contrary to the Constitution, then their representation would have to be reduced accordingly. Why this dread of such an investigation? If what is urged is true, the Northern States may be as seriously affected as the Southern States. I have not heard a protest against such an investigation from the gentleman from Connecticut, for instance, or from the gentleman from Ohio, or from members of the Pennsylvania delegation.

Source: Morrell, Edward De V. "Negro Suffrage: Should the Fourteenth and Fifteenth Amendments Be Repealed?" Speech before the House of Representatives, April 4, 1904. Washington, DC: 1904, pp. 7–13, 19–20, 22–23. Accessed January 3, 2019. https://cdn.loc.gov/service/rbc/lcrbmrp/t2609/t2609.pdf.

Jane Addams Asserts That Women Armed with the "Franchise" Will Redress Social Ills, 1912

Jane Addams was one of the foremost social reformers of the Progressive Era. She was also a champion of women's suffrage. In both private correspondence and public remarks on the latter, Addams's passion for addressing poverty and other social problems frequently informed her arguments for extending the franchise to women. Again and again, she asserted that pressing problems besieging millions of American families—poor housing, abusive employers, polluted cities, limited educational opportunities, legal protections for infants, young children, and pregnant women—would never be satisfactorily addressed in the political sphere until women were given a voice at the ballot box. This theme is evident in a speech that Addams delivered on women's suffrage in Madison, Wisconsin, on January 23, 1912. Excerpts from the speech were in the Chicago Tribune *two weeks later.*

As the first woman suffrage association was planned in 1840 after the women had been refused meats at the anti-slavery convention which met in London, so doubtless these new suffrage societies which are approaching the situation with such valor and heroism are also rooted in a genuine protest that women are not allowed to participate in the legal and formal effort to right ancient wrongs as they arise to the national consciousness, first to disturb it and later to be redressed.

Much of the new demand for political enfranchisement arises from a passionate desire to reform the unsatisfactory and degrading social conditions which are responsible for so much wrong doing and wretchedness. The fate of the unfortunate, the suffering, and the criminal is daily forced upon woman's attention in painful and intimate ways. But because of the tendency to nationalize all industrial and commercial questions, to make the state responsible for the care of the helpless, to safeguard by law the food we eat and the liquid we drink, to subordinate the claims of the individual and the family to the health and well being of the community, contemporary women who are without the franchise are much more outside the real life of the world than any set of disenfranchised men could possibly have been in all history, unless it were the men slaves of ancient Greece, because never before has so large and area of life found civic expression; never since the days of Pericles have politics included so large a portion of human interests.

Never before has Hegel's definition of the state as the realization of the moral ideal been so accurate.

Franchise Necessary to "Players."

The college woman, whether she has made a specialty of economics, of the humanities, or of science, or whether she is leading a purely domestic life, in spite of her widened interests and disciplined mind, if she is without the franchise will find herself outside of the real game. She will find herself trying to win a battle without arms, and resents being obliged to stop in the midst of it in order to forge her weapons with which the men all about her are supplied.

This may be easily illustrated. To take first the college woman who has made a specialty of economics and industrial questions—and their name is legion—they quickly discover that political disability has ever worked itself out in industrial weakness and social impotence; that while the wages of working men have increased from 50 to 100 per cent during the last sixty years, the wages of working women have remained stationary.

In that awful "sweating exhibition" held several years ago in London it was shown that skirts were made for 7 1/2 pence per dozen and that women were working nineteen hours a day for 1 shilling. The latest government investigation in England discloses a number of working women so ill paid that England is perforce developing an entire class of homeless women, too poor to pay for continuous shelter.

The exclusion from all political rights of millions of working women is not only a source of industrial weakness and poverty to themselves, but a danger to national industry. Working women cannot hope to hold their own in industrial matters where their interests clash with those of their enfranchised fellow workers or employers, in whose hands lie the solution of the problems which are at present convulsing the industrial world. They are bound to feel more and more the disadvantages of being shut out from the sphere where questions connected with their wages and hours of labor are being fought out.

Women Are Not Consulted.

In the solution of these problems women themselves are not consulted, even in the laws designed to protect their own health and comfort. Such are:

Anti-sweatshop laws.

Prohibition of tenement house work.

Inspection and licensing.

The minimum wage board first established for woman's work.

Limitation of hours of labor.

Prohibition of night work.

Protection of child bearing women.

Industrial insurance and all of that new legislation embodied in employers' liability acts.

Legal status of trades unions.

Free employment bureaus.

Trade training.

Liquor legislation.

Industrial conciliation and arbitration and that scientific management of industry which goes to show that so often efficiency is only applied mechanics.

To consider next the college woman who has devoted herself to science. The desire for the amelioration of the conditions of human life comes, so to speak, in gusts, and no one can doubt that the wind is now blowing with strength and impelling us onward. It is sweeping into this worldwide effort those who are supposed to represent the least of enthusiasm and the most of cold research—the men and women trained in pure science. No one is more needed at the present moment than the expert in the application of recent scientific discoveries to practical affairs. Much of this application is identified with legislation, and while the researches of scientific women are taken with absolute confidence they are given no vote when it comes to the civic application of their knowledge.

Some Cases in Point.

One can readily instance:

Bacteriological knowledge in relation to the milk supply, to the examination of foods, and to the public water supply.

Prevention of infant mortality.

Care of newborn infants—prevention of blindness.

Regulation of midwifery.

Registration of trained nurses.

Control of contagious diseases.

Vaccination and administration of anti-toxic.

Care of tuberculosis.

Medical supervision of school children.

Housing, sanitation, and ventilation.

Disposal of waste.

Prevention of industrial diseases.

The college woman who studies literature, history, philosophy, whatever treats of the development of human life, of that vast and checkered undertaking of its own moralization to which the human race is committed, quickly feels the [speed] of the franchise. It is inevitable that humanitarian women should wish to vote concerning all the regulation of public charities which have to do with:

The care of dependent children.

Pensions to mothers in distress.

Care of the aged poor.

Care of the homeless—municipal lodging houses and poorhouses.
Care of the mentally defective.
Conditions of jails and penitentiaries.
Conditions of police stations.
Gradual elimination of the social evil.
Extended care of young girls—the age of consent.
The establishment of juvenile courts.
The suppression of gambling.
Protection of the immigrant.
Decent advertising—regulation of billboards.
Municipal art.
Public baths and wash houses.

"Who Keeps Your House?"

To consider next the college woman who is absorbed in domesticity. It is said that certain women are still indifferent to political freedom quite as oriental women are indifferent to personal freedom because they have never seen the implications and consequences which the lack of the franchise entails. A chart has recently been prepared by the Woman's City club of Chicago entitled: "Madam, who keeps your house?" showing the connection which the most domestic woman has with civic affairs. This chart shows a series of sketches of home life connected by a string with the various departments in the city hall that controls them.

A couple being married...Marriage license bureau
A couple hunting a home...Building department
Buying household goods for it...Factory inspection
New wife buying a loaf of bread.....Inspection of foods and markets
Housekeeper taking to milk.....Milk inspector; city health
Lighting gas stove...Commissioner of public works
Putting garbage in pail...........Sanitary inspector of streets and alleys
Getting a drink of water......Commissioner of public works
Baby in nurse's arms......Registered in health department
Children sent to school.....Board of education; health department: medical school inspection.
Smoke pouring out of window...Smoke inspection
Men cleaning streets....Streets and alleys
Signs for contagious diseases....Health department
Crepe on the door......Burial permit

Some Needed Domestic Laws

Even the most indifferent woman who keeps house cannot fail to see this connection and the disaster which must result when she is forced persistently to turn the regulation of such affairs over to others. It is said that the moral trustworthiness of woman in their sense of domestic relation is accepted in our everyday life as part of the natural order of things on which we can rely as implicitly as on the continuity of the forces of nature, but the community is wronged when so much of this integrity is absorbed in a domestic selfishness that a sense of obligation toward the community is never developed. And, perhaps, the women who lead the domestic life, more than any other, are in need of the franchise. One could easily name the regulations of the state which define her status in the community.

DOMESTIC:

Laws regulating marriage and divorce.

Laws defining the legitimacy of children.

Laws defining married women's property rights.

Exemption and homestead laws which protect her when her husband is bankrupt.

Laws concerning nonsupport, which so intimately affect the lives of poorer women and which alone enables them to rear their children.

Laws concerning the co-guardianship which gives a woman an equal right in the care of her children and which until recently have been so manifestly unjust to mothers.

Laws concerning widows' awards.

If we consider next the acts of the state regulating her functions as mother of her children and head of her household there are:

Laws concerning the preparation of food by which alone her children may be protected from poisoning.

Those concerning the manufacture of clothing.

Provision for the education of her children made by the public schools, state universities, etc.

Provision for the recreation of her children, which have lately come to include not only playgrounds but small parks with field houses and gymnasiums.

Child labor laws which protect her children from premature labor.

The newly established laws for vocational guidance and employment supervision which many cities are instituting gradually in connection with their public school systems. Even the factory child averages between six and four-tenths years of education before it enters industry, and it might well seem the duty of the state to keep a supervision over them lest the education which they have gotten at such expense he utterly quenched in work till fitted for the young.

Tariff Greatly Concerns Woman.

These laws I have mentioned defining her status and facilitating the functions of the domestic woman are the most obvious ones. I have not gone into the great question of the tariff and all that it means in raising the price of household commodities for if woman is less the producer than formerly she still determines the kind and quality of production because she is the consumer and purchaser. It is said that English women are most eager to get into the game before the tariff policy is established in England.

Because the college woman is the triumphant heir to the long struggle to secure wider educational opportunities and economic freedom for women, she, above all others, is able to testify that the never changing state inevitably brings about great modifications, not only industrial and social, but domestic and personal as well.

The college woman will know that under the impulsion of new political ideas, the legal forms of society are gradually changing and fresh civic institutions are constantly developed to meet these new wants, and that a government controlled and administered almost exclusively by men, in dealing with these now and peculiar problems which affect all aspects of life, must of necessity fail to deal with them adequately, that all the remedial powers, all the understanding and training, which society possessed must be brought to bear upon them if our nation would hold its own in this complex modern world in which we live.

MISS JANE ADDAMS.

Source: "Jane Addams Tells Why Women Should Vote." *Chicago Daily Tribune*, February 4, 1912, p. 4.

Seventeenth Amendment Provides for "Direct Elections" of U.S. Senators, 1913

When the United States first came into being, the Constitution that laid out its system of government provided for the membership of the U.S. Senate to be filled by elections held by state legislatures. But objections to this state of affairs intensified during the Gilded Age (late nineteenth century) and the Progressive Era (early twentieth century), two periods in which social, economic, and political reformers all railed against the disproportionate influence that powerful industries, business titans, and other special interests exerted over the country's lawmakers. The passage of a constitutional amendment shifting responsibility for electing U.S. senators from state legislatures—which were seen as easily corruptible—to the actual citizens of the states became a major crusade of progressive reformers. Momentum for such an amendment rapidly increased, and on May 13, 1912, Congress passed legislation empowering voters to cast direct votes for U.S. senators. The Seventeenth Amendment was ratified less than eleven months later, on April 8, 1913.

Sixty-second Congress of the United States of America; At the Second Session,

Begun and held at the City of Washington on Monday, the fourth day of December, one thousand nine hundred and eleven.

JOINT RESOLUTION

Proposing an amendment to the Constitution providing that Senators shall be elected by the people of the several States.

Resolved by the Senate and House of Representatives of the United States of America in Congress assembled (two-thirds of each House concurring therein), That in lieu of the first paragraph of section three of Article I of the Constitution of the United States, and in lieu of so much of paragraph two of the same section as relates to the filling of vacancies, the following be proposed as an amendment to the Constitution, which shall be valid to all intents and purposes as part of the Constitution when ratified by the legislatures of three-fourths of the States:

"The Senate of the United States shall be composed of two Senators from each State, elected by the people thereof, for six years; and each Senator shall have one vote. The electors in each State shall have the qualifications requisite for electors of the most numerous branch of the State legislatures.

"When vacancies happen in the representation of any State in the Senate, the executive authority of such State shall issue writs of election to fill such vacancies: *Provided*, That the legislature of any State may empower the executive thereof to make temporary appointments until the people fill the vacancies by election as the legislature may direct.

"This amendment shall not be so construed as to affect the election or term of any Senator chosen before it becomes valid as part of the Constitution."

Source: Joint Resolution proposing an Amendment to the Constitution providing that Senators shall be elected by the people of the several states, May 13, 1912; Enrolled Acts and Resolutions of Congress, Records of the General Government, Record Group 11, National Archives Building, Washington, DC. Accessed January 3, 2019. https://www.archives.gov/legislative/features/17th-amendment/enrolled.html.

Black Writers and Activists Unite to Call for Women's Suffrage, 1915

In 1915 the editors of The Crisis, *the flagship publication of the National Association for the Advancement of Colored People (NAACP), published a long article gathering the statements of a wide range of leaders in the African American community in support of women's suffrage. Among the contributors to the article, titled "Votes for Women: A Symposium of Leading Thinkers of Colored America," was celebrated novelist and lawyer Charles W. Chesnutt and Mary E. Jackson, president of the Rhode Island Association of Colored Women's Clubs and a major figure in the pro-suffrage National Association of Colored Women. Following are the statements provided by Chesnutt and Jackson to* The Crisis *in support of women's suffrage and the overall "broadening of woman's sphere" in American life.*

"Women's Rights" by Charles W. Chesnutt

I believe that all persons of full age and sound mind should have a voice in the making of the laws by which they are governed, or in the selection of those who make those laws. As long as the family was the social unit, it was perhaps well enough for the householder, representing the family, to monopolize the vote. But with the broadening of woman's sphere the situation has changed, and many women have interests which are not concerned with the family.

Experience has shown that the rights and interests of no class are safe so long as they are entirely in the hands of another class—the rights and interests of the poor in the hands of the rich, of the rich in the hands of the poor, of one race in the hands of another. And while there is no such line of cleavage between the sexes as exists between other social classes, yet so far as women constitute a class as differentiated from men, neither can their rights be left with entire safety solely in the hands of men. In the gradual extension of statutory rights, women are in many countries, the equals of men before the law. They have always been subject to the burdens of citizenship. The burden of taxation, generally speaking, falls more heavily upon them, perhaps because they are more honest in returning their personal property for taxation, or less cunning in concealing it. They are subject, equally with men, to the criminal laws, though there, I suspect, for sentimental reasons, the burden has not fallen so heavily upon them. Their rights need protection, and they should be guarded against oppression, and the ballot is the most effective weapon by which these things can be accomplished.

I am not in favor of woman suffrage because I expect any great improvement in legislation to result from it. The contrary, from woman's lack of experience in government, might not unreasonably be expected. Women are certainly no wiser or more logical than men. But they enjoy equal opportunities for education, and large numbers of them are successfully engaged in business and in the professions and have the requisite experience and knowledge to judge intelligently of proposed legislation. Even should their judgment be at fault—as men's judgment too often is—they have fine intuitions, which are many times a safe guide to action; and their sympathies are apt to be in support of those things which are clean and honest and just and therefore desirable—all of which ought to make them a valuable factor in government.

"The Self-Supporting Woman and the Ballot" by Miss M.E. Jackson

Looked at from a sane point of view, all objections to the ballot for women are but protests against progress, civilization, and good sense.

"Woman's place is in the home." Would that the poorly paid toilers in field, work-shop, mill and kitchen, might enjoy the blessed refreshment of their own homes with accompanying assurance that those dependent upon them might be fed, clothed, properly reared and educated.

Each morning's sun beholds a mighty army of 8,000,000 souls marching forth to do battle for daily bread. You inquire who they are? Why, the mothers, wives, sisters, and daughters of the men of America. "The weaker vessels," the majority of whom are constrained from necessity.

There is no field of activity in the country where women are not successfully competing with men. In the agricultural pursuits alone, there are over 900,000. In the ministry 7,000 dare preach the gospel with "Heads uncovered." And 1,010 possess the courage to invade the field of the Solons, bravely interpreting the laws, although their brothers in all but twelve of the forty-five States (so far as the ballot is concerned), class them with criminals, insane and feeble-minded.

The self-supporting woman out of her earnings, pays taxes, into the public treasury and through church, club and civic organization gives her moral backing unstintingly to her Country.

Imagine if you can the withdrawal of this marvelous economic force—the working women of America! It is a fundamental necessity of modern civilization.

The laboring man has discovered beyond peradventure that his most effective weapon of defence is the *ballot in his own hand.* The self-supporting woman asks for and will accept nothing less.

Source: "Votes for Women: A Symposium of Leading Thinkers of Colored America." *The Crisis*, 10, no. 4 (August 1915).

Carrie Chapman Catt Tells Congress That Women's Suffrage Is "Inevitable," 1917

In the late 1910s, the influential women's suffrage advocate Carrie Chapman Catt delivered a standard lecture in which she urged male lawmakers in America to right a historic injustice and give the franchise to women. Framing her address as an "open letter" to the U.S. Congress, she sternly told members that they faced a stark choice: either wake up and support the franchise for women or get rolled over by an international movement that was growing more powerful every day—and that would not be denied. Following are excerpts from Catt's memorable stump speech.

Woman suffrage is inevitable. . . . Three distinct causes make it inevitable.

(1) *The history of our country.* Ours is a nation born of revolution; of rebellion against a system of government so securely entrenched in the customs and traditions of human society that in 1776 it seemed impregnable. From the beginning of things nations had been ruled by kings and for kings, while the people served and paid the cost. The American Revolutionists boldly proclaimed the heresies:

"Taxation without representation is tyranny."

"Governments derive their just powers from the consent of the governed."

Our Theories Make Woman Suffrage Inevitable

The Colonists won and the nation which was established as a result of their victory has held unfailingly that these two fundamental principles of democratic government are not only the spiritual source of our national existence but have been our chief historic pride and at all times the sheer anchor of our liberties.

Eighty years after the Revolution Abraham Lincoln welded those two maxims into a new one:

"Ours is a government of the people, by the people and for the people."

Fifty years more passed an the President of the United States, Woodrow Wilson, in a mighty crisis of the nation, proclaimed to the world: *"We are fighting for the things which we have always carried nearest our hearts—for democracy, for the right of those who submit to authority to have a voice in their own government."*

All the way between these immortal aphorisms political leaders have declared unabated faith in their truth. Not one American has arisen to question their logic in the one hundred and forty-one years of our national existence. However stupidly our country may have evaded the logical application at times, it has never swerved from its devotion to the theory of democracy as expressed by those two axioms.

Not only has it unceasingly upheld the THEORY but it has carried these theories into PRACTICE whenever men made application.

Certain denominations of Protestants, Catholics, Jews, non-land holders, workingmen, Negroes, Indians, were at one time disfranchised in all, or in part, of our country. Class by class they have been admitted to the electorate. Political motives may have played their part in some instances but the only reason given by historians for their enfranchisement is the unassailability of the logic of these maxims of the Declaration.

Meantime the United States opened wide its gates to men of all the nations of the earth. By the combination of naturalization granted the foreigner after a five-years' residence by our national government and the uniform provision of the State constitutions which extends the vote to male citizens, it has been the custom in our country for three generations that any male immigrant, accepted by the national government as a citizen, automatically becomes a voter in any State in which he chooses to reside, subject only to the minor qualifications prescribed by the State. Justifiable exceptions to the general principle might have been entered. Men just emerging from slavery, untrained to think or act for themselves and in most cases wholly illiterate, were not asked to qualify for voting citizenship. Not even as a measure of national caution has the vote ever been withheld from immigrants until they have learned our language, earned a certificate of fitness from our schools or given definite evidence of loyalty to our country. When such questions have been raised, political leaders have replied: "What! Tax men and in return give them no vote; compel men to obey the authority of a government to which they may not give consent! Never. That is un-American." So, it happens that men of all nations and all races, except the Mongolian, may secure citizenship and automatically become voters in any State in the Union, and even the Mongolian born in this country is a citizen and has the vote. With such a history behind it, how can our nation escape the logic it has never failed to follow, when its last unenfranchised class calls for the vote? Behold our Uncle Sam floating the banner with the one hand, "Taxation without representation is tyranny." And with the other seizing the billions of dollars paid in taxes by women to whom he refuses "representation." Behold him again, welcoming the boys of twenty-one and the newly-made immigrant citizen to "a voice in their own government" while he denies that fundamental right of democracy to thousands of women public school teachers from whom many of these men learn all they know of citizenship and patriotism, to women college presidents, to women who preach in our pulpits, interpret law in our courts, preside over our hospitals, write books and magazines and serve in every uplifting moral and social enterprise.

Is there a single man who can justify such inequality of treatment, such outrageous discriminations? Not one.

Woman suffrage became an assured fact when the Declaration of Independence was written. It matters not at all whether Thomas Jefferson and his compatriots though of women when they wrote that immortal document. They conceived and voiced a principle greater than any man. "A Power not of themselves which makes for righteousness" gave them the vision and they proclaimed truisms as immutable as the multiplication table, as changeless as time. The Hon. Champ Clark announced that he had been a woman suffragist ever since he "got the hang of the Declaration of Independence." So it must be with every other American. The amazing thing is that it has required so long a time for a people, most of whom know how to read, "to get the hang of it." Indeed, so inevitable does our history make woman suffrage that any citizen; political party, Congress or Legislature that now blocks its coming by so much as a single day, contributes to the indefensible inconsistency which threatens to make our nation a jest among the onward-moving peoples of the world.

Our Practice Makes Woman Suffrage Inevitable

(2) *The suffrage for women already established in the United States makes woman suffrage for the nation inevitable.* When Elihu Root, as President of the American Society of International Law, at the eleventh annual meeting in Washington, April 26, 1917, said, "The world cannot be half democratic and half autocratic. It must be all democratic or all Prussian. There can be no compromise," he voiced a general truth. Precisely the same intuition has already taught the blindest and most hostile foe of woman suffrage that our nation cannot long continue a condition under which government in half its territory rests upon the consent of half the people and in the other half upon the consent of all the people; a condition which grants representation to the taxed in half its territory and denies it in the other half; a condition which permits women in some States to share in the election of the President, Senators and Representatives and denies them that privilege in others. It is too obvious to require demonstration that woman suffrage now covering half our territory, will eventually be ordained in all the nation. No one will deny it; the only question left is when and how will it be completely established.

Our Leadership Makes Woman Suffrage Inevitable

(3) *The leadership of the United States in world democracy compels the enfranchisement of its own woman.* The maxims of the Declaration were once called "fundamental principles of government." They are now called "American principles" or even "Americanisms." They have become the slogans of every movement toward political liberty the world around; of every effort to widen the suffrage for men or women in any land. Not a people, race or class striving for freedom is there, anywhere in the world that has not made our axioms the chief weapon of the struggle. More all men and women the world around with far-sighted vision into the verities of things, know that the world tragedy of our day is not now being waged over the assassination of an Archduke, nor commercial competition, nor national ambitions, nor the freedom of the seas—it is a death grapple between the forces which deny and those which uphold the truth of the Declaration of Independence.

Our "Americanisms" have become the issue of the great war!

Every day the conviction grows deeper that a world humanity will emerge from the war, demanding political liberty and accepting nothing less. In that new struggle there is little doubt that men and women will demand and attain political liberty together. Today they are fighting the world's battle for democracy together. Men and women are paying the frightful cost of war and bearing its sad and sickening sorrows together. Tomorrow they will share its rewards together in democracies which make no discriminations on account of sex.

These are new times and as an earnest of its sincerity in the battle for democracy, the government of Great Britain has not only pledged votes to its disfranchised men and to its women, but the measure passed the House of Commons in June, 1917, by a vote of 7 to 1 and will be sent to the House of Lords in December with the assurance of Premier Lloyd George that it will shortly become a national law. The measure will apply to England, Scotland, Ireland, Wales and all the smaller British islands.

Canada too has enfranchised the women of all its provinces starting from the Pacific Coast to Northern New York, and the Premiere predicted votes for all Canadian women before the next national election.

Russia, whose opposing forces have made a sad farce of the new poverty, is nevertheless pledged to a democracy which shall include women. It must be remembered that no people ever passed from absolute autocracy into a smoothly running democracy with ready-made constitution and a full set of statutes to cover all conditions. Russia is no exception. She must have time to work out her destiny. Except those maxims of democracy put forth by our own country, it is interesting to note that the only one worthy of immortality is the slogan of the women of New Russia, "Without the participation of women, suffrage is not universal."

France has pledged votes to its women as certainly as a Republic of Italian men have declared woman suffrage an imperative issue when the war is over and have asked its consideration before. The city of Paris (Bohemia) has appointed a Commission to report a new municipal suffrage plan which shall include women. Even autocratic Germany debated the question in the Imperial Reichstag.

In the words of Premier Lloyd George; "There are times in history when the world spins along its destined course so leisurely that for centuries it seems to be at a standstill. Then come awful times when time rushes along at so giddy a pace that the track of centuries is covered in a single year. These are the times in which we now live." . . .

The Logic of the Situation Calls for Immediate Action

It is not clear that American history makes woman suffrage inevitable? That full suffrage in twelve States makes its coming in all forty-eight States inevitable? That the spread of democracy over the world, including votes for the women of many countries, in each case based upon the principles our Republic gave to the world, compels action by our nation? Is it not clear that the world expects such action and fails to understand its delay? . . .

If enfranchisement is to be given to women now, how is it to be done? Shall it be by amendment of State constitutions or by amendment or the Federal

Constitution? There are no other ways. The first sends the question from the Legislature by referendum to all male voters to the State; the other sends the question from Congress to the Legislature of the several States.

Three Reasons for the Federal Method

We elect the Federal method. There are three reasons why we make this choice and three reasons why we reject the state method. We choose the Federal method 1.) because it is the quickest process and justly demands immediate action. If passed by the Sixty-fifth Congress, as it should be, the amendment will go to forty-one Legislatures in 1919, and when thirty-six have ratified it, will become a national law. In 1869 Wyoming led the way and 1919 will round out half a century of the most self-sacrificing struggle any class ever made for the vote. It is enough. The British women's suffrage army will be mustered out at the end of their half century of similar endeavor. Surely men of the land of George Washington will not require a longer time than those of the land of George the Third to discover that taxation without representation is tyranny—no matter whether it be men or women who are taxed! We may justly expect American men to be as willing to grant to the women of the United States generous consideration as those of great Britain have done.

2) Every other country dignifies woman suffrage as a national question. Even Canada and Australia, composed of self-governing states like our own, who regard it. Were the precedent not established our own national government has taken a step which makes the treatment of woman suffrage as a national question imperative. For the first time in our history Congress has imposed a direct tax upon women and has thus deliberately violated the most fundamental and sacred principle of our government, since it offers no compensating "representation" for the tax it imposes. Unless separation is made it becomes the same kind of tyrant as was George the Third. When the exemption for unmarried persons under the Income Tax was reduced to $1000, the Congress laid the tax upon thousands of wage-earning women—teachers, doctors, lawyers, bookkeepers, secretaries and the proprietors of many businesses. Such women are earning their incomes under hard conditions of economic inequalities largely due to their disfranchisement. . . . The national government is guilty of the violation of the principle that the tax and the vote are inseparable; it alone can make amends. Two ways are open: exempt the women the Income Tax or grant them the vote—there can be no compromise. . . .

3) If the entire forty-eight States should severally enfranchise women, their political status would still be inferior to that of men, since no provision for national protection in their right to vote would exist. The women of California or New York are not wholly enfranchised for the national government has not denied the States the right to deprive them of the vote. This protection can come only by Federal action. . . .

Three Reasons against the State Method

The three reasons why we object to the State amendment process are: 1) The constitutions of many States contain such difficult provisions for amending that it is practically impossible to carry and amendment at the polls. . . .

2) The second reason why we object to the State process is far more serious and important than the first. It is because the statutory laws governing elections are so inadequate and defective as to vouchsafe little or no protection to a referendum in most States. . . .

3) The third reason why we object to the State method is even more weighty than either or both of the others. It is because the State method fixes responsibility upon no one. The Legislatures pass the question on to the voters and have no further interest in it. The political parties, not knowing how the election may decide the matter, are loth to espouse the cause of woman suffrage, lest if it loses, they will have alienated from their respective parties the support of enemies of woman suffrage. . . .

You pronounce it unfair that thirty-six States should determine who may vote in the remaining twelve; the possible Republican Northern States should decide who may vote in Democratic Southern States. It is no more unfair than that some counties within a State should decide who may vote in the remaining counties is no more unfair than that the Democratic city of New York should disfranchise the women of the Republican cities of Albany and Rochester as it has just done. Forty-eight States will have the opportunity to ratify the Federal Amendment and every State, therefore, will have its opportunity to disfranchise its own women in this manner. If any State fails to do it, they may agree that that State would probably not enfranchise its own women by the State method, but if it would not so enfranchise them that State is behind the times and is holding our country up to the scorn of other nations. It has failed to catch the vision and the spirit of Democracy sweeping over the world. This nation cannot, must not, wait for any State, ignorant, backward. That State more than all others needs woman suffrage to shake its dry bones, to bring political questions into the home and set discussion going. It needs education, action, stimulation to prevent atrophy. In after years posterity will utter grateful thanks that there was a method which could throw a bit of modernity into it from the outside. . . .

Despite these truths there are among you those who still harbor honest misgivings. Please remember that woman suffrage is coming; you know it is. In this connection, have you ever thought that the women of your own families who may tell you now that they do not want the vote are going to realize someday that there is something insincere in your protestations of chivalry protection and "you are too good to vote, my dear," they are going to discover that the trust, respect, and frank acknowledgment of equality which men of other States have given their women are something infinitely higher and nobler than you have ever offered them? Have you thought that you may now bestow upon them a liberty that they may not yet realize they need, but that tomorrow they may storm your castle and command? . . .

Our nation is in the extreme crisis of its existence and men would search their very souls to find just and reasonable causes for every thought and act. If you, making this search shall find "State's Rights" a sufficient cause to lead you to vote "no" on the Federal Suffrage Amendment, then, with all the gentleness which should accompany the reference to a sacred memory, let us tell you that your cause will bear neither the test of time nor critical analysis, and that your vote will compel your children to apologize for your act. . . .

The framers of the Constitution gave unquestioned authority to Congress to act upon women suffrage. Why not use that authority and use it now to do the big, noble, just thing of catching pace with other nations on this question of democracy? The world and posterity will honor you for it. . . .

We know you will meet opposition. There are a few "woman haters" left, a few "old males of the tribe," as Vance Thompson calls them, whose duty they believe it to be to keep women in the places they have carefully picked out for them. . . . There are women, too, with "slave souls" and "clinging vines" for backbones. There are female dolls and male dandies. But the world does not wait for such as these, nor does Liberty pause to heed the plaint of men and women with a grouch. She does not wait for those who have a special interest to serve, nor a selfish reason for depriving other people of freedom. Holding her torch aloft, Liberty is pointing the way onward and upward and saying to America, "Come." . . . .

Gentlemen, we hereby petition you, our only designated representatives, to redress our grievances by the immediate passage of the influence to secure its ratification in your own state, in order that the women of our nation may be endowed with political freedom that our nation may resume its world leadership in democracy.

Woman suffrage is coming—you know it. Will you, Honorable Senators and Members of the House of Representatives, help or hinder it?

Source: Catt, Carrie Chapman. *Open Letter to Congress on Suffrage for Women, November 1, 1917.* New York: National Woman Suffrage Publishing Company, 1917.

Congresswoman Jeannette Rankin Urges Colleagues to Pass a Suffrage Amendment, 1918

In 1916 Jeannette Rankin became the first elected woman member of the U.S. Congress when the people of Montana elected her to represent them in Washington (although she was not formally seated until April 1917, after a month-long debate in Congress about whether to accept a woman). A Republican, Rankin had run for office on a platform that emphasized women's suffrage and social welfare issues, and she wasted no time in making her views known on those subjects. She also played an important role in getting a special House committee report on the subject of women's suffrage to the floor of Congress for discussion—and was pivotal in organizing a House vote on a suffrage amendment. Her remarks in support of that amendment, delivered to her colleagues and a packed house of suffrage supporters in the balconies on January 10, 1918, have been described as critical in getting the amendment passed (by a narrow 274–136 vote, just barely meeting the two-thirds majority requirement). Although the House amendment fell short of passage when it went to the Senate (the suffrage amendment did not pass on to the states for ratification until it was voted on again by a new Congress eighteen months later), the House of Representatives' January 1918 passage of the amendment nonetheless marked a landmark in the quest by pro-suffrage forces to secure the vote for women across the nation. Following is the full text of the remarks Rankin delivered on the floor of the House on January 10.

Mr. Speaker, we are facing to-day a question of political evolution. International circumstances have forced this question to an issue. Our country is in a state of war. The Nation has had a terrible shock. The result has been a sudden change in our national consciousness. The things we have for years been taking for granted are suddenly assuming a new significance for us.

We as a Nation were born in a land of unparalleled resources, of vast acreage of fertile soil, of minerals, of coal, oil, gas, of timber, and water power. The combinations in which these resources were found, together with our great natural highways, gave us opportunities for development which no other nation could boast. And we had people, people in whose veins ran the blood of all nations, people imbued with the buoyancy of youth, fearless, and with the will and energy to make their dreams of freedom come true.

Without restraint we drew upon the stored treasure of the past. We spent recklessly, and we wasted our natural resources and our human energy with youthful abandon.

And then came the world war, and with its coming our carefree attitude was suddenly replaced by a new seriousness. To-day we are mobilizing all our resources for the ideals of democracy. We are taking stock of our available energy. And we are finding that with all our past wastefulness we still have limitless resources upon which we can count. We have men—men for the Army, for the Navy, for the air; men for the industries, the mines, the fields; men for the Government. And the national leaders are now reaching out and drawing men of talent, picking those with the best minds, with expert knowledge, and with broad perspective, to aid in war work.

But something is still lacking in the completeness of our national effort. With all our abundance of coal, with our great stretches of idle, fertile land, babies are dying from cold and hunger; soldiers have died for lack of a woolen shirt.

Might it not be that the men who have spent their lives thinking in terms of commercial profit find it hard to adjust themselves to thinking in terms of human needs? Might it not be that a great force that has always been thinking in terms of human needs, and that always will think in terms of human needs, has not been mobilized? Is it not possible that the women of the country have something of value to give the Nation at this time?

It would be strange indeed if the women of this country through all these years had not developed an intelligence, a feeling, a spiritual force peculiar to themselves, which they hold in readiness to give to the world. It would be strange if the influence of women through direct participation in the political struggles, through which all social and industrial development proceeds, would not lend a certain virility, a certain influx of new strength and understanding and sympathy and ability to the exhausting effort we are now making to meet the problem before us.

For 70 years, the women leaders of this country have been asking the Government to recognize this possibility. Every great woman who stands out in our history—Susan B. Anthony, Elizabeth Cady Stanton, Clara Barton, Mary Livermore, Harriet Beecher Stowe, Frances Willard, Lucy Stone, Jane Addams, Ella Flagg Young, Alice Stone Blackwell, Anna Howard Shaw, Mrs. Catt—all have asked the Government to permit women to serve more effectively the national welfare. All have felt that the energy, the thought, and the suffering that was spent in trying to obtain permission to serve directly should as quickly as possible be turned to the actual service. And in the meantime they did all they could indirectly. They learned to read and to know each other. They became interested in each others' problems, for they found them to be their own problems. As they were the stabilizing influence in the home and kept the family unity, so they have become a great possible stabilizing influence in society, asking now to help keep the unity of the Nation to its highest standard of service.

The have stood back of the men. They have pioneered with them, rejoiced with them over their successes, and when they failed, encouraged them and helped them to begin again. The women have done all that they were allowed to do, all that the men planned for them to do. But through all their work they have pleaded for the political machinery which would enable them to do more.

To-day as never before the Nation needs its women—needs the work of their hands and their hearts and their minds. Their energy must be utilized in the most effective service they can give. Are we now going to refuse these women the opportunity to serve in the face of their plea—in the face of the Nation's great need? Are you gentlemen representing the South, you who have struggled with your negro problem for half a century, going to retaliate after 50 years for the injustice you believe was done you so long ago? Have you not learned in your struggle for adjustment in the South to be broad and fair and open-minded in dealing with another franchise problem that concerns the whole Nation?

The women of the South have stood by you through every trial. They have backed you in every struggle, and they gave themselves and all they held most dear for the cause for which their men laid down their lives. Now they are asking to help you again in a big, broad, national way. Are you going to deny them the equipment with which to help you effectively simply because the enfranchisement of a child-race 50 years ago brought you a problem you were powerless to handle?

There are more white women of voting age in the South to-day than there are negro men and women together. Are you going to say to these thoughtful women: "After 50 years we have been unable to accomplish more than a temporary adjustment of our problem; and now we refuse to let you disturb us, even to help us?" Dare you say that in the face of our tremendous national crisis—in the face of problems too great to rest upon the old doctrines of our youth, but demanding the action of a Nation united in spirit and using all its power?

These are heroic times, and they call for the strength and the courage and the dignity to think and act in national terms. We thought in national terms when we restricted activities by the prohibition amendment a few weeks ago. Why can we not now think in national terms and extend opportunities?

Our President emphasized the great nationalizing process our country is undergoing when he took over the railroads of the country to meet this crisis. The food and fuel problems must soon be solved by nationalization. We are working and thinking to-day not as separate States but as a Nation. We must discuss public affairs not as Montanans or New Yorkers or Floridians but as Americans, taking always a national perspective and looking toward the welfare of the entire country.

We have made the protection of our child workers a national question. We declared war not State by State but by Federal action. We mobilized and equipped our Army not State by State but through Congress. Shall our women, our home defense, be our only fighters in the struggle for democracy who shall be denied Federal action? It is time for our old political doctrine to give way to the new visions, the new aspects of national and international relations which have come to us already since the war began.

For we have had new visions; we have been aroused to a new way of looking at things. Our President, with his wisdom and astuteness, has helped us to penetrate new problems, to analyze situations, to make fine distinctions. He startled us by urging us to distinguish between the German Government and the German people. We who have been steeped in democratic ideals since the days when our forefathers signed the Declaration of Independence find it difficult to think of government as something separate from the people.

Yet, as we learn to make this distinction for Germany, will not our minds revert to our own situation and be puzzled? How can people in other countries who are trying to grasp our plan of democracy avoid stumbling over our logic when we deny the first steps in democracy to our women? May they not see a distinction between the Government of the United States and the women of the United States?

Deep down in the hearts of the American people is a living faith in democracy. Sometimes it is not expressed in the most effective way. Sometimes it seems almost forgotten. But when the test comes we find it still there, groping and aspiring, and helping men and women to understand each other and their common need. It is our national relation, and it prompts in us the desire for that measure of justices which is based on equal opportunity, equal protection, equal freedom for all. In our hearts we know that this desire can be realized only when "those who submit to authority have a voice in their own government," whether that government be political, industrial, or social.

To-day there are men and women in every field of endeavor who are bending all their energies toward a realization of this dream of universal justice. They believe that we are waging a war for democracy. The farmer who knows the elements of democracy becomes something of an idealist when he contemplates the possibility of feeding the world during this crisis. The woman who knits all day to keep from thinking of the sacrifice she is making wonders what this democracy is which she is denied and for which she is asked to give. The miner is dreaming his dreams of industrial democracy as he goes about 2,000 feet underground, bringing forth from the rock precious metals to help in the prosecution of this war.

The girl who works in the Treasury no longer works until she is married. She knows now that she will work on and on and on. The war has taken from her opportunities for the joys that young girls look forward to. Cheerfully and willingly she makes her sacrifice. And she will pay to the very end in order that the future need not find women paying again for the same cause.

The boys at the front know something of the democracy for which they are fighting. These courageous lads who are paying with their lives testified to the sincerity of their fight when they sent home their ballots in the New York election, and voted two to one in favor of woman suffrage and democracy at home.

These are the people of the Nation. These are the fiber and sinew of war—the mother, the farmer, the miner, the industrial worker, the soldier. These are the people who are given their all for the cause of democracy. These are the people who are resting their faith in the Congress of the United States because they believe that Congress knows what democracy means. These people will not fight in vain.

Can we afford to allow these men and women to doubt for a single instant the sincerity of our protestations of democracy? How shall we answer their challenge, gentlemen; how shall we explain to them the meaning of democracy if the same Congress that voted for war to make the world safe for democracy refuses to give this small measure of democracy to the women of our country?

Source: Rankin, Jeannette. "Woman Suffrage" speech in the House of Representative, January 10, 1918. Washington, DC: Government Printing Office, 1918.

Nineteenth Amendment Granting Women the Vote, 1919

When President Woodrow Wilson announced his support in 1918 for a constitutional amendment in support of suffrage for women, the decades-long crusade that had been waged by thousands of women (and some male supporters) for gender equality at the ballot box finally began to appear as if it would become a reality. The House of Representatives was the first to pass an amendment for women's suffrage, doing so on May 21, 1919. The Senate followed suit two weeks later, on June 4, thus sending the proposed amendment on to the states for ratification (which required approval from three-quarters of the forty-eight states then in the Union). Many states ratified the amendment within days of receiving it, but it did not receive the decisive thirty-sixth vote of approval until August 18, 1920, when Tennessee formally ratified it. Following is the text of the joint congressional resolution that ultimately resulted in the historic Nineteenth Amendment to the Constitution.

Sixty-sixth Congress of the United States of America; At the First Session,

Begun and held at the City of Washington on Monday, the nineteenth day of May, one thousand nine hundred and nineteen.

JOINT RESOLUTION

Proposing an amendment to the Constitution extending the right of suffrage to women.

Resolved by the Senate and House of Representatives of the United States of America in Congress assembled (two-thirds of each House concurring therein), That the following article is proposed as an amendment to the Constitution, which shall be valid to all intents and purposes as part of the Constitution when ratified by the legislature of three-fourths of the several States.

"ARTICLE ———.

"The right of citizens of the United States to vote shall not be denied or abridged by the United States or by any State on account of sex.

Congress shall have power to enforce this article by appropriate legislation."

[endorsements]

Source: U.S. Congress. Joint Resolution Proposing an Amendment to the Constitution Extending the Right of Suffrage to Women." 66th Congress, 1st Session. Approved June 4, 1919; Ratified Amendments, 1795–1992; General Records of the United States Government; Record Group 11; National Archives.

Crystal Eastman Discusses the Work Ahead after the Passage of the Nineteenth Amendment, 1920

Crystal Eastman was a trailblazing labor lawyer, journalist, and political reformer who made notable contributions to both the women's suffrage movement and the wider cause of civil liberties protection (she was a cofounder of the American Civil Liberties Union). Like countless other American women, she exulted when the Nineteenth Amendment was ratified. But in "Now We Can Begin," a speech she delivered in the aftermath of ratification (and subsequently published in The Liberator, *a socialist magazine Eastman cofounded with her brother Max Eastman), she emphasized that the work to achieve true gender equality in American society was far from over.*

Most women will agree that August 23, the day when the Tennessee legislature finally enacted the Federal suffrage amendment, is a day to begin with, not a day to end with. Men are saying perhaps "Thank God, this everlasting woman's fight is over!" But women, if I know them, are saying, "Now at last we can begin." In fighting for the right to vote most women have tried to be either non-committal or thoroughly respectable on every other subject. Now they can say what they are really after; and what they are after, in common with all the rest of the struggling world, is freedom.

Freedom is a large word.

Many feminists are socialists, many are communists, not a few are active leaders in these movements. But the true feminist, no matter how far to the left she may be in the revolutionary movement, sees the woman's battle as distinct in its objects and different in its methods from the workers' battle for industrial freedom. She knows, of course, that the vast majority of women as well as men are without property, and are of necessity bread and butter slaves under a system of society which allows the very sources of life to be privately owned by a few, and she counts herself a loyal soldier in the working-class army that is marching to overthrow that system. But as a feminist she also knows that the whole of woman's slavery is not summed up in the profit system, nor her complete emancipation assured by the downfall of capitalism.

Woman's freedom, in the feminist sense, can be fought for and conceivably won before the gates open into industrial democracy. On the other hand, woman's freedom, in the feminist sense, is not inherent in the communist ideal. All feminists are familiar with the revolutionary leader who "can't see" the woman's movement. "What's the matter with the women? My wife's all right," he says. And his wife, one usually finds, is raising his children in a Bronx flat or a dreary suburb, to which he returns occasionally for food and sleep when all possible excitement and stimulus have been wrung from the fight. If we should graduate into communism tomorrow this man's attitude to his wife would not be changed. The proletarian dictatorship may or may not free women. We must begin now to enlighten the future dictators.

What, then, is "the matter with women"? What is the problem of women's freedom? It seems to me to be this: how to arrange the world so that women can be human beings, with a chance to exercise their infinitely varied gifts in infinitely varied ways, instead of being destined by the accident of their sex to one field of activity—housework and child-raising. And second, if and when they choose housework and child-raising, to have that occupation recognized by the world as work, requiring a definite economic reward and not merely entitling the performer to be dependent on some man.

This is not the whole of feminism, of course, but it is enough to begin with. "Oh, don't begin with economics," my friends often protest, "Woman does not live by bread alone. What she needs first of all is a free soul." And I can agree that women will never be great until they achieve a certain emotional freedom, a strong healthy egotism, and some un-personal sources of joy—that in this inner sense we cannot make woman free by changing her economic status. What we can do, however, is to create conditions of outward freedom in which a free woman's soul can be born and grow. It is these outward conditions with which an organized feminist movement must concern itself.

Freedom of choice in occupation and individual economic independence for women: How shall we approach this next feminist objective? First, by breaking down all remaining barriers, actual as well as legal, which make it difficult for women to enter or succeed in the various professions, to go into and get on in business, to learn trades and practice them, to join trades unions. Chief among these remaining barriers is inequality in pay. Here the ground is already broken. This is the easiest part of our program.

Second, we must institute a revolution in the early training and education of both boys and girls. It must be womanly as well as manly to earn your own living, to stand on your own feet. And it must be manly as well as womanly to know how to cook and sew and clean and take care of yourself in the ordinary exigencies of life. I need not add that the second part of this revolution will be more passionately resisted than the first. Men will not give up their privilege of helplessness without a struggle. The average man has a carefully cultivated ignorance about household matters—from what to do with the crumbs to the grocer's telephone number—a sort of cheerful inefficiency which protects him better than the reputation for having a violent temper. It was his mother's fault in the beginning, but even as a boy he was quick to see how a general reputation for being "no good around the house" would serve him throughout life, and half-consciously he began to cultivate that helplessness until today it is the despair of feminist wives.

A growing number of men admire the woman who has a job, and, especially since the cost of living doubled, rather like the idea of their own wives contributing to the family income by outside work. And of course for generations there have been whole towns full of wives who are forced by the bitterest necessity to spend the same hours at the factory that their husbands spend. But these bread-winning wives have not yet developed homemaking husbands. When the two come home from the factory the man sits down while his wife gets supper, and he does so with exactly the same sense of fore-ordained right as if he were "supporting her." Higher up in the economic scale the same thing is true. The business or professional woman who is married, perhaps engages a cook, but the responsibility is not shifted, it is still hers. She "hires and fires," she orders meals, she does the buying, she meets and resolves all domestic crises, she takes charge of moving, furnishing, settling. She may be, like her husband, a busy executive at her office all day, but unlike him, she is also an executive in a small way every night and morning at home. Her noon hour is spent in planning, and too often her Sundays and holidays are spent in "catching up."

Two business women can "make a home" together without either one being over-burdened or over-bored. It is because they both know how and both feel responsible. But it is a rare man who can marry one of them and continue the homemaking partnership. Yet if there are no children, there is nothing essentially different in the combination. Two self-supporting adults decide to make a home together: if both are women it is a pleasant partnership, more fun than work; if one is a man, it is almost never a partnership—the woman simply adds running the home to her regular outside job. Unless she is very strong, it is too much for her, she gets tired and bitter over it, and finally perhaps gives up her outside work and condemns herself to the tiresome half-job of housekeeping for two.

Cooperative schemes and electrical devices will simplify the business of home-making, but they will not get rid of it entirely. As far as we can see ahead people will always want homes, and a happy home cannot be had without a certain amount of rather monotonous work and responsibility. How can we change the nature of man so that he will honorably share that work and responsibility and thus make the homemaking enterprise a song instead of a burden? Most assuredly not by laws or revolutionary decrees. Perhaps we must cultivate or simulate a little of that highly prized helplessness ourselves. But fundamentally it is a problem of education, of early training—we must bring up feminist sons.

Sons? Daughters? They are born of women—how can women be free to choose their occupation, at all times cherishing their economic independence, unless they stop having children? This is a further question for feminism. If the feminist program goes to pieces on the arrival of the first baby, it is false and useless. For ninety-nine out of every hundred women want children, and seventy-five out of every hundred want to take care of their own children, or at any rate so closely superintend their care as to make any other full-time occupation impossible for at least ten or fifteen years. Is there any such thing then as freedom of choice in occupation for women? And is not the family the inevitable economic unit and woman's individual economic independence, at least during that period, out of the question?

The feminist must have an answer to these questions, and she has. The immediate feminist program must include voluntary motherhood. Freedom of any kind for women is hardly worth considering unless it is assumed that they will know how to control the size of their families. "Birth control" is just as elementary an essential in our propaganda as "equal pay." Women are to have children when they want them, that's the first thing. That ensures some freedom of occupational choice; those who do not wish to be mothers will not have an undesired occupation thrust upon them by accident, and those who do wish to be mothers may choose in a general way how many years of their lives they will devote to the occupation of childraising.

But is there any way of insuring a woman's economic independence while child-raising is her chosen occupation? Or must she sink into that dependent state from which, as we all know, it is so hard to rise again? That brings us to the fourth feature of our program—motherhood endowment. It seems that the only way we can keep mothers free, at least in a capitalist society, is by the establishment of a principle that the occupation of raising children is peculiarly and directly a service to society, and that the mother upon whom the necessity and privilege of performing this service naturally falls is entitled to an adequate economic reward from the political government. It is idle to talk of real economic independence for women unless this principle is accepted. But with a generous endowment of motherhood provided by legislation, with all laws against voluntary motherhood and education in its methods repealed, with the feminist ideal of education accepted in home and school, and with all special barriers removed in every field of human activity, there is no reason why woman should not become almost a human thing.

It will be time enough then to consider whether she has a soul.

Source: Eastman, Crystal. "Now We Can Begin." *The Liberator*, December 1920, pp. 23–24.

Congresses Passes the Indian Citizenship Act of 1924

Prior to World War I, relatively few Native Americans were classified as American citizens, with the full rights conferred by that status, including the right to vote. Before the Civil War, in fact, citizenship in many states and territories was limited to Native Americans who were at least half-white. In the latter half of the nineteenth century, members of some tribes received citizenship by virtue of negotiated treaties with the U.S. government, and many Native American women married to U.S. citizens were themselves awarded citizenship (though they still could not vote). But most Native Americans were unable to claim citizenship until after the Great War, when many Native Americans fought and died bravely under the American flag on the battlefields of Europe. In 1919, one year after the war concluded, the government offered citizenship to Native American veterans of World War I. But this measure still left many Native Americans out in the cold.

To rectify this, Representative Homer Snyder of New York crafted and urged the passage of a law, the Indian Citizenship Act, that granted full citizenship to all "Indians" in the United States. This legislation, which also became known as the Snyder Act, also received support from lawmakers who saw it as a tool for further assimilating Native Americans into mainstream white society. The act succeeded in adding many Native Americans to the voter rolls across the country. Since voting laws remained the province of individual states, however, Native Americans living in states hostile to minority voting rights remained blocked from the ballot box for decades to come.

68th Congress passed act on December 3, 1923

An Act

To authorize the Secretary of the Interior to issue certificates of citizenship to Indians.

Be it enacted by the Senate and House of Representatives of the United States of America in Congress assembled, That all non-citizen Indians born within the territorial limits of the United States be, and they are hereby, declared to be citizens of the United States: *Provided,* that the granting of such citizenship shall not in any manner impair or otherwise affect the right of any Indian to tribal or other property.

Source: *Indian Citizenship Act. U.S. Statutes at Large*, 43 (1924): 233.

3

Civil Rights and the Fight for the Franchise: 1925–1970

Although the federal government had broadened citizenship and voting rights to include women, blacks, Mexicans living on land annexed by the United States, and Native Americans through amendments to the Constitution and legislative action during the nineteenth and early twentieth centuries, states maintained considerable power to determine the time, manner, and place of elections and adopt qualifications for voting. As Southern states in particular adopted formal voting and registration policies and informal practices to restrict black access to the franchise, securing voting rights for all eligible citizens became a paramount goal of civil rights organizations that emerged and expanded during the opening decades of the twentieth century. At the same time, the federal government confronted myriad other issues related to the franchise, such as a lack of standardized procedures for the administration of elections. Lawmakers also sought to implement laws and other measures to ensure that citizens who served in the military were fully enfranchised domestically and when stationed abroad.

WHITE PRIMARIES AND OTHER TOOLS OF VOTER SUPPRESSION

From the early 1920s to the 1960s, the ability of African Americans to freely exercise their constitutional right to political franchise expanded and contracted as cases were brought before the Supreme Court of the United States. Sometimes the court's decisions regarding the power of the states and political parties to adopt policies that limited access to the franchise for African American citizens caused civil rights advocates and black communities to despair. Other times the court issued rulings that resulted in hopefulness and celebration.

Although membership in political parties is voluntary, parties are intricately woven into election processes and procedures in the United States. Access to membership in the nation's dominant parties is thus an important component of enfranchisement, particularly as it relates to participating in political primaries. In the late 1800s and early 1900s, however, nonwhite access to the primary process in several states was limited by the adoption of the "white primary." White primaries were primary elections held in Southern states in which only white voters were permitted to participate. In 1923, for example, Texas adopted a statute that asserted, "[I]n no event shall a Negro be eligible to participate in a Democratic party primary in the state of Texas." Following the passage of the statute, Dr. L. A. Nixon, a black member of the Texas Democratic Party, filed a suit after he was denied a ballot in the 1924 Democratic primary. In *Nixon v. Herndon* (1927), the Supreme Court rejected the defendant's argument that the court lacked jurisdiction because the issue was a political question. Instead, the court ruled that the statute was an "obvious infringement of the Fourteenth [Amendment]." In response to the ruling, the state amended the statute to allow the Democratic Party's state executive committee to set the voting qualifications for Democratic primary elections. Since party leaders were determined to keep blacks out, they passed new rules that effectively restored the all-white primary. In 1932, Nixon again appeared before the Supreme Court, challenging the all-white primary. In *Nixon v. Condon* the court again found the all-white primary unconstitutional. In 1935, however, the court reversed itself. In *Grovey v. Townsend* (1935), the court ruled that the Democratic Party's "white primary" rules were constitutional, making a distinction between discrimination committed by a private organization and that committed by a state. White primaries endured for another nine years, until the Supreme Court declared in *Smith v. Allwright* (1944) that all-white primaries were a violation of the equal protection clause contained in the Fourteenth Amendment. Future Supreme Court Justice Thurgood Marshall, one of the attorneys for the plaintiff in that case, later called the *Smith v. Allwright* decision his most important legal victory during his many years of legal work for the National Association for the Advancement of Colored People (NAACP).

VOTING FOR MILITARY PERSONNEL

During the Civil War, absentee voting was permitted for both Union and Confederate soldiers. In the late 1800s, absentee voting laws were passed in many states to permit voters who were away from home or ill on election day to vote. The number of ballots that were submitted in this manner, however, remained relatively small. Voting for soldiers who were stationed away from home was very challenging. In 1940, the military only allowed one day of leave for voting. Voting for military personnel was additionally complicated because many states that had absentee voting did not allow absentee voting for military personnel. In places where military personnel were permitted to vote, there were often restrictions on the type of elections in which they were permitted to vote. Logistical challenges also complicated matters. Military personnel, for example, were responsible for the cost of postage associated with the absentee voting process. This includes the postage for requesting a registration form, the postage to submit the registration form, the shipping of the ballot to the soldier, and the shipping to return the ballot for counting. Military personnel were also required to pay poll taxes and pass literacy tests and were also subject to grandfather clauses (in states where they were instituted). The ability of military personnel deployed overseas to vote finally changed in 1942 and 1944, when Congress passed laws that permitted citizens who were stationed abroad during World War II to vote.

In December 1941, the United States entered World War II, and, in 1942, Congress passed the Soldier Voting Act. The act required states to create a federal ballot that would allow military personnel to vote for president, vice president, senator, and representative. States could also allow military personnel to vote in state and local races. As the number of military personnel deployed overseas increased, Congress was under pressure to create a bill that would do more to ensure that military personnel could effectively vote. In 1944, Congress amended the 1942 Soldier Voting Act in an effort to standardize procedures. The 1944 act required states to use the federal ballot only if a military voter had not received a requested traditional absentee ballot, the state failed to establish effective absentee voting procedures, and the federal ballot was certified by the state. Another version of the bill that had the support of President Franklin D. Roosevelt would have made military personnel exempt from state devices and tests that suppressed the political power of African Americans and poor whites. While this version of the bill passed in the Senate, it was gutted in the House. The final version of the bill did not include this language, so military personnel remained subject to (potentially discriminatory or otherwise cumbersome) state qualifications for registration and voting.

AN ERA OF LANDMARK CIVIL RIGHTS LEGISLATION

Since the passage of the Fifteenth Amendment, no new federal civil rights legislation had been passed in the United States. As abolitionists and suffragettes worked to push the government to end slavery and extend full citizenship and voting rights to black Americans and women, organized groups continued to utilize coordinated campaigns to push the federal government to proactively address discrimination across the United States. The first piece of civil rights legislation passed following Reconstruction was the Civil Rights Act of 1957. The Civil Rights Act established the United States Commission on Civil Rights, an organization with a mandate "to inform the development of national civil rights policy and enhance enforcement of federal civil rights laws." The act also created the Civil Rights Division in the United States Justice Department and authorized the Attorney General of the United States to obtain court injunctions against individuals, agencies, or organizations that interfered with a citizen—including an African American citizen—trying to exercise his or her constitutional right to vote. Although the Civil Rights Act provided agencies with the power to address discrimination in voting, the Supreme Court of the United States of that era continued to affirm the right of states to determine the qualifications for voting. In 1959, for example, the court ruled in *Lassiter v. Northampton* that literacy tests (which had been transparently passed across the South as a tool to suppress the black vote) did not violate the Fourteenth or Fifteenth Amendment of the United States Constitution.

As African Americans continued to fight to achieve full enfranchisement, voting rights in presidential elections were extended to American citizens who were residents of the District of Columbia (DC) by the Twenty-Third Amendment to the United States Constitution (passed in June 1960; ratified in March 1961). Because DC is not a state, residents were not permitted to vote for president or vice president electors prior. Shortly after voting rights for president and vice president were extended to citizens of the nation's capital, Congress was flooded with new civil rights legislation sparked by the growing civil rights movement in the South. In 1963, a new voting rights bill (H.R. 7152) was introduced in the House by Representative Emanuel Celler (D-New York). The bill, which had been called for by President John F. Kennedy in his 1963 Report to the American People on Civil Rights, asked for legislation that would give "all Americans the right to be served in facilities—hotels, restaurants, theaters, retail stores, and similar establishments." In testimony before the House Judiciary Committee, the Student Nonviolent Coordinating Committee, which was comprised of young civil rights advocates and organizers, offered testimony on the disenfranchisement and discrimination experienced by black Americans in the South and the lack of enforcement of the 1957 Civil Rights Act.

The issue of devices and tests to vote in elections was addressed by the federal government with the passage of the Twenty-Fourth Amendment, which struck down poll taxes. The Twenty-Fourth Amendment, however, only applied to federal elections. Consequently, after its passage and ratification in 1964, citizens were still obligated to pay a poll tax to vote in state and local elections in states where the poll tax had been adopted. In *Harper v. Virginia State Board of Elections* (1966), however, the Supreme Court ruled that "a state violates the Equal Protection Clause of the Fourteenth Amendment to the United States Constitution whenever it makes the affluence of the voters or payment of any fee an electoral standard. Voter qualifications have no relation to wealth." This decision reversed a previous decision in *Breedlove v. Suttles* (1937) in which the court upheld a state's ability to impose a poll tax as a qualification to vote.

In addition to qualifications to vote, state practices pertaining to elections and political representation that dilute the voting strength of citizens were also addressed by the court during the 1960s.

In 1961, the state of Alabama redrew lines such that districts were dramatically unequal. The Alabama constitution required that there be only one representative per county, but after redistricting, some districts contained as many as forty-one times the number of voters as other districts. Because of this strategy, counties that experienced population growth had proportionally less representation than counties with smaller populations. In *Reynolds v. Sims* (1964), the court ruled that the Equal Protection Clause of the Fourteenth Amendment requires that state legislative districts be comprised of roughly equal populations. *Reynolds v. Sims* (1964) was one of many cases in which the Supreme Court considered the question of redistricting and vote dilution. Other cases include *Gomillion v. Lightfoot* (1960), *Baker v. Carr* (1962), *Gray v. Sanders* (1963), *Wesberry v. Sanders* (1964).

In 1965, the landmark Voting Rights Act (VRA) was passed to keep state and local governments from passing or enforcing laws and policies that deny citizens the right to vote based on race. Initially authorized for five years, the VRA prohibited electoral plans (tests and devices) that abridge the right to vote on account of race or color, explicitly prohibited literacy tests, authorized federal litigation against poll taxes in state elections, eliminated state durational residency requirements for presidential elections, and prohibited the erosion of minority political power. The VRA also established a coverage formula in Section 4(b) that was used to determine which jurisdictions were "covered"—required to undergo federal review and approval—before they made any changes to their voting and election rules. The states specifically identified by this aspect of the VRA were those with a long and well-documented history of disenfranchising black voters. The actual procedure by which these identified states needed to secure federal approval for proposed election changes, meanwhile, were laid out in Section 5 of the VRA. In addressing Congress about the need for the Voting Rights Act, President Lyndon B. Johnson noted not only the challenges that black Americans face when trying to enjoy the rights of full enfranchisement and the importance of guaranteeing the right to vote for all citizens but also the role that administrative procedures have played historically in limiting the right to vote for black Americans.

MAKING THE VOTING RIGHTS ACT A REALITY

Although adopted through the legislative process, the implementation of the Voting Rights Act across the United States was not without its challenges. On multiple occasions, states challenged the Voting Rights Act arguing that preclearance violated the Tenth Amendment of the United States Constitution. In both *South Carolina v. Katzenbach* (1966) and *Allen v. State Board of Elections* (1969), the court ruled that Section 5 was constitutional, and most importantly in *Allen v. State Board of Elections* the court ruled that Section 5 was designed to have broad interpretation and any change affecting voting, no matter how minor, was subject to preclearance and approval.

As changes to the electorate were occurring across the nation, the United States entered the Vietnam War. In 1969, a Senate subcommittee hearing on extending the VRA beyond the initial five years was convened. Several positions were presented. The first was to let parts of the act expire. The second was a proposal introduced by Attorney General John Mitchell that would replace Section 5 with an oversight provision that would be more amenable to the South. Lastly, Senator Harrison A. Williams Jr. (D-New Jersey) presented a third option in a letter to the subcommittee. In the letter, Harrison presented statistics that demonstrated the increases after passage of the VRA in nonwhite voter registration in Alabama, Georgia, Louisiana, Mississippi, South Carolina, and Virginia—all states subject to Section 5 of the law. Harrison's goal was to refute claims that the VRA had failed or had served its purpose and should subsequently be allowed to expire. Ultimately, Congress passed the legislation and President Richard M. Nixon signed in 1970 an amendment to the VRA that extended it for another five years. The extension of the VRA, however, did not automatically result in states removing provisions from their constitutions that had the capacity for discriminatory intent, and citizens continued to fight to secure the right to vote through the courts.

Finally, the 1970 Voting Rights Act Amendments also included provisions lowering the voting age to eighteen, but after the Supreme Court struck that provision down on technical grounds, a constitutional amendment to lower the voting age quickly attracted broad support. That amendment—the twenty-sixth in the country's history—was ratified on July 1, 1971.

SOURCES

"'The Act Has Not Failed': A Call to Extend the Voting Rights Act of 1965." Accessed January 29, 2019. http://historymatters.gmu.edu/d/6263/.

Alvarez, R. Michael, Thad E. Hall, and Brian F. Roberts. "Military Voting and the Law: Procedural and Technological Solutions to the Ballot Transit Problem." *Fordham Urban Law Journal*, 34 (2007): 935–996.

Bondi, Chris. "5 Times the Voting Rights Act of 1965 Has Been Challenged by State Legislation." *Newsmax*. Last modified November 8, 2015. https://www.newsmax.com/fastfeatures/voting-rights-act-challenges/2015/11/08/id/701175/.

Brennan Center for Justice at New York University School of Law. "The Voting Rights Act." Accessed January 30, 2019. https://www.brennancenter.org/issues/the-voting-rights-act.

Cobb, Charlie. "The Story of SNCC." SNCC Digital Gateway. Accessed January 20, 2019. https://snccdigital.org/inside-sncc/the-story-of-sncc/.

Guise, Kimberly. "The Wartime Ballot: 1944 Presidential Election." Last modified November 7, 2014. http://www.nww2m.com/2014/11/the-wartime-ballot-1944-presidential-election/.

Kellock, Harold. "Voting in 1944." Editorial research reports 1943 (Vol. II). Washington, DC: CQ Press, 1943. Accessed January 31, 2019. http://library.cqpress.com/cqresearcher/cqresrre1943080600.

Kennedy, John F. "Report to the American People on Civil Rights." June 11, 1963. Accessed January 22, 2019. https://www.jfklibrary.org/learn/about-jfk/historic-speeches/televised-address-to-the-nation-on-civil-rights.

Martin, Boyd A. "The Service Vote in the Elections of 1944." *The American Political Science Review* 39, no. 4 (1945): 720–732.

National Conference of State Legislatures. "Redistricting and the Supreme Court: The Most Significant Cases." Last modified July 19, 2018. http://www.ncsl.org/research/redistricting/redistricting-and-the-supreme-court-the-most-significant-cases.aspx.

United States Commission on Civil Rights. "Mission." Last modified July 10, 2018. https://www.usccr.gov/about/index.php.

United States Department of Justice. "What must be Submitted Under Section 5." Last modified August 6, 2015. https://www.justice.gov/crt/what-must-be-submitted-under-section-5.

"Voting by Mail and Absentee Voting." Massachusetts Institute of Technology (MIT) Election Data and Science Lab. Accessed January 29, 2019. http://www.pbs.org/programs/standing-bears-footsteps/.

PRIMARY DOCUMENTS

Supreme Court Strikes Down All-White Primaries in Texas, 1932

When the Supreme Court ruled in 1927 in Nixon v. Herndon *that a Texas law that barred blacks from voting in the state primaries was a violation of the Fourteenth Amendment, Texas lawmakers formally placed voter eligibility rules in the hands of state party executives. Officials with the Democratic Party, which had dominated the political scene in Texas and other Southern states since Reconstruction, promptly declared that only whites could vote in state primary elections. The National Association for the Advancement of Colored People (NAACP) immediately spearheaded a legal challenge to this racially discriminatory rule, and, in 1932, the Supreme Court weighed in once more on the battle over voting eligibility in Texas primaries. In* Nixon v. Condon, *the court ruled by 5–4 margin that Texas's arrangement was unconstitutional. But the ruling was so narrowly decided—it essentially declared that the state party executives that had imposed the whites-only rules were still relying on the old, discredited state law to carry out their wishes—that Texas lawmakers immediately saw a way to circumvent the court's decision. They just formally repealed all primary election statutes and, unencumbered by any veneer of state guidance, re-established white-only eligibility. This state of affairs remained in place until 1944, when the court finally ruled in* Smith v. Allwright *that primary elections were subject to the Fourteenth Amendment because they were inextricably tied to the operations of the state government.*

CERTIORARI TO THE CIRCUIT COURT OF APPEALS FOR THE FIFTH CIRCUIT

Syllabus

A statute of Texas provided:

"every political party in the State through its State Executive Committee shall have the power to prescribe the qualifications of its own members and shall in its own way determine who shall be qualified to vote or otherwise participate in such political party. . . ."

Acting under this statute, and not under any authorization from the convention of their party, the Executive Committee of the Democratic Party in Texas adopted a resolution that only white Democrats should participate in the primary elections, thereby excluding Negroes.

Held:

1. Whatever inherent power a state political party has to determine the qualifications of its members resides in the party convention, and not in any committee.
2. The power exercised by the Executive Committee in this instance was not the power of the party as a voluntary organization, but came from the statute.

3. The committee's action was therefore state action within the meaning of the Fourteenth Amendment.
4. The resulting discrimination violates that Amendment.
5. Whether, in given circumstances, parties or their committees are agencies of Government within the Fourteenth or the Fifteenth Amendment is a question which this Court must determine for itself.

49 F.2d 1012 reversed. . . .

MR. JUSTICE CARDOZO delivered the opinion of the Court.

The petitioner, a Negro, has brought this action against judges of election in Texas to recover damages for their refusal by reason of his race or color to permit him to cast his vote at a primary election.

This is not the first time that he has found it necessary to invoke the jurisdiction of the federal courts in vindication of privileges secured to him by the Federal Constitution.

In *Nixon v. Herndon,* 273 U. S. 536, decided at the October term, 1926, this Court had before it a statute of the State of Texas (Article 3093a, Revised Statutes, afterwards numbered 3107) whereby the Legislature had said that "in no event shall a Negro be eligible to participate in a Democratic party primary election [held in that State]," and that, "should a Negro vote in a Democratic primary election, such ballot shall be void," and election officials were directed to throw it out. While that mandate was in force, the Negro was shut out from a share in primary elections, not in obedience to the will of the party speaking through the party organs, but by the command of the State itself, speaking by the voice of its chosen representatives. At the suit of this petitioner, the statute was adjudged void as an infringement of his rights and liberties under the Constitution of the United States.

Promptly after the announcement of that decision, the Legislature of Texas enacted a new statute repealing the article condemned by this Court; declaring that the effect of the decision was to create an emergency with a need for immediate action; and substituting for the article so repealed another bearing the same number. By the article thus substituted,

"every political party in this State through its State Executive Committee shall have the power to prescribe the qualifications of its own members and shall in its own way determine who shall be qualified to vote or otherwise participate in such political party; provided that no person shall ever be denied the right to participate in a primary in this State because of former political views or affiliations or because of membership or nonmembership in organizations other than the political party."

Acting under the new statute, the state executive committee of the Democratic party adopted a resolution

"that all white democrats who are qualified under the Constitution and laws of Texas and who subscribe to the statutory pledge provided in Article 3110, Revised Civil Statutes of Texas, and none other, be allowed to participate in the primary elections to be held July 28, 1928, and August 25, 1928,"

and the chairman and secretary were directed to forward copies of the resolution to the committees in the several counties.

On July 28, 1928, the petitioner, a citizen of the United States, and qualified to vote unless disqualified by the foregoing resolution, presented himself at the polls and requested that he be furnished with a ballot. The respondents, the judges of election, declined to furnish the ballot or to permit the vote on the ground that the petitioner was a Negro, and that, by force of the resolution of the executive committee, only white Democrats were allowed to be voters at the Democratic primary. The refusal was followed by this action for damages. In the District Court, there was a judgment of dismissal, which was affirmed by the Circuit Court of Appeals for the Fifth Circuit, 49 F.2d 1012. A writ of certiorari brings the cause here.

Barred from voting at a primary the petitioner has been, and this for the sole reason that his color is not white. The result for him is no different from what it was when his cause was here before. The argument for the respondents is, however, that identity of result has been attained through essential diversity of method. We are reminded that the Fourteenth Amendment is a restraint upon the States, and not upon private persons unconnected with a State. . . . This line of demarcation drawn, we are told that a political party is merely a voluntary association; that it has inherent power, like voluntary associations generally, to determine its own membership; that the new Article of the statute, adopted in place of the mandatory Article of exclusion condemned by this Court, has no other effect than to restore to the members of the party the power that would have been theirs if the lawmakers had been silent; and that qualifications thus established are as far aloof from the impact of constitutional restraint as those for membership in a golf club or for admission to a Masonic lodge. . . .

A narrower base will serve for our judgment in the cause at hand. Whether the effect of Texas legislation has been to work so complete a transformation of the concept of a political party as a voluntary association we do not now decide. Nothing in this opinion is to be taken as carrying with it an intimation that the Court is ready or unready to follow the petitioner so far. As to that, decision must be postponed until decision becomes necessary. Whatever our conclusion might be if the statute had remitted to the party the untrammeled power to prescribe the qualifications of its members, nothing of the kind was done. Instead, the statute lodged the power in a committee, which excluded the petitioner and others of his race not by virtue of any authority delegated by the party, but by virtue of an authority originating or supposed to originate in the mandate of the law.

We recall at this point the wording of the statute invoked by the respondents.

"Every political party in this State through its State Executive Committee shall have the power to prescribe the qualifications of its own members and shall in its own way determine who shall be qualified to vote or otherwise participate in such political party."

Whatever inherent power a state political party has to determine the content of its membership resides in the state convention. There, platforms of principles are announced and the tests of party allegiance made known to the world. What is true in that regard of parties generally is true more particularly in Texas, where the statute is explicit in committing to the state convention the formulation of the party faith (Article 3139). The State Executive Committee, if it is the sovereign organ of the party, is not such by virtue of any powers inherent in its being. It is, as its name imports, a committee, and nothing more—a committee to be chosen by the convention and to consist of a chairman and thirty-one members, one from each senatorial district of the State (Article 3139). To this committee the statute here in controversy has attempted to confide authority to determine of its own motion the requisites of party membership, and, in so doing, to speak for the party as a whole. Never has the state convention made declaration of a will to bar Negroes of the State from admission to the party ranks. Counsel for the respondents so conceded upon the hearing in this Court. Whatever power of exclusion has been exercised by the members of the committee has come to them, therefore not as the delegates of the party, but as the delegates of the State. Indeed, adherence to the statute leads to the conclusion that a resolution, once adopted by the committee, must continue to be binding upon the judges of election though the party in convention may have sought to override it, unless the committee, yielding to the moral force of numbers, shall revoke its earlier action and obey the party will. Power so intrenched is statutory, not inherent. If the State had not conferred it, there would be hardly color of right to give a basis for its exercise. . . .

We discover no significance, and surely no significance favorable to the respondents, in earlier acts of legislation whereby the power to prescribe additional qualifications was conferred on local committees in the several counties of the state. The very fact that such legislation was thought necessary is a token that the committees were without inherent power. We do not impugn the competence of the Legislature to designate the agencies whereby the party faith shall be declared and the party discipline enforced. The pith of the matter is simply this, that, when those agencies are invested with an authority independent of the will of the association in whose name they undertake to speak, they become to that extent the organs of the State itself, the repositories of official power. They are then the governmental instruments whereby parties are organized and regulated to the end that government itself may be established or continued. What they do in that relation, they must do in submission to the mandates of equality and liberty that bind officials everywhere. They are not acting in matters of merely private concern like the directors or agents of business corporations. They are acting in matters of high public interest, matters intimately connected with the capacity of government to exercise its functions unbrokenly and smoothly. Whether in given circumstances parties or their committees are agencies of government within the Fourteenth or the Fifteenth Amendment is a question which this Court will determine for itself. It is not concluded upon such an inquiry by decisions rendered elsewhere. The test is not whether the members of the Executive Committee are the representatives of the State in the strict sense in which an agent is the representative of his principal. The test is whether they are to be classified as representatives of the State to such an extent and in such a sense that the great restraints of the Constitution set limits to their action.

With the problem thus laid bare and its essentials exposed to view, the case is seen to be ruled by *Nixon v. Herndon, supra.* Delegates of the State's power have discharged their official functions in such a way as to discriminate invidiously between white citizens and black. The Fourteenth Amendment, adopted as it was with special solicitude for the equal protection of members of the Negro race, lays a duty upon the court to level by its judgment these barriers of color.

The judgment below is reversed, and the cause remanded for further proceedings in conformity with this opinion.

Source: *Nixon v. Condon*, 286 U.S. 73, No. 265, decided May 1, 1932.

Thurgood Marshall Exults over Voter Registration Trends in the South, 1946

*In the post–World War II era, the National Association for the Advancement of Colored People (NAACP) and other African American civil rights groups began organizing voter registration drives to increase the number of African American voters across the South. In many instances, these included voter education efforts crafted to give black Americans the tools to beat the discriminatory "literacy tests" that had been imposed across the South to suppress the African American vote. These registration efforts were also aided by a key 1944 U.S. Supreme Court decision—*Smith v. Allwright*—that struck down a Texas law that authorized the state Democratic Party to maintain white-only voting restrictions in its primary elections. The court ruled that Texas's decision to outsource the rules of the state's primary elections to political parties did not mean that it could evade responsibility for the discriminatory policies imposed by those parties. According to the court, the state law paving the way for "whites-only" voting pools in primaries was itself unconstitutional because its effect was to deny African American citizens equal protection under the law, as mandated by the Fourteenth Amendment.*

The following 1946 editorial from The Crisis, *the flagship journal of the NAACP, praised the* Smith v. Allwright *decision as a "giant milestone in the progress of Negro Americans toward full citizenship." The editorial, which according to the organization was purportedly written by Thurgood Marshall, a famed NAACP lawyer who later became the nation's first African American justice in the U.S. Supreme Court, also emphasized that as black voters made their presence felt at the ballot box, their needs and priorities would be taken more seriously by lawmakers of all races and political orientations.*

116,000 Georgia Registrants

As this is written, slightly more than 116,000 Negro citizens of George are reported as having registered to vote in the Democratic primary election July 17. It is expected that several thousand more will have registered by the time the books close July 5.

This information, tucked away in an inconspicuous news story in the daily papers, records an American revolution. It is probably the most important step toward erasing racial inequalities that has been taken since Emancipation. It marks the beginning of a new day for the Negro, for the South, and for the nation.

Eugene Talmadge campaigns this year on a platform of race hate. The Ku Klux Klan has renewed its activities with the avowed principal purpose of maintaining white supremacy. But these shall be swept away in a few brief years before the thousands of new white and Negro voters in the South. After bitter election contests and education in between elections, the O'Daniels, Rankins, Bilbos, Coxes, Eastlands, Georges, and McClellands will be no more. More truly representative spokesmen will replace them in Congress.

In home areas, can one imagine a lynching taking place in a county where the sheriff knows there are, say 2,000 registered Negro voters? A governor who knows there are 150,000 to 250,000 registered Negro voters in the state will see that his legislature and his state board of education are fair in their distribution of school funds.

And so it will go in all matters affecting the welfare of citizens. It will not happen overnight, nor in this one election. The Negroes and the whites will make mistakes, and correction of abuses will be delayed, but the handwriting is on the wall: a new day is here for American democracy.

More and more it becomes apparent that the victory of NAACP lawyers in the Texas Primary case in the U.S. Supreme Court in 1944 was a giant milestone in the progress of Negro Americans toward full citizenship.

Source: Editorial [Thurgood Marshall]. "116,000 Georgia Registrants." *The Crisis*, July 1946, p. 201.

Presidential Commission on Civil Rights Condemns Persistent "Negro Disenfranchisement" in the American South, 1947

In December 1946, President Harry S. Truman issued Executive Order 9808 authorizing the creation of a Presidential Commission on Civil Rights to study ways to "strengthen and safeguard the rights of the American people." When the commission delivered its report to the president ten months later, much of its focus was on ways in which America was still falling short on delivering full civil rights protections to African Americans and other citizens of color. The following excerpt from the report highlights ways in which the states of the American South in particular continued to use racist laws and intimidation to keep blacks from exercising their constitutional voting rights.

THE RIGHT TO VOTE

The right of all qualified citizens to vote is today considered axiomatic by most Americans. To achieve universal adult suffrage we have carried on vigorous political crusades since the earliest days of the Republic. In theory the aim has been achieved, but in fact there are many backwaters in our political life where the right to vote is not assured to every qualified citizen. The franchise is barred to some citizens because of race; to others by institutions or procedures which impede free access to the polls. Still other Americans are in substance disfranchised whenever electoral irregularities or corrupt practices dissipate their votes or distort their intended purpose. Some citizens—permanent residents of the District of Columbia—are excluded from political representation and the right to vote as a result of outmoded national traditions. As a result of such restrictions, all of these citizens are limited, in varying degrees, in their opportunities to seek office and to influence the conduct of government on an equal plane with other American citizens.

The denial of the suffrage on account of race is the most serious present interference with the right to vote. Until very recently, American Negro citizens in most southern states found it difficult to vote. Some Negroes have voted in parts of the upper South for the last twenty years. In recent years the situation in the deep South has changed to the point where it can be said that Negroes are beginning to exercise the political rights of free Americans. In the light of history, this represents progress, limited and precarious, but nevertheless progress.

This report cannot adequately describe the history of Negro disfranchisement. At different times, different methods have been employed. As legal devices for disfranchising the Negro have been held unconstitutional, new methods have been improvised to take their places. Intimidation and the threat of intimidation have always loomed behind these legal devices to make sure that the desired result is achieved.

Until 1944, the white primary, by which participation in the Democratic primary is limited to white citizens, was used in Texas, Alabama, Arkansas, Georgia, Louisiana, and Mississippi as the most effective modern "legal" device for disfranchising Negroes. While some southern Negroes succeeded in spite of various obstacles in voting in general elections, almost none voted in the Democratic primaries. Since the Democratic primary is the only election of any significance, the device of the white primary resulted in exclusion of Negroes from government in these states. Over a period of time, advocates of white supremacy had refined this device to the point where it seemed to be constitutionally foolproof. The command of the Fifteenth Amendment, prohibiting states from abridging suffrage because of race or color, was circumvented by purporting to vest the power to exclude Negroes in the political party rather than in the state.

But in 1944, the United States Supreme Court in the case of Smith v. Allwright overruled an earlier decision and held the Texas white primary illegal. It declared that the exclusion rules of the Texas Democratic Party were in effect the rules of the state and were therefore forbidden by the Fifteenth Amendment.

Some states adapted their primary laws to the Supreme Court ruling, others resisted, first, by refusing to open white primaries to Negroes until further litigation made the Texas ruling applicable to them, then, by devising other methods of depriving Negroes of the ballot. Today the effort to preserve the pure white electoral system in these states is continuing.

Two states, Louisiana and Texas, repealed white primary provisions immediately after the Supreme Court decision; Florida, Alabama, and Georgia were forced to do so by further court rulings. South Carolina called a special session of the state legislature at which all state laws in any way regulating primaries were repealed. The theory governing this action was that by placing the primaries entirely outside the law and the structure of government the ruling in *Smith v.*

Allwright would be rendered inapplicable. In a message to the special session of the general assembly, the Governor of the State said:

After these statutes are repealed, in my opinion, we will have done everything within our power to guarantee white supremacy in our primaries of our State insofar as legislation is concerned. Should this prove inadequate, we South Carolinians will use the necessary methods to retain white supremacy in our primaries and to safeguard the homes and happiness of our people.

White supremacy will be maintained in our primaries; let the chips fall where they may.

In 1947 the white primary in South Carolina, resting on its new foundation, was held invalid by the United States District Court for the Eastern District of South Carolina in the case of *Elmore v. Harris*. In its opinion the Court said:

Racial distinctions cannot exist in the machinery that selects the officers and lawmakers of the United States; and all citizens of this State and Country are entitled to cast a free and untrammeled ballot in our elections, and if the only material and realistic elections are clothed with the name "primary", they are equally entitled to vote there.

The case will undoubtedly be carried to the Supreme Court for a final decision.

Alabama took a different course from South Carolina. Instead of repealing the primary laws it sought to continue disfranchisement by establishing "qualifications" standards under which Negroes could be barred by administrative action. The "Boswell amendment" adopted by this state in November, 1946, set up a provision under which voters would be required "to understand and explain" provisions of the state constitution. Exclusion by this kind of device is a familiar southern phenomenon. The tradition is to ignore such tests with respect to white voters but to apply them to Negroes—literally, where there is any possibility of eliminating them under the test; fraudulently, where they meet the test.

In a recent case in the Department of justice files, a Negro school teacher was disqualified under a North Carolina provision requiring an ability to read and interpret the Constitution. The registrar refused to register him on the ground that he had not read the federal Constitution in a satisfactory manner. However, in a statement to the FBI the registrar declared, "my decision not to register him was based solely on the disfranchisement of the colored people in this country rather than on his ability to read, to write and to explain the Constitution." This case was subsequently prosecuted by the Department of Justice and resulted in the conviction of the registrar.

The poll tax—another important legal obstacle to full suffrage in some southern states—limits white as well as Negro suffrage. The poll tax has frequently had an unequal racial effect, since, like the "understand and explain" clauses, it has been administered in a discriminatory manner. It has been very effective as an anti-Negro device. A poll tax simply places the payment of a fee between the voter and the ballot box. In some states it is cumulative; taxes not paid in years when the voter does not go to the polls pile up and he must pay more than one year's tax before he can vote. The poll tax has curtailed the size of the entire electorate, white and Negro. Seven states—Alabama, Arkansas, Mississippi, South Carolina, Tennessee, Texas, and Virginia—still maintain this tax as a prerequisite to voting. Since 1921 four other states have abandoned the poll tax. These are North Carolina, Louisiana, Florida, and Georgia.

It was estimated on the floor of the House of Representatives on July 21, 1947, that:

In the Presidential elections of 1944, 10 percent of the potential voters voted in the seven poll-tax states, as against 49 percent in the free-vote states. In the congressional elections of 1946, the figures are 5 percent for the poll-tax states as compared with 33 percent for the free-voting states.

It has frequently been pointed out that the congressional representation of poll tax states is based on proportionately fewer voters than the representation of other jurisdictions. It has also been urged that the poll tax is in reality a tax levied by the state upon the citizen's federal right to vote for members of Congress. In recent years there has been a strong drive for federal legislation forbidding the requirement of a poll tax as a prerequisite to voting in federal elections. The House of Representatives passed an anti-poll tax bill for the fourth time in July of 1947. The three previous bills passed by the House were killed in the Senate.

In addition to formal, legal methods of disfranchisement, there are the long-standing techniques of terror and intimidation, in the face of which great courage is required of the Negro who tries to vote. In the regions most characterized by generalized violence against Negroes, little more than "advice" is often necessary to frighten them away from the polls. They have learned, through the years, to discover threats in mood and atmosphere. In one case in a deep southern state, a middle-class Negro who had courageously attempted to vote and to complain to the Department of justice when he was refused access to the polls, subsequently became so afraid of reprisal that he indicated uncertainty whether he would be willing to testify in court. He asked, if he should decide to testify, to be given ample notice of the date so that he could first move his family out of the region.

In past years, American Indians have also been denied the right to vote and other political rights in a number of states. Most of these restrictions have been abandoned, but in two states, New Mexico and Arizona, Indians continue to be disfranchised. The constitution of New Mexico withholds suffrage from "Indians not taxed." In Arizona the state constitution has been interpreted to deny the vote to Indians as being "persons under guardianship." Protests against these legal bans on Indian suffrage in the Southwest have gained force with the return of Indian veterans to those states.

The constitutionality of these laws is presently being tested. It has been pointed out that the concept of "Indians not taxed" is no longer meaningful; it is a vestige of the days when most Indians were not citizens and had not become part of the community of people of the United States. Indians are now citizens and subject to federal taxation. They are also subject to state taxes, except for lands held in trust for them by the United States government. There is therefore little justification for denying them the franchise on the assumption that they are excused from the burdens of other citizens.

Source: President's Committee on Civil Rights. "The Right to Vote." In *To Secure These Rights: The Report of the President's Committee on Civil Rights.* October 1947, pp. 35–40. Accessed April 17, 2019. https://www.trumanlibrary.org/civilrights/srights1.htm.

President Truman Urges the Passage of Absentee Voting Reforms for Military Personnel, 1952

The only American president to experience combat in World War I, President Harry S. Truman remembered how difficult it had been for him and many of his fellow servicemen to vote in American elections while stationed overseas (in 1918, the last year of the Great War, only twenty-eight states had absentee voting systems in place for military personnel stationed in other states or deployed overseas). Congress took some measures to make it easier for members of the armed forces to vote during World War II, but problems persisted, and in March 1952 Truman formally asked Congress to craft a new law that would ensure that all military personnel serving their country overseas (and civilian support personnel) had the same opportunity to vote in American elections as civilians back home. His request (reprinted below) was based on recommendations from a special task force he had appointed to study the issue, but Southern Democrats blocked it because it would give the vote to African American soldiers and sailors (and civilian support personnel) hailing from their states. These opponents of enfranchisement for black Americans insisted on making the Truman administration's guidelines voluntary, for states to follow or ignore as they pleased. And in the case of white-controlled states across the South carrying out Jim Crow practices of disenfranchisement, the guidelines were widely disregarded until the Voting Rights Act was passed in 1965. With disenfranchisement of African Americans no longer an incentive for opposition, reforms to make it easier for Americans serving their country overseas to vote quickly followed.

To the Congress of the United States:

About 2,500,000 men and women in the armed forces are of voting age at the present time. Many of those in uniform are serving overseas, or in parts of the country distant from their homes. They are unable to return to their States either to register or to vote. Yet these men and women, who are serving their country and in many cases risking their lives, deserve above all others to exercise the right to vote in this election year. At a time when these young people are defending our country and its free institutions, the least we at home can do is to make sure that they are able to enjoy the rights they are being asked to fight to preserve.

All of us agree that the men and women in our armed services ought to be able to exercise the right to vote. Yet there are many barriers in the way.

Traditionally, procedures for voting have been laid down by the States, not only in State elections but also in elections to federal office. There are many variations among State laws on voting. In some States, absentee voting is either impossible or is encumbered with such difficult procedural requirements that it is of little value to persons in military service. The resulting patch-work quilt of complicated-and conflicting regulations has, in the past, deprived many of our service people of the chance to vote.

Efforts were made during World War II to improve and standardize procedures. Many State laws were passed to facilitate voting by persons in the services, and the Congress intervened to confirm the right of service people to vote in Federal elections, to provide simpler procedures for obtaining ballots for persons overseas, and, in some cases, to provide a Federal ballot to be used when State ballots could not be used.

As a result, over 2½ million of the 9 million persons of voting age in the armed forces voted in 1944. The record was not good, but it was better than it is likely to be this year, unless prompt action is taken. In many States, the laws which facilitated voting in 1944 have now expired. Since 1942, Federal Statutes have affirmed the right of absent service people to vote without registering in person, but even this basic right may be ignored in some States this year unless vigorous action is taken.

Recognizing that the situation required careful examination, I requested the American Political Science Association on October 23, 1951, to make a special study of voting in the armed forces, reviewing the history of Federal and State laws and procedures on the subject, "to be sure that we have a completely effective program for voting in the armed services." The American Political Science Association set up a Special Committee on Service Voting, composed of qualified experts, which conducted a comprehensive inquiry. The results of their study and their recommendations are embodied in their report to me, which I am transmitting, with this message, to the Congress.

In this report, the Special Committee of the American Political Science Association has set forth a Servicemen's Bill of Voting Rights, which I believe is so sound and right that it deserves the support of the Congress and the country:

"We believe that all servicemen of voting age, whether in the United States or overseas, should have the right:

"1. To vote without registering in person.
"2. To vote without paying a poll tax.
"3. To vote without meeting unreasonable residence requirements.
"4. To vote without meeting unreasonable literacy and educational requirements.
"5. To use the Federal postcard application for a ballot.
"6. To receive ballots for primary and general elections in time to vote.
"7. To be protected in the free exercise of their voting rights.
"8. To receive essential information concerning candidates and issues.
"9. To receive essential information concerning the methods by which the right to vote may be exercised.
"10. To receive essential information on the duty of 'citizens in uniform' to defend our democratic institutions by using, rather than ignoring, their voting rights."

In contrast to these standards, there are twenty-four of our States—exactly half—in which many of our soldiers, sailors and airmen will be unable to vote effectively and easily in 1952. Seven of these States appear to have laws that are in conflict with the provisions of the Servicemen's Voting Act of 1946. These States either make no provision at all for absentee voting, or require registration by servicemen in person. In addition, there are seventeen States in which the statutory interval permitted between the sending out of the absentee ballots and the time when the ballots must be returned is so short that it will deprive service people overseas of a decent chance to get their ballots back on time.

The report I am transmitting to the Congress recommends ways of overcoming these defects, either through special action by State legislatures, or through more efficient and flexible administration of State laws, or through court action. It also recommends that the States take action to permit voting by spouses and dependents of persons serving in the armed forces, and by other civilians serving overseas. I hope all State officials concerned will take these recommendations to heart, and do all they can to improve the situation in their respective States. The best and most effective way to assure our service people of their right to vote is through State action.

Some of the recommendations of the report are directed at the Executive Branch of the Federal Government, and are designed particularly to strengthen the administration of soldier voting in the Department of Defense. I am sending the report to the Secretary of Defense, requesting him to consider these recommendations, to act on them where possible, and to report progress to me. The Department of Defense has the important duty, not only to facilitate voting, but also to see to it that the information that service voters receive is presented in a completely fair and non-partisan manner.

The members of the Congress will be particularly interested in the recommendations made for Federal legislation. The Committee recommends a long-range program which will encourage service voting, provide adequate voting information to service people, and require regular reports to the Congress on the manner and extent of soldier voting.

As a first step, the Committee recommends that the Congress continue in effect existing statutory provisions affirming the right of service people to vote. These provisions, which are contained in the first two sections of the Servicemen's Voting Act of 1946, are, by their terms, effective only "in time of war", and will therefore lapse when the Peace Treaty with Japan comes into effect. I have already called this problem to the attention of the Congress in my communication to the Vice President and the Speaker of the House concerning the proposed Emergency Powers Extension Act.

In addition, the Committee recommends that the Secretary of Defense report biennially to the Congress, commencing in January, 1953, on action taken by the respective States in carrying out the Servicemen's Voting Act. The Committee further recommends that the Secretary of Defense, in cooperation with the Bureau of the Census and the several States, be required to compile and publish statistical reports on the number of applications and executed ballots received from servicemen in each State, as well as the number of servicemen of voting age in each State. Such information will serve as a basis for improving existing laws and procedures in the light of experience. In order to acquaint servicemen with their voting privileges and responsibilities, the Committee recommends legislative support for an effective information and education program designed to bring to absent servicemen some of the voting information available to all citizens in their own communities.

With one dissent, the report of the Committee recommends the use of a Federal ballot this year in those cases where State laws are not sufficiently improved in time to give soldiers from those States the right to vote. There are administrative and legal difficulties in the use of a Federal ballot, and our experience with it under the cumbersome procedures set up by the Federal law of 1944 was not encouraging, but the findings of the Committee point out ways of avoiding some of the difficulties experienced in that year.

I agree with the Committee that, in spite of the obvious difficulties in the use of the Federal ballot, the Congress should not shrink from accepting its responsibility and exercising its constitutional powers to give soldiers the right to vote where the States fail to do so. Of course, if prompt action is taken by the States, as it should be, it may be possible to avoid the use of a Federal ballot altogether. I believe, however, that the Congress should consider this matter with great care, and provide emergency legislation which will overcome the obstacles to soldier voting that may still exist in State laws as the elections draw near. Any such legislation by Congress should be temporary, since it should be possible to make all the necessary changes in State laws before the Congressional elections of 1954.

Our experience during and after World War II conclusively demonstrates that unless early action is taken, hundreds of thousands of servicemen and women of voting age will be deprived of their constitutional right to vote this year. I am confident that all Members of Congress and all State officials will join me in the determination that those who are on the front line in the defense of our freedom shall have a chance to exercise one of the great rights associated with that freedom.

HARRY S. TRUMAN

Source: Truman, Harry S. "Special Message to the Congress on Absentee Voting by Members of the Armed Forces." March 28, 1952. *Public Papers of the Presidents of the United States: Harry S. Truman, 1952–1953.* Washington, DC: Government Printing Office, 1966.

The Civil Rights Act of 1957

As the first major events of the civil rights movement took place during the mid-1950s—events such as the landmark 1954 school desegregation ruling by the U.S. Supreme Court in Brown v. Board of Education *and the 1955–1956 Montgomery Bus Boycott launched in protest of Rosa Parks' conviction for refusing to give up her seat on a Montgomery, Alabama, city bus to a white man—the Eisenhower administration felt growing pressure to address the systemic racial discrimination that permeated American society, and which was particularly pernicious in the American South. In 1957, President Eisenhower proposed new legislation to bolster civil rights protections for African Americans, especially in the realm of voting rights. Among other things, the administration wanted Congress to pass a law that would establish a special division of the Justice Department specifically for civil rights enforcement, give federal authorities the power to prosecute those who engaged in vote denial or suppression activities, and create a federal Civil Rights Commission authorized to investigate alleged cases in which constitutionally protected voting rights were being violated. Despite angry opposition from white Southern lawmakers in Congress, all these measures were included in the final legislation signed by Eisenhower on September 9, 1957.*

An Act

to provide means of further securing and protecting the civil rights of persons within the jurisdiction of the United States.

Be it enacted by the Senate and House of Representatives of the United States of America in Congress assembled,

PART I. ESTABLISHMENT OF THE COMMISSION ON CIVIL RIGHTS

Section 101.

(a) There is created in the executive branch of the Government a Commission on Civil Rights (hereinafter called the "Commission").
(b) The Commission shall be composed of six members who shall be appointed by the President by and with the advice and consent of the Senate. Not more than three of the members shall at any one time be of the same political party.
(c) The President shall designate one of the members of the Commission as Chairman and one as Vice Chairman. The Vice Chairman shall act as Chairman in the absence or disability of the Chairman, or in the event of a vacancy in that office.
(d) Any vacancy in the Commission shall not affect its powers and shall be filled in the same manner, and subject to the same limitations with respect to party affiliations as the original appointment was made.
(e) Four members of the Commission shall constitute a quorum. . . .

[Sections 102 and 103 described the "Rules of Procedure" and "Compensation" for the Commission and its membership]

Section 104. Duties of the Commission

(a) The Commission shall—
    (1) investigate allegations in writing under oath or affirmation that certain citizens of the United States are being deprived of their right to vote and have that vote counted by reason of their color, race, religion, or national origin; which writing, under oath or affirmation, shall set forth the facts upon which such belief or beliefs are based;
    (2) study and collect information concerning legal developments constituting a denial of equal protection of the laws under the Constitution; and
    (3) appraise the laws and policies of the Federal Government with respect to equal protection of the laws under the constitution.
(b) The Commission shall submit interim reports to the President and to the Congress at such times as either the Commission or the President shall

deem desirable, and shall submit to the President and to the Congress a final and comprehensive report of its activities, findings and recommendations not later than two years from the date of the enactment of this Act.

(c) Sixty days after the submission of its final report and recommendations the Commission shall cease to exist.

Section 105. Powers of the Commission

(a) There shall be a full-time staff director for the Commission who shall be appointed by the President by and with the advice and consent of the Senate and who shall receive compensation at a rate, to be fixed by the President, not in excess of $22,500 a year. The President shall consult with the Commission before submitting the nomination of any person for appointment to the position of staff director. Within the limitations of its appropriations, the Commission may appoint such other personnel as it deems advisable, in accordance with the civil service and classification laws, and may procure services as authorized by section 15 of the Act of August 2, 1946 (60 Stat. 810; 5 U.S.C. 55a), but at rates for individuals not in excess of $50 per diem.

(b) The commission shall not accept or utilize services of voluntary or uncompensated personnel, and the term "whoever" as used in paragraph (g) of section 102 hereof shall be construed to mean a person whose services are compensated by the United States.

(c) The Commission may constitute such advisory committees within States composed of citizens of that State and may consult with governors, attorneys general, and other representatives of State and local governments, and private organizations, as it deems advisable.

(d) Members of the Commission, and members of advisory committees constituted pursuant to subsection (c) of this section, shall be exempt from the operation of sections 281, 283, 284, 434, and 1914 of title 18 of the United States Code, and section 190 of the Revised Statutes (5 U.S.C. 99).

(e) All Federal agencies shall cooperate fully with the Commission to the end that it may effectively carry out its functions and duties.

(f) The Commission, or on the authorization of the Commission any subcommittee of two or more members, at least one of whom shall be of each major political party, may, for the purpose or carrying out the provisions of this Act, hold such hearings and act at such times and places as the Commission or such authorized subcommittee may deem advisable. Subpenas for the attendance and testimony of witnesses or the production of written or other matter may be issued in accordance with the rules of the Commission as contained in section 102 (j) and (k) of this Act, over the signature of the Chairman of the Commission or of such subcommittee, and may be served by any person designated by such Chairman.

(g) In case of contumacy or refusal to obey a subpena, any district court of the United States or the United States court of any Territory or

> possession, or the District Court of the United States for the District of Columbia, within the jurisdiction of which the inquiry is carried on or within the jurisdiction of which said person guilty of contumacy or refusal to obey is found or resides or transacts business, upon application by the Attorney General of the United States shall have jurisdiction to issue to such person an order requiring such person to appear before the Commission or a subcommittee thereof, there to produce evidence is so ordered, or there to give testimony touching the matter under investigation; and any failure to obey such order of the court may be punished by said court as a contempt thereof. . . .

PART III. TO STRENGTHEN THE CIVIL RIGHTS STATUTES, AND FOR OTHER PURPOSES

Section 121.

Section 1343 of title 28, United States Code, is amended as follows:

(a) Amend the catch line of said section to read: "Section 1343. Civil Rights and elective franchise"
(b) Delete the period at the end of paragraph (3) and insert in lieu thereof a semicolon.
(c) Add a paragraph as follows: "(4) to recover damages or to secure equitable or other relief under any Act of Congress providing for the protection of civil rights, including the right to vote."

Section 122.

Section 1989 of the Revised Statutes (42 U.S.C. 1993) is hereby repealed.

PART IV. TO PROVIDE MEANS OF FURTHER SECURING AND PROTECTING THE RIGHT TO VOTE

Section 131.

Section 2004 of the Revised statutes (42 U.S.C. 1971), is amended as follows:

(a) Amend the catch line of said section to read, "Voting rights".
(b) Designate its present text with the subsection symbol "(a)".
(c) Add, immediately following the present text, four new subsections to read as follows:

"(b) No person, whether acting under color of law or otherwise, shall intimidate, threaten coerce, or attempt to intimidate, threaten or coerce any other person for the purpose of interfering with the right of such other person to vote or to vote as he may choose, or of causing such other person to vote for, or not to vote for, any candidate for the office of President, Vice President, presidential elector, Member of the Senate, or Member of the house of Representatives, Delegates or Commissioners from the Territories or possessions, at any general special, or primary election held solely or in part for the purpose of selecting or electing any such candidate.

"(c) whenever any person has engaged or there are reasonable grounds to believe that any person is about to engage in any act or practice which would deprive any other person of any right or privilege secured by a subsection (a) or (b), the Attorney General may institute for the United States, or in the name of the

United States, a civil action or other proper proceeding for preventive relief, including an application for a permanent or temporary injunction, restraining order, or other order. In any proceeding hereunder the United States shall be liable for costs the same as a private person.

"(d) the district courts of the United States shall have jurisdiction of the proceedings instituted pursuant to this section and shall exercise the same without regard to whether the party aggrieved shall have exhausted any administrative or other remedies that may be provided by law.

"(e) Any person cited for an alleged contempt under this Act shall be allowed to make his full defense by counsel learned in the law; and the court before which he is cited or tried, or some judge thereof, shall immediately, upon his request, assign to him such counsel, not exceeding two, as he may desire, who shall have free access to him at all reasonable hours. He shall be allowed, in his defense to make any proof that he can produce by lawful witnesses, and shall have the like process of the court to compel his witnesses to appear at his trial or hearing, as is usually granted to compel witnesses to appear on behalf of the prosecution. If such person shall be found by the court to be financially unable provide for such counsel, it shall be the duty of the court to provide such counsel."

PART V. TO PROVIDE TRIAL BY JURY FOR PROCEEDINGS TO PUNISH CRIMINAL CONTEMPTS OF COURT GROWING OUT OF CIVIL RIGHTS CASES AND TO AMEND THE JUDICIAL CODE RELATING TO FEDERAL JURY QUALIFICATIONS.

Section 151.

All cases of criminal contempt arising under the provisions of this Act, the accused, upon conviction, shall be punished by fine or imprisonment or both: Provided however, That in case the accused is a natural person the fine to be paid shall not exceed the sum of $1,000, nor shall imprisonment exceed the term of six months: Provided Further, that in any such proceeding for criminal contempt, at the discretion of the judge, the accused may be tried with or without a jury: Provided further, however, That in the event such proceeding for a criminal contempt be tried before a judge without a jury and the sentence of the court upon conviction is a fine in excess of the sum of $30 or imprisonment in excess of forty-five days, the accused in said proceeding, upon demand therefor, shall be entitled to a trial de novo before a jury which shall conform as near as may be to the practice in other criminal cases. . . .

Source: Civil Rights Act of 1957. *Public Law 85–315. U.S. Statutes at Large*, 71 (1957): 634.

The Supreme Court Upholds Literacy Tests in *Lassiter v. Northampton County Board of Elections*, 1959

In the late 1950s, an African American resident of the state of North Carolina, Louise Lassiter, mounted a legal challenge to an article in the state constitution that mandated that all voters "should be able to read and write any section of the

Constitution in the English language." Lassiter and her attorneys argued that this literacy test violated the Fourteenth and Fifteenth Amendments, noting that long-standing inequities in education between white and black students in the state made such tests harder for African Americans. The case eventually reached the U.S. Supreme Court, which turned aside Lassiter's legal challenge in a unanimous decision. The majority opinion, written by William O. Douglas and delivered on June 8, 1959, asserted that since the North Carolina literacy test statute applied to all voters, it did not violate the Fourteenth or Fifteenth Amendments.

North Carolina's victory, however, was short lived. When the Voting Rights Act of 1965 was signed into law, it contained specific language in Section 2 forbidding states from enforcing literacy tests for voting, because such tests had the practical effect of disproportionately restricting African American enfranchisement.

Justice Douglas delivered the opinion of the Court

This controversy started in a Federal District Court. Appellant, a Negro citizen of North Carolina, sued to have the literacy test for voters prescribed by that State declared unconstitutional and void. A three-judge court was convened. That court noted that the literacy test was part of a provision of the North Carolina Constitution that also included a grandfather clause. It said that the grandfather clause plainly would be unconstitutional under *Guinn v. United States*, 238 U.S. 347 (1915). It noted, however, that the North Carolina statute which enforced the registration requirements contained in the State Constitution had been superseded by a 1957 Act and that the 1957 Act does not contain the grandfather clause or any reference to it. But being uncertain as to the significance of the 1957 Act and deeming it wise to have all administrative remedies under that Act exhausted before the federal court acted, it stayed its action, retaining jurisdiction for a reasonable time to enable appellant to exhaust her administrative remedies and obtain from the state courts an interpretation of the statute in light of the State Constitution. 152 F. Supp. 295.

Thereupon the instant case was commenced. It started as an administrative proceeding.

Appellant applied for registration as a voter. Her registration was denied by the registrar because she refused to submit to a literacy test as required by the North Carolina statute. She appealed to the County Board of Elections. On the de novo hearing before that Board appellant again refused to take the literacy test and she was again denied registration for that reason. She appealed to the Superior Court which sustained the Board against the claim that the requirement of the literacy test violated the Fourteenth, Fifteenth, and Seventeenth Amendments of the Federal Constitution. Preserving her federal question, she appealed to the North Carolina Supreme Court which affirmed the lower court. 248 N.C. 102, 102 S. E. 2d 853. The case came here by appeal, 28 U.S.C. 1257 (2), and we noted probable jurisdiction.

The literacy test is a part of 4 of Art. VI of the North Carolina Constitution. That test is contained in the first sentence of 4. The second sentence contains a so-called grandfather clause. The entire 4 reads as follows:

> Every person presenting himself for registration shall be able to read and write any section of the Constitution in the English language. But no male person who was, on January 1, 1867, or at any time prior thereto, entitled to vote under the laws of any state in the United States wherein he then resided, and no lineal descendant of any such person, shall be denied the right to register and vote at any election in this State by reason of his failure to possess the educational qualifications herein prescribed: Provided, he shall have registered in accordance with the terms of this section prior to December 1, 1908. The General Assembly shall provide for the registration of all persons entitled to vote without the educational qualifications herein prescribed, and shall, on or before November 1, 1908, provide for the making of a permanent record of such registration, and all persons so registered shall forever thereafter have the right to vote in all elections by the people in this State, unless disqualified under section 2 of this article.

Originally Art. VI contained in 5 the following provision:

> That this amendment to the Constitution is presented and adopted as one indivisible plan for the regulation of the suffrage, with the intent and purpose to so connect the different parts, and to make them so dependent upon each other, that the whole shall stand or fall together.

But the North Carolina Supreme Court in the instant case held that a 1945 amendment to Article VI freed it of the indivisibility clause. That amendment rephrased 1 of Art. VI to read as follows:

"Every person born in the United States, and every person who has been naturalized, twenty-one years of age, and possessing the qualifications set out in this article, shall be entitled to vote . . . "

That court said that "one of those qualifications" was the literacy test contained in 4 of Art. VI; and that the 1945 amendment "had the effect of incorporating and adopting anew the provisions as to the qualifications required of a voter as set out in Article VI, freed of the indivisibility clause of the 1902 amendment. And the way was made clear for the General Assembly to act." 248 N.C., at 112, 102 S. E. 2d 860, 861.

In 1957 the Legislature rewrote General Statutes 163-28 as we have noted. Prior to that 1957 amendment 163-28 perpetuated the grandfather clause contained in Art. VI of the Constitution and 163-32 established a procedure for registration to effectuate it. But the 1957 amendment contained a provision that "All laws and clauses of laws in conflict with this Act are hereby repealed." The federal three-judge court ruled that this 1957 amendment eliminated the grandfather clause from the statute.

The Attorney General of North Carolina, in an amicus brief, agrees that the grandfather clause contained in Art. VI is in conflict with the Fifteenth Amendment. Appellee maintains that the North Carolina Supreme Court ruled that the invalidity of that part of Art. VI does not impair the remainder of Art. VI since the 1945 amendment to Art VI freed it of its indivisibility clause. Under that view Art. VI would impose the same literacy test as that imposed by the 1957 statute and neither would be linked with the grandfather clause which, though present in print, is separable from the rest and void. We so read the opinion of the North Carolina Supreme Court.

Appellant argues that that is not the end of the problem presented by the grandfather clause.

. . .We come then to the question whether a State may consistently with the Fourteenth and Seventeenth Amendments apply a literacy test to all voters irrespective of race or color. The Court in *Guinn v. United States* (1915) disposed of the question in a few words, "No time need be spent on the question of the validity of the literacy test considered alone since as we have seen its establishment was but the exercise by the State of a lawful power vested in it not subject to our supervision, and indeed, its validity is admitted."

The States have long been held to have broad powers to determine the conditions under which the right of suffrage may be exercised, *Pope v. Williams*, 193 U.S. 621, 633 (1904), absent of course the discrimination which the Constitution condemns. Article I, 2 of the Constitution in its provision for the election of members of the House of Representatives and the Seventeenth Amendment in its provision for the election of Senators provide that officials will be chosen "by the People." Each provision goes on to state that "the Electors in each State shall have the Qualifications requisite for Electors of the most numerous Branch of the State Legislature." So while the right of suffrage is established and guaranteed by the Constitution (*Ex parte Yarbrough*, 110 U.S. 651, 663–665 (1884); *Smith v. Allwright*, 321 U.S. 649, 661–662 (1944) it is subject to the imposition of state standards which are not discriminatory and which do not contravene any restriction that Congress, acting pursuant to its constitutional powers, has imposed. See *United States v. Classic*, 313 U.S. 299, 315 (1941). While 2 of the Fourteenth Amendment, which provides for apportionment of Representatives among the States according to their respective numbers counting the whole number of persons in each State (except Indians not taxed), speaks of "the right to vote," the right protected "refers to the right to vote as established by the laws and constitution of the State." *McPherson v. Blacker*, 146 U.S. 1, 39 (1892).

We do not suggest that any standards which a State desires to adopt may be required of voters. But there is wide scope for exercise of its jurisdiction. Residence requirements, age, previous criminal record (*Davis v. Beason*, 133 U.S. 333, 345–347 [1890]) are obvious examples indicating factors which a State may take into consideration in determining the qualifications of voters. The ability to read and write likewise has some relation to standards designed to promote intelligent use of the ballot. Literacy and illiteracy are neutral on race, creed, color, and sex, as reports around the world show. Literacy and intelligence are obviously not synonymous. Illiterate people may be intelligent voters. Yet in our society where newspapers, periodicals, books, and other printed matter canvass and debate campaign issues, a State might conclude that only those who are literate should exercise the franchise. It was said last century in Massachusetts that a literacy test was designed to insure an "independent and intelligent" exercise of the right of suffrage. North Carolina agrees. We do not sit in judgment on the wisdom of that policy. We cannot say, however, that it is not an allowable one measured by constitutional standards.

Of course a literacy test, fair on its face, may be employed to perpetuate that discrimination which the Fifteenth Amendment was designed to uproot. No such influence is charged here. On the other hand, a literacy test may be unconstitutional on its face. In *Davis v. Schnell*, 336 U.S. 933 (1949), the test was the citizen's ability to "understand and explain" an article of the Federal Constitution. The legislative setting of that provision and the great discretion it vested in the registrar made clear that a literacy requirement was merely a device to make racial discrimination easy. We cannot make the same inference here. The present requirement, applicable to members of all races, is that the prospective voter "be able to read and write any section of the Constitution of North Carolina in the English language." That seems to us to be one fair way of determining whether a person is literate, not a calculated scheme to lay springs for the citizen. Certainly we cannot condemn it on its face as a device unrelated to the desire of North Carolina to raise the standards for people of all races who cast the ballot.

Affirmed.

Source: *Lassiter v. Northampton County Board of Elections*, 360 U.S. 45 (1959).

Congress Gives Washington, DC, Residents a Voice in Presidential Elections, 1961

On June 16, 1960, the U.S. Congress passed a constitutional amendment crafted to give residents of the District of Columbia, home of the nation's capital city of Washington, the right to vote in presidential elections. It was ratified and became law on March 29, 1961, when Ohio became the thirty-eighth state to ratify the amendment (thus fulfilling the constitutional requirement that amendments be approved by at least three-quarters of the states). Prior to the passage and ratification of this amendment, residents of Washington, DC, could only vote in presidential elections if they had valid voter registration in an American state. The Twenty-Third Amendment, however, did not grant residents of Washington, DC, any representation in either the House of Representatives or the Senate. Efforts to rectify that inequity—a clear-cut example of "taxation without representation" since DC residents are subject to both local and federal taxes—have regularly been launched in the nearly sixty years since the ratification of the Twenty-Third Amendment. But these bids have consistently been blocked (despite the fact that Washington, DC, actually has more residents than either Wyoming or Vermont), most recently by Republicans who fear that granting the District of Columbia statehood or otherwise giving it representation in Congress would benefit the Democratic Party.

XXIII AMENDMENT

Section 1. The District constituting the seat of Government of the United States shall appoint in such manner as the Congress may direct:

A number of electors of President and Vice President equal to the whole number of Senators and Representatives in Congress to which the District would be entitled if it were a State, but in no event more than the least populous State; they shall be in addition to those appointed by the States, but they shall be considered, for the purposes of the election of President and Vice President, to be electors appointed by a State; and they shall meet in the District and perform such duties as provided by the twelfth article of amendment.

Section 2. The Congress shall have the power to enforce this article by appropriate legislation.

Source: Amendment XXIII to the U.S. Constitution. National Archives.

Waves of Violence against African American Voter Registration Efforts in One Mississippi Town, 1963

As activists worked across the American South to register black voters and ensure that they could exercise their constitutional voting rights, they often encountered threats and violence from white citizens. This was true even in the "black belt" counties—counties where black residents outnumbered white ones. The following March 12, 1963, report from one civil rights group working on voter registration, the Student Nonviolent Coordinating Committee (SNCC), details some of the harrowing conditions and threats that both activists and black residents faced across the South in the early 1960s.

VIOLENCE STALKS VOTER-REGISTRATION WORKERS IN MISSISSIPPI

Staff members of the Student Nonviolent Coordinating Committee, working on voter registration in Leflore county, Mississippi, have been the object of a new wave of violence in the past few weeks. The town of Greenwood has been the scene of these recent efforts to terrorize student workers who have also helped to secure food for Negro sharecroppers denied Federal surplus food relief.

On February 25th and 26th, over 150 Negroes attempted to register to vote in Greenwood, Mississippi. This is the largest number of Negroes who have attempted to register in Greenwood or any Black Belt County. Hunger and violence are apparently being used to curtail voter-registration efforts.

Since February 20, 1963:

***Four (4) Negro businesses destroyed by fire!

***SNCC Field Secretary sentenced to six months in jail!

***Student worker shot in neck when attacked by passing car!

***Second shooting injures four (4) voter-registration workers!

BUSINESS PLACES BURNED TO GROUND

February 20: Four small business places, located on the same street as the Greenwood office of SNCC, were destroyed by fire early Wednesday morning, February 20.

The belief that the real target was the SNCC office finds support in the call reported by Mrs. Nancy Brand, worker in that office. She received an anonymous phone call the morning of the fire from a man who asked if she ever went to the office. When she answered "yes," the caller said, "You won't be going there any more. That's been taken care of."

The destroyed businesses were Jackson's Garage, George's Café, Porter's Pressing Shop, and the Esquire club.

SNCC WORKER ARRESTED ON WASHINGTON'S BIRTHDAY

February 22: Samuel Block, SNCC field secretary, was arrested in front of his office in Greenwood, Mississippi, on Friday, February 22. He was taken to an unknown jail and charged with "circulating breach of the peace." When tried on Monday, February 25, the charge was changed to "issuing statements calculated to breach the peace," and Block was sentenced to six months in jail and fined $500.00.

The judge who pronounced sentence told Mr. Block that he would reduce the fine to $250.00 and suspend sentence if he would leave Mississippi for good. Samuel Block was born and reared in Mississippi.

STUDENT SHOT AND CRITICALLY WOUNDED

February 28: James Travis, 20 year old SNCC staff member, narrowly missed death when the car which he was driving was shot into by three white men, seven miles outside Greenwood on Thursday evening, February 28.

Travis was accompanied by Robert Moses, director of SNCC's statewide Mississippi registration program, and Randolph Blackwell, field director of southwide Voter Education Project. An untagged 1962 white Buick passed Travis' car on the highway to Greenville, Mississippi, and fired several blasts into his car. Both front windows were demolished, seven bullets pierced the side of the car, and a bullet passed through Travis' shoulder and lodged at the back of his head, behind the spine. He was operated on the next day at University Hospital in Jackson, Mississippi.

SECOND SHOOTING INJURES FOUR

March 7: Four voter registration workers were cut by flying glass when the car in which they were sitting was fired into on Wednesday night, March 7. This was the second such shooting in Greenwood in less than ten days.

Those cut by the shattered front window of their car were Sam Block, 23, Willie Peacock, 25, Miss Peggy Marye, 19, and Miss Essie Broome, 24. The four your persons had just left a church meeting dealing with food and clothing needs of the county.

OTHER PERTINENT FACTS:

***There are 19,806 Negroes and 6,881 whites in Leflore County, Mississippi.

***Some 22,000 people were denied Federally supplied surplus commodities. County officials said they could not pay workers to distribute the food; yet no employees were laid off when the 22,000 were deprived of this relief.

***Samuel Block is one of the twenty young Mississippi Negroes working with the Student Nonviolent Coordinating Committee's voter-registration program.

***Black has been arrested seven times, beaten twice, and was forced to jump from a second story window last August to flee a lynch mob of white men carrying chains, ropes, and iron pipes.

Source: Student Nonviolent Coordinating Committee (SNCC). "Violence Stalks Voter-Registration Workers in Mississippi." March 12, 1963. Accessed February 6, 2019. https://www.crmvet.org/docs/6303_sncc_ms-violence.pdf.

Fannie Lou Hamer Remembers the "Freedom Summer" Fight for Voting Rights, 1964

Mississippi native Fannie Lou Hamer was one of the giants of the early civil rights movement. Born into abject poverty and routinely subjected to systemic racism in her home state, Hamer became politically active with the Student Nonviolent Coordinating Committee (SNCC), one of the nation's leading civil rights groups, after her repeated attempts to register to vote were thwarted by state authorities. She became heavily involved in voter registration, desegregation, and poverty relief programs across the state. In June 1963 she suffered a brutal beating at the hands of Winona, Mississippi, police and other jail inmates after she and several other activists sat at a whites-only bus station lunch counter. The attack left her with injuries that bothered her for the rest of her life. But still she persevered, joining SNCC and Congress of Racial Equality (CORE) activists and volunteers in the famous 1964 "freedom summer" campaign to register black Mississippians to vote. That same year, Hamer became a Congressional candidate for the Mississippi Freedom Democratic Party (MFDP), a group founded for the specific purpose of challenging the state Democratic Party, which was fiercely pro-segregation and anti-black voting rights in its orientation. Hamer's bid to unseat the incumbent Democrat in the party primary fell short, but her subsequent appearance at the Democratic National Convention (DNC) in Atlantic City, New Jersey, in which she castigated the national party for its continued coddling of pro-segregation elements in Mississippi and other Southern states, was deeply embarrassing to President Lyndon B. Johnson and other party leaders. Following is the testimony that Hamer gave to the DNC's Credentials Committee—the group that ultimately sided with Mississippi's racist state Democratic Party over the MFDP—in Atlantic City on August 22, 1964.

Mr. Chairman, and the Credentials Committee, my name is Mrs. Fanny Lou Hamer, and I live at 626 East Lafayette Street, Ruleville, Mississippi, Sunflower County, the home of Senator James O. Eastland, and Senator Stennis.

It was the 31st of August in 1962 that 18 of us traveled 26 miles to the country courthouse in Indianola to try to register to try to become first-class citizens. We was met in Indianola by policemen, Highway Patrolmens and they only allowed two of us in to take the literacy test at the time.

After we had taken this test and started back to Ruleville, we was held up by the City Police and the State Highway Patrolmen and carried back to Indianola where the bus driver was charged that day with driving a bus the wrong color.

After we paid the fine among us, we continued on to Ruleville, and Reverend Jeff Sunny carried me four miles in the rural area to where I had worked as a time-keeper and sharecropper for 18 years. I was met there by my children, who told me that the plantation owner was angry because I had gone down to try to register. After they told me, my husband came, and said that the plantation owner was raising cain because I had tried to register, and before he quit talking the plantation owner came, and said, "*Fanny Lou, do you know—did Pap tell you what I said?*"

And I said, "*Yes, sir.*"

He said, "*I mean that.*" He said, "*If you don't go down and withdraw your registration, you will have to leave.*" [He] said, "Then if you go down and withdraw," he said, "*you still might have to go because we are not ready for that in Mississippi.*"

And I addressed him and told him and said, "*I didn't try to register for you. I tried to register for myself.*" I had to leave that same night.

On the 10th of September 1962, 16 bullets was fired into the home of Mr. and Mrs. Robert Tucker for me. That same night two girls were shot in Ruleville, Mississippi. Also Mr. Joe McDonald's house was shot in.

And June the 9th, 1963, I had attended a voter registration workshop; was returning back to Mississippi. Ten of us was traveling by the Continental Trailway bus. When we got to Winona, Mississippi, which is Montgomery County, four of the people got off to use the washroom, and two of the people—to use the restaurant—two of the people wanted to use the washroom.

The four people that had gone in to use the restaurant was ordered out. During this time I was on the bus. But when I looked through the window and saw they had rushed out I got off of the bus to see what had happened. And one of the ladies said, "*It was a State Highway Patrolman and a Chief of Police ordered us out.*"

I got back on the bus and one of the persons had used the washroom got back on the bus, too. As soon as I was seated on the bus, I saw when they began to get the five people in a Highway Patrolman's car. I stepped off of the bus to see what was happening and somebody screamed from the car that the five workers was in, and said, "*Get that one there.*" When I went to get in the car, when the man told me I was under arrest, he kicked me.

I was carried to the county jail and put in the booking room. They left some of the people in the booking room and began to place us in cells. I was placed in a cell with a young woman called Miss Euvester Simpson. After I was placed in the cell I began to hear sounds of licks and screams, I could hear the sounds of licks and horrible screams. And I could hear somebody say, "*Can you say, 'yes, sir,' n****r? Can you say 'yes, sir'?*" And they would say other horrible names.

She would say, "*Yes, I can say 'yes, sir.'*"

"*So, well, say it.*"

She said, "*I don't know you well enough.*"

They beat her, I don't know how long. And after a while she began to pray, and asked God to have mercy on those people.

And it wasn't too long before three white men came to my cell. One of these men was a State Highway Patrolman and he asked me where I was from. I told him Ruleville and he said, "*We are going to check this.*"

They left my cell and it wasn't too long before they came back. He said, "*You are from Ruleville all right,*" and he used a curse word. And he said, "*We are going to make you wish you was dead.*"

I was carried out of that cell into another cell where they had two Negro prisoners. The State Highway Patrolmen ordered the first Negro to take the blackjack. The first Negro prisoner ordered me, by orders from the State Highway Patrolman, for me to lay down on a bunk bed on my face. I laid on my face and the first Negro began to beat. I was beat by the first Negro until he was exhausted. I was holding my hands behind me at that time on my left side, because I suffered from polio when I was six years old.

After the first Negro had beat until he was exhausted, the State Highway Patrolman ordered the second Negro to take the blackjack. The second Negro began to beat and I began to work my feet, and the State Highway Patrolman ordered the first Negro who had beat me to sit on my feet—to keep me from working my feet. I began to scream and one white man got up and began to beat me in my head and tell me to hush.

One white man—my dress had worked up high—he walked over and pulled my dress—I pulled my dress down and he pulled my dress back up.

I was in jail when Medgar Evers was murdered.

All of this is on account of we want to register, to become first-class citizens. And if the Freedom Democratic Party is not seated now, I question America. Is this America, the land of the free and the home of the brave, where we have to sleep with our telephones off the hooks because our lives be threatened daily, because we want to live as decent human beings, in America?

Thank you.

Source: Hamer, Fannie Lou. Testimony before the Democratic National Convention Credentials Committee, August 22, 1964. Accessed February 5, 2019. https://www.crmvet.org/docs/flh_ac.htm.

A Baptist Minister's Call for "Lawful" Civil Rights Activism, 1964

Many modern Americans assume that during the civil rights era of the 1950s and 1960s, black individuals and communities divided into one of two camps. They either supported the peaceful civil disobedience campaigns and marches championed by Martin Luther King Jr. and other civil rights activists or they subscribed to the more radical "black power" rhetoric of fiery figures like Malcolm X and Stokely Carmichael. But considerable numbers of African Americans who wanted to secure voting rights and social equality for themselves and their families were skeptical or fearful of both of these paths. They believed that the safest—and ultimately the most productive—course of action was to follow the law, avoid causing any fuss or controversy, vote for candidates sympathetic to their cause, show white America the contributions that they could make to the nation, and wait patiently for lawmakers to pass legislation that would put them on equal footing with whites at the ballot box and elsewhere.

One of the most prominent advocates of this position was Joseph H. Jackson, a prominent Chicago minister who was the longest-serving president (from 1953 to 1982) in the history of the National Baptist Convention. A political conservative, Jackson was extremely critical of King and his nonviolent brand of civil protests, as well as of those who advocated for black nationalism or violent revolution against racism. His views are well represented in the following excerpt from a September 10, 1964, address that Jackson gave at the 84th Annual Session of the National Baptist Convention in Detroit, Michigan.

Much time and space is given in the public press to the problem of civil rights. It has engaged the minds of our congressmen, and has occasioned many days of debate and deliberation. In the name of civil rights thousands have marched through the streets of our cities, boycotts have been staged, picket lines have been thrown around places of businesses, institutions of learning; and in every nook and corner of the country voices have been heard in the defense of and in the interest of civil rights.

What is this struggle for civil rights? I answer, it is an effort of American citizens to get full equality of opportunity. It is the resolution and the determination that there shall be in these United States one class of citizens and that is first class citizens. This is a struggle to adopt in practice as well as theory the concept of man on which the Declaration of Independence is based, and to fully implement the Federal Constitution, one of the greatest documents for human freedom since the writing of the Magna Carta. The civil rights struggle is a struggle for full freedom, justice, and equality before the law. It is a struggle to bring from paper the lofty ideals of America, and to apply them in practice to the lives and actions of all Americans. In reality it is America's struggle to be herself, to fulfill the highest promises of her being, and to build a social order after the pattern and dreams of our founding fathers and in the light of the wisdom of the ages. . . .

SOME SUGGESTIONS TO THE AMERICAN NEGRO

But we as a people must keep ever before us the true meaning of our struggle so that we will never be used as tools in the hands of those who love not the nation's cause but seek the nation's hurt and not our help. Hence there are some things that we must do.

1. In our struggle for civil rights we must remain always in the mainstream of American democracy. Our cause must never be divorced from the American cause, and our struggle must not be separated from the American struggle. We must stick to law and order, for as I have said in the past I say now, there are no problems in American life that cannot be solved through commitment to the highest laws of our land and in obedience to the American philosophy and way of life. In spite of criticisms and not-with-standing threats and open attacks, I have not retreated from

this position and never will as long as America is the America of the Federal Constitution and a land of due process of law. We cannot win our battle through force and unreasonable intimidation. As a minority group we cannot win outside of the protection and power of the just laws of this land. Read history with open eyes and attentive minds, and we will discover that no minority group has and can win in a struggle by the direct confrontation of the majority and by employing the same type of pressures and powers that the majority possess in abundance. The hope of the minority struggle is with the just laws of the land and the moral and constructive forces that are germane to this nation's life and character.

While we must be determined to achieve the best, we must not be guided by a spirit of revenge, blind emotions, and uncontrolled temper. When we act by these baser emotions we find ourselves contradicting ourselves. We will deny freedom of speech to those who differ with us, and will seek to do the things that will embarrass others however costly it may be to us and to them. When we are guided by revenge we do not choose our program of action wisely. There are some groups who are thus motivated, will go in, sit in, or lie in, in places that have objected to their presence. These same groups when they are dissatisfied in places that have accepted them, will give up their achieved rights and walk out in protest and revenge. Our actions must be guided both by logic and by law.

2. The methods that we employ in the present struggle must not lead us into open opposition to the laws of the land. In some cases the technique of direct action and demonstrations have led to mob violence and to vandalism. At least some who have desired to practice these negative methods have used the technique of so-called direct action.

3. Negroes must become registered voters and fight their battles in the polling booth. In the coming campaign we must not allow our prejudices, our hatred for individuals, to lead us into emotional outbursts and disrespect. The candidates contending for the presidency of the United States deserve, and should enjoy, the respect from every American citizen. It is beneath the dignity of this fair land of ours to seek to howl down, and to boo from platforms any candidate whom we do not favor. We must make choice of the candidate whom we think will serve the best interest of this nation and the nation's cause, and then take our ballot and help to elect our choice. As I told this convention in 1956, I tell you again, the ballot is our most important weapon. We must not neglect it, forfeit or sell it, but use it for the protection of the nation, the promotion of freedom, the promotion of every citizen, and for the glory of the United States of America. What I said in 1956 I still say now.
4. Negroes must still make their own leaders. We must not expect the public press, radio, and television to do this job for us. These news media are too busy with other responsibilities to be assigned the task

of choosing Negro leaders to represent the race in these days of stress and strain. Negroes must not forget that we have many fields in which leaders are necessary and important, and we should accept and follow the leaders in their respective field; that is, when they are right. We have political leaders, many of whom are worthy of our confidence and our respect. We shall follow them and show our appreciation for them. We have some dedicated civil rights leaders. We should respect them and follow them in their chosen field when they are right. We have religious leaders. We should respect and follow them when they are committed to the task of human betterment, human uplift, and the work of re-making the social order in the name of justice, righteousness, and peace.

We have worthy business leaders who can show us the way to improve our economic status, and to develop our available economic resources. Let us follow them. We have educators who are making their contribution in the field of thought and of mental growth. Let us honor them and respect them, and let us not discourage Negro educators by advocating directly or indirectly, that they are by nature inferior to educators in other racial groups.

We have athletes and comedians. Let us still applaud our athletes when they achieve on the field of competition, and let us join with others and freely laugh at the jokes that our comedians give. But we must not confuse these various fields. There must not develop any dictatorship of any one field, and athletes and comedians must not make the mistake of assuming the role of political, religious, and cultural leaders. We as a race must see to it that each man serves in his field, and we must not allow the white community to pick our leaders or to tell us what Negro we should follow.

5. Let us be courageous enough not only to oppose the wrong and the un-American actions in our nation, but we must also appreciate and rejoice in the achievements of our nation. There are some recent achievements which give us reason for hope, grounds for trust, and basis for rejoicing.

Ten years ago the Supreme Court of the United States rose above its old concept of separate but equal, and declared that segregation had no place in America's system of public education. This year, after a long, hard, and laborious fight, the Congress of the United States passed the strongest civil rights bill in its history, and the president signed into law a document that said that segregation has no place in American life and destiny. The call is to all of us to accept these facts and build on them. We must not ignore the constructive laws of our land, we must not organize, condone, or support mobs that parade in the name of freedom. We must not turn aside from decency and the constructive American standards in our quest for freedom. In our haste let us not be haughty. In our determination we must not become detrimental, and in our demonstrations we cannot afford to damn the nation of which we are a vital part.

6. . . . We have heard much in recent months about direct action in terms of boycotts, pickets, sit-ins, and demonstrations of various kinds. In each case the purpose as stated is a lofty one; namely, the winning of civil rights and the achievement of the equality of opportunity. I repeat, these are worthy ends and desirable goals, but this kind of direct action is orientated against others, and for the most part, must be classified in the negative since they have been designed to stop, arrest, or hinder certain orderly procedures in the interest of civil rights. In some cases however, these actions have been against practices and laws considered to be both evil and unjust.

Today, I call for another type of direct action; that is, direct action in the positive which is orientated towards the Negro's ability, talent, genius, and capacity. Let us take our economic resources, however insignificant and small, and organize and harness them, not to stop the economic growth of others, but to develop our own and to help our own community. If our patronage withdrawn from any store or business enterprise will weaken said enterprise, why not organize these resources and channel them into producing enterprises that we ourselves can direct and control. In the act of boycotting, our best economic talents are not called into play, and we ourselves are less productive and seek to render others the same. Why not build for ourselves instead of boycotting what others have produced? We must not be guilty of possessing the minds and actions of a blind Sampson who pulled a massive building down upon him-self as well as his enemies, and died with them in a final act of revenge. No act of revenge will lift a race from thralldom, and any direct actions that reduce the economic strength and life of the community is sure to punish the poor as well as the rich. Direct actions that encourage and create more tensions, ill will, hostility, and hate, will tend to make more difficult the mental, moral, and spiritual changes essential to new growth and creativity in human relations. Remember that when we seek to change certain acquired notions and habits of men we are seeking to change that which is very vital in human nature. When we labor to change segregationists and racists who believe they are right, we are facing the task of re-conditioning human emotions and building within. new patterns of thought, and changing human nature itself. In addition to that type of direct action which is negative and aimed at the correction of others, we need the type of direct action also that starts with ourselves which tends to produce a higher type of life within us as well as within others, and which aims to build a better community in which the available moral forces may be used to create new attitudes and new dispositions where human beings will regard others as they regard them-selves. Why should we expect direct actions against others to bear immediate fruit, and then procrastinate and postpone the direct actions that will make us better business men, better statesmen, better thinkers, and better men and women with better homes and better fellowship NOW? Now must not only be applied to the needs for changes and attitudes of segregationists, it must also be applied to us as as people and as a race when we aspire for the best and seek the more constructive and creative methods of life. We can be better now. We can acquire a better education now, we can organize our capital now and receive our share in this economy of free enterprise now. In spite of all that we have attained as a people we have not exhausted our possibilities, and the past does not define the limits of our potential. Are we not as well equipped to respond to the call of the right, the just, the good, the highest, and the best as are the white segregationists against whom we fight? Has not the great God put in our souls the thirst for truth and righteousness? Are we not endowed as co-workers with the great creative spirit of the universe? Then we need not wait until all is well before we harness our resources and venture upon new ways of life and creativity. . .

The progress of the race lies not in continued street demonstrations, and the liberation of an oppressed people shall not come by acts of revenge and retaliation but by the constructive use of all available opportunities and a creative expansion of the circumstances of the past into stepping stones to higher things.

Source: Jackson, Joseph H. "Participating in the Struggle of America." Remarks delivered at the 84th Annual Session of the National Baptist Convention, September 19, 1964. Accessed April 17, 2019. https://teachingamericanhistory.org/library/document/address-to-84th-annual-session-of-the-national-baptist-convention/.

The Twenty-Fourth Amendment Strikes Down Poll Taxes, 1964

One of the methods by which white Southern lawmakers kept black citizens from exercising their right to vote was by imposing a financial cost, known as a "poll tax," on state residents. Since systemic racism was pervasive across the economic, educational, and legal systems of these states, most African Americans were so deeply impoverished that paying a poll tax constituted a significant economic hardship (it also posed a hardship to poor white voters, giving more affluent white residents of the state's disproportionate influence at the ballot box). Numerous legal challenges to poll taxes were mounted, but again and again the Supreme Court asserted that such state laws were constitutional.

In 1962, poll taxes were still enforced in Alabama, Arkansas, Mississippi, Texas, and Virginia, to the dismay of a civil rights movement that was growing stronger by the day. That same year, however, President John F. Kennedy urged Congress to pass a constitutional amendment to prevent states from imposing such taxes (or literacy tests, another favorite voting suppression tool of white Southern politicians). The amendment, which passed despite uniform condemnation from Southern white lawmakers in August 1963, was subsequently ratified by the states less than six months later, on January 23, 1964.

XIV Amendment to the Constitution

Section 1

The right of citizens of the United States to vote in any primary or other election for President or Vice President, for electors for President or Vice President, or for Senator or Representative in Congress, shall not be denied or abridged by the United States or any State by reason of failure to pay poll tax or other tax.

Section 2
The Congress shall have power to enforce this article by appropriate legislation.

Source: Amendment XXIV, U.S. Constitution. National Archives.

Warren Court Establishes "One Person, One Vote" as a Constitutional Standard, 1964

Reynolds v. Sims *(1964) was one of the most momentous Supreme Court rulings of the civil rights era. It established that states needed to maintain similar population totals within their electoral districts rather than craft districts with dramatically different population levels. The court accepted the argument posed by the plaintiffs in the case—voters in Jefferson County, Alabama, which contained more than forty times as many eligible voters as those in another district of the state—that the imbalance meant that voters in low-population districts had a greater say in the political process (including electing representatives) than those from high-population districts. The arrangement violated the Constitution's Equal Protection Clause, which forbids any state from denying "any person within its jurisdiction the equal protection of the laws."*

The court's 8–1 decision was handed down on June 15, 1964. The majority opinion, written by Chief Justice Earl Warren, enshrined a basic pillar of what became known as the "one person, one vote" standard in election law—the belief that one person's vote should carry no more or less influence than that of another person in the state. Following are excerpts from Warren's majority opinion.

A predominant consideration in determining whether a State's legislative apportionment scheme constitutes an invidious discrimination violative of rights asserted under the Equal Protection Clause is that the rights allegedly impaired are individual and personal in nature. As stated by the Court in *United States v. Bathgate,* "[t]he right to vote is personal. . . ." While the result of a court decision in a state legislative apportionment controversy may be to require the restructuring of the geographical distribution of seats in a state legislature, the judicial focus must be concentrated upon ascertaining whether there has been any discrimination against certain of the State's citizens which constitutes an impermissible impairment of their constitutionally protected right to vote. Like *Skinner v. Oklahoma,* such a case "touches a sensitive and important area of human rights," and "involves one of the basic civil rights of man," presenting questions of alleged "invidious discriminations . . . against groups or types of individuals in violation of the constitutional guaranty of just and equal laws."

Undoubtedly, the right of suffrage is a fundamental matter in a free and democratic society. Especially since the right to exercise the franchise in a free and unimpaired manner is preservative of other basic civil and political rights, any alleged infringement of the right of citizens to vote must be carefully and meticulously scrutinized. Almost a century ago, in *Yick Wo v. Hopkins,* the Court referred to "the political franchise of voting" as "a fundamental political right, because preservative of all rights."

Legislators represent people, not trees or acres. Legislators are elected by voters, not farms or cities or economic interests. As long as ours is a representative form of government, and our legislatures are those instruments of government elected directly by and directly representative of the people, the right to elect legislators in a free and unimpaired fashion is a bedrock of our political system. It could hardly be gainsaid that a constitutional claim had been asserted by an allegation that certain otherwise qualified voters had been entirely prohibited from voting for members of their state legislature. And, if a State should provide that the votes of citizens in one part of the State should be given two times, or five times, or 10 times the weight of votes of citizens in another part of the State, it could hardly be contended that the right to vote of those residing in the disfavored areas had not been effectively diluted. It would appear extraordinary to suggest that a State could be constitutionally permitted to enact a law providing that certain of the State's voters could vote two, five, or 10 times for their legislative representatives, while voters living elsewhere could vote only once. And it is inconceivable that a state law to the effect that, in counting votes for legislators, the votes of citizens in one part of the State would be multiplied by two, five, or 10, while the votes of persons in another area would be counted only at face value, could be constitutionally sustainable. Of course, the effect of state legislative districting schemes which give the same number of representatives to unequal numbers of constituents is identical. Overweighting and overvaluation of the votes of those living here has the certain effect of dilution and undervaluation of the votes of those living there. The resulting discrimination against those individual voters living in disfavored areas is easily demonstrable mathematically. Their right to vote is simply not the same right to vote as that of those living in a favored part of the State. Two, five, or 10 of them must vote before the effect of their voting is equivalent to that of their favored neighbor. Weighting the votes of citizens differently, by any method or means, merely because of where they happen to reside, hardly seems justifiable. One must be ever aware that the Constitution forbids "sophisticated, as well as simple-minded, modes of discrimination." As we stated in *Wesberry v. Sanders, supra:*

"We do not believe that the Framers of the Constitution intended to permit the same vote-diluting discrimination to be accomplished through the device of districts containing widely varied numbers of inhabitants. To say that a vote is worth more in one district than in another would . . . run counter to our fundamental ideas of democratic government. . . ."

State legislatures are, historically, the fountainhead of representative government in this country. A number of them have their roots in colonial times, and substantially antedate the creation of our Nation and our Federal Government. In fact, the first formal stirrings of American political independence are to be found, in large part, in the views and actions of several of the colonial legislative bodies. With the birth of our National Government, and the adoption and ratification of the Federal Constitution, state legislatures retained a most important place in our Nation's governmental structure. But representative government is, in essence, self-government through the medium of elected representatives of the people, and each and every citizen has an inalienable right to full and effective participation in the political processes of his State's legislative bodies. Most citizens can achieve this participation only as qualified voters through the election of legislators to represent them. Full and effective participation by all citizens in state government requires, therefore, that each citizen have an equally effective voice in the election of members of his state legislature. Modern and viable state government needs, and the Constitution demands, no less.

Logically, in a society ostensibly grounded on representative government, it would seem reasonable that a majority of the people of a State could elect a majority of that State's legislators. To conclude differently, and to sanction minority control of state legislative bodies, would appear to deny majority rights in a way that far surpasses any possible denial of minority rights that might otherwise be thought to result. Since legislatures are responsible for enacting laws by which all citizens are to be governed, they should be bodies which are collectively responsive to the popular will. And the concept of equal protection has been traditionally viewed as requiring the uniform treatment of persons standing in the same relation to the governmental action questioned or challenged. With respect to the allocation of legislative representation, all voters, as citizens of a State, stand in the same relation regardless of where they live. Any suggested criteria for the differentiation of citizens are insufficient to justify any discrimination, as to the weight of their votes, unless relevant to the permissible purposes of legislative apportionment. Since the achieving of fair and effective representation for all citizens is concededly the basic aim of legislative apportionment, we conclude that the Equal Protection Clause guarantees the opportunity for equal participation by all voters in the election of state legislators. Diluting the weight of votes because of place of residence impairs basic constitutional rights under the Fourteenth Amendment just as much as invidious discriminations based upon factors such as race, *Brown v. Board of Education,* or economic status, *Griffin v. Illinois, Douglas v. California.* Our constitutional system amply provides for the protection of minorities by means other than giving them majority control of state legislatures. And the democratic ideals of equality and majority rule, which have served this Nation so well in the past, are hardly of any less significance for the present and the future.

Source: Majority Opinion of Chief Justice Warren. *Reynolds v. Sims,* 377 U.S. 533, 1964.

Congress Passes the Voting Rights Act, 1965

The Voting Rights Act of 1965, signed into law by President Lyndon B. Johnson on August 6, 1965, was a powerful, long-overdue response to decades of ruthless black voter suppression across the American South. This landmark legislation, crafted in an environment in which peaceful African American civil rights activists and their allies were being murdered, assaulted, harassed, and subjected to economic punishment in many parts of the South, outlawed all forms of racial discrimination in voting, including poll taxes and literacy tests, the main mechanisms that Southern whites had employed to keep blacks from the voting booth for generations. Section 5 of the law also established the federal government as a watchdog of sorts over "covered jurisdictions"—state and local governments with a history of hostility to black voters. Following are key provisions in this legislation, which finally gave federal authorities the power to enforce the voting rights enshrined in the Fourteenth and Fifteenth Amendments.

AN ACT To enforce the fifteenth amendment to the Constitution of the United States, and for other purposes.

Be it enacted by the Senate and House of Representatives of the United States of America in Congress assembled, That this Act shall be known as the "Voting Rights Act of 1965."

SEC. 2. No voting qualification or prerequisite to voting, or standard, practice, or procedure shall be imposed or applied by any State or political subdivision to deny or abridge the right of any citizen of the United States to vote on account of race or color.

SEC. 3. (a) Whenever the Attorney General institutes a proceeding under any statute to enforce the guarantees of the fifteenth amendment in any State or political subdivision the court shall authorize the appointment of Federal examiners by the United States Civil Service Commission in accordance with section 6 to serve for such period of time and for such political subdivisions as the court shall determine is appropriate to enforce the guarantees of the fifteenth amendment (1) as part of any interlocutory order if the court determines that the appointment of such examiners is necessary to enforce such guarantees or (2) as part of any final judgment if the court finds that violations of the fifteenth amendment justifying equitable relief have occurred in such State or subdivision: Provided, That the court need not authorize the appointment of examiners if any incidents of denial or abridgement of the right to vote on account of race or color (1) have been few in number and have been promptly and effectively corrected by State or local action, (2) the continuing effect of such incidents has been eliminated, and (3) there is no reasonable probability of their recurrence in the future.

(b) If in a proceeding instituted by the Attorney General under any statute to enforce the guarantees of the fifteenth amendment in any State or political subdivision the court finds that a test or device has been used for the purpose or with the effect of denying or abridging the right of any citizen of the United States to vote on account of race or color, it shall suspend the use of tests and devices in such State or political subdivisions as the court shall determine is appropriate and for such period as it deems necessary.

(c) If in any proceeding instituted by the Attorney General under any statute to enforce the guarantees of the fifteenth amendment in any State or political subdivision the court finds that violations of the fifteenth amendment justifying equitable relief have occurred within the territory of such State or political subdivision, the court, in addition to such relief as it may grant, shall retain jurisdiction for such period as it may deem appropriate and during such period no voting qualification or prerequisite to voting, or standard, practice, or procedure with respect to voting different from that in force or effect at the time the proceeding was commenced shall be enforced unless and until the court finds that such qualification, prerequisite, standard, practice, or procedure does not have the purpose and will not have the effect of denying or abridging the right to vote on account of race or color: Provided, That such qualification, prerequisite, standard, practice, or procedure may be enforced if the qualification, prerequisite, standard, practice, or procedure has been submitted by the chief legal officer or other appropriate official of such State or subdivision to the Attorney General and the Attorney General has not interposed an objection within sixty days after such submission, except that neither the court's finding nor the Attorney General's failure to object shall bar a subsequent action to enjoin enforcement of such qualification, prerequisite, standard, practice, or procedure.

SEC. 4. (a) To assure that the right of citizens of the United States to vote is not denied or abridged on account of race or color, no citizen shall be denied the right to vote in any Federal, State, or local election because of his failure to comply with any test or device in any State with respect to which the determinations have been made under subsection (b) or in any political subdivision with respect to which such determinations have been made as a separate unit, unless the United States District Court for the District of Columbia in an action for a declaratory judgment brought by such State or subdivision against the United States has determined that no such test or device has been used during the five years preceding the filing of the action for the purpose or with the effect of denying or abridging the right to vote on account of race or color: Provided, That no such declaratory judgment shall issue with respect to any plaintiff for a period of five years after the entry of a final judgment of any court of the United States, other than the denial of a declaratory judgment under this section, whether entered prior to or after the enactment of this Act, determining that denials or abridgments of the right to vote on account of race or color through the use of such tests or devices have occurred anywhere in the territory of such plaintiff. An action pursuant to this subsection shall be heard and determined by a court of three judges in accordance with the provisions of section 2284 of title 28 of the United States Code and any appeal shall lie to the Supreme Court. The court shall retain jurisdiction of any action pursuant to this subsection for five years after judgment and shall reopen the action upon motion of the Attorney General alleging that a test or device has been used for the purpose or with the effect of denying or abridging the right to vote on account of race or color.

If the Attorney General determines that he has no reason to believe that any such test or device has been used during the five years preceding the filing of the action for the purpose or with the effect of denying or abridging the right to vote on account of race or color, he shall consent to the entry of such judgment.

(b) The provisions of subsection (a) shall apply in any State or in any political subdivision of a state which (1) the Attorney General determines maintained on November 1, 1964, any test or device, and with respect to which (2) the Director of the Census determines that less than 50 percentum of the persons of voting age residing therein were registered on November 1, 1964, or that less than 50 percentum of such persons voted in the presidential election of November 1964.

A determination or certification of the Attorney General or of the Director of the Census under this section or under section 6 or section 13 shall not be reviewable in any court and shall be effective upon publication in the Federal Register.

(c) The phrase "test or device" shall mean any requirement that a person as a prerequisite for voting or registration for voting (1) demonstrate the ability to read, write, understand, or interpret any matter, (2) demonstrate any educational achievement or his knowledge of any particular subject, (3) possess good moral character, or (4) prove his qualifications by the voucher of registered voters or members of any other class.

(d) For purposes of this section no State or political subdivision shall be determined to have engaged in the use of tests or devices for the purpose or with the effect of denying or abridging the right to vote on account of race or color if (1) incidents of such use have been few in number and have been promptly and effectively corrected by State or local action, (2) the continuing effect of such incidents has been eliminated, and (3) there is no reasonable probability of their recurrence in the future.

(e) (1) Congress hereby declares that to secure the rights under the fourteenth amendment of persons educated in American-flag schools in which the predominant classroom language was other than English, it is necessary to prohibit the States from conditioning the right to vote of such persons on ability to read, write, understand, or interpret any matter in the English language. (2) No person who demonstrates that he has successfully completed the sixth primary grade in a public school in, or a private school accredited by, any State or territory, the District of Columbia, or the Commonwealth of Puerto Rico in which the predominant classroom language was other than English, shall be denied the right to vote in any Federal, State, or local election because of his inability to read, write, understand, or interpret any matter in the English language, except that, in States in which State law provides that a different level of education is presumptive of literacy, he shall demonstrate that he has successfully completed an equivalent level of education in a public school in, or a private school accredited by, any State or territory, the District of Columbia, or the Commonwealth of Puerto Rico in which the predominant classroom language was other than English.

SEC. 5. Whenever a State or political subdivision with respect to which the prohibitions set forth in section 4(a) are in effect shall enact or seek to administer any voting qualification or prerequisite to voting, or standard, practice, or procedure with respect to voting different from that in force or effect on November 1, 1964, such State or subdivision may institute an action in the United States District Court for the District of Columbia for a declaratory judgment that such qualification, prerequisite, standard, practice, or procedure does not have the purpose and will not have the effect of denying or abridging the right to vote on account of race or color, and unless and until the court enters such judgment no person shall be denied the right to vote for failure to comply with such qualification, prerequisite, standard, practice, or procedure: Provided, That such qualification, prerequisite, standard, practice, or procedure may be enforced without such proceeding if the qualification, prerequisite, standard, practice, or procedure has been submitted by the chief legal officer or other appropriate official of such State or subdivision to the Attorney General and the Attorney General has not interposed an objection within sixty days after such submission, except that neither the Attorney General's failure to object nor a declaratory judgment entered under this section shall bar a subsequent action to enjoin enforcement of such qualification, prerequisite, standard, practice, or procedure. Any action under this section shall be heard and determined by a court of three judges in accordance with the provisions of section 2284 of title 28 of the United States Code and any appeal shall lie to the Supreme Court.

SEC. 6. Whenever (a) a court has authorized the appointment of examiners pursuant to the provisions of section 3(a), or (b) unless a declaratory judgment has been rendered under section 4(a), the Attorney General certifies with respect to any political subdivision named in, or included within the scope of, determinations made under section 4(b) that (1) he has received complaints in writing from twenty or more residents of such political subdivision alleging that they have been denied the right to vote under color of law on account of race or color, and that he believes such complaints to be meritorious, or (2) that, in his judgment (considering, among other factors, whether the ratio of nonwhite persons to white persons registered to vote within such subdivision appears to him to be reasonably attributable to violations of the fifteenth amendment or whether substantial evidence exists that bona fide efforts are being made within such subdivision to comply with the fifteenth amendment), the appointment of examiners is otherwise necessary to enforce the guarantees of the fifteenth amendment, the Civil Service Commission shall appoint as many examiners for such subdivision as it may deem appropriate to prepare and maintain lists of persons eligible to vote in Federal, State, and local elections. Such examiners, hearing officers provided for in section 9(a), and other persons deemed necessary by the Commission to carry out the provisions and purposes of this Act shall be appointed, compensated, and separated without regard to the provisions of any statute administered by the Civil Service Commission, and service under this Act shall not be considered employment for the purposes of any statute administered by the Civil Service Commission, except the provisions of section 9 of the Act of August 2, 1939, as amended (5 U.S.C. 118i), prohibiting partisan political activity: Provided, That the Commission is authorized, after consulting the head of the appropriate department or agency, to designate suitable persons in the official service of the United States, with their consent, to serve in these positions. Examiners and hearing officers shall have the power to administer oaths.

SEC. 7. (a) The examiners for each political subdivision shall, at such places as the Civil Service Commission shall by regulation designate, examine applicants concerning their qualifications for voting. An application to an examiner shall be in such form as the Commission may require and shall contain allegations that the applicant is not otherwise registered to vote.

(b) Any person whom the examiner finds, in accordance with instructions received under section 9(b), to have the qualifications prescribed by State law not inconsistent with the Constitution and laws of the United States shall promptly be placed on a list of eligible voters. A challenge to such listing may be made in accordance with section 9(a) and shall not be the basis for a prosecution under section 12 of this Act. The examiner shall certify and transmit such list, and any supplements as appropriate, at least once a month, to the offices of the appropriate election officials, with copies to the Attorney General and the attorney general of the State, and any such lists and supplements thereto transmitted during the month shall be available for public inspection on the last business day of the month and, in any event, not later than the forty-fifth day prior to any election. The appropriate State or local election official shall place such names on the official voting list. Any person whose name appears on the examiner's list shall be entitled and allowed to vote in the election district of his residence unless and until the appropriate election officials shall have been notified that such person has been removed from such list in accordance with subsection (d): Provided, That no person shall be entitled to vote in any election by virtue of this Act unless his name shall have been certified and transmitted on such a list to the offices of the appropriate election officials at least forty-five days prior to such election.

(c) The examiner shall issue to each person whose name appears on such a list a certificate evidencing his eligibility to vote.

(d) A person whose name appears on such a list shall be removed therefrom by an examiner if (1) such person has been successfully challenged in accordance with the procedure prescribed in section 9, or (2) he has been determined by an examiner to have lost his eligibility to vote under State law not inconsistent with the Constitution and the laws of the United States.

SEC. 8. Whenever an examiner is serving under this Act in any political subdivision, the Civil Service Commission may assign, at the request of the Attorney General, one or more persons, who may be officers of the United States, (1) to enter and attend at any place for holding an election in such subdivision for the purpose of observing whether persons who are entitled to vote are being permitted to vote, and (2) to enter and attend at any place for tabulating the votes cast at any election held in such subdivision for the purpose of observing whether votes cast by persons entitled to vote are being properly tabulated. Such persons so assigned shall report to an examiner appointed for such political subdivision, to the Attorney General, and if the appointment of examiners has been authorized pursuant to section 3(a), to the court.

SEC. 9. (a) Any challenge to a listing on an eligibility list prepared by an examiner shall be heard and determined by a hearing officer appointed by and responsible to the Civil Service Commission and under such rules as the Commission shall by regulation prescribe. Such challenge shall be entertained only if filed at such office within the State as the Civil Service Commission shall by regulation designate, and within ten days after the listing of the challenged person is made available for public inspection, and if supported by (1) the affidavits of at least two persons having personal knowledge of the facts constituting grounds for the challenge, and (2) a certification that a copy of the challenge and affidavits have been served by mail or in person upon the person challenged at his place of residence set out in the application. Such challenge shall be determined within fifteen days after it has been filed. A petition for review of the decision of the hearing officer may be filed in the United States court of appeals for the circuit in which the person challenged resides within fifteen days after service of such decision by mail on the person petitioning for review but no decision of a hearing officer shall be reversed unless clearly erroneous. Any person listed shall be entitled and allowed to vote pending final determination by the hearing officer and by the court.

(b) The times, places, procedures, and form for application and listing pursuant to this Act and removals from the eligibility lists shall be prescribed by regulations promulgated by the Civil Service Commission and the Commission shall, after consultation with the Attorney General, instruct examiners concerning applicable State law not inconsistent with the Constitution and laws of the United States with respect to (1) the qualifications required for listing, and (2) loss of eligibility to vote.

(c) Upon the request of the applicant or the challenger or on its own motion the Civil Service Commission shall have the power to require by subpoena the attendance and testimony of witnesses and the production of documentary evidence relating to any matter pending before it under the authority of this section. In case of contumacy or refusal to obey a subpoena, any district court of the United States or the United States court of any territory or possession, or the District Court of the United States for the District of Columbia, within the jurisdiction of which said person guilty of contumacy or refusal to obey is found or resides or is domiciled or transacts business, or has appointed an agent for receipt of service of process, upon application by the Attorney General of the United States shall have jurisdiction to issue to such person an order requiring such person to appear before the Commission or a hearing officer, there to produce pertinent, relevant, and nonprivileged documentary evidence if so ordered, or there to give testimony touching the matter under investigation, and any failure to obey such order of the court may be punished by said court as a contempt thereof.

SEC. 10. (a) The Congress finds that the requirement of the payment of a poll tax as a precondition to voting (i) precludes persons of limited means from voting or imposes unreasonable financial hardship upon such persons as a precondition to their exercise of the franchise, (ii) does not bear a reasonable relationship to any legitimate State interest in the conduct of elections, and (iii) in some areas has the purpose or effect of denying persons the right to vote because of race or color. Upon the basis of these findings, Congress declares that the constitutional right of citizens to vote is denied or abridged in some areas by the requirement of the payment of a poll tax as a precondition to voting.

(b) In the exercise of the powers of Congress under section 5 of the fourteenth amendment and section 2 of the fifteenth amendment, the Attorney General is authorized and directed to institute forthwith in the name of the United States such actions, including actions against States or political subdivisions, for declaratory judgment or injunctive relief against the enforcement of any requirement of the payment of a poll tax as a precondition to voting, or substitute therefor enacted after November 1, 1964, as will be necessary to implement the declaration of subsection (a) and the purposes of this section. . . .

SEC. 11. (a) No person acting under color of law shall fail or refuse to permit any person to vote who is entitled to vote under any provision of this Act or is otherwise qualified to vote, or willfully fail or refuse to tabulate, count, and report such person's vote.

(b) No person, whether acting under color of law or otherwise, shall intimidate, threaten, or coerce, or attempt to intimidate, threaten, or coerce any person for voting or attempting to vote, or intimidate, threaten, or coerce, or attempt to intimidate, threaten, or coerce any person for urging or aiding any person to vote or attempt to vote, or intimidate, threaten, or coerce any person for exercising any powers or duties under section 3(a), 6, 8, 9, 10, or 12(e).

(c) Whoever knowingly or willfully gives false information as to his name, address, or period of residence in the voting district for the purpose of establishing his eligibility to register or vote, or conspires with another individual for the purpose of encouraging his false registration to vote or illegal voting, or pays or offers to pay or accepts payment either for registration to vote or for voting shall be fined not more than $10,000 or imprisoned not more than five years, or both: Provided, however, That this provision shall be applicable only to general, special, or primary elections held solely or in part for the purpose of selecting or electing any candidate for the office of President, Vice President, presidential elector, Member of the United States Senate, Member of the United States House of Representatives, or Delegates or Commissioners from the territories or possessions, or Resident Commissioner of the Commonwealth of Puerto Rico.

(d) Whoever, in any matter within the jurisdiction of an examiner or hearing officer knowingly and willfully falsifies or conceals a material fact, or makes any false, fictitious, or fraudulent statements or representations, or makes or uses any false writing or document knowing the same to contain any false, fictitious, or fraudulent statement or entry, shall be fined not more than $10,000 or imprisoned not more than five years, or both. . . .

SEC 19. If any provision of this Act or the application thereof to any person or circumstances is held invalid, the remainder of the Act and the application of the provision to other persons not similarly situated or to other circumstances shall not be affected thereby.

Approved August 6, 1965.

Source: Voting Rights Act of 1965. Public Law 89–110, U.S. Statutes at Large, 79 (1965): 437, codified at U.S. Code 42, 1973.

President Johnson's "American Promise" Speech, 1965

On the evening of March 7, 1965, tens of millions of American television viewers watched footage from earlier that day of peaceful civil rights demonstrators in Selma, Alabama, being brutally attacked by state troopers, local police, and white civilians when they tried to cross Selma's Edmund Pettus Bridge as part of a civil rights march. The ugly, stunning images from "Bloody Sunday," as that dark day in Selma came to be known, produced a seismic change in American perceptions of the struggle for voting rights and other civil rights being waged by African Americans across the American South. The images also had a tremendous impact on President Lyndon B. Johnson. The appalling footage from Selma convinced him that securing the civil rights of the nation's black people was not only a moral imperative but necessary to keep the country from tearing itself apart.

Eight days after Selma, Johnson appeared before a joint session of Congress to deliver a speech titled "The American Promise." In his remarks, Johnson declared his intention to send muscular voting rights legislation to Congress—and he demanded that Congress act on it. "On this issue, there must be no delay, or no hesitation, or no compromise with our purpose. We cannot, we must not, refuse to protect the right of every American to vote in every election that he may desire to participate in. And we ought not, and we cannot, and we must not wait before we get a bill. We have already waited 100 years and more and the time for waiting is gone." Johnson's American Promise speech, which helped lay the groundwork for the landmark Voting Rights Act he signed into law a mere five months later, is regarded by many historians as the greatest and most consequential speech of his presidency.

Mr. Speaker, Mr. President, Members of the Congress:

I speak tonight for the dignity of man and the destiny of democracy.

I urge every member of both parties, Americans of all religions and of all colors, from every section of this country, to join me in that cause.

At times history and fate meet at a single time in a single place to shape a turning point in man's unending search for freedom. So it was at Lexington and Concord. So it was a century ago at Appomattox. So it was last week in Selma, Alabama.

There, long-suffering men and women peacefully protested the denial of their rights as Americans. Many were brutally assaulted. One good man, a man of God, was killed.

There is no cause for pride in what has happened in Selma. There is no cause for self-satisfaction in the long denial of equal rights of millions of Americans. But there is cause for hope and for faith in our democracy in what is happening here tonight.

For the cries of pain and the hymns and protests of oppressed people have summoned into convocation all the majesty of this great Government—the Government of the greatest Nation on earth.

Our mission is at once the oldest and the most basic of this country: to right wrong, to do justice, to serve man.

In our time we have come to live with moments of great crisis. Our lives have been marked with debate about great issues; issues of war and peace, issues of prosperity and depression. But rarely in any time does an issue lay bare the secret heart of America itself. Rarely are we met with a challenge, not to our growth or abundance, our welfare or our security, but rather to the values and the purposes and the meaning of our beloved Nation.

The issue of equal rights for American Negroes is such an issue. And should we defeat every enemy, should we double our wealth and conquer the stars, and still be unequal to this issue, then we will have failed as a people and as a nation.

For with a country as with a person, "What is a man profited, if he shall gain the whole world, and lose his own soul?"

There is no Negro problem. There is no Southern problem. There is no Northern problem. There is only an American problem. And we are met here tonight as Americans—not as Democrats or Republicans—we are met here as Americans to solve that problem.

This was the first nation in the history of the world to be founded with a purpose. The great phrases of that purpose still sound in every American heart, North and South: "All men are created equal"—"government by consent of the governed"—"give me liberty or give me death." Well, those are not just clever words, or those are not just empty theories. In their name Americans have fought and died for two centuries, and tonight around the world they stand there as guardians of our liberty, risking their lives.

Those words are a promise to every citizen that he shall share in the dignity of man. This dignity cannot be found in a man's possessions; it cannot be found in his power, or in his position. It really rests on his right to be treated as a man equal in opportunity to all others. It says that he shall share in freedom, he shall choose his leaders, educate his children, and provide for his family according to his ability and his merits as a human being.

To apply any other test—to deny a man his hopes because of his color or race, his religion or the place of his birth—is not only to do injustice, it is to deny America and to dishonor the dead who gave their lives for American freedom.

THE RIGHT TO VOTE

Our fathers believed that if this noble view of the rights of man was to flourish, it must be rooted in democracy. The most basic right of all was the right to choose your own leaders. The history of this country, in large measure, is the history of the expansion of that right to all of our people.

Many of the issues of civil rights are very complex and most difficult. But about this there can and should be no argument. Every American citizen must have an equal right to vote. There is no reason which can excuse the denial of that right. There is no duty which weighs more heavily on us than the duty we have to ensure that right.

Yet the harsh fact is that in many places in this country men and women are kept from voting simply because they are Negroes.

Every device of which human ingenuity is capable has been used to deny this right. The Negro citizen may go to register only to be told that the day is wrong, or the hour is late, or the official in charge is absent. And if he persists, and if he manages to present himself to the registrar, he may be disqualified because he did not spell out his middle name or because he abbreviated a word on the application.

And if he manages to fill out an application he is given a test. The registrar is the sole judge of whether he passes this test. He may be asked to recite the entire Constitution, or explain the most complex provisions of State law. And even a college degree cannot be used to prove that he can read and write.

For the fact is that the only way to pass these barriers is to show a white skin.

Experience has clearly shown that the existing process of law cannot overcome systematic and ingenious discrimination. No law that we now have on the books—and I have helped to put three of them there—can ensure the right to vote when local officials are determined to deny it.

In such a case our duty must be clear to all of us. The Constitution says that no person shall be kept from voting because of his race or his color. We have all sworn an oath before God to support and to defend that Constitution. We must now act in obedience to that oath.

GUARANTEEING THE RIGHT TO VOTE

Wednesday I will send to Congress a law designed to eliminate illegal barriers to the right to vote.

The broad principles of that bill will be in the hands of the Democratic and Republican leaders tomorrow. After they have reviewed it, it will come here formally as a bill. I am grateful for this opportunity to come here tonight at the invitation of the leadership to reason with my friends, to give them my views, and to visit with my former colleagues.

I have had prepared a more comprehensive analysis of the legislation which I had intended to transmit to the clerk tomorrow but which I will submit to the clerks tonight. But I want to really discuss with you now briefly the main proposals of this legislation,

This bill will strike down restrictions to voting in all elections—Federal, State, and local—which have been used to deny Negroes the right to vote.

This bill will establish a simple, uniform standard which cannot be used, however ingenious the effort, to flout our Constitution.

It will provide for citizens to be registered by officials of the United States Government if the State officials refuse to register them.

It will eliminate tedious, unnecessary lawsuits which delay the right to vote.

Finally, this legislation will ensure that properly registered individuals are not prohibited from voting.

I will welcome the suggestions from all of the Members of Congress—I have no doubt that I will get some—on ways and means to strengthen this law and to make it effective. But experience has plainly shown that this is the only path to carry out the command of the Constitution.

To those who seek to avoid action by their National Government in their own communities; who want to and who seek to maintain purely local control over elections, the answer is simple:

Open your polling places to all your people.

Allow men and women to register and vote whatever the color of their skin.

Extend the rights of citizenship to every citizen of this land.

THE NEED FOR ACTION

There is no constitutional issue here. The command of the Constitution is plain.

There is no moral issue. It is wrong—deadly wrong—to deny any of your fellow Americans the right to vote in this country.

There is no issue of States fights or national rights. There is only the struggle for human rights.

I have not the slightest doubt what will be your answer.

The last time a President sent a civil rights bill to the Congress it contained a provision to protect voting rights in Federal elections. That civil rights bill was passed after 8 long months of debate. And when that bill came to my desk from the Congress for my signature, the heart of the voting provision had been eliminated.

This time, on this issue, there must be no delay, no hesitation and no compromise with our purpose.

We cannot, we must not, refuse to protect the right of every American to vote in every election that he may desire to participate in. And we ought not and we cannot and we must not wait another 8 months before we get a bill. We have already waited a hundred years and more, and the time for waiting is gone.

So I ask you to join me in working long hours—nights and weekends, if necessary—to pass this bill. And I don't make that request lightly. For from the window where I sit with the problems of our country I recognize that outside this chamber is the outraged conscience of a nation, the grave concern of many nations, and the harsh judgment of history on our acts.

WE SHALL OVERCOME

But even if we pass this bill, the battle will not be over. What happened in Selma is part of a far larger movement which reaches into every section and State of America. It is the effort of American Negroes to secure for themselves the full blessings of American life.

Their cause must be our cause too. Because it is not just Negroes, but really it is all of us, who must overcome the crippling legacy of bigotry and injustice. And we shall overcome.

As a man whose roots go deeply into Southern soil I know how agonizing racial feelings are. I know how difficult it is to reshape the attitudes and the structure of our society.

But a century has passed, more than a hundred years, since the Negro was freed. And he is not fully free tonight.

It was more than a hundred years ago that Abraham Lincoln, a great President of another party, signed the Emancipation Proclamation, but emancipation is a proclamation and not a fact.

A century has passed, more than a hundred years, since equality was promised. And yet the Negro is not equal.

A century has passed since the day of promise. And the promise is unkept.

The time of justice has now come. I tell you that I believe sincerely that no force can hold it back. It is right in the eyes of man and God that it should come. And when it does, I think that day will brighten the lives of every American.

For Negroes are not the only victims. How many white children have gone uneducated, how many white families have lived in stark poverty, how many white lives have been scarred by fear, because we have wasted our energy and our substance to maintain the barriers of hatred and terror?

So I say to all of you here, and to all in the Nation tonight, that those who appeal to you to hold on to the past do so at the cost of denying you your future.

This great, rich, restless country can offer opportunity and education and hope to all: black and white, North and South, sharecropper and city dweller. These are the enemies: poverty, ignorance, disease. They are the enemies and not our fellow man, not our neighbor. And these enemies too, poverty, disease and ignorance, we shall overcome.

AN AMERICAN PROBLEM

Now let none of us in any sections look with prideful righteousness on the troubles in another section, or on the problems of our neighbors. There is really no part of America where the promise of equality has been fully kept. In Buffalo as well as in Birmingham, in Philadelphia as well as in Selma, Americans are struggling for the fruits of freedom.

This is one Nation. What happens in Selma or in Cincinnati is a matter of legitimate concern to every American. But let each of us look within our own hearts and our own communities, and let each of us put our shoulder to the wheel to root out injustice wherever it exists.

As we meet here in this peaceful, historic chamber tonight, men from the South, some of whom were at Iwo Jima, men from the North who have carried Old Glory to far corners of the world and brought it back without a stain on it, men from the East and from the West, are all fighting together without regard to religion, or color, or region, in Viet-Nam. Men from every region fought for us across the world 20 years ago.

And in these common dangers and these common sacrifices the South made its contribution of honor and gallantry no less than any other region of the great Republic—and in some instances, a great many of them, more.

And I have not the slightest doubt that good men from everywhere in this country, from the Great Lakes to the Gulf of Mexico, from the Golden Gate to the harbors along the Atlantic, will rally together now in this cause to vindicate the freedom of all Americans. For all of us owe this duty; and I believe that all of us will respond to it.

Your President makes that request of every American.

PROGRESS THROUGH THE DEMOCRATIC PROCESS

The real hero of this struggle is the American Negro. His actions and protests, his courage to risk safety and even to risk his life, have awakened the conscience of this Nation. His demonstrations have been designed to call attention to injustice, designed to provoke change, designed to stir reform.

He has called upon us to make good the promise of America. And who among us can say that we would have made the same progress were it not for his persistent bravery, and his faith in American democracy.

For at the real heart of battle for equality is a deep-seated belief in the democratic process. Equality depends not on the force of arms or tear gas but upon the force of moral right; not on recourse to violence but on respect for law and order.

There have been many pressures upon your President and there will be others as the days come and go. But I pledge you tonight that we intend to fight this battle where it should be fought: in the courts, and in the Congress, and in the hearts of men.

We must preserve the right of free speech and the right of free assembly. But the right of free speech does not carry with it, as has been said, the right to holier fire in a crowded theater. We must preserve the right to free assembly, but free assembly does not carry with it the right to block public thoroughfares to traffic.

We do have a right to protest, and a right to march under conditions that do not infringe the constitutional rights of our neighbors. And I intend to protect all those rights as long as I am permitted to serve in this office.

We will guard against violence, knowing it strikes from our hands the very weapons which we seek—progress, obedience to law, and belief in American values.

In Selma as elsewhere we seek and pray for peace. We seek order. We seek unity. But we will not accept the peace of stifled rights, or the order imposed by fear, or the unity that stifles protest. For peace cannot be purchased at the cost of liberty.

In Selma tonight, as in every—and we had a good day there—as in every city, we are working for just and peaceful settlement. We must all remember that after this speech I am making tonight, after the police and the FBI and the Marshals have all gone, and after you have promptly passed this bill, the people of Selma and the other cities of the Nation must still live and work together. And when the attention of the Nation has gone elsewhere they must try to heal the wounds and to build a new community.

This cannot be easily done on a battleground of violence, as the history of the South itself shows. It is in recognition of this that men of both races have shown such an outstandingly impressive responsibility in recent days—last Tuesday, again today,

RIGHTS MUST BE OPPORTUNITIES

The bill that I am presenting to you will be known as a civil rights bill. But, in a larger sense, most of the program I am recommending is a civil rights program. Its object is to open the city of hope to all people of all races.

Because all Americans just must have the right to vote. And we are going to give them that right.

All Americans must have the privileges of citizenship regardless of race. And they are going to have those privileges of citizenship regardless of race.

But I would like to caution you and remind you that to exercise these privileges takes much more than just legal right. It requires a trained mind and a healthy body. It requires a decent home, and the chance to find a job, and the opportunity to escape from the clutches of poverty.

Of course, people cannot contribute to the Nation if they are never taught to read or write, if their bodies are stunted from hunger, if their sickness goes untended, if their life is spent in hopeless poverty just drawing a welfare check.

So we want to open the gates to opportunity. But we are also going to give all our people, black and white, the help that they need to walk through those gates.

THE PURPOSE OF THIS GOVERNMENT

My first job after college was as a teacher in Cotulla, Texas, in a small Mexican-American school. Few of them could speak English, and I couldn't speak much Spanish. My students were poor and they often came to class without breakfast, hungry. They knew even in their youth the pain of prejudice. They never seemed to know why people disliked them. But they knew it was so, because I saw it in their eyes. I often walked home late in the afternoon, after the classes were finished, wishing there was more that I could do. But all I knew was to teach them the little that I knew, hoping that it might help them against the hardships that lay ahead.

Somehow you never forget what poverty and hatred can do when you see its scars on the hopeful face of a young child.

I never thought then, in 1928, that I would be standing here in 1965. It never even occurred to me in my fondest dreams that I might have the chance to help the sons and daughters of those students and to help people like them all over this country.

But now I do have that chance—and I'll let you in on a secret—I mean to use it. And I hope that you will use it with me.

This is the richest and most powerful country which ever occupied the globe. The might of past empires is little compared to ours. But I do not want to be the President who built empires, or sought grandeur, or extended dominion.

I want to be the President who educated young children to the wonders of their world. I want to be the President who helped to feed the hungry and to prepare them to be taxpayers instead of taxeaters.

I want to be the President who helped the poor to find their own way and who protected the right of every citizen to vote in every election.

I want to be the President who helped to end hatred among his fellow men and who promoted love among the people of all races and all regions and all parties.

I want to be the President who helped to end war among the brothers of this earth.

And so at the request of your beloved Speaker and the Senator from Montana; the majority leader, the Senator from Illinois; the minority leader, Mr. McCulloch, and other Members of both parties, I came here tonight—not as President Roosevelt came down one time in person to veto a bonus bill, not as President Truman came down one time to urge the passage of a railroad bill—but I came down here to ask you to share this task with me and to share it with the people that we both work for. I want this to be the Congress, Republicans and Democrats alike, which did all these things for all these people.

Beyond this great chamber, out yonder in 50 States, are the people that we serve. Who can tell what deep and unspoken hopes are in their hearts tonight as they sit there and listen. We all can guess, from our own lives, how difficult they often find their own pursuit of happiness, how many problems each little family has. They look most of all to themselves for their futures. But I think that they also look to each of us.

Above the pyramid on the great seal of the United States it says—in Latin—"God has favored our undertaking."

God will not favor everything that we do. It is rather our duty to divine His will. But I cannot help believing that He truly understands and that He really favors the undertaking that we begin here tonight.

Source: Johnson, Lyndon B. "American Promise" speech to Joint Session of Congress, March 15, 1965. *Public Papers of the Presidents of the United States: Lyndon B. Johnson, 1965.* Volume I, entry 107, pp. 281–287. Washington, DC: Government Printing Office, 1966.

President Johnson Calls for Lowering Voting Age to Eighteen, 1968

On June 27, 1968, President Lyndon B. Johnson issued a formal call for Congress to pass a constitutional amendment to lower the voting age to eighteen from twenty-one. Johnson's stance was very much a product of the times: U.S. involvement in the Vietnam War was at its height in 1968, and millions of Americans argued that if young men between the ages of eighteen and twenty were old enough to be drafted and fight in Vietnam, they were old enough to have a voice at the ballot box. Johnson's request was not granted during his presidency, but a Twenty-Sixth Amendment to the Constitution officially lowering the voting age to eighteen was passed by Congress on March 23, 1971, and ratified on July 1, 1971. The official language of the amendment stated that "the right of citizens of the United States, who are eighteen years of age or older, to vote shall not be denied or abridged by the United States or by any State on account of age."

To the Congress of the United States:

The ballot box is the great anvil of democracy, where government is shaped by the will of the people. It is through the ballot that democracy draws its strength, renews its processes, and assures its survival.

Throughout the life of our Republic, no single, enduring question has so engaged generation after generation of Americans as this: Who among our citizens shall be eligible to participate as voters in determining the course of our public affairs?

On four occasions we have amended our Constitution to enlarge or to protect that participation. In recent years, Congress itself has been attentive to sheltering and assuring the free exercise of the right to vote.

Such a concern is altogether fitting. Under a government of, by and for the people, the right to vote is the most basic right of all. It is the right on which all others finally stand.

Such a right is not to be idly conferred or blindly withheld. But the stability of our Republic from the beginning has been served—well and faithfully—by the willingness of Americans to lay aside the constraints of custom and tradition and heed the appeals of reason and reality to welcome into the American electorate those of our citizens fitted by the precepts of our society's values to participate in the exercise of the ultimate right of citizenship.

At the inception of the Republic, the promise of the new Nation was strengthened because our forefathers cast aside tests of religion and property.

At midpassage, America's moral strength was fortified when the test of color was removed by the Fifteenth Amendment. The Voting Rights Act of 1965 has reinforced this principle for all time.

At the beginning of the modern era in this twentieth century, reason and reality wisely prevailed when the women of America—through the Nineteenth Amendment to the Constitution—were granted the equality of citizenship so long denied them.

In 1961, the Twenty-Third Amendment to the Constitution gave citizens of the Nation's capital the right to vote for President and Vice President.

Four years ago, the Twenty-Fourth Amendment struck down the tests of the poll tax which had for almost a century disenfranchised thousands of Americans.

ENLARGING THE AMERICAN FRANCHISE

In all these instances time has affirmed the wisdom and the right of these decisions to enlarge participation in the Nation's affairs. Time, too, has already affirmed the wisdom and justice of our continuing efforts in the last decade to perfect, protect and shelter the right of all citizens to vote and to put an end to the unconscionable techniques of studied discrimination.

Today, I believe it is time once more for Americans to measure the constraints of custom and tradition against the compelling force of reason and reality in regard to the test of age. The hour has come to take the next great step in the march of democracy. We should now extend the right to vote to more than ten million citizens unjustly denied that right. They are the young men and women of America between the ages of 18 and 21.

The practice of admitting young Americans to the electorate at the age of twenty-one has its roots in the dim and distant mists of medieval England—but it is a practice and limitation without roots in the American experience.

Throughout our history as a young Nation, young people have been called upon by the age of eighteen to shoulder family responsibilities and civic duties identical with their elders.

At the age of eighteen, young Americans are called upon to bear arms.

At the age of eighteen, young Americans are treated as adults before many courts of law and are held responsible for their acts.

The age of eighteen, far more than the age of twenty-one, has been and is the age of maturity in America—and never more than now.

Reason does not permit us to ignore any longer the reality that eighteen year old young Americans are prepared—by education, by experience, by exposure to public affairs of their own land and all the world—to assume and exercise the privilege of voting.

The essential stability of our system is not served, the moral integrity of our cause is not strengthened, the value we place on the worth of the individual is not honored by denying to more than ten million citizens—solely because of their age—the right to full participation in determining our country's course.

This denial of the right to vote limits our democracy. It diminishes every modern concept of citizenship.

The young people of America in this decade are far more ready, far better qualified, far more able to discharge the highest duty of citizenship than any generations of the past.

We know—and the young men and women know also—that this is so.

They are better educated than their counterparts of a generation ago. They graduate from high school and enter college in greater proportions. Already this group—although many have not yet completed their schooling—have a higher education level than the general electorate.

Mass communication and greater opportunities for travel expose them earlier and more frequently to the issues of the day than the young men and women of the 1940's, or even the 1950's.

The young men of today serve their Nation in uniform with the same devotion as their fathers and brothers of earlier days showed. But duties unknown a decade ago have summoned the devotion of young men and women alike, by the tens of thousands. Their participation in the Peace Corps, in VISTA, and in other community ventures has elevated our national life and brought new meaning to the concept of service.

For myself, I deeply believe that America can only prosper from the infusion of youthful energy, initiative, vigor and intelligence into our political processes.

We live in a world that is young and growing younger each year. Of all nations, none has more generously invested in preparing its young people for constructive citizenship and none has been more faithfully served by its young than has America.

Today, the young people of America are asking the opportunity to give of their talents and abilities, their energies and enthusiasms, to the greater tasks of their times. I believe their proper request can and must be properly answered by a national affirmation of our faith in them. For a nation without faith in its sons and daughters is a nation without faith in itself.

WHAT I PROPOSE

I accordingly propose that the Congress of the United States approve and submit for ratification of the legislatures of three-fourths of the States an amendment to the Constitution of the United States to provide, as follows:

"The right of any citizen of the United States to vote shall not be denied or abridged by the United States or by any State on account of age if a citizen is eighteen years of age or older."

In proposing submission of such an amendment I am mindful that:

—The State of Georgia since 1943, and the State of Kentucky, since 1955, have permitted eighteen year old residents to vote.

—The two new States of Alaska and Hawaii have permitted nineteen and twenty year old residents, respectively, to vote.

—The first proposal for such an amendment was advanced in 1942 by Senator Arthur Vandenberg.

—President Dwight D. Eisenhower, in his 1954 State of the Union Address, urged an Amendment to lower the voting age to eighteen.

—In the 90th Congress, more than fifty proposed Constitutional Amendments to extend voting rights to eighteen year old citizens have been introduced, and many of these measures have broad bi-partisan support.

The concept has been tried and tested. Its merit has been established. Its rightness is now beyond dispute.

FULL PARTICIPATION IN OUR AMERICAN DEMOCRACY

The time has come to grant our youth what we ask of them but still deny to them—full and responsible participation in our American democracy.

In this year of national decision, as Americans in every State prepare to choose their leadership for the decisive and fateful years before us, the Congress has a rare opportunity through the submission of this amendment to signify to our young people that they are respected, that they are trusted, that their commitment to America is honored and that the day is soon to come when they are to be participants, not spectators, in the adventure of self-government.

Every time before, when America has extended the vote to citizens whose hour has come, new vitality has been infused into the lifestream of the Nation, and America has emerged the richer.

Now the hour has come again to take another step in Democracy's great journey.

LYNDON B. JOHNSON
The White House
June 27, 1968

Source: Johnson, Lyndon B. "Special Message to Congress: To Vote at Eighteen—Democracy Fulfilled and Enriched." *Public Papers of the Presidents of the United States: Lyndon B. Johnson, 1968. Book I: January 1 to June 30.* Washington, DC: Government Printing Office, 1969.

Top Civil Rights Official Condemns a Nixon Administration Scheme to Roll Back Voting Rights, 1969

When Republican nominee Richard M. Nixon won the 1968 presidential election over Democrat Hubert Humphrey, many observers credited his so-called Southern strategy—a conscious decision to court white conservative voters in the American South—as central to his victory. So when Nixon was inaugurated in January 1969, some civil rights advocates expressed anxiety about the 1965 Voting Rights Act (VRA), several provisions of which were set to expire in August 1970 unless they were renewed. They emphasized that while the VRA had opened long-locked gates to political participation for African Americans, it would take a long time for historical patterns of voting suppression to be wholly eradicated. As journalist Ari Berman noted in his book Give Us the Ballot *(2015, 76), "the number of black registered voters had doubled in the seven Southern states covered under Section 5 [from 1965 to 1969], and the number of black elected officials had increased from sixty-five to four hundred across the South. But there were still no black members of Congress or statewide officials from the Southern states, and the black voter registration rate lagged twenty-four points behind whites. Jurisdictions throughout the South had changed their electoral procedures, making it harder for black candidates to run for and win elected office."*

In June 1969, the Nixon administration unveiled several proposed changes to the VRA, all of which enjoyed broad support from conservative white Southern lawmakers. The administration proposed to completely eliminate Section 5, which forced states with a history of black voter suppression to get approval from federal authorities before making any voting-related changes, and extend VRA's reach nationwide—a change that would overwhelm the resources of U.S. Department of Justice's Civil Rights division.

A special subcommittee of the House Judiciary Committee immediately held hearings to study the Nixon White House proposal. Many of the committee members expressed deep alarm about the proposed changes to Attorney General John Mitchell, who testified on behalf of the administration. Subcommittee chairman Emanuel Celler (D-New York), for example, told Mitchell that "Your amendment gives the appearance of value and merit but actually will disappoint and deceive. . . . Its effect would turn the bill of the Voting Rights Act of 1965 into smoke and ashes" by freeing Southern states to return to their old voter suppression ways. Another prominent critic was Father Theodore Hesburgh, president of the University of Notre Dame (from 1952 to 1987) and chairman of the U.S. Civil Rights Commission (1969 to 1972). In the following letter to Mitchell that was included in the subcommittee hearings, Hesburgh condemned the Nixon administration's attitude toward the Voting Rights Act and urged it to support a clean reauthorization of all of its provisions (in 1972, Hesburgh was dismissed from the commission because of his repeated clashes with the Nixon White House over civil rights issues).

Hon. JOHN N. MITCHELL,
Attorney General,
Washington, D.C.

DEAR MR. ATTORNEY GENERAL: I am writing to express my deep concern about the amendments to the Voting Rights Act which you proposed to the Subcommittee of the House Judiciary Committee on Thursday, June 26, 1969. The Commission staff is preparing a more detailed analysis which will be provided to you. Your fourth proposal—to eliminate existing protection against manipulative changes in voting laws—is in no sense an advance in protection of the voting rights of American citizens. It is a distinct retreat. It is an open invitation to those States which denied the vote to minority citizens in the past to resume doing so in the future, through insertion of disingenuous technicalities and changes in their election laws.

Under the present act, they cannot make such changes without prior approval of the United States District Court for the District of Columbia or of the Justice Department. Even so, at least one municipality in Mississippi's election last month changed election procedures without approval and in violation of the law, a defiance which your statement recognizes has not been unusual. Your proposed alternative would turn back the clock to 1957, relying on the slow process of litigation to try to keep up with rapidly enacted changes in the laws. It would mean that the Department of Justice would not have notice of such changes before they went into effect. The inadequacy of litigation as the sole technique of protecting the right to vote was recognized by Congress when it passed the

Voting Rights Act of 1965. Now is not the time to gut one of that act's key provisions.

I am also disturbed by your fifth proposal, which would add to the United States Government yet another new Federal commission, this one called a "national advisory commission" to concern itself with voting discrimination and corrupt practices relating to voting. You State that this new agency would be set up to study the effects which literacy tests have on minority groups, to study the problem of election frauds, and to report to Congress its findings and recommendations for any new legislation pertaining to the right to vote.

I am unable to understand what purpose such a new commission would serve that is not already within the authority granted by the Congress to the United States Commission on Civil Rights. The Commission on Civil Rights is, as you know, a bipartisan, independent agency, proposed by President Eisenhower and Attorney General Brownell in 1956 and established by Congress in 1957. Attorney General Brownell said at that time: "When there are charges that by one means or another the Vote is being denied, we must find out all of the facts—the extent, the methods, the result * * *. The study should be objective and free from partisanship."

Under its statute as amended, the Commission on Civil Rights has been directed to: "investigate allegations, made in writing and under oath or affirmation, that citizens of the United States are unlawfully being accorded or denied the right to vote, or to have their votes properly counted, in any election of presidential electors, Members of the United States Senate, or of the House of Representatives, as a result of any patterns or practice of fraud or discrimination in the conduct of such election * * *" 78 Stat. 251, 42 U.S.C. § 1975c (a) (5).

Thus the Commission on Civil Rights has an ample mandate to investigate fraud in such elections, as well as to: "investigate allegations in writing and under oath or affirmation that certain citizens of the United States are being deprived of their right to vote and have that vote counted by reason of their color, race, religion, or national origin * * *" 71 Stat. 635, as amended, 42 U.S.C. § 1977c.(a)(1).

The Commission has been vigorous over the years in investigating denials of the franchise and fraudulent election processes. Indeed, it was work by this Commission which helped lay the factual base for the Civil Rights Acts of 1960 and 1964 as well as the 1965 Voting Rights Act. Our investigations have not been confined to cases of election fraud which involve discrimination against members of minority groups, though we have consistently found that the most flagrant frauds and abuses were directed against minorities.

Our investigations have not flagged. You have been provided a copy of a recent staff memorandum on the May 1969 elections in Mississippi. The Commission's numerous hearings and reports are filled with the results of our research on voting. Our publications which deal especially with voting rights include: Political Participation (1968); The Voting Rights Act of 1965: The First Months (1965); Voting in Mississippi (1965); Voting (1961); Report of the Commission (1959).

The Commission's budget proposal for fiscal year 1970 already requests funds for a study of political participation of minority groups outside the South. The Commission on Civil Rights, as you know, has recommended abolition of literacy requirements for voting throughout the nation. I gather from your testimony that you agree. Certainly, however, this recommendation would not prevent the Commission from re-examining that question thoroughly and with an Open mind if Congress so desires.

It is generally conceded that the Commission on Civil Rights has developed great expertise in investigating complaints of violations of voting rights and in recommending steps for their correction. Indeed, the document on voting complaints outside the states covered by the 1965 Act, which you submitted for the record of the Subcommittee, was a staff paper of this Commission. It would be totally incongruous to establish a new body, staff it, and fund it in order to duplicate the tasks which the Commission on Civil Rights was established under President Eisenhower to perform and continues to perform.

President Nixon on January 30 spoke of the need for: "cutting expenditures, increasing efficiency in Government operations, abolishing unnecessary agencies and eliminating duplication of efforts."

At a time when funds for all domestic programs are severely limited, and when the President in April asked his Advisory Council on Executive Organization to look for ways to eliminate duplication and waste, it would make no sense to spend millions of dollars, lose valuable start-up and staffing time, and add still another agency to the federal bureaucracy to do a job that, to the extent our funds permit, is already being done. If more effort needs to be put forth, the Commission on Civil Rights stands ready to use its skilled staff and years of experience, to the extent Congress will provide the money. This nation should not waste the limited domestic funds which are available. I hope you will withdraw the proposal.

Sincerely yours,

THEODORE M. HESBURGH, Chairman.

Source: Letter from Theodore M. Hesburgh, Chairman, U.S. Civil Rights Commission to U.S. Attorney General John Mitchel. Voting Rights Act extension: Hearings before Subcommittee no. 5 . . . 91-1, on H.R. 4249, H.R. 5538, and similar proposals . . . May 14, 15, June 19, 26, July 1, 1969, serial no. 3, pp. 301–302.

President Nixon Signs the Voting Rights Act Amendments, 1970

When major provisions of the landmark Voting Rights Act (VRA) of 1965 came up for renewal in 1970, the Nixon administration pushed a package of legislative "reforms" to the act that alarmed and angered voting rights advocates. It proposed, for example, to completely eliminate Section 5 of the VRA, the linchpin of the law's goal of stopping Southern states from engaging in black voter suppression. Section 5 forced states with particularly virulent histories of black disenfranchisement to gain approval from federal authorities—charged with protecting voting rights enshrined in the Fourteenth and Fifteenth Amendments—before making any changes to their voting laws or procedures. The Nixon White House also wanted to make the VRA a truly national law rather than one focused primarily on former Jim Crow Southern states. This latter proposal sounded idealistic on the surface, but civil rights leaders and their allies in Congress charged that such a change would so overwhelm the resources of the U.S. Department of Justice that it would not be able to effectively monitor disenfranchisement efforts in the South. The fact that Nixon's bill also included a national ban on literacy tests for voting and a call for a federal commission to investigate voter discrimination did not assuage concerns that the president's proposed terms for VRA renewal would dramatically roll back black voter protections.

For a brief period of time, it appeared that Nixon's bill, which was supported by white conservative lawmakers across the South (both Democrat and Republican), might actually prevail. On December 12, 1969, the House of Representatives narrowly passed the administration's legislation. But the Senate refused to go along. A bipartisan coalition led by Republican Hugh Scott of Pennsylvania instead passed a version that preserved Section 5 and other key provisions of the original law. It also strengthened the 1965 VRA by lowering the voting age to eighteen in state and federal elections, banning literacy tests across the country, and easing voting residency requirements. The Senate version subsequently sailed through the House to land on Nixon's desk.

Nixon felt considerable pressure from his conservative white base to veto the bill, but he ultimately felt that the political price he might pay for such a move was too great a risk. So on June 22, 1970, he signed the legislation into law. In his signing remarks, he expressed misgivings about the legality of the provision lowering the voting age but otherwise tried to frame the passage of the VRA amendments as a positive for both the nation and his administration. As it turned out, Nixon was right about the provision lowering the voting age—later that year the U.S. Supreme Court ruled in Oregon v. Mitchell *that Congress could only set voting ages for federal elections, not local or state elections. That ruling prompted the passage and ratification of the Twenty-Sixth Amendment to the Constitution, which lowered the voting age to eighteen for all elections, in 1971.*

June 22, 1970

On Wednesday, Congress completed action on a bill extending and amending the Voting Rights Act of 1965, and sent it to me for signature. As passed, the bill contained a "rider" which I believe to be unconstitutional: a provision lowering the voting age to 18 in Federal, State, and local elections. Although I strongly favor the 18-year-old vote, I believe—along with most of the Nation's leading constitutional scholars—that Congress has no power to enact it by simple statute, but rather it requires a constitutional amendment.

Despite my misgivings about the constitutionality of this one provision, I have today signed the bill. I have directed the Attorney General to cooperate fully expediting a swift court test of the constitutionality of the 18-year-old provision.

An early test is essential because of the confusion and uncertainty surrounding an act of doubtful constitutionality that purports to extend the franchise. Until this uncertainty is resolved, any elections—including primary elections even local referenda on such questions school bond issues—could have their results clouded by legal doubt.

If I were to veto, I would have to veto the entire bill—voting rights and all. If the courts hold the voting-age provisions unconstitutional, however, only that one section of the act will be affected. Because the basic provisions of this act are of great importance, therefore, I am giving it my approval and leaving the decision on the disputed provision to what I hope will be a swift resolution by the courts.

The Voting Rights Act of 1965 has opened participation in the political process. Although this bill does not include all of the administration's recommendations, it does incorporate improvements which extend its reach still further, suspending literacy tests nationwide and also putting an end to the present welter of State residency requirements for voting for President and Vice President. Now, for the first time, citizens who move between elections may vote without long residency requirements.

In the 5 years since its enactment, close to I million Negroes have been registered to vote for the first time and more than 400 Negro officials have been elected to local and State offices. These are more than election statistics; they are statistics of hope and dramatic evidence that the American system works. They stand as an answer to those who claim that there is no recourse except to the streets.

The time has also come to give 18-year olds the vote, as I have long urged. The way to do this is by amending the Constitution. Because of the likelihood that the 18-year-old vote provision of this law will not survive its court test, the constitutional amendment pending before the Congress should go forward to the States for ratification now.

I therefore call upon the Congress to act now upon the constitutional amendment to avoid undue delay in its approval by the States should this provision of the new law be held unconstitutional.

Source: Nixon, Richard M. Statement on Signing the Voting Rights Act Amendments of 1970. June 22, 1970. *Public Papers of the Presidents of the United States: Richard M. Nixon, 1970.* Washington, DC: Government Printing Office, 1971.

4

A Period of (Relative) Stability and Incremental Expansion of Voting Rights: 1970–2000

Following the 1971 ratification of the Twenty-Sixth Amendment, which lowered the voting age to eighteen, the political and legal maneuvering over voting rights and restrictions and the conduct of elections headed back to the courts, as they have done so often over the course of American history. Some of the most notable clashes over the next several years concerned the rights of demographically smaller groups of Americans, such as the homeless. In most states, people seeking to register to vote are required to have a permanent address. The address is used to not only determine where you vote in states that have precinct-based voting but also to determine what political and geographic area you live in for representation at the local, state, and federal level. For transient and homeless populations, the requirement for a permanent address limits their ability to register and vote.

VOTING ASSISTANCE FOR ARMED FORCES, THE HOMELESS, AND PEOPLE WITH DISABILITIES

Homelessness became a potent political issue in the 1980s, driven by apparent growth in the sheer number of homeless Americans due to economic downturns and efforts by corporations and industries to downsize their workforces. When the population of homeless citizens began to grow, however, many states came to the realization that their laws did not adequately address how citizens who did not have a home would register to vote. As with other marginalized groups, the integration of homeless citizens into the franchise was facilitated by a series of State Supreme, U.S. District, and U.S. Supreme Court decisions, including *Pitts v. Black* (1984), *Collier v. Menzel* (1985), *Walters v. Weed* (1988), *Coalition for the Homeless v. Jensen* (1992), among others. The decisions resulting from these cases permit homeless individuals to list the place where they sleep as their residence even if the location is a nontraditional home, register to vote by swearing under oath that they lack a permanent home, use their prior residence for registration if they have not found a new residence, use the address of a shelter, and ensure that homeless citizens are not subject to more extensive questioning than others who register to vote. Meanwhile, people with disabilities who had long struggled to overcome physical barriers to polling places finally received relief with the passage of the Voting Accessiblity for the Elderly and Handicapped Act of 1984 and the 1990 Americans with Disabilities Act.

Addressing the ability of displaced citizens to register and vote continued to be a priority for the federal government, particularly as it related to military personnel, their families, and overseas citizens. The Federal Voting Assistance Program (FVAP) is a voter assistance and education program within the Department of Defense. FVAP works to ensure that military personnel and other citizens who are overseas are aware of their right to vote and have the tools necessary to do so and administers the Uniformed and Overseas Citizens Absentee Voting Act (UOCAVA). The Uniformed and Overseas Citizens Absentee Voting Act (UOCAVA) was enacted by Congress in 1986 with the express purpose of requiring states and territories to allow certain groups of citizens to register and vote absentee in federal elections. Individuals who are covered by UOCAVA are members of the United States armed forces and merchant marine; their eligible family members; and American citizens residing outside of the United States. One of the key provisions of UOCAVA was the Federal Post Card Application, which allows service members and overseas citizens to simultaneously register to vote and request an absentee ballot. UOCAVA also provides for a "back-up ballot" for federal offices, the Federal Write-In Absentee Ballot, which can be used by voters who are covered by the act if they submitted their absentee ballot application on time but did not receive their regular ballot. The 2009 Military and Overseas Voter Empowerment Act (MOVE) amended UOCAVA by providing more protections for citizens who are covered by UOCAVA. As an example, the MOVE Act requires states to send absentee ballots to UOCAVA voters at least forty-five days before federal elections.

REPRESENTATION AND ELECTION REFORM

Although the Supreme Court had repeatedly ruled that racial gerrymanders that dilute the voting strength of minority voters were unconstitutional, the way voters are divided for political representation continued to matter as the court had yet to consider if political gerrymanders were unconstitutional. In 1985, a group of Democrats challenged Indiana's state apportionment strategy. They argued that the strategy resulted in partisan gerrymanders, which diluted their votes and violated their right to equal protection as outlined in the Fourteenth Amendment to the U.S. Constitution. The court ruled in *Davis v. Bandemer* (1986) that Indiana's redistricting plan did not violate the equal protection clause of the Fourteenth Amendment. Specifically, while the plan may have had discriminatory effects, the effect was not "sufficiently adverse." The issue of partisan gerrymandering remains one of great importance as cases are continually brought before the court in which the argument is made that constitutionally protected rights to political representation and voting rights are being violated or otherwise compromised. In the last decade, many of these legal challenges have resulted in the redistricting plan being struck down as unconstitutional.

Critics of the two-stage registration and voting process in the United States assert that it makes voting costlier and more cumbersome than in other democracies and contributes to levels of turnout that are generally lower than in other democracies. In essence, when the cost of voting outweighs the benefits, voters abstain. When the benefits outweigh the costs, voters participate. Although costs exist for all voters, the costs are not distributed equally across all racial, ethnic, and socioeconomic groups. Costs can be correlated with not only the administrative procedures that are associated with registration and voting but also the information resources associated with registration and casting a ballot. Given this, many of the approaches to address challenges in voting have focused on lowering the costs of voting. Efforts to lower the cost or make registration and voting more accessible and convenient have been adopted not only by the federal government but also by some individual states.

Many of the costs associated with registration and voting have been addressed by federal legislation and/or legal decisions made by the Supreme Court of the United States. As an example, the Civil Rights Act (1964) invalidated the use of different voter registration qualifications for potential voters. The Voting Rights Act (1965) made it illegal to use devices or tests to determine the eligibility of voters. While these two pieces of legislation had the express purpose of increasing accesses to political participation and public spaces for African Americans, more recent federal legislation has centered on reducing the cost of participation for all voters and improving the administration of elections in the United States. The 1993 National Voter Registration Act (NVRA) created new opportunities for citizens to register to vote by requiring public agencies to provide potential voters with voter registration forms. The NVRA requires states without Election Day registration policies in place to establish mail-in and agency-based programs and eliminate the practice of removing registrants from the registration rolls solely because they do not vote.

One provision of the NVRA requires "each state [to] include a voter registration application form for election for Federal office as part of an application for state motor vehicle driver's license." It is from this provision that the NVRA gets its nickname "Motor Voter." Because of this provision, when citizens obtain a new license or renew their license at a driver licensing office, they are offered the opportunity to register to vote. In some states, the registration is automatically transmitted from the licensing office. In others, the voter will be provided a voter registration form that they must complete and submit. Through agency-based registration, the goal of motor voter was to increase voter turnout and reduce the participation gap that existed between economically disadvantaged voters and those with more financial resources. Following the implementation of the NVRA, the number of registered voters across the nation increased, as did the number of low-income citizens who were registered to vote. The gains in registration, however, often did not translate into an actual increase in voter turnout.

OREGON PIONEERS NEW VOTING REFORMS

As the federal government was working to ease the burden of voting for citizens, states experimented with new and innovative ways to reduce the cost of voting for citizens. One such innovation was all-mail elections. Although states had provisions that permitted select eligible voters to vote by mail since before the Civil War, vote by mail was not frequently used by citizens to cast ballots. In 1998, however, Oregon became the first state to conduct all of their elections by mail, after years of incremental progress toward that goal.

In 1981, the Oregon State Legislature approved a test of vote by mail for local elections. By 1987, vote by mail for local and special elections was made permanent. In June 1993, the first statewide special election Oregon conducted by mail resulted in 39 percent voter turnout. In 1995, the state legislature passed a proposal to expand vote by mail to primary and general elections. The bill, however, was vetoed by the governor. Two years later a similar bill was approved by the House of Representatives but died in the Senate. As all-mail elections continued to be used in the state to conduct elections, the use of permanent absentee voting by citizens also increased. In 1998, Oregon became the first state to have more ballots cast by mail than in person on Election Day. In June 1998 those who supported the expansion of vote by mail to include primary and general elections used the initiative process to put the issue on the November ballot. In November 1998, voters decided to expand vote by mail to primary and general elections (69.39% to 30.61%). Other examples of state innovations to expand access include Election Day Registration, same day registration, early (in person) voting, "no excuse" absentee voting, and portable voter registration.

Even as efforts were being made to expand access to the vote and reduce the cost for votes, some American citizens still did not have full citizenship or enfranchisement rights. In 1921 Congress passed the Hawaiian Homes Commission Act (HHCA) to facilitate the rehabilitation of native Hawaiians. Native Hawaiians were defined as "a descendant of not less than one-half part of the blood of the races inhabiting the Hawaiian Islands, previous to 1778" and "Hawaiians"—a larger class that includes "native Hawaiians"—as descendants of the peoples inhabiting the Hawaiian Islands in 1778. When Hawaii became a state in 1959, Hawaii was granted title to public lands as long as those lands, and the proceeds and incomes generated by the lands were held as a public trust and used for a variety of reasons, including improving the lives of native Hawaiians. In 1978, Hawaii established the Office of Hawaiian Affairs (OHA). The agency was to be independent of other branches of the state government and responsible for programs belonging to native Hawaiians. Importantly, the OHA was responsible for the administration of the lands that were given to Hawaii at the time of statehood. The OHA was governed by a board of trustees. The trustees were required by state statute to be elected by Hawaiians. If a citizen was not Hawaiian as defined by the 1778 definition and they applied to vote in the election of OHA trustees, their application was denied. In 1996 Harold F. Rice, a citizen of Hawaii who was not Hawaiian as defined by the 1778 statue, filed a suit arguing that by being excluded from the election, his Fourteenth and Fifteenth Amendment rights were being violated. In *Rice v. Cayetano* (2000), the U.S. Supreme Court ruled that Hawaii's denial of Rice's right to vote in OHA trustee elections is a violation of the Fifteenth Amendment because the state created a race-based qualification for voting.

SOURCES

Downs, Anthony. *An Economic Theory of Democracy*. New York: Harper and Row Publishers, 1957.

Federal Election Commission. "Implementing the National Voter Registration Act: A Report to State and Local Election Officials on Problems and Solutions Discovered 1995–1996." 1998. Accessed January 4, 2019. https://www.eac.gov/assets/1/28/Implementing%20the%20NVRA--Report%20to%20State%20and%20Local%20Election%20Of.pdf.

Highton, Benjamin. "Easy Registration and Voter Turnout." *The Journal of Politics*, 59, no. 7 (1997): 565–575.

Knack, Stephen. "Drivers Wanted: Motor Voter and the Election of 1996." *PS: Political Science and Politics*, 32, no. 2 (1999): 237–243.

Li, Michael, Thomas Wolf, and Annie Lo. "The State of Redistricting Litigation." *The Brennan Center for Justice at New York University School of Law*. June 17, 2019. Last modified January 26, 2019. https://www.brennancenter.org/blog/state-redistricting-litigation.

National Coalition for the Homeless. "Court Decisions on Homeless People's Voting Rights." Last modified Auburn 10, 2012. http://www.nationalhomeless.org/projects/vote/court.html.

Oregon Secretary of State. "Oregon Vote-by-Mail." Accessed January 31, 2019. https://sos.oregon.gov/elections/Documents/statistics/vote-by-mail-timeline.pdf.

Smith, Edward J. "Disenfranchisement of Homeless Persons." *Washington University Journal of Urban and Contemporary Law*, 31 (1987): 225–239.

United States Department of Justice. "The Uniformed and Overseas Citizen Absentee Voting Act." Last modified February 26, 2018. https://www.justice.gov/crt/uniformed-and-overseas-citizens-absentee-voting-act.

PRIMARY DOCUMENTS

The Twenty-Sixth Amendment Lowers the Voting Age to Eighteen, 1971

The Fourteenth Amendment to the United States Constitution, enacted in 1868, established a right to vote for the "male inhabitants of [each] state, being twenty-one years of age, and citizens of the United States." States still had the option of lowering the voting age, but none chose to do so until 1943, when Georgia lowered its voting age to eighteen for local and state elections. That decision was spurred to a large degree by Congress's vote (with encouragement from President Franklin D. Roosevelt) in November 1942 to lower the military draft age from twenty-one to eighteen.

As American military involvement in Vietnam deepened in the 1960s—and tens of thousands of eighteen-, nineteen-, and twenty-year-old draftees were sent there to fight—many Americans came to feel that if young American men were "old enough to fight," they were also "old enough to vote." In 1970, the Supreme Court narrowly ruled in Oregon v. Mitchell *that Congress could only lower the voting age in federal elections, not state or local elections. This did not sit well with millions of Americans who felt that the voting age should be lowered for all elections. Sensitive to the direction of the political winds that were blowing over this issue, the U.S. Congress quickly proposed a new amendment to the Constitution that would lower the voting age to eighteen for all elections—local, state, and federal. This amendment—the twenty-sixth addition to the Constitution in that document's history—passed Congress on March 23, 1971, and was ratified a little more than three months later, on July 1, 1971.*

Section 1

The right of citizens of the United States, who are eighteen years of age or older, to vote shall not be denied or abridged by the United States or by any State on account of age.

Section 2

The Congress shall have power to enforce this article by appropriate legislation.

Source: Amendment XXVI to the U.S. Constitution. National Archives.

Shirley Chisholm's Presidential Announcement Speech, 1972

Shirley Chisholm (1924–2005) was a pioneering American politician and educator. In 1968 she became the first black woman ever elected to the U.S. Congress (representing a district in New York City), and four years later she made history by becoming both the first woman and the first African American to announce her candidacy for the Democratic Party's presidential nomination. By all accounts Chisholm knew that she had virtually no chance of winning the party's nomination (it eventually went to South Dakota Senator George McGovern), but she saw her campaign as an opportunity to publicize issues that mattered to her, including racial injustice and gender discrimination. Following are excerpts from the speech she gave announcing her candidacy.

I stand before you today as a candidate for the Democratic nomination for the presidency of the United States of America. I am not the candidate of black America, although I am black and proud. I am not the candidate of the women's movement of this country, although I am a woman and I'm equally proud of that. I am not the candidate of any political policies or fatcats or special interests. I stand here now, without endorsements from many big name politicians or celebrities or any other kind of prop, I do not intend to offer you the tired clichés that have too long been an accepted part of our political life. I am the candidate of the people of America. Fellow Americans, we have looked in vain to the Nixon administration for the courage, the spirit, the character, and the words to lift us, to bring out the best in us, to rekindle in each of us the faith of the American dream. Yet all that we have received in return is just another smooth exercise in political manipulation, deceit and deception, callousness and indifference to our individual problems, and the disgusting playing of divisive politics, pitting the young against the old, labor against management, North against South, blacks against whites. The abiding concern of this administration has been one of political expediency rather than the needs of man's nature. The president has broken his promises to us, and has therefore lost his claim to our trust and confidence in him.

I cannot believe—[applause] I cannot believe that this administration would ever have been elected four years ago if we had known then what we know today. What we are entering—we are entering a new era, in which we must, as Americans, demand stature and size from our national leadership—leadership which is fresh, leadership which is open, and leadership which is receptive to the problems of all Americans. I have faith in the American people. I believe that we are smart enough to correct our mistakes. I believe that we are intelligent enough to recognize the talent, energy, and dedication that all Americans, including women and minorities, have to offer. I know from my travels to the cities and the small towns of America that we have vast potential which can and must be put to constructive use in getting this great nation together. I know that millions of Americans from all walks of life agree with me, that leadership does not mean putting the air to the ground, to follow public opinion, but to have the vision of what is necessary, and the courage to make it possible. Americans all over are demanding a new sensibility, a new philosophy of government from Washington. Instead of sending spies to snoop on participants at Earth Day, I would welcome the efforts of concerned citizens of all ages to stop the abuse of our environment. Instead of watching a football game on television while young people beg for the attention of their president concerning our actions abroad, I would encourage them to speak out, organize for peaceful change, and vote in November. Instead of blocking efforts to control the huge amounts of money given political candidates by the rich and the powerful, I would provide certain limits on such amounts, and encourage all the people of this nation to contribute small sums to the candidates of their choice. Instead of calculating the political costs, this or that policy, and [inaudible] in favor of this or that group, depending on whether that group voted for me in 1968, I would remind all

Americans at this hour of the words of Abraham Lincoln, "a house divided cannot stand." We Americans are all fellow countrymen. One day confronting the judgment of history in our country, we are all God's children, and the will of each of us is as precious as the will of the most powerful general or corporate millionaire.

And my presence before you now symbolizes a new era in American political history. I've always earnestly believed the great potential of America. Our constitutional democracy will soon celebrate its 200th anniversary, effective testimony to the longevity of our cherished Constitution and its unique Bill of Rights which continuously give to the world an inspirational message of freedom and liberty. . . . I do not believe that in 1972 the great majority of Americans will continue to harbor such narrow and petty prejudices. I am convinced that the American people are in a mood to discard the politics and political personalities of the past. I believe that they will show in 1972, and thereafter, that they intend to make independent judgments on the merits of a particular candidate, based on that candidate's intelligence, character, physical ability, competence, integrity, and honesty. It is, I feel, the duty of responsible leaders in this country to encourage and maximize, not to dismiss and minimize, such judgement . . . Our will can create a new America in 1972, one where there's freedom from violence and war at home and abroad. Where there's freedom from poverty and discrimination. Where there exists at least a feeling that we are making progress and ensuring for everyone medical care and employment and decent housing. Where we more decisively clean up our streets, our water, and our air. We work together, black and white, to rebuild our neighborhoods and to make our city twice as attractive and efficient and, fundamentally, where we live in the confidence that every man and every woman in America has at long last the opportunity to become all that he was created of being such as his ability.

In conclusion, all of you who share this vision, from New York to California, from Wisconsin to Florida, our brothers and sisters on the road to national unity and a new America. [applause] Those of you who were locked outside of the convention hall in 1968, those of you who can now vote for the first time, those of you who agree with me that the institutions of this country belong to all of the people who inhabit it, those of you who have been neglected, left out, ignored, forgotten, or shunned aside for whatever reason, give me your help at this hour. Join me in an effort to reshape our society and regain control of our destiny as we go down the Chisholm trail of 1972. [applause]

Reporter: You represent a trend for more women and specifically black women to get involved with politics and go after elected office in this country.

Chisholm: Yes I specifically recommend, do I recommend a trend for more women and specifically black women to enter in to politics . . .

Reporter: Elected office.

Chisholm: Elected office. Yes I definitely am feeling and recognizing that as a result of over 20 years in political life, only emerging 8 years ago publicly, there is a great need for more women in the political arena. I happen to believe that there's certain aspects of legislation that probably would be given much more attention if we had more women's voices in the halls of the legislatures on the city, state, and national level. And I will—legislation that pertains to daycare centers, education, social services, mental services—the kind of legislation that has to do with the conservation and preservation of the most important resources that any nation has, and that is its human resources.

Source: Chisholm, Shirley. Announcement of 1972 presidential candidacy. January 25, 1972. Accessed February 4, 2019. https://www.commonlit.org/en/texts/shirley-chisholm-s-presidential-announcement-speech-transcript.

President Carter Calls for Same-Day Voter Registration and Other Election Reforms, 1977

On March 22, 1977, President Jimmy Carter formally urged Congress to pass legislation making several important changes to America's voting laws. The proposal that attracted the most attention was one for national same-day voter registration for federal elections, but Carter lobbied for several other reforms as well, such as abolishment of the Electoral College in favor of electing the president by national popular vote.

Several of Carter's proposed reforms, which he framed as a necessary response to declining election participation, initially received bipartisan support. This included same-day registration, which was the president's highest priority. But conservative groups pressed the Republicans to reconsider on that issue, warning that most of the increase in voters that would result from the passage of a same-day registration law would benefit the president's own Democratic Party. The Republican National Committee subsequently declared that same-day registration would "endanger the integrity of the franchise and open American elections to serious threat of fraud," and Republicans across Congress announced their opposition. Once GOP support for his reform package collapsed, Carter's proposal went nowhere.

Following are excerpts from Carter's address to Congress.

The Vice President and I have developed these proposals in order to meet our commitment to the American people to work toward an electoral process which is open to the participation of all our citizens, which meets high ethical standards, and which operates in an efficient and responsive manner. I know that you in the Congress share these goals, and I applaud your efforts which are already underway to achieve them.

Voter Registration

My first proposal, and the one on which I am proposing a specific bill to the Congress, is designed to open up our system of voter registration.

The basis of our democratic system is the right of every eligible citizen to vote. In the 200 years of its history, this Nation has greatly expanded the opportunity to vote to wider and wider groups of citizens.

Despite this progress, we have in recent years witnessed a disturbing trend toward lower and lower levels of voting by our citizens. I am deeply concerned that our country ranks behind at least twenty other democracies in its level of voter participation.

Our country's disappointing record cannot be remedied by any one solution or any single piece of legislation. But, millions of Americans are prevented or discouraged from voting in every election by antiquated and overly restrictive voter registration laws. We can take one immediate step toward solving this serious problem by removing antiquated and unnecessary obstacles which prevent voters from participating in the electoral process.

I am proposing to remove the unnecessary and unfair barriers by creating a method of universal voter registration. Under the legislation I will propose to the Congress, citizens qualified to vote under state laws could go to their polling places on the day of a Federal election and register there after proving their eligibility. The states would 'be encouraged to adopt a similar system of registration for state and local elections.

Under this plan, state and local officials will continue to administer voter registration and elections, and will still register as many voters as possible prior to election day in the usual manner, in order to avoid congestion at the polls.

We would offer financial assistance to the states to employ additional registrars and to help pay the cost of registration by mail, traveling registrars, or any other pre-election day registration efforts the state might choose.

State and local officials would also have the option of using the money they receive under the plan to modernize what are often outmoded and poorly equipped systems of election administration. A new office within the Federal Election Commission would distribute the Federal funds and oversee the program.

I also propose that we enact very strong safeguards to protect the integrity of the election process. Willful fraud in registering to vote should bear the strong criminal penalties of five years imprisonment and a $10,000 fine already found in the Voting Rights Act. Any person who takes part in a scheme to falsely identify or register voters should be similarly punished, and multiple convictions should lead to even stiffer penalties. The government should seek injunctive relief in Federal court to stop any patterns of fraudulent activity which might arise.

States should be allowed to require all persons registering at the polls to prove their identity and place of residence by approved forms of identification. All registrants should he informed of the state's qualifications for voting and be required to sign a statement, under oath and criminal penalty, that they meet those qualifications.

While these safeguards are important and necessary, I am optimistic that they will rarely be tested and the record suggests that they will rarely be needed.

This system of election-day registration is already employed in a number of states, and the record shows that it has usually increased voter participation without increasing voter fraud. Four out of five states with the highest voter turnout rates in the 1976 election permitted citizens to register and vote on election day.

Campaign Financing

My second recommendation deals with the way in which we pay the costs of Congressional campaigns.

In 1974, Congress took the historic step of establishing a system of public financing for Presidential primary and general elections. I urge the Congress to extend this important reform to campaigns for both the House and the Senate.

The record of the first publicly financed Presidential campaign has demonstrated that public financing is workable and widely accepted by the American people. Public financing of candidates not only minimizes even the appearance of obligation to special interest contributors, but also provides an opportunity for qualified persons who lack funds to seek public office. It would be a tragic irony if the 1974 law, which reduced the pressure special interests could place on Presidential candidates, increased the pressures on candidates for Congress as the large contributors look for new means of gaining influence with their political funds.

The method we select should allow each American the option of deciding whether to participate in public funding. The check-off provision on the income tax form accomplishes this goal for Presidential campaign financing. The check-off method should also be used to raise the funds necessary to support Congressional candidates.

Congress is best suited to decide on an exact formula for financing campaigns. However, I believe there are several features which should be part of any plan:

First, the plan should require that candidates demonstrate substantial public support before they get public funds to help finance their campaigns. This would guard against frivolous candidates depleting the limited public funds available. The matching formula in the Presidential primaries provided a successful link between total public funds received and a candidate's ability to demonstrate citizen support through small private donations.

Second, the limit on overall expenditures should not be excessively low so as to prevent an adequate presentation of candidates and their platforms to the people.

Third, we should ensure that candidates who accept public financing are not placed at a serious disadvantage in competing with opponents who have extraordinarily abundant private funds. Under 'the recent Supreme Court ruling, if a candidate refuses to accept public financing, then no limitation can be imposed on the amount of personal or other private funds which may be spent on the campaign. But if a less wealthy opponent does accept public financing, stricter spending limits would be imposed on him than on his opponent. I hope Congress will address this problem.

Fourth, I favor the broadest possible application of public financing. It should apply to primaries as well as general elections. I hope the Congress will act soon to pass legislation so that public financing can be available for the 1978 Congressional campaigns. It is important to begin now with public financing for general elections, even if a plan for primaries cannot be adopted this year.

Strengthening the Federal Election Campaign Act

While public financing of the last Presidential election was highly successful, my third suggestion is for certain modifications which our experience has shown could make the system work even better.

We noticed, for example, that there was less activity than in the past at the state and local level during the general election campaign. Opportunities should be available for more grass-roots participation in Presidential races. This could be accomplished by allowing Presidential candidates to designate one committee in each state to raise and spend a limited amount of money for campaign activities within the state. A reasonable limit for this activity might be 2¢ per eligible voter. Such committees could be allowed to delegate spending authority to local committees, but they should still be responsible for reporting contributions and expenditures. Also, when Congressional candidates mention in their advertising the Presidential nominee of their party, the expenditure should not have to be reported by the Presidential candidate.

Another useful change would be to grant Presidential candidates an additional amount to cover the great costs of complying with election laws—for example, filing the many necessary financial reports. We should prohibit the private raising of funds for this purpose.

We could also simplify the reporting of contributions and expenditures by directing the Federal Election Commission to establish common reporting and accounting systems to be used by all candidates.

Finally, we must clarify the law as it applies to the financial aspects of the delegate selection process. Contributions to delegates, or candidates for delegate, should be charged against a Presidential candidate only when such delegates are pledged to the specific candidate. Also, a delegate's expenses for attending conventions should not be considered as contributions or expenditures for the candidate he or she supports.

Direct Popular Election of the President

My fourth recommendation is that the Congress adopt a Constitutional amendment to provide for direct popular election of the President.

Such an amendment, which would abolish the Electoral College, will ensure that the candidate chosen by the voters actually becomes President. Under the Electoral College, it is always possible that the winner of the popular vote will not be elected. This has already happened in three elections, 1824, 1876, and 1888. In the last election, the result could have been changed by a small shift of votes in Ohio and Hawaii, despite a popular vote difference of 1.7 million.

I do not recommend a Constitutional amendment lightly. I think the amendment process must be reserved for an issue of overriding governmental significance. But the method by which we elect our President is such an issue.

I will not be proposing a specific direct election amendment. I prefer to allow the Congress to proceed with its work without the interruption of a new proposal.

Political Rights of Federal Employees

My fifth and final recommendation concerns the political fights of federal employees.

Over 2.8 million federal employees, including postal workers and workers for the District of Columbia, are now denied a full opportunity to participate in the electoral process. Unlike other Americans, they cannot run as a partisan candidate for any public office, cannot hold party office, and cannot even do volunteer work in a partisan political campaign.

I favor revising the Hatch Act to free those federal employees not in sensitive positions from these restrictions. There should be exceptions for those employees who must retain both the appearance and the substance of impartiality. For employees in such sensitive positions who are not subject to Senate confirmation, restrictions on political activity are necessary. Acting on standards prescribed by Congress, the Civil Service Commission should determine which positions should be treated as sensitive in all relevant government agencies.

Under such a Hatch Act revision, the vast majority of federal employees would be able to participate in federal, state and local elections and other political functions. But, federal employees have a special obligation not to abuse their public service responsibility. I favor strong penalties for any federal employee who attempts to influence or coerce another federal employee into political activity, or who engages in political activity while on the job. I also favor maximum reliance on a strong Civil Service Commission to vigorously prosecute employees who violate regulations against this kind of behavior.

Source: Carter, Jimmy. "Election Reform Message to the Congress." March 22, 1977. *Public Papers of the Presidents of the United States: Jimmy Carter, 1977. Book 1.* Washington, DC: Government Printing Office, 1978, pp. 481–485.

President Carter Describes Voting as the Key to Building a Better America, 1979

On May 20, 1979, President Jimmy Carter gave the commencement address at Cheyney State College in Cheyney, Pennsylvania. Founded in 1837, Cheyney State College was the first historically black university to be founded in the United States. In his speech to the school's graduating class, Carter emphasized the importance of political engagement in making America a more prosperous nation for all its citizens—and he described exercising one's voting rights as the purest and most important expression of citizenship. Following are excerpts from his remarks.

As President, I have a special opportunity to take part in the stream of history and also to study the course of history. Tonight, for instance, I will sleep in the same room where Abraham Lincoln slept when he was President, only a few steps from the place where he signed the Emancipation Proclamation.

Thursday, I met in the White House with several hundred black leaders, dozens of whom were instrumental in bringing about the Supreme Court decision, *Brown versus the Board of Education,* which occurred 25 years ago on that date, which struck down the separate but equal doctrine that had perpetuated segregation in the schools of a nation which has always claimed to be free and to provide equality of opportunity.

Not long ago, when I was in Memphis, I went with Mrs. Martin Luther King, Jr., to the balcony of a motel to visit the spot where her own husband was assassinated.

These events and others like them are profoundly moving, personal experiences. But I also feel a sense of history as I stand here today.

Many of you are the first in your family who ever had a chance to go to college. Neither my father nor any of his ancestors ever had a chance to finish high school or to go to college. So, I share the pride that you feel. And I also know the hardship that has gone into this achievement which is taking place today.

Ours, yours and mine, is a very special generation, the generation that Dr. Martin Luther King, Jr., was thinking of when he expressed his dream for America with an eloquence and a moral power that never will be forgotten.

One part of Dr. King's dream had a special meaning for me because of the State where he and I were born. He said, "I have a dream that one day on the red hills of Georgia, sons of former slaves and sons of former slaveholders will be able to sit down at the table of brotherhood."

And now when Andrew Young and I, two Georgians, sit down in the White House with other Cabinet members to hammer out foreign policy for the United States of America, it truly is a table of brotherhood.

I'm proud that we are working together for human rights around the world and for a majority rule, equality, and the end of racism and apartheid in southern Africa.

But I have not come to Cheyney State to boast about what my administration has done in foreign policy or civil rights or any other field. I'm not here to soothe you with promises that everything is going to be all right just because I happen to be in the White House or just because almost 200 superb black leaders now work with me to establish the policies of our Nation's Government. Instead, I'm here to talk to you very briefly today about some problems and to offer a challenge.

Our country does face extremely difficult problems—problems like inflation, energy shortages, inequality, discrimination, unemployment, and worldwide threats to peace. Each of these problems brings with it a tendency toward withdrawal from responsibility and sometimes crippling fears, fears that stand in the doorway between us and needed solutions. These fears of an uncertain future affect our daily lives. All of us, for instance—consumers, public officials, students, working people, business executives—hesitate to make individual sacrifices that we know are needed to fight inflation, because we are afraid that someone else may get a better deal.

We've seen the panic gasoline buying in California when everyone knows that this only makes our energy problems worse. Some people are afraid of losing their jobs. And this gives rise to racial bigotry and hatred.

All of us, if we are sane, are afraid of nuclear war, but the horror of the thought that mankind might actually be destroyed does not yet bring us together in a spirit of brotherhood and sisterhood to work for peace.

If our bellies are full and we are safe and secure, these fears, among others, contribute to our own sense of selfishness and the avoidance of responsibility. People are so concerned with getting ahead, with preserving what we have, with beating the system, that we refuse to become involved with anything outside our own personal lives. By taking refuge in either complacency or hopelessness, we mistakenly believe that we can grab and hold the best deal for ourselves in a difficult world.

Our problems are serious and they are real. They will not disappear if we ignore them. There are powerful special interests in our country which feed on the apathy of ordinary citizens. They enjoy the special privilege of power and influence, and they are determined to block positive change.

Those among you who believe in change—in improvement—those who are committed to making our country a greater country, must let your voices be heard if we are to defeat these special interests.

We know we need better programs in welfare, health care, education, and jobs. We know we need to control inflation, eliminate racial discrimination, have universal voter registration, control nuclear weapons, and help bring about majority rule in southern Africa.

The Congress of the United States can either make these decisions or block these decisions—decisions which affect every person in America.

I usually do not like polls. But I would like to take a little poll right here in the quadrangle. All of you who care about jobs, peace, eliminating racism, and ensuring justice for men and women, black and white, would you please raise your hand? Now, put your hands down. That's the easy part.

Tell the truth. Now all of you who voted in the last congressional election, 1978, in November, would you raise your hand? That's much better than the national average. [Laughter]

The question I would like to ask you is, why did the others not vote? Martin Luther King, Jr., was willing to risk and even give up his life so that you might have the right to vote—the right to shape the actions of your own Government. And he was not the only one. A lot of brave people have suffered and some have died to win that basic right. But that right is hollow, that right is empty, unless you use it.

When the Brown decision was handed down 25 years ago last Thursday, the school doors did not open up the following Monday. Do you know when they really began to let little black children into the schools that had been all white? I'll tell you when it began—when the voting rights bill was passed, that's when it began.

Both political candidates and incumbents have got to know that you will both vote and act. How are we going to have leadership to fight for equal opportunity and affirmative action in jobs, schools, and housing if even the act of voting is too great an effort?

Last November, two-thirds of the registered American adults did not vote. I ask you to join me in overcoming fear about the future, in battling apathy, and in fighting for change. One place to begin, for instance, is to keep the pressure on for equal opportunity in education and jobs.

Our economy has added 250,000 jobs for black and other minority teenagers since I became President. This year, we've committed $3.4 billion for youth employment and training—twice what we were spending 3 years ago. But we must do better. That's why I've asked Vice President Mondale to head a Cabinet-level task force to review everything both government and private industry is doing in youth employment and in training.

We're going to make sure these programs work. And we're going to look for ways to get private business to do its part as well. . . .

The struggle for civil rights is not over. Talk to the members of the Congressional Black Caucus. They are deeply concerned about the attitude in the United States Congress toward civil rights.

We have made progress, but we've not achieved what we need to accomplish. The *Brown* decision and the voting rights act tore the mask of legality from the face of racism, and you and I are never going to let this mask of racism be put back on.

Before these legal actions, there were only a few thousand black students in State colleges all across the country. Now more than a million black students are going to colleges all over America, mostly in publicly supported colleges like this one.

These numbers do indicate that progress has been made. These numbers are important, because education leads to jobs—good jobs. . . .

I'm going to tell it to you straight, because I care about the things you care about, because you and others like you are the reason that I'm President, and because one day, one of you may have the job that I hold now. I don't know if you'll want it or not. [Laughter]

Change—change does not come easy. Changing the course of society is not like changing the channel on a television set.

In 1896, for example, the Supreme Court issued the evil principle of separate but equal. It took 58 years—more than one half a century—of losing court battles, marches, arrests, courage, sacrifice, before a new court finally killed the ghost of Jim Crow. But it happened because people like you, mostly blacks, many students, made it happen.

There were a lot of heroes. One of those heroes died last week, A. Philip Randolph. He was 90 years old. He spent his long life fighting against discrimination in jobs, in defense industries, in the Armed Forces of his own country. He fought more battles than he won, but he won enough to change the face of this Nation and the lives of all of us.

His fight, your fight, our fight, goes on. We've written the promise of equality into our laws. But we must have the means and the tools now to keep that promise.

There are still unlawful, documented racial discrimination practices in housing in our country, for instance, especially in our cities. That's why we are struggling in Congress now to give Patricia Harris, the Secretary of the Housing and Urban Development Department, cease-and-desist orders, so that the victims of discrimination in housing will no longer have to have the burden, very expensive burden, of enforcing the very laws designed to protect them.

We're not going to get this change into law through Congress without your political participation. The very least we need is your vote on election day. But we also need for every Member of the Congress to know that you are interested.

We have an energy crisis in our country. Yet too few of our people, and even fewer of our politicians, are willing to face that reality.

I proposed a windfall profits tax to develop very good programs for the poor, who bear the extra burdens of rising energy costs, to provide mass transit, to give us other forms of energy, and to keep the oil companies from pocketing billions of dollars in unearned, excess profits. When the time comes for a vote in Congress, you can be sure that the oil company lobbyists will still be there. And you can provide—and no one but you and other American citizens can provide—the countervailing force that will curb the power of the lobbyists. If your voice is not heard, the oil companies will prevail again.

The most basic human right is the right of a person to live in peace. Today, as you march down this aisle to receive your diplomas, I'm thankful that none of you will have to march off to die in battle. I'm thankful that instead of fighting a war, we're debating a new step toward limiting the nuclear arms race. Peace and freedom are both precious gifts, and that's why the fight over ratification of the strategic arms limitation talks treaty is so important. As did Martin Luther King, Jr., you must make your voices heard in this battle for sanity and for peace.

Here at home, inflation threatens all the progress we have made. Again, I want to tell it to you straight, because inflation robs the poor, it robs minorities, and it robs those just starting out in life, like you, as surely as it robs old people who have to live on fixed incomes.

Inflation forces the Government to tighten the budget and to cut back on many programs that might help some of you. And inflation destroys some of the resources of business and industry needed to provide jobs for you and other Americans.

When Congress makes the tough choices on what has to be cut, who will stand with me to put people first unless you use your influence and your power?

I did not come here today to ask you to make my job easier. I came to urge you to help me make the job of every single elected officer in the United States tougher, more difficult, by insisting that government be more responsive, more compassionate, and more open to hear the voices of America. . . .

I'm not here only to let you hear my voice, but so that we in government can be sure to hear your voice, and that together our voices will be too strong to be ignored; so that together we'll have the courage to win more victories which we can place alongside the great ones that we've won.

Most of the progress that has been initiated and achieved has not come from government. This progress has come from voices outside of government that slowly but surely were united in shouting for justice and equality in our own Nation, and slowly—often after many years, even generations—government finally listened.

The long struggle for civil rights, for equal rights, for human rights has been a cycle of action, and then reaction, of lash and then backlash, for the cancer of racial injustice has always been near the heart of America.

Three hundred and sixty years ago, the first slaves were unloaded on the east coast of this continent in chains. One year later, the pilgrims landed on Plymouth Rock searching for freedom. The story of America has been the struggle and agony of a people trying to heal that contradiction—and it's been painful, and it's not over.

A great victory still remains to be won where we are sure about our future, where we are sure about justice, sure about equality, sure about the morals and commitments of our Nation, sure that government accurately represents what our people are and what they would like to be. It can be done. Much has been done already. If it had not, you would not be here and I would not be here.

We must continue to fight our battles and to overcome our fears together, or we will not be able to stand together for these purposes tomorrow.

In his Nobel Prize acceptance speech, Dr. King said, "I have the audacity to believe that peoples everywhere can have three meals a day for their bodies, education and culture for their minds, and dignity, equality and freedom for their spirits."

I share that audacious dream. And I ask you to join each other, and to join with me, in the struggle to make that dream come true.

Thank you very much.

Source: Carter, Jimmy. "Address at the Commencement Exercises at Cheyney State College." May 20, 1979. *Public Papers of the Presidents of the United States: Jimmy Carter, 1979. Book I, January 1 to June 29, 1979.* Washington, DC: Government Printing Office, 1980.

A Senator Urges the Passage of the Voting Accessibility for the Elderly and Handicapped Act, 1983

In 1984, Congress passed and President Ronald Reagan signed the Voting Accessibility for the Elderly and Handicapped Act (VAEHA). The purpose of this legislation was to ensure "the fundamental right to vote by improving access for handicapped and elderly individuals to registration facilities and polling places for Federal elections." This law, combined with the Americans with Disabilities Act that came along six years later, dramatically improved access to polling stations and the overall voting process for people with disabilities and the elderly.

VAEHA enjoyed broad bipartisan support, with both Democrats and Republicans rallying behind the bill. David Durenberger, a Republican senator from Minnesota, offered a representative defense of the bill at a House task-force hearing on the proposed legislation on July 14, 1983. His remarks are excerpted below.

Mr. Chairman, there is no principle more important in our democratic system of government than each citizen's right to vote. We deny the right to criminals and residents not yet citizens, but our great battles have been fought over the denial of this right to citizens who haven't done anything other than being born minority or handicapped. Congress, though legislation such as the Voting Rights Act of 1965, and its reauthorization passed last year, has consistently demonstrated its commitment to ensuring this fundamental right to every citizen.

But the right to vote and the capacity to vote are not necessarily the same. For the 35 million elderly and disabled Americans, physical barriers have often provided as great an obstacle to voter participation as have legal barriers. To understand the real impact of these barriers on human beings consider how you would respond to any of the following situations:

Suppose you were elderly or disabled, and arrived at a polling site only to find that the polls have been set up on the second or third floor of a building that lacks elevator access.

Suppose you were in a wheelchair and arrived at the polls only to find that architectural barriers physically barred you from access to the polling place.

Imagine that you lost your hearing and discovered, upon arriving at the voting booth, that only oral—rather than written—directions were provided.

These problems arise every year, in every election. To most of us, they may be nothing more than a minor inconvenience. To some Americans they are the difference between exercising a constitutional right and isolation from the democratic process.

The barriers these individuals face are not legislatively imposed—they are the darkness of blindness, the frustration of physical paralysis, and the frailty of age. The States, however, have done little to assist these citizens to overcome the barriers to the electoral process. According to a recent study, prepared by the Institute for Public Awareness, only four States mandate accessibility to polling places. Similarly, only seven States mandate accessibilit, but allow exemptions, twelve states encourage accessibility of polling places, and four provide for alternative voting by handicapped citizens.

The legislation which I have introduced in the Senate and which the Committee is considering today—Equal Access to Voting Rights Act, H.R. 1250—is designed to overcome these barriers and offer all qualified voters the freedom to exercise their right to vote.

It will overcome the distress of an elderly woman who wakes up on election day to find her arthritis so painful she cannot get out of bed. In seventeen States, handicapped individuals must have a doctor's verification of disability before they can file an absentee ballot. Those suffering from sporadic illness can only hope for a flare-up when they seek absentee status.

It will overcome the disappointment of a citizen confined to a wheelchair, who arrives at the polls on election day only to find there is no way to enter. A simple flight of stairs may be the only barrier standing in the way, but it effectively means that his or her opinion will not be heard.

Most important, Mr. Chairman, the legislation being considered today will overcome the fear of these obstacles. It is the fear of inaccessibility that keeps untold numbers of elderly and handicapped citizens away from the polls.

The Equal Access to Voting Rights Act removes barriers to voter participation. Its provisions are simple and inexpensive, yet offer a real chance for thousands of disabled and elderly voters to participate in the electoral process.

Today there is no legal requirement that Federal election polls be accessible to the handicapped. This bill would require the Attorney General of the United States, in consultation with the Secretary of the Department of Health and Human Services, to set minimum standards for registration and voting sites used in national elections to ensure that physical barriers associated with these facilities do not prevent the elderly and handicapped from voting. Wherever practical, polling and registration facilities will be located in buildings with either temporary or permanent ramp access.

Registration and voting facilities must also be accessible to the elderly. A voting booth up three flights of stairs with no elevator denies an older American the opportunity to vote. This legislation would ensure that voting and registration sites are located on the ground floor of multistory buildings, or in an area of multistory buildings accessible by elevator.

Other provisions of the bill include a requirement that voter information notices, already required by Federal law, be printed in large type to assist the visually impaired. The bill would also require that in Federal elections, absentee ballot provisions be avilable not only to those who are physically absent from the jurisdiction on the date of the vote, but also to those whose age or physical handicap would be likely to prevent their presence at the polling place.

Access to the polls should not be contingent upon two strong legs, perfect vision and robust physical health. Every member of society loses when access to the electoral process is abridged. . . .

We have fought and gained the legal right to suffrage through constitutional amendment. Let us back up this voting right with the means to make it truly possible for every American to exercise his or her right to vote. We cannot afford to be flexible in guaranteeing that right—it must be afforded to all who are entitled to exercise their franchise. As Abraham Lincoln said in his final public address: "Important principles may and must be inflexible."

Source: Durenberger, David. Statement. *Equal Access to Voting for Elderly and Disabled Persons.* Hearings Held Before the Task Force on Elections of the Committee on House Administration. 98th Congress, 1st Session, on H.R. 1250. July 14, 1983. Washington, DC: GOP, 1983, pp. 50–51.

Protecting the Voting Rights of Homeless Americans, 1985

During the 1980s and 1990s, courts across the country issued rulings that, by and large, strengthened protections for homeless people seeking to exercise their constitutional right to vote. One such case was Collier v. Menzel, *which was heard by the California Court of Appeals in 1985. The plaintiffs in* Collier v. Menzel *were three homeless individuals whose voter registration applications had been rejected by Santa Barbara County because they listed a local public park as their residence. The appeals court ruled in favor of the plaintiffs, noting not only that all Americans had a constitutional right to vote but also that the city park could qualify as the fixed residence necessary for registration. The court also emphasized that homeless people particularly needed to have their voices heard in the political process. Excerpts from the decision are below.*

This and other pro-enfranchisement legal decisions concerning the homeless prompted a number of states to pass legislation during the 1990s and 2000s, protecting their voting rights. But even in those states, homeless people face numerous hurdles that complicate their efforts to vote. Although no states require voters to live in a traditional residential home or apartment—people can list homeless shelters or specific locales within a park, for instance—many of them require a valid mailing address at which they can receive mail or valid government-issued forms of personal identification (such as a driver's license). Moreover, states without strict voter ID laws still typically require first-time or infrequent voters to provide some sort of documentation (driver's license, bank statement, electricity bill, etc.) to confirm their local or state residency. Obviously, furnishing such documentation is impossible for many homeless people.

Appellants filed a petition for writ of mandate in superior court seeking to compel respondent, the Santa Barbara County Clerk-Recorder, to allow appellants to register to vote. They appeal the trial court's denial of their petition.

Appellants, three persons identifying themselves as "homeless" citizens and indigents of Santa Barbara County, submitted affidavits of registration to vote to respondent in September 1984. The address appellants listed as their residence on their affidavits was "100 Montecito Street." A park owned by the City of Santa Barbara and commonly known as Fig Tree Park is located at this address, a gathering place for homeless persons. Camping or sleeping overnight on park grounds is prohibited by city ordinance.

After receiving their registration affidavits, respondent sent appellants a letter informing them that the address listed on their registration applications was insufficient as a residence address and therefore prevented respondent from determining appellants' correct voting precinct. The letter enclosed blank registration forms so that appellants could clarify their addresses. It also informed appellants that they were legally entitled to vote in the precincts of their former residences until they established new residences.

Appellants contend that their registration applications complied with statutory requirements for voter registration. They further claim that respondent's failure to process these applications violated their right to the equal protection of the laws under the United States Constitution.

We conclude the affidavits were sufficient for voter registration purposes and reverse the judgment below. We also conclude that, as a consequence of the denial of these affidavits, appellants were unjustifiably deprived of their right to vote on an equal basis with other citizens.

I. State Registration Requirements

Appellants argue that respondent abused its administrative discretion by failing to accept their registration affidavits because California law does not require that a voter registrant live in an actual building. Appellants assert they have complied with state voter registration laws since they are citizens of California, they live in Santa Barbara, and have the intent to remain there permanently. Respondent counters that its rejection of appellants' registration affidavits was proper as appellants listed for their addresses a place where there are no living facilities. Thus, respondent contends, appellants have not established an essential factor which would demonstrate a domicile in Santa Barbara.

[1] A review of state election laws supports appellants' position. The California Constitution provides that a "United States citizen 18 years of age and a resident in the state may vote." (Cal. Const., art. II, § 2.) [2] Even if a person may be qualified to vote under constitutional standards, he/she may not be entitled to vote if compliance with state registration laws has not been met. . . .

In order to be properly registered, an elector must be a resident of an election precinct. . . . Since Fig Tree Park, the alleged residence of appellants, lies within Santa Barbara City, a county election precinct is determinable on the basis of appellants' registration affidavits.

[3] The next issue for consideration is whether appellants are residents of the park. Election Code, section 200, subdivision (a), defines a person's "residence" as his/her "domicile." "The domicile of a person is that place in which his or her habitation is fixed, wherein the person has the intention of remaining, and to which, whenever he or she is absent, the person has the intention of returning . . ."

For voting purposes then, the Legislature has set up the following residential requirements: (1) a fixed habitation, and (2) an intention of remaining at that place and of returning to it after temporary absences. Appellants have satisfied both statutory requirements of fixed habitation and intent to remain. . . .

More important, the Legislature has not adopted the traditional notion that a dwelling or habitation for voter registration signifies four walls. Section 207 of the Election Code provides: "Residence in a trailer or vehicle or at any public camp or camping ground may constitute a domicile for voting purposes if the registrant complies with other requirements of this article." Implicit in this language is that a public camping ground itself without residence in a vehicle or trailer is deemed a fixed habitation. We find that the designation of a public park as a residence for voting purposes likewise can qualify as a place of fixed habitation. While a park may not be legally designated as a place for camping, it is a physical area where a person can sleep and otherwise use as a dwelling place. . . .

It is important to point out that, pursuant to city ordinance, the city park appellants designate as their residence is legally forbidden for use as a residence. Since appellants have "no right" to use the park for a habitation, do they have the required intent to remain there? Yes. Appellants' intent to remain in the park is legally independent of any intent to violate the ordinance. We do not hold that respondent cannot enforce its ordinance making it illegal to live in a public park. We do hold that so long as petitioners actually reside there, they may register to vote in that precinct.

II. Equal Protection

Appellants contend that respondent's refusal to register them to vote discriminates against them as a class of homeless or indigent persons. Appellants do not challenge the constitutionality of the statutory requirement that voter registrants must be residents of an election precinct. Their assertion is that respondent has unconstitutionally interpreted and applied this requirement since appellants have demonstrated they are residents of an election precinct in the City of Santa Barbara. . . .

[9] The right to vote on an equal basis with other citizens is a fundamental right in our democratic society and one of the basic civil rights of man which preserves all other rights. Classifications denying this right deserve the strictest scrutiny. Under this stringent standard, the government must not only demonstrate that it has a compelling public interest in utilizing the classification, it must also show that the classification is necessary to serve its objectives.

[10] Respondent contends it is not necessary to find a compelling public interest in order to sustain the validity of statutory residence requirements for voting. Respondent is partially correct. States and their political subdivisions have the unquestioned constitutional authority to restrict availability of the ballot to those persons who reside within their borders. . . .

[11] Although registration laws are valid if reasonable, these laws and the interpretation of them will receive strict scrutiny if they deny certain classes of residents the right to vote. . . .Thus, a governmental entity is not justified in excluding otherwise qualified voters who have no way of making themselves eligible to vote. . . .

[12] We have concluded that appellants' affidavits showed appellants are residents of Santa Barbara. We also find that respondent's rejection of appellants' registration affidavits absolutely denied them the right to vote. Hence, respondent's interpretation and application of state registration laws deserve strict scrutiny.

[13] Respondent argues that appellants were not completely denied the right to vote because they have the ability under registration laws to vote in the precinct of their last established domicile. We disagree. Requiring appellants to travel to their former place of residence unnecessarily burdens their right to vote, particularly in view of their alleged indigent status, and, consequently, their restricted mobility.

Does respondent therefore assert a compelling interest in rejecting appellants' affidavits? Further, is it necessary for respondent to reject the affidavits in order to serve its objectives or are there alternative means which will not restrict appellants' right to vote?

[14] Respondent urges that it has a compelling interest in requiring appellants to list known residential addresses since the location of a voter's domicile determines which measures appear on the ballot the voter casts. . . . Respondent also claims it is interested in preventing the importation of voters in close elections and in preserving the concept of political community. Federal courts have indeed found that states have compelling interests in preventing voting fraud and in maintaining an orderly election procedure.

Nevertheless, do the means justify the ends in the instant case? We conclude they do not. Respondent's election goals do not warrant its refusal to register appellants to vote.

With regard to the interest in preventing fraudulent voting, respondent presented no evidence that appellants were more likely to commit fraud than persons who were not homeless. Without such evidence, the status of homelessness raises no presumption that homeless persons are more prone to commit voter fraud than any other group.

Appellants further point out the existence of a statutory framework in California to deter dual registration and other voter fraud problems. There is no reason to believe that these statutes would not be effective to deter fraud by a class of homeless registrants. It may have been feasible in 1850 to influence the outcome of an election by rounding up the impecunious and the thirsty, furnishing them with free liquor, premarked ballots, and transportation to the polls; to do so now, if possible at all, would require the coordinated skills of a vast squadron of computer technicians. . . .

[15] Respondent's other primary concern is administrative feasibility. It asks how it can, as a practical matter, handle affidavits of registration which on their face do not list as residences places where people reside. First of all, there is no statutory authority for the proposition that a residence cannot be a place where there are no living facilities. In other words, the old adage, "A man's home is where he makes it," is not statutorily proscribed. We therefore agree with appellants that whether people "sleep under a bush or a tree or in the open air is immaterial regarding their right to vote." The type of place a person calls home has no relevance to his/her eligibility to vote if compliance with registration has been achieved, that is, the designation of a fixed habitation, the declaration of an intent to remain at that place and to return to it after temporary absences, and the designation of an address where mail can be received.

Respondent concedes it is not necessary to live in a house or apartment in order to be allowed to vote. It further states that the standard for establishing a residence for voting purposes found in *Pitts v. Black*, supra, 608 F. Supp. 696, is an appropriate standard for determining the residence of a homeless person.

Pitts resolves respondent's asserted administrative dilemma of ascertaining a person's election precinct when he/she does not live in a house or apartment or any other building. The federal court there found that it was not administratively infeasible to register homeless individuals to vote who lived in a city park which had no postal address and which spread over several election districts. As long as a homeless person could identify a specific spot within the park where he/she regularly slept, such as a park bench, election officials would be able to determine that person's election district. Furthermore, the court found that the identification of a specific "home base" within a district together with the designation of a place where messages could be received satisfied a stringent domicile standard.

Similarly, although Fig Tree Park has no building numbers, respondent can identify an election precinct for appellants. This is particularly feasible as the park encompasses a small geographical area. Appellants' designation of a fixed premises and a post office box also establishes their domicile within a particular locality. This, in turn, allows them to vote without disturbing the integrity of the political community.

Admittedly, allowing appellants to vote produces a different set of circumstances for respondent to deal with and may result in additional administrative burdens. However, respondent has not only failed to show that registering appellants has created a situation incapable of administrative resolution, it has not shown that any administrative burdens it may face outweigh appellants' fundamental interest in participating in the electoral process.

It can be argued that permitting the "homeless" to vote will impart a sense of responsibility to those people by giving them a political stake in their future and a sense of caring about their community. Unlike other minority groups or disadvantaged persons, the "homeless," by the very nature of their living circumstances, have been unable to exercise any political influence in order to make their particular problems and needs known.

It is patently unjust that society ignores the homeless and yet also denies them the proper avenues to remedy the situation. Even more compelling, the denial of the vote to the "homeless" denies them electoral power. Powerlessness breeds apathy, and apathy is the greatest danger to society. . . .

[17] . . . the Equal Protection Clause prohibits using the affluence of the voter as an electoral standard since voter qualifications have no relation to wealth. (*Harper v. Virginia Bd. of Elections.*) A citizen who is a qualified voter is no more nor no less so because he or she lives in an unconventional place. "'This is the clear and strong command of our Constitution's Equal Protection Clause. This is an essential part of the concept of a government of laws and not men. This is at the heart of Lincoln's vision of government of the people, by the people and for the people. The Equal Protection Clause demands no less than substantially equal representation for all citizens, of all places as well as of all races.'" Denying the opportunity to vote to a resident merely because he or she cannot afford housing denies a citizen's vote on the basis of economic status and is therefore an impermissible basis for determining the entitlement to vote.

We conclude that appellants are entitled to a writ of mandamus directing respondent to allow appellants to register to vote on the ground that their submitted affidavits of registration comply with state registration laws. We further conclude that respondent's refusal to register appellants is not necessary to promote respondent's proffered election goals and is therefore violative of appellants' right to vote under equal protection standards.

The judgment appealed from is reversed and remanded to superior court for the issuance of a writ and the determination of costs at trial and on appeal.

Source: California Court of Appeals, Opinion. *Collier v. Menzel,* December 20, 1985. 176 Cal. App. 3d 24, 221 Cal. Rptr. 110.

Supreme Court Sends Mixed Signals about Gerrymandering in *Davis v. Bandemer,* 1986

In 1985 the U.S. Supreme Court heard arguments in Davis v. Bandemer*, a case that proved influential for many years in setting the limits and terms by which the courts could intervene in clashes over gerrymandering, the practice of setting the boundaries of electoral district by one political party to gain a political advantage over other parties.* Davis v. Bandemer *was brought by several Indiana Democrats who alleged that the apportionment scheme implemented by Indiana's Republican-controlled state legislature in 1981 diluted the impact of Democratic votes in important districts in ways that constituted a violation of the Equal Protection Clause of the Fourteenth Amendment to the U.S. Constitution. On June 30, 1986, the Court ruled in a 7–2 decision that the state's redrawing of districts did not rise to the level of being a partisan gerrymander. It also emphasized that the courts should tread carefully before wading into politically based gerrymandering squabbles. But supporters of the plaintiffs were mildly heartened by one victory. The majority did hold that the courts had the legal authority to consider—a term known as "justiciability"—cases in which egregious partisan gerrymandering violated the Equal Protection Clause.*

Following are excerpts from Byron White's majority opinion in Davis v. Bandemer, *including remarks in response to arguments made by Justice Lewis Powell, one of the court's two dissenting voices in the case.*

Here, none of the identifying characteristics of a nonjusticiable political question are present. Disposition of the case does not involve this Court in a matter more properly decided by a coequal branch of the Government. There is no risk of foreign or domestic disturbance. Nor is this Court persuaded that there are no judicially discernible and manageable standards by which political gerrymandering cases are to be decided. The mere fact that there is no likely arithmetic presumption, such as the "one person, one vote" rule, in the present context does not compel a conclusion that the claims presented here are nonjusticiable. The claim is whether each political group in the State should have the same chance to elect representatives of its choice as any other political group, and this Court declines to hold that such claim is never justiciable. That the claim is submitted by a political group, rather than a racial group, does not distinguish it in terms of justiciability.

JUSTICE WHITE, joined by JUSTICE BRENNAN, JUSTICE MARSHALL, and JUSTICE BLACKMUN, concluded in Parts III and IV that the District Court erred in holding that appellees had alleged and proved a violation of the Equal Protection Clause.

(a) A threshold showing of discriminatory vote dilution is required for a *prima facie* case of an equal protection violation. The District Court's findings of an adverse effect on appellees do not surmount this threshold requirement. The mere fact that an apportionment scheme makes it more difficult for a particular group in a particular district to elect representatives of its choice does not render that scheme unconstitutional. A group's electoral power is not unconstitutionally diminished by the fact that an apportionment scheme makes winning elections more difficult, and a failure of proportional representation alone does not constitute impermissible discrimination under the Equal Protection Clause. As with individual districts, where unconstitutional vote dilution is alleged in the form of statewide political gerrymandering, as here, the mere lack of proportional representation will not be sufficient to prove unconstitutional discrimination. Without specific supporting evidence, a court cannot presume in such a case that those who are elected will disregard the disproportionally underrepresented group. Rather, unconstitutional discrimination occurs only when the electoral system is arranged in a manner that will consistently degrade a voter's or a group of voters' influence on the political process as a whole. The District Court's apparent holding that *any* interference with an opportunity to elect a representative of one's choice would be sufficient to allege or prove an equal protection violation, unless justified by some acceptable state interest, in addition to being contrary to the above-described conception of an unconstitutional political gerrymander, would invite attack on all or almost all reapportionment statutes.

(b) Relying on a single election to prove unconstitutional discrimination, as the District Court did, is unsatisfactory. Without finding that, because of the 1981 reapportionment, the Democrats could not in one of the next few elections secure a sufficient vote to take control of the legislature, that the reapportionment would consign the Democrats to a minority status in the legislature throughout the 1980's, or that they would have no hope of doing any better in the reapportionment based on the 1990 census, the District Court erred in concluding that the 1981 reapportionment violated the Equal Protection Clause. Simply showing that there are multimember districts, and that those districts are constructed so as to be safely Republican or Democratic, in no way bolsters the contention that there has been a *statewide* discrimination against Democratic voters.

(c) The view that intentional drawing of district boundaries for partisan ends, and for no other reason, violates the Equal Protection Clause would allow a constitutional violation to be found where the only proven effect on a political party's electoral power was disproportionate results in one election (possibly two elections), and would invite judicial interference in legislative districting whenever a political party suffers at the polls. Even if a state legislature redistricts with the specific intention of disadvantaging one political party's election prospects, there has been no unconstitutional violation against members of that party unless the redistricting does, in fact, disadvantage it at the polls. As noted, a mere lack of proportionate results in one election cannot suffice in this regard.

JUSTICE O'CONNOR, joined by THE CHIEF JUSTICE and JUSTICE REHNQUIST, concluding that the partisan gerrymandering claims of major political parties raise a nonjusticiable political question, would reverse the District Court's judgment on the grounds that appellees' claim is nonjusticiable. The Equal Protection Clause does not supply judicially manageable standards for resolving purely political gerrymandering claims, and does not confer group rights to an equal share of political power. Racial gerrymandering claims are justiciable because of the greater warrant the Equal Protection Clause gives the federal courts to intervene for protection against racial discrimination, and because of the stronger nexus between individual rights and group interests that is present in the case of a discrete and insular racial group. But members of the major political parties cannot claim that they are vulnerable to exclusion from the political process, and it has not been established that there is a need or a constitutional basis for judicial intervention to resolve political gerrymandering claims. The costs of judicial intervention will be severe, and such intervention requires courts to make policy choices that are not of a kind suited for judicial discretion. Nor is there any clear stopping point to prevent the gradual evolution of a requirement of roughly proportional representation for every cohesive political group. Accordingly, political gerrymandering claims present a nonjusticiable political question. . . .

Relying on a single election to prove unconstitutional discrimination is unsatisfactory. The District Court observed, and the parties do not disagree, that Indiana is a swing State. Voters sometimes prefer Democratic candidates, and sometimes Republican. The District Court did not find that, because of the 1981 Act, the Democrats could not, in one of the next few elections, secure a sufficient vote to take control of the assembly. Indeed, the District Court declined to hold that the 1982 election results were the predictable consequences of the 1981 Act, and expressly refused to hold that those results were a reliable prediction of future ones. The District Court did not ask by what percentage the statewide Democratic vote would have had to increase to control either the House or the Senate. The appellants argue here, without a persuasive response from the appellees, that, had the Democratic candidates received an additional few percentage points of the votes cast statewide, they would have obtained a majority of the seats in both houses. Nor was there any finding that the 1981 reapportionment would consign the Democrats to a minority status in the Assembly throughout the 1980's, or that the Democrats would have no hope of doing any better in the reapportionment that would occur after the 1990 census. Without findings of this nature, the District Court erred in concluding that the 1981 Act violated the Equal Protection Clause.

In response to our approach, JUSTICE POWELL suggests an alternative method for evaluating equal protection claims of political gerrymandering. In his view, courts should look at a number of factors in considering these claims: the nature of the legislative procedures by which the challenged redistricting was accomplished and the intent behind the redistricting; the shapes of the districts and their conformity with political subdivision boundaries; and "evidence concerning population disparities and statistics tending to show vote dilution." . . . The District Court in this case reviewed these factors in reaching its ultimate conclusion that unconstitutional vote dilution had occurred, and JUSTICE POWELL concludes that its findings on these factors—and on the ultimate question of vote discrimination—should be upheld. According to JUSTICE POWELL, those findings adequately support a conclusion that "the boundaries of the voting districts have been distorted deliberately and arbitrarily to achieve illegitimate ends." This deliberate and arbitrary distortion of boundaries, in turn, apparently distinguishes gerrymandering in a "loose" sense, "the common practice of the party in power to choose the redistricting plan that gives it an advantage at the polls," *post* at 164, from gerrymandering in an "unconstitutional" sense.

Although we are not completely clear as to the distinction between these two categories of gerrymander, the crux of JUSTICE POWELL's analysis seems to be that—at least in some cases—the intentional drawing of district boundaries for partisan ends and for no other reason violates the Equal Protection Clause in and of itself. We disagree, however, with this conception of a constitutional violation. Specifically, even if a state legislature redistricts with the specific intention of disadvantaging one political party's election prospects, we do not believe that there has been an unconstitutional discrimination against members of that party unless the redistricting does in fact disadvantage it at the polls.

Moreover, as we discussed above, a mere lack of proportionate results in one election cannot suffice in this regard. We have reached this conclusion in our cases involving challenges to individual multimember districts, and it applies equally here. In the individual multimember district cases, we have found equal protection violations only where a history of disproportionate results appeared in conjunction with strong indicia of lack of political power and the denial of fair representation. In those cases, the racial minorities asserting the successful equal protection claims had essentially been shut out of the political process. In the statewide political gerrymandering context, these prior cases lead to the analogous conclusion that equal protection violations may be found only where a history (actual or projected) of disproportionate results appears in conjunction with similar indicia. The mere lack of control of the General Assembly after a single election does not rise to the requisite level.

This requirement of more than a showing of possibly transitory results is where we appear to depart from JUSTICE POWELL. Stripped of its "factors" verbiage, JUSTICE POWELL's analysis turns on a determination that a lack of proportionate election results can support a finding of an equal protection violation, at least in some circumstances. Here, the only concrete effect on the Democrats in Indiana in terms of election results that the District Court had before it was one election in which the percentage of Democrats elected was lower than the percentage of total Democratic votes cast. In JUSTICE POWELL's view, this disproportionality, when combined with clearly discriminatory intent on the part of the 1981 General Assembly and the manipulation of district lines in the apportionment process, is sufficient to conclude that fair representation has been denied.

The factors other than disproportionate election results, however, do not contribute to a finding that Democratic voters have been disadvantaged in fact. They support a finding that an intention to discriminate was present, and that districts were drawn in accordance with that intention, but they do not show any actual disadvantage beyond that shown by the election results: it surely cannot be an actual disadvantage in terms of fair representation on a group level just to be placed in a district with a supermajority of other Democratic voters or a district that departs from preexisting political boundaries. Only when such placement affects election results and political power statewide has an actual disadvantage occurred.

Consequently, JUSTICE POWELL's view would allow a constitutional violation to be found where the only proven effect on a political party's electoral power was disproportionate results in one (or possibly two) elections. This view, however, contains no explanation of why a lack of proportionate election results should suffice in these political gerrymandering cases while it does not in the cases involving racial gerrymandering. In fact, JUSTICE POWELL's opinion is silent as to the relevance of the substantive standard developed in the multimember district cases to these political gerrymandering cases.

In rejecting JUSTICE POWELL's approach, we do not mean to intimate that the factors he considers are entirely irrelevant. The election results obviously are relevant to a showing of the effects required to prove a political gerrymandering claim under our view. And the district configurations may be combined with vote projections to predict future election results, which are also relevant to the effects showing. The other factors, even if not relevant to the effects issue, might well be relevant to an equal protection claim. The equal protection argument would proceed along the following lines: if there were a discriminatory effect and a discriminatory intent, then the legislation would be examined for valid underpinnings. Thus, evidence of exclusive legislative process and deliberate drawing of district lines in accordance with accepted gerrymandering principles would be relevant to intent, and evidence of valid and invalid configuration would be relevant to whether the districting plan met legitimate state interests.

This course is consistent with our equal protection cases generally, and is the course we follow here: we assumed that there was discriminatory intent, found that there was insufficient discriminatory effect to constitute an equal protection violation, and therefore did not reach the question of the state interests (legitimate or otherwise) served by the particular districts as they were created by the legislature. Consequently, the valid or invalid configuration of the districts was an issue we did not need to consider.

It seems inappropriate, however, to view these separate components of an equal protection analysis as "factors" to be considered together, without regard for their separate functions or meaning. This undifferentiated consideration of the various factors confuses the import of each factor and disguises the essential conclusion of JUSTICE POWELL's opinion: that disproportionate election results alone are a sufficient effect to support a finding of a constitutional violation.

In sum, we decline to adopt the approach enunciated by JUSTICE POWELL. In our view, that approach departs from our past cases and invites judicial interference in legislative districting whenever a political party suffers at the polls. We recognize that our own view may be difficult of application. Determining when an electoral system has been "arranged in a manner that will consistently degrade a voter's or a group of voters' influence on the political process as a whole," is of necessity a difficult inquiry. Nevertheless, we believe that it recognizes the delicacy of intruding on this most political of legislative functions, and is at the same time consistent with our prior cases regarding individual multimember districts, which have formulated a parallel standard.

In sum, we hold that political gerrymandering cases are properly justiciable under the Equal Protection Clause. We also conclude, however, that a threshold showing of discriminatory vote dilution is required for a *prima facie* case of an equal protection violation. In this case, the findings made by the District Court of an adverse effect on the appellees do not surmount the threshold requirement. Consequently, the judgment of the District Court is

Reversed.

Source: Majority Decision, Justice White. *Davis v. Bandemer,* 478 U.S. 109 (1986).

Voting Becomes Easier for Overseas Military and Civilians, 1986

For much of its history, the United States struggled to protect the voting rights of active-duty military personnel deployed outside America's borders. The process for voting was so cumbersome, in fact, that Newsweek *reported that in 1942—the second year of American military engagement in World War II—only twenty-eight thousand out of five million soldiers voted in the presidential election. In the years following the 1945 conclusion of the war, the United States passed a number of laws, most notably the Federal Voting Assistance Act (1955) and the Overseas Citizens Voting Rights Act (1975), to make it easier for American military personnel and civilians to vote in U.S. elections. Then, in 1986, Congress passed and President Ronald Reagan signed the Uniformed and Overseas Citizens Absentee Voting Act (UOCAVA), a piece of legislation that combined many of the provisions of the 1955 and 1975 acts into a single law that greatly eased absentee voter registration and the voting process for members of the U.S. military and other Americans living overseas. Following is the Title I of UOCAVA, as modified by the National Defense Authorization Act for fiscal year 2005.*

TITLE I—REGISTRATION AND VOTING BY ABSENT UNIFORMED SERVICE VOTERS AND OVERSEAS VOTERS IN ELECTIONS FOR FEDERAL OFFICE

SEC. 101. FEDERAL RESPONSIBILITIES.

(a) PRESIDENTIAL DESIGNEE.—The President shall designate the head of an executive department to have primary responsibility for Federal functions under this title.

(b) DUTIES OF PRESIDENTIAL DESIGNEE.—The Presidential designee shall—

(1) consult State and local election officials in carrying out this title, and ensure that such officials are aware of the requirements of this Act;
(2) prescribe an official post card form, containing both an absentee voter registration application and an absentee ballot application, for use by the States as required under section 102(4);
(3) carry out section 103 with respect to the Federal write-in absentee ballot for absent uniformed services voters and overseas voters in general elections for Federal office;
(4) prescribe a suggested design for absentee ballot mailing envelopes for use by the States as recommended in section 104;
(5) compile and distribute (A) descriptive material on State absentee registration and voting procedures, and (B) to the extent practicable, facts relating to specific elections, including dates, offices involved, and the text of ballot questions;
(6) not later than the end of each year after a Presidential election year, transmit to the President and the Congress a report on the effectiveness of assistance under this title, including a separate statistical analysis of uniformed services voter participation, a separate statistical analysis of overseas nonmilitary participation, and a description of State-Federal cooperation; and
(7) prescribe a standard oath for use with any document under this title affirming that a material misstatement of fact in the completion of such a document may constitute grounds for conviction of perjury.

(c) DUTIES OF OTHER FEDERAL OFFICIALS—

(1) IN GENERAL.—The head of each Government department, agency, or other entity shall, upon request of the Presidential designee, distribute balloting materials and otherwise cooperate in carrying out this title.

(2) ADMINISTRATOR OF GENERAL SERVICES.—As directed by the Presidential designee, the Administrator of General Services shall furnish official post card forms (prescribed under subsection (b)) and Federal write-in absentee ballots (prescribed under section 103).

SEC. 102. STATE RESPONSIBILITIES

(a) IN GENERAL.—Each State shall—

(1) permit absent uniformed services voters and overseas voters to use absentee registration procedures and to vote by absentee ballot in general, special, primary, and runoff elections for Federal office;

(2) accept and process, with respect to any election for Federal office, any otherwise valid voter registration application and absentee ballot application from an absent uniformed services voter or overseas voter, if the application is received by the appropriate State election official not less than 30 days before the election;

(3) permit absent uniformed services voters and overseas voters to use Federal write-in absentee ballots (in accordance with section 103) in general elections for Federal office;

(4) use the official post card form (prescribed under section 101) for simultaneous voter registration application and absentee ballot application; and

(5) if the State requires an oath or affirmation to accompany any document under this title, use the standard oath prescribed by the Presidential designee under section 101(b)(7).

(b) DESIGNATION OF SINGLE STATE OFFICE TO PROVIDE INFORMATION ON REGISTRATION AND ABSENTEE BALLOT PROCEDURES FOR ALL VOTERS IN THE STATE.—

(1) IN GENERAL.—Each State shall designate a single office which shall be responsible for providing information regarding voter registration procedures and absentee ballot procedures to be used by absent uniformed services voters and overseas voters with respect to elections for Federal office (including procedures relating to the use of the Federal write-in absentee ballot) to all absent uniformed services voters and overseas voters who wish to register to vote or vote in any jurisdiction in the State.

(2) RECOMMENDATION Regarding Use of Office to Accept and Process Materials.—Congress recommends that the State office designated under paragraph (1) be responsible for carrying out the State's duties under this Act, including accepting valid voter registration applications,

absentee ballot applications, and absentee ballots (including Federal write-in absentee ballots) from all absent uniformed services voters and overseas voters who wish to register to vote or vote in any jurisdiction in the State.

(c) REPORT ON NUMBER OF ABSENTEE BALLOTS TRANSMITTED AND RECEIVED.—Not later than 90 days after the date of each regularly scheduled general election for Federal office, each State and unit of local government which administered the election shall (through the State, in the case of a unit of local government) submit a report to the Election Assistance Commission (established under the Help America Vote Act of 2002) on the combined number of absentee ballots transmitted to absent uniformed services voters and overseas voters for the election and the combined number of such ballots which were returned by such voters and cast in the election, and shall make such report available to the general public.

(d) REGISTRATION NOTIFICATION.—With respect to each absent uniformed services voter and each overseas voter who submits a voter registration application or an absentee ballot request, if the State rejects the application or request, the State shall provide the voter with the reasons for the rejection.

SEC. 103. FEDERAL WRITE-IN ABSENTEE BALLOT IN GENERAL ELECTIONS FOR FEDERAL OFFICE FOR ABSENT UNIFORMED SERVICES VOTERS AND OVERSEAS VOTERS

(a) IN GENERAL.—The Presidential designee shall prescribe a Federal write-in absentee ballot (including a secrecy envelope and mailing envelope for such ballot) for use in general elections for Federal office by absent uniformed services voters and overseas voters who make timely application for, and do not receive, States, absentee ballots.

(b) SUBMISSION AND PROCESSING.—Except as otherwise provided in this title, a Federal write-in absentee ballot shall be submitted and processed in the manner provided by law for absentee ballots in the State involved. A Federal write-in absentee ballot of an absent uniformed services voter or overseas voter shall not be counted.

   (1) in the case of a ballot submitted by an overseas voter who is not an absent uniformed services voter, if the ballot is submitted from any location in the United States;

   (2) if the application of the absent uniformed services voters or overseas voter for a State absentee ballot is received by the appropriate State election official after the latter of—

      (A) the deadline of the State for receipt of such application; or

      (B) the date that is 30 days before the general election; or

   (3) if a State absentee ballot of an absent uniformed services voters or overseas voter is received by the appropriate State election official

not later than the deadline for receipt of the State absentee ballot under State law.

(c) SPECIAL RULES.—The following rules shall apply with respect to Federal write-in absentee ballots:

(1) In completing the ballot, the absent uniformed services voters or overseas voter may designate a candidate by writing in the name of the candidate or by writing in the name of political party (in which case the ballot shall be counted for the candidate of that political party).

(2) In the case of the offices of President and Vice President, a vote for a named candidate or a vote by writing in the name of a political party shall be counted as a vote for the electors supporting the candidate involved.

(3) Any abbreviation, misspelling, or other minor variation in the form of the name of a candidate or a political party shall be disregarded in determining the validity of the ballot, if the intention of the voter can be ascertained.

(d) SECOND BALLOT SUBMISSION; INSTRUCTION TO ABSENT UNIFORMED SERVICES VOTER OR OVERSEAS VOTER.—

An absent uniformed services voter or overseas voter who submits a Federal write-in absentee ballot and later receives a State absentee ballot, may submit the State absentee ballot. The Presidential designee shall assure that the instructions for each Federal write-in absentee ballot clearly state that an absent uniformed services voter or overseas voter who submits a Federal write-in absentee ballot and later receives and submits a State absentee ballot should make every reasonable effort to inform the appropriate State election official that the voter has submitted more than one ballot.

(e) USE OF APPROVED STATE ABSENTEE BALLOT IN PLACE OF FEDERAL WRITE-IN ABSENTEE BALLOT.

The Federal write-in absentee ballot shall not be valid for use in a general election if the State involved provides a State absentee ballot that—

(1) at the request of the State, is approved by the Presidential designee for use in place of the Federal write-in absentee ballot; and

(2) is made available to absent uniformed services voters and overseas voters at least 60 days before the deadline for receipt of the State ballot under State law.

(f) CERTAIN STATES EXEMPTED.—A State is not required to permit use of the Federal write-in absentee ballot, if, on and after the date of the enactment of the title, the State has in effect a law providing that—

(1) a State absentee ballot is required to be available to any voter described in section 107(5)(A) at least 90 days before the general election involved; and

(2) a State absentee ballot is required to be available to any voter described in section 107(5)(B) or (C), as soon as the official list of candidates in the general election is complete.

SEC. 104. USE OF SINGLE APPLICATION FOR ALL SUBSEQUENT ELECTIONS.

(a) IN GENERAL.—If a State accepts and processes an official post card form (prescribed under section 101) submitted by an absent uniformed services voter or overseas voter for simultaneous voter registration and absentee ballot application (in accordance with section 102(a)(4)) and the voter requests that the application be considered an application for an absentee ballot for each subsequent election for Federal office held in the State through the next 2 regularly scheduled general elections for Federal office (including any runoff elections which may occur as a result of the outcome of such general elections), the State shall provide an absentee ballot to the voter for each such subsequent election.

(b) EXCEPTION FOR VOTERS CHANGING REGISTRATION.—Subsection (a) shall not apply with respect to a voter registered to vote in a State for any election held after the voter notifies the State that the voter no longer wishes to be registered to vote in the State or after the State determines that the voter has registered to vote in another State.

(c) REVISION OF OFFICIAL POST CARD FORM.—The Presidential designee shall revise the official post card form (prescribed under section 101) to enable a voter using the form to—

   (1) request an absentee ballot for each election for Federal office held in a State during a year; or

   (2) request an absentee ballot for only the next scheduled election for Federal office held in a State.

(d) NO EFFECT ON VOTER REMOVAL PROGRAMS.—Nothing in this section may be construed to prevent a State from removing any voter from the rolls of registered voters in the State under any program or method permitted under section 8 of the National Voter Registration Act of 1993.

(e) PROHIBITION OF REFUSAL OF APPLICATION ON GROUNDS OF EARLY SUBMISSION.—A State may not refuse to accept or process, with respect to any election for Federal office, any otherwise valid voter registration application or absentee ballot application (including the postcard form prescribed under section 101) submitted by an absent uniformed services voter during a year on the grounds that the voter submitted the application before the first date on which the State otherwise accepts or processes such applications for that year submitted by absentee voters who are not members of the uniformed services.

SEC. 105. ENFORCEMENT

The Attorney General may bring a civil action in an appropriate district court for such declaratory or injunctive relief as may be necessary to carry out this title.

SEC. 106. EFFECT ON CERTAIN OTHER LAWS

The exercise of any right under this title shall not affect, for purposes of any Federal, State, or local tax, the residence or domicile of a person exercising such right.

SEC. 107. DEFINITIONS

(1) "absent uniformed services voter" means—
  (A) a member of a uniformed service on active duty who, by reason of such active duty, is absent from the place of residence where the member is otherwise qualified to vote;
  (B) a member of the merchant marine who, by reason of service in the merchant marine, is absent from the place of residence where the member is otherwise qualified to vote; and
  (C) a spouse or dependent of a member referred to in subparagraph (A) or (B) who, by reason of the active duty or service of the member, is absent from the place of residence where the spouse or dependent is otherwise qualified to vote;

(2) "balloting materials" means official post card forms (prescribed under section 101), Federal write-in absentee ballots (prescribed under section 103), and any State balloting materials that, as determined by the Presidential designee, are essential to the carrying out of this title;

(3) "Federal office" means the office of President or Vice President, or of Senator or Representative in, or Delegate or Resident Commissioner to, the Congress

(4) "member of the merchant marine" means an individual (other than a member of a uniformed service or an individual employed, enrolled, or maintained on the Great Lakes or the inland waterways)—
  (A) employed as an officer or crew member of a vessel documented under the laws of the United States, or a vessel owned by the United States, or a vessel of foreign-flag registry under charter to or control of the United States; or
  (B) enrolled with the United States for employment or training for employment, or maintained by the United States for emergency relief service, as an officer or crew member of any such vessel;

(5) "overseas voter" means—
  (A) an absent uniformed services voter who, by reason of active duty or service is absent from the United States on the date of the election involved;
  (B) a person who resides outside the United States and is qualified to vote in the last place in which the person was domiciled before leaving the United States; or
  (C) a person who resides outside the United States and (but for such residence) would be qualified to vote in the last place in which the person was domiciled before leaving the United States;

(6) "State" means a State of the United States, the District of Columbia, the Commonwealth of Puerto Rico, Guam, the Virgin Islands, and American Samoa;

(7) "uniformed services" means the Army, Navy, Air Force, Marine Corps, and Coast Guard, the commissioned corps of the Public Health Service, and the commissioned corps of the National Oceanic and Atmospheric Administration; and

(8) "United States", where used in the territorial sense, means the several States, the District of Columbia, the Commonwealth of Puerto Rico, Guam, the Virgin Islands, and American Samoa.

Source: Uniformed and Overseas Citizens Absentee Voting Act (UOCAVA). *U.S. Department of Justice; Civil Rights Division; Voting Section.* 1986. Accessed March 28, 2019. http://www.fvap.gov/laws/uocavalaw.html.

President Clinton Signs the National Voter Registration Act, 1993

The National Voter Registration Act was an important piece of legislation that made it easier for millions of Americans to register to vote in federal elections. The law contained a number of significant provisions, but the most momentous was the "motor voter" section that required states to allow people seeking to obtain or renew their driver's license to register to vote at the same time. Following are excerpts from President Bill Clinton's May 20, 1993, signing statement for the law, which went into effect in 1995.

Getting to know the young people across this country, beginning in New Hampshire, who pushed the motor voter bill, was one of the most rewarding parts of the 1992 campaign. But the effort that we come here to celebrate today has a long and venerable heritage.

A few moments ago, you heard the voice of President Johnson crossing the chasm of time back to 1965 as he signed the Voting Rights Act into law. As a southerner and as President, his words have special significance to me. During my childhood, no family's dinner table, no church congregation, no community, and no place of work was immune from the searing struggle for civil rights. To hear Johnson's voice is to make vivid for me once again those difficult, yet glorious years of struggle, difficult and terrible because so many people gave their lives moving the stone of freedom up the side of a mountain, glorious because the years of contention eventually gave way to an overdue season of reconciliation and renewal, and gave our region and our country a second chance to fulfill our promise.

The victory we celebrate today is but the most recent chapter in the overlapping struggles of our Nation's history to enfranchise women and minorities, the disabled, and the young with the power to affect their own destiny and our common destiny by participating fully in our democracy. When blacks and women won the right to vote, when we outlawed the poll tax and literacy test, when the voting age was lowered to 18, and when finally we recognized the rights of disabled Americans, it was because the forces of change overcame the indifference of the majority and the resistance by the guardians of the status quo. And who prevailed? Brave people working at the grassroots, impatient with an always imperfect democracy and dedicated to widening the circle of liberty to encompass more and more of our fellow citizens.

I have said many times in many places that in this country we don't have a person to waste. Surely the beginning of honoring that pledge is making sure the franchise is extended to and used by every eligible American. Today we celebrate our noble tradition by signing into law our newest civil rights law, the National Voter Registration Act of 1993, which all of us know and love as "motor voter."

An extraordinary coalition of organizations, many of whom played historic roles in our expanding democratic rights, joined many years ago with the hope that they would see this day come. I'm honored to share this podium with representatives with three fighters for freedom: the NAACP, the League of Women Voters, and Human Serve. I want to pay special tribute to Disabled and Able To Vote, to Project Vote, and to Rock the Vote, and literally, the scores of other groups for whom the goal of full voter participation has been a durable and lasting dream. I want to pay special tribute to the young people who lobbied me personally for motor voter and who voted with renewed energy and conviction for their own futures in the election last November.

They all labored hard because this bill was necessary. As many as 35 percent of otherwise eligible voters in our Nation are not registered, and the failure to register is the primary reason given by eligible citizens for their not voting. The principle behind this legislation is clear: Voting should be about discerning the will of the majority, not about testing the administrative capacity of a citizen.

The State of Washington instituted a similar measure during the 1992 election, and their motor voter program registered in that State alone an additional 186,000 people. Motor voter works at registering voters and people who register vote.

With this law and its appropriate implementation by States, voters can register by applying for a driver's license, through uniform mail application, or by applying in person at various agencies designated by the States. As a result, registration for Federal election will become as accessible as possible, while the integrity of the electoral process is clearly preserved.

As I said, I have long supported the idea of motor voter. More than a year ago, I promised as President that I would sign H.R. 2 and fight for its passage. I'm pleased to be able to keep the promise today that I made on this Rock the Vote card which still has my signature back in New Hampshire.

I also want to point out that all the President does is lobby for and sign laws. If the Congress doesn't pass them, they don't get passed. The Rock the Vote card that I signed here says, "Why don't politicians want you to vote?" Well, there are a lot of Members of the Congress here from both parties who do want you to vote, and I want to thank not only those on the platform here but all of those out in the audience who, after all, passed this bill into law. It was their votes that made this day possible.

This bill in its enactment is a sign of a new vibrancy in our democracy. With all the challenges and difficulties, with the years of accumulated economic problems we face, with all the divisions among our people, there is a new determination to make progress. You can see it in many ways: Voter participation was up in November, and after the election it didn't stop. Here at the White House, mail has climbed to unprecedented levels. After I had been in office 14 weeks, the White House had received more mail than was received in all of 1992. We have had the switchboards jammed, the E-mail system full. And if you haven't gotten an answer to your letter, we're working on it. [Laughter]

This country is pulsing with the power of individual citizens' ideas in their determination to get something done. The legislators who worked so hard to adopt this bill, the organizations that gave themselves so completely to its endeavor, the young people, the activists, MTV, all of them tapped a powerful current of energy that is still flowing in this country. . . .

The current of reform is moving in this country. And those of you who helped to bring this bill to pass can take a large share of credit not only for this bill but for the general movement and energy and involvement and determination of all of our fellow citizens. It was never right to sit on the sidelines of our democracy. And now with motor voter, there will be fewer and fewer excuses for anyone to do so.

Let us remember this in closing: Voting is an empty promise unless people vote. Now there is no longer the excuse of the difficulty of registration. It is the right of every American to vote. It is also the responsibility of every American to vote. We have taken an important step this morning to protect that right. And I want to challenge Joel and all the young people who did so much to register voters for the last election, and all of you who did so much to bring this voting rights bill to law and all the ones that preceded it, to make sure now that we keep the rights alive by making sure that the responsibility to exercise it is exercised by every eligible American.

When we leave here today, we ought to say: This voting rights bill and the others will not be in vain. Every year from now on, we're going to have more registered voters and more people voting. We're going to make the system work. The law empowers us to do it. It's now up to us to assume the responsibility to see that it gets done.

Source: Clinton, Bill. Remarks upon signing the National Voter Registration Act of 1993, May 20, 1993. *Public Papers of the Presidents of the United States: William J. Clinton, 1993, Book I.* Washington, DC: Government Printing Office, 1994, pp. 706–708.

Oregon Voters Approve Nation's First Federal Vote-by-Mail Voting System, 1998

In 1998 Oregon became the first state in the nation to establish a voting system that was exclusively vote-by-mail (VBM). The state had first put such a voting option—also sometimes known as a vote-at-home (VAH)—in place for local elections in the early 1980s. This option worked so well that in 1998 citizen supporters managed to get a measure on the ballot that would establish a vote-by-mail system for all elections, including primaries and federal elections. This referendum, known as Measure 60, passed by a resounding margin, with approval from approximately 70 percent of Oregonian voters.

Since that time, vote-by-mail systems have gradually spread to other states. Both Washington and Colorado have moved to complete VBM systems, while counties and cities in several other states have implemented VBM elections. In Utah, for example, twenty-seven of twenty-nine counties used exclusively mail-in voting in 2018, and Anchorage, Alaska, moved to a VBM system that year as well. Meanwhile, as of early 2018 a majority of states—twenty-seven of them, plus the District of Columbia—send VBM absentee ballots to voters upon request, no questions asked (the remaining twenty states require a valid excuse before they will grant a request for an absentee ballot).

Voting rights advocates are virtually unanimous in praising the shift toward vote-by-mail systems. They contend that such systems are a godsend for voters who are disabled, elderly, work on election days, or have difficulty securing reliable transportation to polling places. They also claim that VBM is more cost effective and secure than the traditional polling station. As the following excerpts from Oregon's 1998 voter guide show, these arguments were prominent in the campaign to get VBM approved in the first place. Oregonians were swayed by the "Arguments in Favor" included in the guide, and generally did not find the "Arguments in Opposition" to be convincing.

Be It Enacted by the People of the State of Oregon:

Section 1. ORS 254.465 is amended to read:

254.465. The following rules apply to elections conducted by mail:

1) A presidential preference primary election described in ORS 254.056 shall be conducted by mail in all counties, under the supervision of the Secretary of State
2) *[Except as provided in subsection (1) of this section,]* An election held on the date of the biennial primary or general election shall *[not]* be conducted by mail.
3) A state election not described in subsections (1) or (2) of this section may be conducted by mail. The Secretary of State by rule shall direct that a state election authorized to be conducted by mail under this subsection be conducted uniformly by mail or at polling places.
4) A county clerk may conduct an election not described in subsections (1) to (3) of this section by mail in the county, in a city, or in a district defined in ORS 255.012, under the supervision of the Secretary of State. In deciding to conduct an election by mail, the county clerk may consider requests from the governing body of the county, city, or district and shall consider whether conducting the election by mail will be economically and administratively feasible.
5) The Secretary of State shall adopt rules to provide for uniformity in the conduct of state elections by mail.

EXPLANATORY STATEMENT

This measure requires that the primary and general elections by conducted by mail. The primary and general elections are held in May and November of even-numbered years. Current law prohibits conducting the primary and general elections by mail.

Under current law, the following rules apply:

1. The primary and general elections may not be conducted by mail.
2. Voters may sign up to become permanent absentee voters and receive all ballots by mail.
3. The presidential primary election in March of presidential election years is required to be conducted by mail.
4. Special state elections and local elections may be conducted by mail.

Currently, voters may vote by going to a polling place on election day or by some form of absentee voting, including permanent absentee or single-election absentee.

This measure would eliminate polling places for primary and general elections. Voters could return their ballots by mail or drop them off at designated sites.

This measure would not affect the current law that allows voters to obtain absentee ballots or to vote at the elections office. It would also not affect the current laws that allow the Secretary of State to decide whether to conduct special state elections by mail, or that allow the county election officials to decide whether to conduct local elections by mail. . . .

ARGUMENT IN FAVOR

Ballot measure 60 makes sense:

Voter sense . . . taxpayer sense . . . Common sense

The people who conduct your local, state, and federal elections, the election officials of Oregon, ask for your YES vote on Ballot measure 60, which brings the Primary and General elections into the same system as all other Oregon elections. Passage means that all elections can be conducted by mail.

It is the common sense thing to do. Why? Our 16-year history with conducting elections by mail shows that voter turnout improves with elections by mail, tax dollars are saved when elections are conducted by mail and elections by mail help keep our voter registration files among the cleanest in the nation.

If you could improve voter turnout, save up to $4 million in property tax dollars, make voting more convenient for everyone, why wouldn't you do it? . . .

No longer will you need to worry about finding the time in your busy schedule on a Tuesday during limited hours to get to your polling place to cast your ballot.

Your ballot will be mailed to you for every election and you can return it by mail, deposit it at a secure official ballot dropsite, or go to a site designated by your elections office and vote in a voting booth if that is what you prefer. The options are yours.

Meanwhile you will have your ballot, at your home with your voter pamphlet, and be able to vote at your own pace. You will have your ballot in time to call and ask questions of candidates or ballot measure campaigns.

As those you have elected and chosen to oversee your elections process, we recommend a "YES" vote on measure 60.

It just makes sense.

The Election Officials of Oregon

ARGUMENT IN FAVOR

The American Association of Retired Persons (AARP) supports Ballot Measure 60.

VOTE BY MAIL.

We support Vote By Mail for all primary and general elections because it enhances the fundamental right to vote, increases voter turnout, has greater protections against fraud and gives more convenient access for everyone to vote.

Measure 60—Vote By Mail is a non-partisan issue that enjoys bipartisan support.

The Right to Vote

Most basic of all political rights is the RIGHT TO VOTE. We feel that one of the most important aspects of a democracy is voter participation and citizen involvement in the democratic process. The essence of a democracy is that citizens exercise their civic responsibility by voting. The act of voting is what is valuable, regardless of where one does it.

Increases Voter Participation

We support the efforts to promote and enhance the ability of all Oregonians to vote. Vote By Mail assures greater voter participation. AARP favors **increasing** the number of citizens voting in elections. . . .

Higher Safeguards Against Fraud

Retired persons do not take the privilege of voting lightly. It is important to retired persons to vote their own convictions and make their own decisions when voting on issues and candidates. Over 15 years of conducting elections by mail in Oregon has proven that Vote By Mail does not deny privacy nor does it encourage fraud. In fact, higher safeguards against fraud and intimidation exist in Vote By Mail elections [than] in a traditional polling place election.

More Convenient

Vote By Mail gives more convenient access to everyone to vote. It provides convenient access for employed persons to vote. It also enables the frail, elderly and persons with disabilities to vote—people whom otherwise may not make it to the polls.

AARP URGES YOU TO VOTE YES ON MEASURE #60—VOTE BY MAIL!

ARGUMENT IN FAVOR

The Time Has Come to Expand Vote By Mail

As current and former Governors and Secretaries of State, both Republicans and Democrats alike, we urge you to vote Yes on Measure 60. In an age where good ideas unfortunately become bogged down in partisan politics, we all agree that Vote By Mail—Measure 60 is an idea whose time has come.

Oregon has always led the country in new and innovative ideas, and Vote By Mail is another step in that proud tradition. Vote By Mail began in Oregon over 15 years ago and we have personally seen it progress to the point that all elections are now conducted by mail **except** for the biennial primary and general. The time has come to **expand Vote By Mail to all elections.**

Oregon also has a proud tradition of active citizen involvement in their political process and high voter turnout when compared with the rest of the country. Sadly, we are seeing this tradition slowly disappearing. We are now saddled with a costly and confusing dual election system that drives down voter turnout while increasing costs.

Most of us grew up voting at a polling place. While some of us may miss the polling place experience, we understand that the question now is **not** polling places Vs voting by mail. Rather it is replacing our current dual election system—one that is costly, confusing and rives down voter turnout—with the simplicity, convenience and efficiency of Voting By Mail.

Obviously every Oregonian should be concerned about fraud, coercion and intimidation in any election. However, over 15 years of conducting elections by mail in Oregon have proven that Vote By Mail elections can be conducted with the highest standards of integrity.

As leaders we have seen that Oregonians value ideas that make sense, improve our government and increase civic involvement. The time has come to expand Vote By Mail to all elections. We urge you to vote Yes on Measure 60!

Governor John Kitzhaber
Secretary of State Phil Keisling
Fmr Secretary of State, Governor and U.S. Senator Mark Hatfield
Fmr Secretary of State and State Treasurer Clay Myers

ARGUMENT IN FAVOR

VOTE-BY-MAIL IS IN THE PUBLIC INTEREST

Vote Yes on Measure 60

OSPIRG urges the passage of Measure 60. As a public interest watchdog organization with 25,000 citizen members, OSPIRG has a history of supporting policies that would enhance public participation in the political process. Efforts such as campaign finance reform, motor voter, and defense of the initiative process do this, and so does Vote-By-Mail. Simply put, when more people participate in our democracy, the true public interest will be more likely to prevail. . . .

Vote-by-Mail has overwhelming public support

With so many opportunities in politics today for the public to be cynical or angry, it's nice to have a measure we can all feel good about. Measure 60 has been brought forward by a broad coalition of citizens and civic organizations. This inspiring effort is in the product tradition of Oregon's citizen initiative process.

VOTE YES ON MEASURE 60!

Submitted by
Maureen Kirk
Executive Director
Oregon State Public Interest Research Group

ARGUMENT IN FAVOR

VOTE-BY-MAIL: MYTH AND REALITY

As a supporter of Vote-by-Mail, I have heard a number of objections to this innovation. These have failed to deter the growing support for Voting-By-Mail. However, there is also such a hodge-podge of mythology about this process that additional information is needed.

First myth: that voting is a "social function." The act of voting is not a meet-and-greet gabfest. It is the noblest expression of the democratic process and it is so wherever you do it, in a kitchen or a campground or a courthouse. In fact, Vote-By-Mail doesn't even deprive the polling place fan. They can drive to their clerk's office on election day and vote with all the ceremony and camaraderie they want.

Second myth: fraud. Fraud is <u>less</u> possible in mail elections, where every signature is verified, than in poll elections where they are not.

Third myth: coercion. People who have looked for it haven't found it. But anyone who has the slightest fear of coercion can prevent it. Designate on your registration card to send your ballot to a place where you feel safe and free from coercion. If sometime tries to interfere with your vote, destroy your ballot. Later, report the action to your clerk, receive a new ballot and vote unhindered.

Fourth myth: Vote-By-Mail voters miss out on "late revelations about candidates." The "late revelations" just <u>before</u> election day are really just "attack ads" and mudslinging. In a Vote-by-Mail election the ads have to come <u>three weeks</u> early and can be effectively rebutted. The voter can vote or wait for more information, whichever he or she prefers.

To believe that voting in a public setting is somehow superior to voting in a private setting puts too high a value on ostentation. No, with voting, as with prayer, what matters is what is in your heart and your head and not where you happen to be standing at the time.

David Buchanan
Executive Director
Oregon Common Cause

ARGUMENT IN OPPOSITION

<u>Eliminating "Election Day Voting" at local polls.</u> Officials would mail out ballots far ahead of "election day" to all registered voters, whether or not they request ballots. Recipients then must dispose of the ballots, whether or not interested in voting. Such casual broadcast of blank ballots to people who have not requested

them invites more vote scams, fosters corruption, trivializes voting, and deprives everyone of the option of casting a secret ballot in a protected and secured voting place.

Broadcast mailing of ballots far ahead of time surrenders the state responsibility for providing citizens access to ballots and turns this solemn duty over to a semi-privatized federal agency. It increases chances of delay, intrusion, loss, theft, premature voting, and low turnout. . . .

Depriving all voters of the private refuge of the polling place eliminates the truly secret ballot, exposing many voters to undue pressures and promptings while actually voting. Mail-out ballots facilitate "helpers" intruding and dominating voting by recipients unlikely to vote independently.

Secure, secret, intentional, and accurate voting might cost a bit more than indiscriminate broadcast mailings of official ballots later collected as rubbish. Shouldn't a voter's security in voting have greater worth than a recycling effort? Don't vote us back to the mess of corrupted elections that Americans reformed by adopting the secret ballot a century ago! . . .

(This information furnished by Fred W. Decker, Treasurer, Citizens for Choice of Voting).

ARGUMENT IN OPPOSITION

Let's call it what it is: an elimination of your ability to choose how to vote and new opportunity for corruption to our election process. Mandatory vote by mail does not assure the sacred agreement that the state must uphold with its citizens: one ballot, one vote, assurance of privacy, and the freedom to choose how your ballot is cast.

Facts:

- Saving dollars is not the answer to every problem. I would no more ask for substandard materials for a bridge to save money than I would to jeopardize the voting system for the sake of saving money.
- We do not have a statewide-computerized voter registration system. A single voter can be registered in more than one county and receive more than one ballot. Counties verify signatures, however, they do not automatically talk to 35 other counties to see if someone is registered in multiple jurisdictions. Therefore, multiple casting of ballots can occur.
- Proponents state that no fraud exists because there are no reports of fraud. . . . What family member would report to authorities another for tampering with a voting decision? We must not quickly brush aside the issue of "domestic coercion" simply because it is not being reported.
- Requests to bring your ballots to the church, union hall, employee meetings, senior luncheon so that individuals and "vote as a unified group" or "get questions answered" will be highly intimidating situations.

Intimidation, coercion, thousands of ballots sent from inaccurate and outdated registration lists, counties lacking the ability to daily and accurately exchange or compare data with each other, and lack of privacy all [contain] potential for dramatic corruption. . . .

Vote NO on Mandatory Vote by Mail.

(This information furnished by Representative Lynn Snodgrass.)

Source: Oregon, State of. "Measure No. 60." *Official 1998 General Election Voters Pamphlet—Statewide Measures.* 1998, pp. 61–67.

5

Partisanship Clouds Battles over Voting Rights and Election Integrity: 2000–2016

The 2000 election and the subsequent *Bush v. Gore* Supreme Court decision that paved the way for George W. Bush's inauguration as the nation's forty-third president ushered in a series of administrative reforms for voting and registration in the United States. While these reforms aimed at creating more administrative consistency across the United States, states also amended and adopted policies that changed the way citizens register and vote. The connection between voting and registration reforms and political participation for certain segments of the electorate also created opportunities for political parties to use the rules to facilitate participation for voters that are more likely to identify with their political party or limit opportunities for participation for voters that are less likely to identify with their political party. Over a short period of time, the conversation around election administration shifted from one focused on procedure to one deeply embedded in politics.

THE FRANCHISE AFTER *BUSH v. GORE*

In the aftermath of the politically charged and enormously controversial *Bush v. Gore* ruling, the United State Congress enacted the Help America Vote Act in 2002. The Help America Vote Act, or HAVA, ushered in several administrative reforms. HAVA not only provided federal funds to states to purchase new voting equipment but also "imposed a number of requirements on the states with respect to election administration, created a new independent agency, made some changes to improve military and overseas voting, and authorized other election reform activities" (Burrus and Fischer, 2016). Under HAVA, for example, the Election Assistance Commission (EAC) was created. The EAC is an independent bipartisan agency, tasked with providing guidelines for states for the administration of elections, and for the distribution of funds for grant programs. HAVA authorized

$3.65 billion in payments to states to replace voting systems and meet the requirements of the act. The EAC was responsible for distributing the funds. Most recently, following concerns raised about cyber threats to the integrity of American elections after the 2016 election, the EAC was tasked with distributing an additional $380 million in grants to states (Election Assistance Commission, 2018). The funds from the grants can be used by states to replace voting equipment, implement post-audit systems, upgrade election-related computer systems, facilitate cybersecurity training, implement cybersecurity best practices, and fund other activities that will improve election security (Election Assistance Commission, 2018).

In the years that followed *Bush v. Gore*, states began to adopt and amend election administration reforms both increasing and decreasing opportunities for citizens to participate. As an example, no-excuse absentee ballots allow a voter to cast a ballot without providing an excuse for their absence from the voting precinct at the time of the election. In 2004, twenty-five states allowed no-excuse absentee voting; as of 2019, that number has increased to twenty-eight states (plus DC) (National Conference of State Legislatures, 2019).

Research has suggested changes to voting and registration do not have an equal effect across all segments of the electorate. To the contrary, these changes have different levels of impact depending on the race and socioeconomic status of citizens. Many studies have found that the use of in-person early voting (which allows a voter to cast a ballot prior to election day) in the states, for example, varies by an individual's income and does little to mobilize the young, less educated, minorities, or individuals with low incomes. This coupled with our two-party system, in which racial minorities and the poor are more likely to be Democrats, has put the administration of elections in the crosshairs of politics, and such changes are framed as hurting or helping one party over the other as opposed to being focused on the rights of citizens.

SHELBY v. HOLDER RULING GUTS ENFORCEMENT OF THE VOTING RIGHTS ACT

In 2013, the Supreme Court decided in *Shelby v. Holder* that Section 4b of the 1965 Voting Rights Act was unconstitutional. Section 4b contains the coverage formula that was used to determine which states or jurisdictions were required to receive preclearance from the courts or the Department of Justice under Section 5 of the VRA before making any changes to their voting or registration laws. Following the court's dramatic ruling, many states that were previously covered by Section 5 moved to change their voting laws. Of the changes that were adopted by the states, voter-identification requirements received the most scrutiny. Several states rushed to tighten previously existing voter ID laws or adopted strict photo ID laws.

Although the pace at which states adopted strict voter ID laws accelerated during the 2000s, voter ID laws have existed in the United States since the 1950s. South Carolina became the first state to request that voters show some type of identification at the polls. The identification did not require a photo but had to include the voter's name. Hawaii (1970), Texas (1971), Florida (1977), and Alaska (1980) followed South Carolina. By 2000, fourteen states had adopted laws that requested voters to present some form of identification. In 2005, the Commission on Federal Election Reform (also known as the Carter-Baker Commission) made a bipartisan recommendation that voters show identification at the polls. Shortly after the commission's recommendation, Georgia and Indiana adopted new voter-identification policies that required voters to show identification. Both laws went into effect in 2008 after Indiana's law was found constitutional in *Crawford v. Marion County* (2008). The adoption of voter identification laws continued across the United States for the next several years, with blue and red states alike adopting policies that range from ID requested but not required to strict photo voter-identification requirements. As states adopted voter ID requirements, challenges to their constitutionality were made by nonprofit, advocacy, and civil and voting rights organizations. These groups argued that they placed an undue burden on minority and poor voters—voters who overwhelmingly identify with the Democratic party.

FELONY DISENFRANCHISEMENT

Similar arguments were made during this period about the voting rights of citizens with felony convictions. Felony disenfranchisement, in which a citizen is stripped of his or her right to vote after being convicted of a felony level offense, has had an extensive history in the United States. Like many laws in the United States, the practice of felony disenfranchisement is a carryover from English law and colonization. The legal tradition in England included the imposition of civil disabilities, or the loss of rights or privileges, on those who were convicted for crimes (Pettus, 2005; Reiman, 1995). Civil disabilities included the forfeiture of property, corruption of the blood, and the loss of civil rights. Essentially, the imposition of civil disabilities left the lawbreaker with no legal status and his descendants unable to access any inheritance (Pettus, 2005). Although this particular law was not adopted by all of the would-be states, from 1776 to 1821 eleven states adopted statutes in their state constitutions that denied votes to those convicted of a felony or provided the state legislature with the authority to deny such a right. Before the Civil War, nineteen of the thirty-four states had provisions that excluded citizens with felony convictions from the ballot box, and between 1865 and 1900, eighteen states adopted laws that restricted voting rights for citizens with felony convictions.

State felony disenfranchisement policies in the United States fall into one of five categories: no disenfranchisement; voting rights restored automatically after release from prison; voting rights restored after release from prison and discharge from parole (probationers may vote); voting rights restored after completion of sentence (incarceration, parole, probation); and permanent disenfranchisement for some or all felony offenses. As of early 2019, only two states, Maine and Vermont, allow *all* felons to vote, including those who are currently incarcerated.

Following civil rights challenges to felony disenfranchisement laws, several states changed their laws to provide for the return of voting rights to certain segments of the disenfranchised population. In spite of this handful of reversals, however, experts estimate that more than six million citizens with felony convictions were ineligible to vote in the November 2016 election. More than three out of four of these disenfranchised citizens were unable to vote even though they had completed their sentences, been released on parole, or were on supervised probation.

Florida, Kentucky, Iowa, Maryland, and Virginia are examples of states that have since 2000 amended their felony disenfranchisement policies to expand voting rights for citizens with felony convictions. During this period, many of the expanded policies that were adopted were rescinded, lasting only a short time before they again limited the voting rights of citizens with felony convictions. In the 2018 midterm election, for example, Florida voters passed Amendment 4, which changed the process of rights restoration for citizens with felony convictions in Florida. It automatically restored voting rights for individuals who have not been convicted of murder or a felony sexual offense. In May 2019, however, legislation was passed in the Republican-controlled state legislature that requires citizens with felony convictions to pay off all court fines, fees, and restitution before they can regain their voting rights. On June 28, 2019, Governor Ron DeSantis (R) signed the bill.

Given the overrepresentation of racial minorities in the population of citizens who are disenfranchised due to felony conviction, the political consequences of the restoration or withholding of voting rights for citizens with felony convictions have not gone unnoticed. Citizens with felony convictions have shown a preference for Democratic political candidates in both presidential and senate elections (Uggen and Manza, 2002). One 2002 study found that Democratic candidates would have received 70 percent of votes cast by citizens with felony convictions in fourteen of the last fifteen Senate elections from 1972 to 2000. This same study found that if citizens with felony convictions had been able to vote, the popular vote margin of victory for Democratic Party candidate Al Gore would have been greater than one million. When specifically focused on Florida, Gore would have had more than enough votes to win the state—and thus the presidential election that year (Uggen and Manza, 2002, 792).

RENEWED FOCUS ON GERRYMANDERING

In addition to administrative practices and the rules for access to the voting booth, the rules of representation also came under increased scrutiny during this era.

Redistricting is the process that is used to determine the geographic boundaries for representation at various levels of government, most notably in state legislatures and the House of Representatives. Although drawing district boundaries is an administrative process, it is also political. Through the districting process, geographic boundaries can be drawn that predetermine what party or candidate will win a seat. In most states this process, which occurs at least every ten years after the decennial census, is controlled by the political party that is the majority in the state legislature (Brennan Center for Justice, "Who Draws the Maps," 2019). The Supreme Court of the United States has ruled that using the redistricting process as a tool to dilute the voting strength of racial minorities by gerrymandering voting districts is unconstitutional. The constitutionality of partisan gerrymanders, however, remains unsettled. Partisan gerrymanders in some instances, according to a decision by the court in *Cooper v. Harris* (2016), are de facto racial gerrymanders because of the racial and ethnic alignment of minority groups with the Democratic Party and the intent underlying the creation of the district(s). While many hoped the court would settle the issue in 2019, in June 2019 the court ruled the issue of partisan gerrymanders, as a political question, is beyond the scope of the court.

SOURCES

Brennan Center for Justice. "Who Draws the Maps? Legislative and Congressional Redistricting." Brennan Center for Justice. January 30, 2019. Accessed June 25, 2019. https://www.brennancenter.org/analysis/who-draws-maps-states-redrawing-congressional-and-state-district-lines.

Burrus, Arthur L., and Eric A. Fischer. "The Help America Vote Act and Election Administration: Overview and Selected Issues for the 2016 Election." Congressional Research Service. 2016. Accessed June 25, 2019. https://fas.org/sgp/crs/misc/RS20898.pdf.

Election Assistance Commission. "HAVA Funds State Chart View." March 30, 2018. Accessed June 25, 2019. https://www.eac.gov/payments-and-grants/hava-funds-state-chart-view/.

National Conference of State Legislatures. "Absentee and Early Voting." April 3, 2019. Accessed June 25, 2019. http://www.ncsl.org/research/elections-and-campaigns/absentee-and-early-voting.aspx.

National Conference of State Legislatures. "Voter ID History." May 5, 2017. Accessed June 25, 2019. http://www.ncsl.org/research/elections-and-campaigns/voter-id-history.aspx.

Neely, Grant, and Lilliard Richardson. "Who Is Early Voting? An Individual Level Examination." *Social Science Journal*, 38 (2001): 381–392.

Pettus, Katherine. *Felony Disenfranchisement in America: Historical Origins, Institutional Racism, and Modern Consequences*. New York: LFB Scholarly Publications, Inc., 2005.

Reiman, Jeffrey. *The Rich Get Richer and the Poor Get Prison*. 4th ed. Boston, MA: Allyn & Bacon, 1995.

Stein, Robert. "Introduction: Early Voting." *Public Opinion Quarterly*, 62, no. 1 (1998): 57–69.

Stein, Robert, and Patricia Garcia-Monet. "Voting Early But Not Often." *Social Science Quarterly*, 78, no. 3 (1997): 657–671.

Teixeira, Ruy. *The Disappearing American Voter*. Washington, DC: The Brookings Institution, 1992.

Timpone, Richard. "Structure, Behavior and Voter Turnout in the United States." *American Political Science Review*, 92, no. 1 (1998): 145–158.

Uggen, Christopher, Angela Behrens, and Jeff Manza. "Criminal Disenfranchisement." *Annual Review of Law in Social Science*, 1 (2005): 307–322.

Uggen, Christopher, Ryan Larson, and Sarah Shannon. "6 Million Lost Voters: State-level Estimates of Felony Disenfranchisement." 2016. The Sentencing Project. Accessed June 25, 2019. https://www.sentencingproject.org/publications/6-million-lost-voters-state-level-estimates-felony-disenfranchisement-2016/.

Uggen, Christopher, and Jeff Manza. "Democratic Contraction? Political Consequences of Felon Disenfranchisement in the United States." *American Sociological Review*, 67 (2002): 777–803.

PRIMARY DOCUMENTS

Commission Calls for Voting Reforms in the Wake of Disputed Bush-Gore Election, 2001

The 2000 presidential election was extremely close and clouded with controversy about the vote count in Florida. With neither Republican nominee George W. Bush nor Democratic nominee Al Gore certain who would ultimately be named the victor in that state—and thus receive the necessary electoral votes to win the presidency—the entire nation endured weeks of uncertainty and legal maneuverings that put the country on edge. Bush became president only after Florida's conservative Supreme Court shut down Gore's request for a statewide recount of the state's popular vote on what many independent legal scholars saw as legally dubious grounds.

The entire episode left America's faith in the integrity of its elections so shaken that both Democrats and Republicans endorsed the creation of a bipartisan National Commission on Federal Election Reform. In August 2001, the commission released its report, which included thirteen specific recommendations for federal voting reform. "It is critical that all Americans have confidence in our electoral system," stated the Commission, "and we should strive to eliminate any reasonable perception that the basic mechanisms of democratic participation favor some citizens over others. No voter should ever feel that the process of voting was intimidating or that there were improper barriers, either intentional or unintentional, that prevented the exercise of their right to vote."

Several of the Commission's proposed reforms to better ensure that every legitimate vote is counted—though not all of them—became law one year later with the passage of the Help America Vote Act of 2002. Supporters of that law described it as an important advance in reforming American election practices, but critics said that Congress could have done much more to protect voting rights and election integrity if it had embraced all of the commission's proposed reforms. Following are introductory remarks from the commission report, To Assure Pride and Confidence in the Electoral Process, *as well as a summary of its recommendations.*

Letter to the American People

In 2000 the American electoral system was tested by a political ordeal unlike any in living memory. From November 7 until December 12 the outcome of the presidential election was fought out in bitter political and legal struggles that ranged throughout the state of Florida and ultimately extended to the Supreme Court of the United States. The American political system proved its resilience. But we must think about the future.

The ordinary institutions of election administration in the United States, and specifically Florida, just could not readily cope with an extremely close election. Many aspects of the election process were put under a microscope and viewed by an anxious nation. With dismay and growing anger we saw controversial ballot design; antiquated and error-prone voting machines; subjective and capricious processes for counting votes; voter rolls that let unqualified voters vote in some counties and turned away qualified voters in others; confusion in the treatment of overseas military ballots; and a political process subjected to protracted litigation.

Stepping back from Florida, the picture is no more encouraging. The chief election official of Georgia, Cathy Cox, testified to our Commission that: "As the presidential election drama unfolded in Florida last November, one thought was foremost in my mind: there but for the grace of God go I. Because the truth is, if the presidential margin had been razor thin in Georgia and if our election systems had undergone the same microscopic scrutiny that Florida endured, we would have fared no better. In many respects, we might have fared even worse." Across America, we have heard from official after official who feels the same way.

There is good news, though. In the last few years, and now spurred by the events last year, election reform has returned to the legislative agenda in many states. In much of the country cadres of able and dedicated election administrators are in place who can show what is possible and carry reforms into practice. In a world of problems that often defy any solution, the weaknesses in election administration are, to a very great degree, problems that government actually can solve.

In this report we and our colleagues offer very specific recommendations on what should be done. In other words, Americans can and should expect their electoral system to be a source of national pride and a model to all the world.

Gerald R. Ford
Jimmy Carter
Robert H. Michel
Lloyd N. Cutler
Co-Chairs of the National Commission on Federal Election Reform

Summary of Principal Recommendations

The Goals of Federal Election Reform

When they choose the president, the vice president, and members of Congress, the American people should expect all levels of government to provide a democratic process that:

- Maintains an accurate list of citizens who are qualified to vote;
- Encourages every eligible voter to participate effectively;
- Uses equipment that reliably clarifies and registers the voter's choices;
- Handles close elections in a foreseeable and fair way;
- Operates with equal effectiveness for every citizen and every community; and
- Reflects limited but responsible federal participation.

For Americans, democracy is a precious birthright. But each generation must nourish and improve the processes of democracy for its successors. In the near-term, the next three to five years for instance, we envision a country where each state maintains accurate, computerized lists of who can vote, networked with local administrators. Using that system, qualified voters in our mobile society would be able to vote throughout their state without being turned away because of the vagaries of local administration. Using the system we recommend here, millions of military and other overseas voters would find it easier to get and return their ballots. Election Day would be held on a national holiday, freeing up more people to serve as poll workers and making polling places more accessible. Voting machines would meet a common standard of excellent performance. Each state would have its uniform, objective definitions of what constitutes a vote. News organizations would exert necessary restraint in predicting election outcomes. Every jurisdiction and every official would obey the Voting Rights Act and other statutes that secure the franchise and prohibit discrimination. In all of this there would be a delicate balance of shared responsibilities between levels of government, and between officials and the voters they serve.

This report sets forth our recommendations for the next, immediate steps on the road to attainment of these goals.

Policy Recommendation 1

Every state should adopt a system of statewide voter registration.

1. The statewide computerized voter file should be networked with and accessible to every election jurisdiction in the state so that any level can initiate registrations and updates with prompt notification to the others. It should include provisions for sharing data with other states.
2. When a citizen either applies for a driver's license or registers to vote, each state should obtain residential address and other information, such as a digitized signature, in a form that is equally usable for both the motor vehicle and voter databases. The address information can then be linked to a statewide street index.
3. Each state's driver's license and voter registration applications should require applicants to provide at least the last four digits of their Social Security number. States should also ask applicants if they are registered in another state, so that that state can be notified of the new registration.
4. Each state's voter registration applications should require a separate and specific affirmation that the applicant is a U.S. citizen.

Policy Recommendation 2

Every state should permit provisional voting by any voter who claims to be qualified to vote in that state.

1. Provisional voting authorizes any person whose name does not appear on the list of registered voters, but who wishes to vote, to be issued a ballot. The ballot shall be counted only upon verification by election officials that the provisional voter is eligible and qualified to vote within the state and only for the offices for which the voter is qualified to vote.

2. Another option, for states with statewide computerized voting lists, would be to let a voter who is not on the list submit proof of identification and swear to or affirm an appropriate affidavit of eligibility to vote in that jurisdiction. This information could then be used as an application for voter registration and the voter list would be amended accordingly. If qualified, the voter could either be issued a regular ballot or, if the state preferred, be allowed to vote provisionally pending confirmation of the voter's eligibility.

Policy Recommendation 3

Congress should enact legislation to hold presidential and congressional elections on a national holiday.

1. Holding national elections on a national holiday will increase availability of poll workers and suitable polling places and might make voting easier for some workers.
2. One approach, which this Commission favors, would be to specify that in even-numbered years the Veterans Day national holiday be held on the Tuesday next after the first Monday in November and serve also as our Election Day.

Policy Recommendation 4

Congress should adopt legislation that simplifies and facilitates absentee voting by uniformed and overseas citizens.

1. Each state should designate a responsible official for absentee voting by uniformed and overseas citizens who are residents of that state. That official should become the single point of contact for the citizens of that state who are served by the Federal Voting Assistance Program, which helps such uniformed and overseas citizens.
2. In 1986 Congress passed the Uniformed and Overseas Citizens Absentee Voting Act (UOCAVA) to help eligible members of the armed services and their families, and other citizens overseas, to vote. Utilizing standardized forms for voter registration and absentee ballot requests, all UOCAVA-covered residents from a home state should be authorized to mail these applications to the designated official for their state. If that state uses a statewide voter registration system networked to local jurisdictions, as we have recommended, the state official should be authorized to act directly on these applications or to forward them for action by the appropriate local jurisdiction. States should accept one absentee ballot application as a valid application for all subsequent elections being held by that state in that year.
3. The designated state official should be authorized to accept either a voted ballot being returned for any jurisdiction of that state or a standardized Federal Write-In Absentee Ballot that is an option for a UOCAVA-covered citizen. States should be obliged to accept and tally a

Federal Write-In Absentee Ballot for those contests in which they determine the voter was eligible to vote.

4. Properly filed absentee ballots should be accepted if they have been received by the time the polls of that state have closed on Election Day. States and the Federal Voting Assistance Program should develop common standards for validation of ballots that have been voted and mailed on or before Election Day, even if they are received after that date.

Policy Recommendation 5

Each state should allow for restoration of voting rights to otherwise eligible citizens who have been convicted of a felony once they have fully served their sentence, including any term of probation or parole.

Policy Recommendation 6

The state and federal governments should take additional steps to assure the voting rights of all citizens and to enforce the principle of one person, one vote.

1. Federal and state governments should intensify efforts to enforce compliance with the several statutes guaranteeing the right to vote and prohibiting various forms of discrimination in voting and registration.
2. The methods for funding and administering elections—from investments in equipment through voter education to procedures at the polling place—should seek to ensure that every qualified citizen has an equal opportunity to vote and that every individual's vote is equally effective. No individual, group, or community should be left with a justified belief that the electoral process works less well for some than for others.
3. Federal and state governments should consider uses of technology, for example when developing voting equipment system standards, that will make it feasible to provide greater assistance to language minorities.

Policy Recommendation 7

Each state should set a benchmark for voting system performance, uniform in each local jurisdiction that conducts elections. The benchmark should be expressed as a percentage of residual vote (the combination of overvotes, spoiled votes, and undervotes) in the contest at the top of the ballot and should take account of deliberate decisions of voters not to make a choice.

1. Benchmarks should consider the results obtained by best practices within that state, taking local circumstances into account. In general, we suggest that the benchmarks in the next election cycle should be set no higher than 2%, with the goal of further reductions in succeeding cycles.
2. Each state should require its election jurisdictions to issue a public report on the number of residual votes after every statewide election, including the probable causes of error, if any.
3. Each state should determine for itself how to hold its election jurisdictions accountable for achieving the benchmarks.

Policy Recommendation 8

The federal government should develop a comprehensive set of voting equipment system standards for the benefit of state and local election administration.

1. Congress should grant statutory authority to an appropriate federal agency to develop such standards in consultation with state and local election officials.
2. The scope of the voting system standards should include security (including a documentary audit for non-ballot systems), procedures for decertification as well as certification of both software and hardware, assessment of human usability, and operational guidelines for proper use and maintenance of the equipment. The agency should maintain a clearinghouse of information about experience in practice.
3. Voters should have the opportunity to correct errors at the precinct or other polling place, either within the voting equipment itself or in the operational guidelines to administrators for using the equipment.
4. Each voting tally system certified for use should include, as part of the certification, a proposed statement of what constitutes a proper vote in the design and operation of the system.
5. New voting equipment systems certified either by the federal government or by any state should provide a practical and effective means for voters with physical disabilities to cast a secret ballot.
6. In addition to developing the voting system standards, the federal agency should provide its own certification and decertification of hardware and software, including components in voter registration systems. These federal certifications and decertifications, like the remainder of the standards, will be recommendations to states which they can adopt or not.
7. This federal service should include selection and oversight of a federally supervised set of independent testing authorities who will apply the standards in assessing equipment. After the federal agency develops and approves the relevant voluntary voting system standards in consultation with state and local administrators, this further, technical task should be delegated to the highly regarded and relatively independent National Institute of Standards and Technology (NIST) of the Department of Commerce.

Policy Recommendation 9

Each state should adopt uniform statewide standards for defining what will constitute a vote on each category of voting equipment certified for use in that state. Statewide recount, election certification, and contest procedures should take account of the timelines for selection of presidential electors.

1. Statewide standards for defining a vote in advance of an election should be uniform and as objective as possible.
2. Each state should reevaluate its election code to consider adopting a predictable sequence of:

a) vote tabulation and retabulation;
b) machine or manual recounts to encompass the entire jurisdiction of the office being recounted, triggered by whatever threshold the state may choose;
c) certification of a final count; followed then by
d) contests of the certification limited to allegations of fraud or other misconduct.

3. In such a sequence, each state should allow at least 21 days before requiring certification of the final count. But we recommend retention of a federal deadline under which the "safe harbor" for conclusive state determination of presidential electors will expire.
4. Each state should also develop a uniform design for the federal portion of the state ballot, for use in each of that state's certified voting equipment systems.

Policy Recommendation 10

News organizations should not project any presidential election results in any state so long as polls remain open elsewhere in the 48 contiguous states. If necessary, Congress and the states should consider legislation, within First Amendment limits, to protect the integrity of the electoral process.

1. In practice, this would mean that news organizations would voluntarily refrain from projecting the outcomes of the presidential elections in any state until 11:00 p.m. Eastern Standard Time (8:00 p.m. Pacific Standard Time).Voluntary restraint is preferable to government action.
2. If news organizations refuse to exercise voluntary restraint, Congress and the states should consider prohibiting any public disclosure by government entities of official tallies in the race for president and vice-president at the precinct level and above until 11:00 p.m. EST (8:00 p.m. PST), where such regulations are consistent with existing provisions for public observation of the vote tabulation process.
3. If news organizations refuse to exercise voluntary restraint and other measures cannot protect the integrity of the electoral process, Congress should impose a plan for uniform poll closing hours in the continental United States for presidential elections.
4. National television broadcasters should provide, during the last thirty days of the presidential campaign, at least five minutes each night of free prime television time to each presidential candidate who has qualified for federal matching funds. They or their local affiliates should further make free time available for state and local election officials to provide necessary voter education.

Policy Recommendation 11

The federal government, on a matching basis with the governments of the 50 states, should provide funds that will add another $300–400 million to the level of annual spending on election administration in the United States. The federal share will require a federal contribution totaling $1–2 billion spread out over two or three years to help capitalize state revolving funds that will provide long-term assistance.

1. These responsibilities should be apportioned about 50–50 between the federal government and the states, so that the federal contribution has the effect of raising the annual federal and state level of spending on election administration by an added $150–200 million. This is a modest sum, lower than some other current estimates about what is needed.
2. The federal expenditures should be made in the form of matching grants to the states, and the states should directly administer the disbursement of funds for administration at the state, county, and local level.
3. Instead of planning on permanent expenditures of federal funds, Congress should instead consider leveraging temporary funding over a two- or three-year period in an amount, totaling perhaps $1–2 billion, that will be sufficient to capitalize the federal share of state revolving funds. These funds can leverage the initial federal contribution, after it has been matched by the states, to create a long-term source of federal and state support to election administration. The capitalization should be sufficient to sustain our proposed federal increment of $150–200 million of continued additional spending on election administration that, when matched by state contributions to the funds, will reach the $300–400 million annual nationwide target.
4. Such state revolving funds would be used to carry out flexible state programs, allowing the states to support a variety of election administration activities undertaken by state, county, and local governments and do so with a variety of financing options that can include grants, loans at or below market rates, loan guarantees, and other arrangements. States would assess relative needs among their election jurisdictions and be accountable for maintaining the fund.
5. Federal funds should be allocated among the states in proportion to the electoral votes that each state will cast in the presidential election of 2004. This reflects a slight per capita weighting toward rural states. Such a modest weighting is appropriate, given the greater average per capita cost of election administration in rural counties.

Policy Recommendation 12

The federal responsibilities envisioned in this report should be assigned to a new agency, an Election Administration Commission (EAC).

1. The number of governing commissioners in this agency should be small; the members should be distinguished citizens with a reputation for integrity.
2. The commission should:
    a) develop federal voting system standards in consultation with state and local election administrators;

  - b) oversee the implementation of these standards in conjunction with the National Institute of Standards and Technology;
  - c) maintain a national clearinghouse of information on best practices in election administration; and
  - d) administer the limited federal assistance program to the states.
3. Enforcement of other federal election laws should remain a separate function, centered in the Civil Rights and Criminal Divisions of the Department of Justice.
4. States that do not have them should also consider establishing nonpartisan election commissions.

Policy Recommendation 13

Congress should enact legislation that includes federal assistance for election administration, setting forth policy objectives for the states while leaving the choice of strategies to the discretion of the states. The Commission as a whole takes no position on whether Congress should use the powerful incentive of conditional grants or instead establish requirements or mandates wholly independent of funding. A majority of the Commission members suggests the approach described below. However, a minority suggests a more direct federal role as detailed in an additional statement of views appended to this report.

1. Congress should enact legislation to create a new federal election administration agency, to facilitate military and overseas citizen voting, to address a national election holiday, to constrain—if necessary—premature official disclosure of presidential election results, and to appropriate federal assistance in election administration.
2. To be eligible for federal assistance, states shall:
   - a) match the federal assistance with an added contribution of their own in the proportion fixed by Congress;
   - b) adopt legislation that will establish a statewide voter registration system networked to every local jurisdiction in that state, with provisions for sharing data with other states;
   - c) permit on-site provisional voting by every voter who claims to be qualified to vote in that state, or adopt an alternative that achieves the same objective;
   - d) set a uniform statewide benchmark for voting system performance in each local jurisdiction administering elections expressed as a percentage of residual vote in the contest at the top of the ballot, and require local jurisdictions to report data relevant to this benchmark;
   - e) either agree to comply with the federal voting system standards and certification processes or develop their own state voting system standards and processes that, at a minimum: i. give voters the opportunity to correct errors, either within the voting equipment itself or in the operational guidelines to administrators for using the equipment at a precinct or other polling place and ii. require that new

voting systems should provide a practical and effective means for voters with physical disabilities to cast a secret ballot; and

f) adopt uniform statewide standards that define what will constitute a vote on each category of voting equipment certified for use in that state;

g) certify that they are in compliance with existing federal voting rights statutes.

3. Specific choices on how to comply with these conditions should be left to the discretion of the states.
4. States that qualify for federal assistance should have broad discretion in how they disburse this money, so long as the money is expended on:
    a) establishing and maintaining accurate lists of eligible voters;
    b) encouraging eligible voters to vote;
    c) improving verification of voter identification at the polling place;
    d) improving equipment and methods for casting and counting votes;
    e) recruiting and training election officials and poll workers;
    f) improving the quantity and quality of available polling places; and
    g) educating voters about their rights and responsibilities.

Source: National Commission on Federal Election Reform. *To Assure Pride and Confidence in the Electoral Process.* August 2001, pp. 1, 5–13. Accessed June 25, 2019. http://web1.millercenter.org/commissions/comm_2001.pdf.

A Democratic Congressman Charges Florida with Voter Suppression, 2001

In the aftermath of the hotly contested 2000 presidential election, which culminated with a narrow and extremely controversial Supreme Court decision that awarded the presidency to Republican nominee George W. Bush, a number of special hearings were convened at Capitol Hill to investigate various aspects of the election. During one of these hearings—a hearing convened by a House committee to examine the confusing election night coverage provided by the nation's television networks—Democratic Representative Sherrod Brown of Ohio brought up another issue raised by many observers: a charge that it has become standard practice for GOP elected officials to suppress the vote of Democrat-leaning African Americans and other minorities, both in Florida and around the country.

Chairman [Billy] Tauzin. The Chair recognizes the gentleman, Mr. Brown.

Mr. [Sherrod] Brown. I thank the chairman. While the networks deserve criticism from the Congress and the public, I am amazed that this committee is holding a hearing about election night coverage while this Congress and the Bush administration are not moving legislation to correct the flaws in the system, to standardize ballots, to establish uniform poll closing, to modernize election procedures, and equipment.

This Congress must act to end Republican efforts to suppress minority voters. The revelations of voter intimidation tactics in Florida are one example of the practices that national and State GOP officials have been using for more than 20 years to keep voters, especially minority voters, from the polls. For 8 years as the Ohio Secretary of State I saw the kind of voter intimidation, suppression and harassment created and carried out by the Republican Party at the highest levels.

The evidence of voter intimidation in Florida reminded me of the 1981 gubernatorial race in New Jersey. Sponsored by the national and State Republican Party, the National Ballot Security Task Force, comprised of off duty deputy sheriffs and local policemen, monitored polling places in predominantly African American precincts. They wore arm bands that identified them as members of the Ballot Security Task Force. They posted warning signs that they were patrolling the area and it was a crime to violate election laws. The Republican Party acknowledged doing that in a settlement later.

We saw in Florida 2000 a kinder, gentler version of the Ballot Security Task Force. We know of the purging of thousands of voters, mostly black voters, illegally from voter rolls. We know of police checkpoints established near polling places. We know of requests for additional forms of ID in predominantly African American precincts. All of these tactics were created and executed by Republican officials, usually high ranking GOP officials.

The media had the responsibility to tell the public more about these voter suppression tactics. These forms of intimidation diminish the electoral process.

Similar to the suppression tactics, the media repeated some of the same mistakes when reporting on the Florida recount. I was in Florida during the recount and witnessed firsthand the media's reluctance to fully examine statements the Republicans made about the recount process. In Palm Beach County I stood 20 feet from Governor Pataki of New York as he repeatedly said four recounts had been conducted. Four recounts had been conducted. Like birds off a telephone wire, every Republican elected official repeated this mantra. All fair-minded people know that the four-recount charge was simply not true.

In another instance I stood by as Senator Lugar from Indiana stated that his State doesn't do hand recounts. A simple call to his elections office confirmed that the Hoozier State does conduct hand recounts. But the media allowed Lugar and Pataki and countless other Republicans to repeat this mantra generally unchallenged.

These statements reflected a series of distortions backed up by a conservative, corporate-owned media too lazy to scrutinize such allegations and too eager to manufacture drama. The media have the responsibility to check the facts for their audience. I asked the news executives here today, scrutinize our observations, refrain from adopting a ``he said, she said'' approach to news coverage because the ``he said, she said'' coverage causes politicians to exaggerate, to distort and even to lie.

Florida surely taught us that. Do not accept what we say. Make us tell the truth. This task is a challenge of today's 24 hours news cycle. I ask you to resist merely filling the time with talking heads. I hope that the media does its job better. I hope that we in Congress do our jobs better as well.

Source: Brown, Sherrod. Remarks. "Election Night Coverage by the Networks." Hearing before the Committee on Energy and Commerce, U.S. House of

Representatives, 107th Congress, 1st Session, February 14, 2001. Accessed June 25, 2019. https://www.govinfo.gov/content/pkg/CHRG-107hhrg71490/html/CHRG-107hhrg71490.htm.

Attorney General John Ashcroft Announces New Justice Department Focus on Voter Fraud, 2002

During Republican President George W. Bush's two terms in the White House (2001–2009), voting rights advocates expressed growing concerns that unfounded or unsubstantiated fears about voter fraud might produce "remedies" that would actually make it more difficult for many Americans to exercise their constitutional voting rights.

Complaints about alleged voter fraud had intensified in the wake of the 2000 presidential election, which Bush had won despite losing the popular vote (he owed his victory to his narrow edge in the electoral college). Conservative media outlets ran stories insinuating that voter fraud was a massive problem, and some Republican lawmakers echoed these charges and demanded that steps be taken to shore up U.S. election integrity. Critics, however, contended that these charges were overblown or unsupported by fact—and that some of them were being used to cast doubt on legitimate Democratic election victories or implement partisan laws and policies that would disproportionately suppress the votes of Democratically inclined voting constituencies (such as college students and African Americans).

In 2002 Bush administration Attorney General John Ashcroft announced that the U.S. Department of Justice was embarking on a major new investigation of voter fraud called the Voting Access and Integrity Initiative. He then invited all ninety-three U.S. attorneys to a special Justice Department "Voting Integrity Symposium," during which he asserted that "votes have been bought, voters intimidated and ballot boxes stuffed. Voters have been duped into signing absentee ballots believing they were applications for public relief. And the residents of cemeteries have infamously shown up at the polls on Election Day."

Over the ensuing four years, prosecutors in the Justice Department launched more than three hundred investigations of alleged voter fraud and misconduct across the country. But when the campaign concluded in July 2006, those investigations only resulted in eighty-six convictions. "The worst examples," reported Lisa Rab in a 2017 story for Politico, *"were vote-buying schemes in eastern Kentucky and West Virginia that helped keep local politicians in power. Cases that had fixated GOP officials . . . were not substantiated. Instead, most of the cases involved individuals who had cast a single ballot that they shouldn't have, or hadn't even voted at all but simply had registered improperly." Meanwhile, the Bush administration fired several U.S. attorneys who refused to prosecute cases that they felt were too weak or flimsy. When the political motivations behind these firings came to light, several top Bush White House officials were forced to resign (including Alberto Gonzalez, who succeeded Ashcroft as head of the Justice Department in 2005).*

Following is the full text of Ashcroft's prepared remarks at the Voting Integrity Symposium conference that marked the launch of the Justice Department's four-year investigation.

Today, we gather at a unique moment in America's history; a time in which the work of those who dedicate their lives to protecting America, our citizens, and our values has never been more important. One year and twenty-six days ago, enemies of liberty struck this nation, leaving us with two choices: to succumb to fanatics who seek to extinguish political and religious freedom, fanatics who would enslave women, corrupt education and kill Americans wherever and whenever they can; or to fight in defense of lives and liberties—in defense of freedom to speak, freedom to worship, the freedom to educate boys and girls, freedom to work, and the freedom from fear.

America has chosen to fight. And chief among the values for which we fight is our right to chart our own national destiny. The right of citizens to vote and have their vote count is the cornerstone of our democracy—the necessary precondition of government of the people, by the people and for the people.

Enforcing the laws that guarantee voting rights and punish voting fraud is the duty of the Department of Justice. More than mere law enforcement, our responsibility to protect the access to and integrity of elections is the responsibility of upholding freedom itself. Today, four weeks from elections that will determine one-third of the membership of the United States Senate and the entire membership of the House of Representatives, electoral accessibility and integrity are the urgent challenges of our democracy, and they are the reasons for this unprecedented gathering of the nation's justice officials.

America is a nation whose founding documents and most inspired words uphold the ideal of democratic self-government as a model for the world. The opening phrases of the Declaration of Independence declare that governmental power, if it is to be just, must be derived from the consent of the governed. The Constitution begins, purposefully and deliberately, with these three words: "We the people . . ."

These words have inspired millions of freedom seeking people throughout the world. But we cannot consummate—we cannot honor—the ideal of democracy with our words alone. Our actions demonstrate our commitment to self-government far above our ability to add or detract with mere words—and our actions have not always been exemplary.

All Americans know—or should know—of the instances in our history when our deeds have fallen short of our commitment to democracy. For long periods of our history, America failed to grant African-Americans and women the right to vote. Later in our history, subtler but no less insidious forms of disenfranchisement occurred. Laws were passed that required African-Americans to take a reading test or interpret a passage of the Constitution in order to vote. Some people were not allowed to register to vote unless they brought along someone already registered who would vouch for their, quote, "good character."

And America has failed too often to uphold the right of every citizen's vote, once cast, to be counted fairly and equally. Votes have been bought, voters intimidated and ballot boxes stuffed. The polling process has been disrupted or not completed. Voters have been duped into signing absentee ballots believing they were applications for public relief. And the residents of cemeteries have infamously shown up at the polls on election day.

Political war stories like these are often told with a grin, but these failures of our democracy are no laughing matter. There is nothing funny about winning an election with stolen votes. And there is no occasion for mirth by the campaigns that commit these offenses. All of us pay the price for voting fraud. For when the right to vote is infringed, self-government is damaged. The national will is thwarted. The democratic ideal itself is assaulted.

The strength of our democracy demands that we fulfill the rights of both ballot access and ballot integrity—to guarantee to every citizen, in accordance with the law, the right to vote, and to every voter the right to be counted.

So we come together today to renew our democratic compact with the American people. We gather here, in this Great Hall of Justice, to begin a new ethic of enforcement of our voting rights.

On October 1st, I issued a directive to all United States Attorneys announcing the creation of a Department-wide Voting Access and Integrity Initiative. Leading this initiative are Assistant Attorney General of the Civil Rights Division, Ralph Boyd, and Assistant Attorney General of the Criminal Division, Michael Chertoff.

We have created this precedent-setting Voting Access and Integrity Initiative for two reasons: first, to enhance our ability to deter discrimination and election fraud, and second, to prosecute violators vigorously whenever and wherever these offenses occur.

- Our goal is to work cooperatively with civil rights leaders and state and local election officials to prevent election offenses and to bring violators to justice.
- Our means are a national mobilization of the resources of the Department of Justice.
- And our message is clear and unequivocal: the Department of Justice will investigate and prosecute voting rights and election fraud offenses.

To provide on-the-ground investigative and prosecutorial coordination, I have asked each United States Attorney to designate a District Election Officer responsible for the 2002 election cycle. These officers are experienced Assistant U.S. Attorneys whose mission is to help guarantee access, honesty and integrity at the polls on election day.

Today, we have brought together all designated District Election Officers for this day of intensive training in voting rights and election offenses. Throughout the day, these officers will hear from officials in the Civil Rights Division who are charged with enforcing the laws prohibiting racial discrimination and voter intimidation. Enforcement of the laws governing absentee voting for uniformed and overseas citizens as well as elderly citizens and citizens with disabilities will be covered in detail. And election officers will renew our commitment to providing language assistance to voters with limited proficiency in English.

The Civil Rights Division has already had considerable success, working with the Department of Commerce, in facilitating the capacity of all citizens to participate fully in the electoral process. Earlier this year, the Civil Rights Division worked successfully with the Commerce Department to secure the early release of 2000 Census data that will determine which districts receive language assistance. As a result, thousands of citizens in 80 jurisdictions who would not have received assistance before will be provided help in exercising fully their voting rights on election day. Fulfilling this obligation took extraordinary effort on behalf of Secretary Don Evans, Commerce Department staff and Civil Rights Division officials. I commend all of those individuals who made possible this enhancement of our voting rights.

Election officers have also heard from the leadership of the Criminal Division—the men and women who supervise the enforcement of the laws against voter fraud. These experts have prosecuted dozens of cases involving voting rights abuses, and they will share what they have learned with those here today.

Tomorrow, our District Election Officers will take this training out into their own districts. I have asked each U.S. Attorney and FBI Special Agent in Charge to meet with state officials who handle election violations in each district, in order to underscore the Department's commitment to preventing—and, if necessary, investigating and prosecuting—election fraud and voting rights offenses. I am also asking U.S. Attorneys, Election Officers and FBI officials to explore ways in which the Department can work more closely with state and local election and law enforcement authorities to deter and detect discrimination, prevent electoral corruption, and bring violators to justice.

And on election day, the Justice Department will dedicate all available resources to ensuring access and integrity at the polls through our Election Day Program. This Program was established more than a quarter of a century ago to respond to public concerns about the integrity of the election process. When the polls open, every available resource of the Department of Justice—both in Washington and in the U.S. Attorneys' districts—will be available to handle complaints, open investigations and prosecute offenses. Every office will be open. All federal investigators and prosecutors will be on call to help ensure the accessibility, honesty, and integrity of the election.

In the past several weeks, I have met personally with state and local officials. I have met personally with leaders in the civil rights community and leaders of national ethnic groups. My message to them is my message to you: the Department of Justice will use all available means within the law to provide access, prevent fraud and prohibit the intimidation of voters on November 5.

This is our compact with the American people. Our role is to train, to educate and ultimately to enforce—when and if the laws are violated. Our pledge is to ensure justice for all American voters.

But we recognize also the indispensable role that states and counties play in the administration of elections. We appreciate and acknowledge the volunteers, the poll workers, and the state and county election officials.

All of us depend on the dedication of these Americans for the opportunity to exercise our voting rights—to make our voices heard in the great American commitment to democracy.

Today, it is more important than ever before that we embrace the privilege that makes us unique among the peoples, nations and societies of human history. Our way of life is not a given, and our freedom is not an accident. Liberty is a rare gift for which millions have worked and suffered and sacrificed and died. It now falls to us to guard this gift from those who would destroy it. It falls to us, the free, to ensure that the cornerstone of our freedom—government of the people, by the people, and for the people—does not perish from the earth.

Thank you very much.

Source: Ashcroft, John. Prepared Remarks. Voting Integrity Symposium. Washington, DC. October 8, 2002. Accessed June 25, 2019. https://www.justice.gov/archive/ag/speeches/2002/100802ballotintegrity.htm.

President Bush Signs the Voting Rights Act Reauthorization and Amendments Act of 2006

In the summer of 2006, Republican President George W. Bush became the fourth president in U.S. history to sign an extension of the Voting Rights Act (VRA), which became one of the pillars of the civil rights movement when it was first passed in 1965. The bipartisan reauthorization bill, which extended the VRA for another twenty-five years, reached Bush's desk after passage in the House of Representatives by a 390–33 vote on July 13 and a unanimous vote in the Senate on July 20. Following are President George W. Bush's remarks from the July 27 signing ceremony.

Thank you. Good morning. Welcome. Thanks for being here on this special day. Please be seated. America began with a declaration that all men are created equal. This declaration marked a tremendous advance in the story of freedom, yet it also contained a contradiction: Some of the same men who signed their names to this self-evident truth owned other men as property. By reauthorizing this act, Congress has reaffirmed its belief that all men are created equal, its belief that the new founding started by the signing of the bill by President Johnson is worthy of our great Nation to continue.

I'm proud to be here with our Attorney General, members of my Cabinet, leaders of the United States Senate and House of Representatives. I thank the bill sponsors. I thank the members of the Judiciary Committee. I appreciate so very much representatives of the Hamer family who have joined us, representatives of the Rosa and Raymond Parks Institute who have joined us, and members of the King family, in particular Reverend Bernice King and Martin Luther King. Thank you all for coming.

I'm honored to be here with civil rights leaders like Dr. Dorothy Height, Julian Bond, the chairman of the NAACP. Bruce Gordon—thank you, Bruce. Reverend Lowery—it's good to see you again, sir—fortunately, I got the mike this time.

[*Laughter*] I'm proud to be here with Marc Morial. Thanks for coming, Marc. Juanita Abernathy is with us today. Jesse Jackson—good to see you, Jesse. Al Sharpton, Dr. Benjamin Hooks and Frances are with us. A lot of other folks who care deeply about this issue, we welcome you here.

It's good to welcome the mayor. Mr. Mayor, good to see you. Thanks for coming—Tony Williams. Everything is fine in the neighborhood; I appreciate it. [*Laughter*] And the mayor of Selma, Alabama, James Perkins, is with us. Mr. Mayor, proud you're here. Welcome, sir.

The right of ordinary men and women to determine their own political future lies at the heart of the American experiment, and it is a right that has been won by the sacrifice of patriots. The Declaration of Independence was born on the stand for liberty taken at Lexington and Concord. The amendments to our Constitution that outlawed slavery and guaranteed the right to vote came at the price of a terrible civil war.

The Voting Rights Act that broke the segregationist lock on the ballot box rose from the courage shown on a Selma bridge one Sunday afternoon in March of 1965. On that day, African Americans, including a Member of the United States Congress, John Lewis, marched across the Edmund Pettus Bridge in a protest intended to highlight the unfair practices that kept them off the voter rolls.

The brutal response showed America why a march was necessary. When the marchers reached the far side of the bridge, they were met by State troopers and civilian posse bearing billy clubs and whips, weapons they did not hesitate to use. The images of policemen using night sticks on peaceful protesters were carried on television screens across the country, and they stung the conscience of a slumbering America.

One week after Selma, President Lyndon Johnson took to the airwaves to announce that he planned to submit legislation that would bring African Americans into the civic life of our Nation. Five months after Selma, he signed the Voting Rights Act into law in the rotunda of our Nation's Capitol. In a little more than a year after Selma, a newly enfranchised black community used their power at the ballot box to help defeat the sheriff who had sent men with whips and clubs to the Edmund Pettus Bridge on that bloody Sunday.

For some parts of our country, the Voting Rights Act marked the first appearance of African Americans on the voting rolls since Reconstruction. And in the primaries and elections that followed the signing of this act, many African Americans pulled the voting lever for the first time in their lives.

Eighty-one-year-old Willie Bolden was the grandson of slaves, and in the spring of 1966, he cast his first ballot in Alabama's Democratic primary. He told a reporter, "It felt good to me. It made me think I was sort of somebody." In the America promised by our Founders, every citizen is a somebody, and every generation has a responsibility to add its own chapter to the unfolding story of freedom.

In four decades since the Voting Rights Act was first passed, we've made progress toward equality, yet the work for a more perfect union is never ending. We'll continue to build on the legal equality won by the civil rights movement to help ensure that every person enjoys the opportunity that this great land of liberty offers. And that means a decent education and a good school for every child, a chance to own their own home or business, and the hope that comes from knowing that you can rise in our society by hard work and God-given talents.

Today we renew a bill that helped bring a community on the margins into the life of American democracy. My administration will vigorously enforce the provisions of this law, and we will defend it in court. This legislation is named in honor of three heroes of American history who devoted their lives to the struggle of civil rights: Fannie Lou Hamer, Rosa Parks, and Coretta Scott King. And in honor of their memory and their contributions to the cause of freedom, I am proud to sign the Voting Rights Act Reauthorization and Amendments Act of 2006.

Source: Bush, George W. "Remarks on Signing the Fannie Lou Hamer, Rosa Parks, and Coretta Scott King Voting Rights Act Reauthorization and Amendments Act of 2006." July 27, 2006. *Public Papers of the Presidents of the United States: George W. Bush, 2006, Book 2.* Washington, DC: Government Printing Office, 2010, pp. 1448–1449.

The Brennan Center for Justice Debunks Claims of Widespread "Voter Fraud," 2007

In 2007 the Brennan Center for Justice, a nonpartisan public policy institute focusing on voting rights and other pillars of American democracy, published a report that aimed to address growing controversies about whether voter fraud in U.S. elections was a significant problem—or just an excuse for political partisans to suppress the vote of Americans more likely to cast their votes for political opponents. The study, which was authored by Justin Levitt, an attorney and scholar specializing in election law and voting rights, examined all types of allegations of voter fraud and found scant evidence that they were anything other than very occasional honest mistakes. Levitt's examination found no evidence to support claims that voter fraud constituted any sort of threat to the integrity of American elections. Following are excerpts (footnotes removed) from Levitt's report. (Full details on various types of alleged fraud, including findings on selected case studies, can be found in the full report.)

Introduction

Allegations of election-related fraud make for enticing press. Many Americans remember vivid stories of voting improprieties in Chicagoland, or the suspiciously sudden appearance of LBJ's alphabetized ballot box in Texas, or Governor Earl Long's quip: "When I die, I want to be buried in Louisiana, so I can stay active in politics." Voter fraud, in particular, has the feel of a bank heist caper: roundly condemned but technically fascinating, and sufficiently lurid to grab and hold headlines.

Perhaps because these stories are dramatic, voter fraud makes a popular scapegoat. In the aftermath of a close election, losing candidates are often quick to blame voter fraud for the results. Legislators cite voter fraud as justification for various new restrictions on the exercise of the franchise. And pundits trot out the same few anecdotes time and again as proof that a wave of fraud is imminent.

Allegations of widespread voter fraud, however, often prove greatly exaggerated. It is easy to grab headlines with a lurid claim ("Tens of thousands may be voting illegally!"); the follow-up—when any exists—is not usually deemed newsworthy. Yet on closer examination, many of the claims of voter fraud amount to a great deal of smoke without much fire. The allegations simply do not pan out.

These inflated claims are not harmless. Crying "wolf" when the allegations are unsubstantiated distracts attention from real problems that need real solutions. If we can move beyond the fixation on voter fraud, we will be able to focus on the real changes our elections need, from universal registration all the way down to sufficient parking at the poll site.

Moreover, these claims of voter fraud are frequently used to justify policies that do not solve the alleged wrongs, but that could well disenfranchise legitimate voters. Overly restrictive identification requirements for voters at the polls—which address a sort of voter fraud more rare than death by lightning—is only the most prominent example. The Brennan Center for Justice at NYU School of Law carefully examines allegations of fraud to get at the truth behind the claims. The Brennan Center has analyzed purported fraud cited by state and federal courts; multipartisan and bipartisan federal commissions; political party entities; state and local election officials; and authors, journalists, and bloggers. Usually, only a tiny portion of the claimed illegality is substantiated—and most of the remainder is either nothing more than speculation or has been conclusively debunked.

This paper seeks to distill our findings: the truth about voter fraud. It first offers a straightforward definition to avoid the common trap of discussing election irregularities that involve neither voters nor fraud as if they showed voter fraud. It then discusses different alternative reasons more credible than voter fraud to explain many of the recurring allegations. The paper then analyzes, scenario by scenario, some of the more common types of alleged voter fraud and their more likely causes and policy solutions. Finally, the paper presents individual case studies of notorious instances of alleged voter fraud, and finds those allegations to be grossly inflated. . . .

What Is Voter Fraud?

"Voter fraud" is fraud by voters.

More precisely, "voter fraud" occurs when individuals cast ballots despite knowing that they are ineligible to vote, in an attempt to defraud the election system.

This sounds straightforward. And yet, voter fraud is often conflated, intentionally or unintentionally, with other forms of election misconduct or irregularities.

There are many such problems that are improperly lumped under the umbrella of "voter fraud." Some result from technological glitches, whether sinister or benign:

for example, voting machines may record inaccurate tallies due to fraud, user error, or technical malfunction. Some result from honest mistakes by election officials or voters: for example, a person with a conviction may honestly believe herself eligible to vote when the conviction renders her temporarily ineligible, or an election official may believe that certain identification documents are required to vote when no such requirement exists. And some irregularities involve fraud or intentional misconduct perpetrated by actors other than individual voters: for example, flyers may spread misinformation about the proper locations or procedures for voting; thugs may be dispatched to intimidate voters at the polls; missing ballot boxes may mysteriously reappear. These are all problems with the election administration system but they are not "voter fraud."

Conflating these concerns is not merely a semantic issue. First, the rhetorical sloppiness fosters the misperception that fraud by voters is prevalent. That is, when every problem with an election is attributed to "voter fraud," it appears that fraud by voters is much more common than is actually the case. This, in turn, promotes inappropriate policy. By inflating the perceived prevalence of fraud by voters, policy-makers find it easier to justify restrictions on those voters that are not warranted by the real facts.

Moreover, mislabeling problems as "voter fraud" distracts attention from the real election issues that need to be resolved. It draws attention away from problems best addressed, for example, by resource allocation or poll worker education or implementation of longstanding statutory mandates, and instead improperly focuses on the voter as the source of the problem. . . .

Voter Fraud and the Press for Photo ID

The most common example of the harm wrought by imprecise and inflated claims of "voter fraud" is the call for in-person photo identification requirements. Such photo ID laws are effective only in preventing individuals from impersonating other voters at the polls—an occurrence more rare than getting struck by lightning.

By throwing all sorts of election anomalies under the "voter fraud" umbrella, however, advocates for such laws artificially inflate the apparent need for these restrictions and undermine the urgency of other reforms.

Moreover, as with all restrictions on voters, photo identification requirements have a predictable detrimental impact on eligible citizens. Such laws are only potentially worthwhile if they clearly prevent more problems than they create. If policymakers distinguished real voter fraud from the more common election irregularities erroneously labeled as voter fraud, it would become apparent that the limited benefits of laws like photo ID requirements are simply not worth the cost.

Royal Masset, the former political director for the Republican Party of Texas, concisely tied all of these strands together in a 2007 *Houston Chronicle* article concerning a highly controversial battle over photo identification legislation in Texas. Masset connected the inflated furor over voter fraud to photo identification laws and their expected impact on legitimate voters:

> Among Republicans it is an "article of religious faith that voter fraud is causing us to lose elections," Masset said. He doesn't agree with that, but does believe that requiring photo IDs could cause enough of a dropoff in legitimate Democratic voting to add 3 percent to the Republican vote.

This remarkably candid observation underscores why it is so critical to get the facts straight on voter fraud. The voter fraud phantom drives policy that disenfranchises actual legitimate voters, without a corresponding actual benefit. Virtuous public policy should stand on more reliable supports.

Source: Levitt, Justin. *The Truth about Voter Fraud.* Brennan Center for Justice at New York University School of Law, 2007, pp. 3–4, 6. The complete document is available at https://www.brennancenter.org/sites/default/files/legacy/The%20Truth%20About%20Voter%20Fraud.pdf. Used by permission of the Brennan Center for Justice.

U.S. Supreme Court Puts Stamp of Approval on Voter Photo ID Laws, 2008

When Republican lawmakers in the state of Indiana passed a new law requiring most citizens voting in person at primary or general elections to present a current driver's license or other government-recognized form of photo identification, Democrats cried foul. They claimed that the statute was partisan in nature because it would disproportionately impact constituencies that were more likely to vote for Democrats, like college students and minorities. Critics also asserted that the law purported to address a nonexistent problem: voter fraud. But by a 6–3 margin, the Supreme Court let stand a lower court ruling supporting the law. In essence, the court found that the plaintiffs had not provided evidence that the statute was discriminatory, that American history was peppered with instances of voter fraud, and that federal election laws passed with bipartisan support over the previous two decades had included photo ID measures. The court also voiced support for the argument made by proponents of the law that photo ID requirements would spark greater public confidence in the integrity and accuracy of the state's election system. Following are excerpts from the Supreme Court's decision, which was delivered on April 28, 2008.

Justice Stevens announced the judgment of the Court and delivered an opinion in which The Chief Justice and Justice Kennedy join.

At issue in these cases is the constitutionality of an Indiana statute requiring citizens voting in person on election day, or casting a ballot in person at the office of the circuit court clerk prior to election day, to present photo identification issued by the government.

Referred to as either the "Voter ID Law" or "SEA 483," the statute applies to in-person voting at both primary and general elections. The requirement does not apply to absentee ballots submitted by mail, and the statute contains an exception for persons living and voting in a state-licensed facility such as a nursing home. A voter who is indigent or has a religious objection to being photographed may cast a provisional ballot that will be counted only if she executes an appropriate affidavit before the circuit court clerk within 10 days following the election. A voter who has photo identification but is unable to present that identification on election day may file a provisional ballot that will be counted if she brings her photo identification to the circuit county clerk's office within 10 days. No photo identification is required in order to register to vote, and the State offers free photo identification to qualified voters able to establish their residence and identity.

Promptly after the enactment of SEA 483 in 2005, the Indiana Democratic Party and the Marion County Democratic Central Committee (Democrats) filed suit in the Federal District Court for the Southern District of Indiana against the state officials responsible for its enforcement, seeking a judgment declaring the Voter ID Law invalid and enjoining its enforcement. A second suit seeking the same relief was brought on behalf of two elected officials and several nonprofit organizations representing groups of elderly, disabled, poor, and minority voters. The cases were consolidated, and the State of Indiana intervened to defend the validity of the statute.

The complaints in the consolidated cases allege that the new law substantially burdens the right to vote in violation of the Fourteenth Amendment; that it is neither a necessary nor appropriate method of avoiding election fraud; and that it will arbitrarily disfranchise qualified voters who do not possess the required identification and will place an unjustified burden on those who cannot readily obtain such identification.

After discovery, District Judge Barker prepared a comprehensive 70-page opinion explaining her decision to grant defendants' motion for summary judgment. She found that petitioners had "not introduced evidence of a single, individual Indiana resident who will be unable to vote as a result of SEA 483 or who will have his or her right to vote unduly burdened by its requirements." She rejected "as utterly incredible and unreliable" an expert's report that up to 989,000 registered voters in Indiana did not possess either a driver's license or other acceptable photo identification. She estimated that as of 2005, when the statute was enacted, around 43,000 Indiana residents lacked a state-issued driver's license or identification card.

A divided panel of the Court of Appeals affirmed. The majority first held that the Democrats had standing to bring a facial challenge to the constitutionality of SEA 483. Next, noting the absence of any plaintiffs who claimed that the law would deter them from voting, the Court of Appeals inferred that "the motivation for the suit is simply that the law may require the Democratic Party and the other organizational plaintiffs to work harder to get every last one of their supporters to the polls." It rejected the argument that the law should be judged by the same strict standard applicable to a poll tax because the burden on voters was offset by the benefit of reducing the risk of fraud. The dissenting judge, viewing the justification for the law as "hollow"—more precisely as "a not-too-thinly-veiled attempt to discourage election-day turnout by certain folks believed to skew Democratic"—would have applied a stricter standard, something he described as "close to 'strict scrutiny light.'" In his view, the "law imposes an undue burden on a recognizable segment of potential eligible voters" and therefore violates their rights under the First and Fourteenth Amendments to the Constitution.

Four judges voted to grant a petition for rehearing en banc. Because we agreed with their assessment of the importance of these cases, we granted certiorari. We are, however, persuaded that the District Court and the Court of Appeals correctly concluded that the evidence in the record is not sufficient to support a facial attack on the validity of the entire statute, and thus affirm . . .

II

The State has identified several state interests that arguably justify the burdens that SEA 483 imposes on voters and potential voters. While petitioners argue that the statute was actually motivated by partisan concerns and dispute both the significance of the State's interests and the magnitude of any real threat to those interests, they do not question the legitimacy of the interests the State has identified. Each is unquestionably relevant to the State's interest in protecting the integrity and reliability of the electoral process.

The first is the interest in deterring and detecting voter fraud. The State has a valid interest in participating in a nationwide effort to improve and modernize election procedures that have been criticized as antiquated and inefficient. The State also argues that it has a particular interest in preventing voter fraud in response to a problem that is in part the product of its own maladministration—namely, that Indiana's voter registration rolls include a large number of names of persons who are either deceased or no longer live in Indiana. Finally, the State relies on its interest in safeguarding voter confidence. Each of these interests merits separate comment.

Election Modernization

Two recently enacted federal statutes have made it necessary for States to reexamine their election procedures. Both contain provisions consistent with a State's choice to use government-issued photo identification as a relevant source of information concerning a citizen's eligibility to vote.

In the National Voter Registration Act of 1993 (NVRA), Congress established procedures that would both increase the number of registered voters and protect the integrity of the electoral process. The statute requires state motor vehicle driver's license applications to serve as voter registration applications. While that requirement has increased the number of registered voters, the statute also contains a provision restricting States' ability to remove names from the lists of registered voters. These protections have been partly responsible for inflated lists of registered voters. For example, evidence credited by Judge Barker estimated that as of 2004 Indiana's voter rolls were inflated by as much as 41.4%, and data collected by the Election Assistance Committee in 2004 indicated that 19 of 92 Indiana counties had registration totals exceeding 100% of the 2004 voting-age population.

In HAVA, Congress required every State to create and maintain a computerized statewide list of all registered voters. HAVA also requires the States to verify voter information contained in a voter registration application and specifies either an "applicant's driver's license number" or "the last 4 digits of the applicant's social security number" as acceptable verifications. If an individual has neither number, the State is required to assign the applicant a voter identification number.

HAVA also imposes new identification requirements for individuals registering to vote for the first time who submit their applications by mail. If the voter is casting his ballot in person, he must present local election officials with written identification, which may be either "a current and valid photo identification" or another form of documentation such as a bank statement or paycheck. If the voter is voting by mail, he must include a copy of the identification with his ballot. A voter may also include a copy of the documentation with his application or provide his driver's license number or Social Security number for verification. Finally, in a provision entitled "Fail-safe voting," HAVA authorizes the casting of provisional ballots by challenged voters.

Of course, neither HAVA nor NVRA required Indiana to enact SEA 483, but they do indicate that Congress believes that photo identification is one effective method of establishing a voter's qualification to vote and that the integrity of elections is enhanced through improved technology. That conclusion is also supported by a report issued shortly after the enactment of SEA 483 by the Commission on Federal Election Reform chaired by former President Jimmy Carter and former Secretary of State James A. Baker III, which is a part of the record in these cases. In the introduction to their discussion of voter identification, they made these pertinent comments:

"A good registration list will ensure that citizens are only registered in one place, but election officials still need to make sure that the person arriving at a polling site is the same one that is named on the registration list. In the old days and in small towns where everyone knows each other, voters did not need to identify themselves. But in the United States, where 40 million people move each year, and in urban areas where some people do not even know the people living in their own apartment building let alone their precinct, some form of identification is needed.

"There is no evidence of extensive fraud in U. S. elections or of multiple voting, but both occur, and it could affect the outcome of a close election. The electoral system cannot inspire public confidence if no safeguards exist to deter or detect fraud or to confirm the identity of voters. Photo identification cards currently are needed to board a plane, enter federal buildings, and cash a check. Voting is equally important."

Voter Fraud

The only kind of voter fraud that SEA 483 addresses is in-person voter impersonation at polling places. The record contains no evidence of any such fraud actually occurring in Indiana at any time in its history. Moreover, petitioners argue that provisions of the Indiana Criminal Code punishing such conduct as a felony provide adequate protection against the risk that such conduct will occur in the future. It remains true, however, that flagrant examples of such fraud in other parts of the country have been documented throughout this Nation's history by respected historians and journalists, that occasional examples have surfaced in recent years, and that Indiana's own experience with fraudulent voting in the 2003 Democratic primary for East Chicago Mayor—though perpetrated using absentee ballots and not in-person fraud—demonstrate that not only is the risk of voter fraud real but that it could affect the outcome of a close election.

There is no question about the legitimacy or importance of the State's interest in counting only the votes of eligible voters. Moreover, the interest in orderly administration and accurate recordkeeping provides a sufficient justification for carefully identifying all voters participating in the election process. While the most effective method of preventing election fraud may well be debatable, the propriety of doing so is perfectly clear.

In its brief, the State argues that the inflation of its voter rolls provides further support for its enactment of SEA 483. The record contains a November 5, 2000, newspaper article asserting that as a result of NVRA and "sloppy record keeping," Indiana's lists of registered voters included the names of thousands of persons who had either moved, died, or were not eligible to vote because they had been convicted of felonies. The conclusion that Indiana has an unusually inflated list of registered voters is supported by the entry of a consent decree in litigation brought by the Federal Government alleging violations of NVRA. Even though Indiana's own negligence may have contributed to the serious inflation of its registration lists when SEA 483 was enacted, the fact of inflated voter rolls does provide a neutral and nondiscriminatory reason supporting the State's decision to require photo identification.

Safeguarding Voter Confidence

Finally, the State contends that it has an interest in protecting public confidence "in the integrity and legitimacy of representative government." While that interest is closely related to the State's interest in preventing voter fraud, public confidence in the integrity of the electoral process has independent significance, because it encourages citizen participation in the democratic process. As the Carter-Baker Report observed, the "electoral system cannot inspire public confidence if no safeguards exist to deter or detect fraud or to confirm the identity of voters." . . .

V

In their briefs, petitioners stress the fact that all of the Republicans in the General Assembly voted in favor of SEA 483 and the Democrats were unanimous in opposing it. In her opinion rejecting petitioners' facial challenge, Judge Barker noted that the litigation was the result of a partisan dispute that had "spilled out of the state house into the courts." It is fair to infer that partisan considerations may have played a significant role in the decision to enact SEA 483. If such considerations had provided the only justification for a photo identification requirement, we may also assume that SEA 483 would suffer the same fate as the poll tax at issue in *Harper*.

But if a nondiscriminatory law is supported by valid neutral justifications, those justifications should not be disregarded simply because partisan interests may have provided one motivation for the votes of individual legislators. The state interests identified as justifications for SEA 483 are both neutral and sufficiently strong to require us to reject petitioners' facial attack on the statute. The application of the statute to the vast majority of Indiana voters is amply justified by the valid interest in protecting "the integrity and reliability of the electoral process."

The judgment of the Court of Appeals is affirmed.

It is so ordered.

Source: *Crawford v. Marion County Election Board* 553 U.S.181 (2008).

A Voting Rights Expert Condemns Restrictive Voting Measures, 2012

In April 2012, Wendy R. Weiser, director of the Democracy Program at the New York School of Law's Brennan Center for Justice, appeared before a hearing of the House Judiciary Committee's Subcommittee on the Constitution. She presented the views of the Brennan Center, one of the best-known voting rights and public policy research institutes in the nation, on a fresh wave of proposed voting restrictions that had been proposed—primarily by Republican-controlled legislatures—across the United States since the election of Democrat Barack Obama in 2008. Weiser criticized these proposed measures as violative of constitutional rights and unnecessary given the lack of actual evidence of voter fraud in modern America. She also described enforcement of the Section 5 of the Voting Rights Act (VRA) of 1965 as essential in keeping these voting rights rollbacks from becoming law. Fourteen months after Weiser's testimony, however, the Supreme Court struck down Section 5 of the VRA, a decision that paved the way for many of the voting restrictions described by Weiser to be implemented.

In my testimony today, I will focus on: (1) the recent state legislative developments affecting voting and elections, including laws requiring government-issued photo ID to vote; (2) the impacts of the new laws, including those that are being examined by the Department of Justice and the courts; (3) the Department's efforts to enforce federal voting laws; and (4) the need for additional steps to improve the election system for all eligible Americans.

I. New Laws Restricting Voting in the States

For decades, our nation has expanded the franchise and knocked down old barriers to full electoral participation. The last two years have seen an abrupt change in course, with a wave of state laws and legislation that create new restrictions on voting access. These laws take many forms—from eliminating election-day registration, to restricting voter registration drives by community groups, to reducing the number of days for early voting and limiting the number of days for voter registration.

As of today, during the 2011-12 legislative sessions, twenty-four (24) laws and executive actions restricting access to the polls were passed, and at least seventy-four (74) measures are still pending in state legislatures across the country. . . .

a. Restrictive Photo ID

By far the most common election-related legislation introduced and passed in 2011 and thus far in 2012 is legislation requiring voters to produce certain forms of photo ID to vote. Prior to 2011, only two states had imposed strict photo ID requirements. During the 2011 and 2012 legislative sessions, however, seven states have passed strict "no-photo, no-vote" voter ID laws for citizens who vote in person; and three of those extended the new photo ID requirements to absentee voters. Mississippi similarly adopted a strict photo ID requirement for all voters via a ballot measure to amend the state constitution. Rhode Island passed a photo ID law that allows voters without ID to cast a ballot that will count if their identities are later verified by signature match.

Overall, thirty-four (34) states saw bills introduced requiring photo IDs for voting. Of the states that do not have voter ID laws, only three—Oregon, Vermont and Wyoming—did not consider voter ID legislation this year or last. In five states, governors' vetoes prevented photo ID legislation from becoming law. In Minnesota, voters will consider a ballot initiative to require photo ID for voting in November 2012; and Missouri voters may also consider a voter ID ballot initiative, depending on the resolution to a legal challenge.

In addition, Virginia's legislature recently sent a voter ID bill to Republican Governor Bob McDonnell, who just last week stated that he would not sign the law unless the legislature softened the requirement to present a photo ID in order to cast a ballot. His proposed amendments included an expansion of the list of acceptable IDs, an increase in the time voters have to provide the required ID, and a proposal to count the provisional ballots of voters who lack the required identification after signature verification.

b. Proof of Citizenship

At least seventeen (17) states saw legislation introduced that would require documentary proof of citizenship in order to register or vote. Very few official documents actually establish citizenship: birth certificates, naturalization certificates, and passports are among the rare examples. Proof of citizenship laws passed this past year in Alabama, Kansas, and Tennessee. Alabama and Kansas will require all new voter registration applicants to produce documentary proof of citizenship, while Tennessee will require individuals flagged by state officials as potential non-citizens to produce such documentation. Until this year, only two states (Arizona, through its controversial Ballot Proposition 200, and Georgia) had passed proof of citizenship laws, and only one (Arizona) had such a requirement in effect. In contrast, all other states rely on the affidavit signed by a new registrant, under penalty of perjury, swearing that she is a U.S. citizen and that she meets all other voting eligibility requirements.

c. Making Voter Registration Harder

At least sixteen (16) states saw bills introduced to end highly popular Election Day and same-day voter registration, limit voter registration mobilization efforts, and reduce other registration opportunities. Florida and Wisconsin passed laws making it more difficult for people who move to stay registered and vote. Ohio and Maine, meanwhile, eliminated same-day voter registration, used by tens of thousands in 2008 alone, although the people of Maine voted to restore same-day voter registration, and Ohio's law is now being challenged by ballot referendum in November 2012.

Florida, Illinois, and Texas passed laws restricting voter registration drives and other community-based voter registration activity. Florida enacted a law which effectively shut down registration drives that previously registered hundreds of thousands of citizens in that state. Florida's new law now requires that groups and individuals who wish to help voters register first pre-register with the state, submit within 48 hours every voter registration application received, continually submit extensive forms and reports, and keep track of every voter registration application they distribute. While Texas law had already required private citizens to be deputized by a local election official before they could register anyone to vote, the new law now requires these individuals to complete certain training requirements, which may include a final exam, before they can help register any new voters.

d. Reducing Early and Absentee Voting

At least nine (9) states saw bills introduced to reduce their early voting periods, and four tried to reduce absentee voting opportunities. Florida, Georgia, Ohio, Tennessee, and West Virginia succeeded in enacting bills reducing early voting. These cutbacks were proposed in spite of the fact that early voting was used by nearly one-third of all voters in 2008. Five states—Florida, Georgia, Ohio, Tennessee, and West Virginia—enacted laws that shortened the early voting period. In the law that will be put before voters this November, Ohio cut the state's previous early voting period of thirty-five days and eliminated early voting on Saturday afternoon and Sunday. Florida shortened the early voting period from two weeks to one, and eliminated voting on the Sunday before Election Day.

e. Making It Harder to Restore Voting Rights

Governors Terry Branstad of Iowa and Rick Scott of Florida both issued executive actions reversing previously adopted policies of restoring voting rights to citizens with past felony convictions. In Iowa, 80,000 citizens in the last six years had their voting rights restored under this now reversed policy. In Florida, about 150,000 citizens had their rights restored between 2007 and 2010. In fact, up to one million people could have benefited from the practice reversed by Governor Scott and his clemency board; based on the prior rates of restoration, we estimate that approximately 100,000 Floridians would have had their voting rights restored by 2012 but for that executive action.

South Dakota recently passed a law imposing further restrictions on voting by citizens with past felony convictions by disenfranchising persons on probation.

This new law adds to the state's existing requirement that an individual complete any term of imprisonment or parole before his or her voting rights can be restored.

II. The Impact of the New Voting Laws

The new laws significantly alter the rules by which many Americans register and vote, placing new restrictions on the ways citizens can register and requiring more administrative steps in order to vote. In October, the Brennan Center estimated that these changes will make it harder for five million eligible Americans to vote. To put that number in perspective, it is larger than the margin of victory in two of the last three presidential elections.

The litany of new state voting laws will have a disproportionately large impact on certain voters—especially the young, students, the elderly, minorities, women, low-income, and disabled voters. The new laws hit these groups hardest for multiple reasons. Some are less likely to have access to the type of documentation required by the new laws, or lack documentation with a current name or address. And some may rely on methods of voting and registration eliminated or restricted by the laws at higher levels than the general population. Below is some statistical evidence of how each of these groups may be especially affected by particular laws that have been passed.

a. The Impact of Photo ID Laws

Before examining the data concerning the impact of the new photo ID laws, it is worth noting that not all photo ID laws are created equal. Photo ID laws in place before the 2011 and 2012 legislative sessions were by and large less restrictive than the current crop of ID laws in three key ways: they accepted more forms of ID; they provided more exemptions and failsafe options for those without conforming IDs; and they made it easier for voters without photo IDs to obtain such IDs, through affirmative education and outreach and, in Indiana's case, by having far greater citizen access to ID-issuing offices. In contrast, for example, unlike in Indiana and Georgia, the new South Carolina and Texas laws exclude state-issued employee photo IDs, and the new laws in Kansas and Wisconsin provide *no* mechanism for *any* voters without photo ID to vote a ballot that would count at the polls. Unfortunately, this means that there is a far higher likelihood that lack of ID will prevent citizens in these states from voting.

As the Brennan Center published in our report, *Citizens Without Proof*, based on a national survey conducted by the Opinion Research Corporation, 11% of voting-age Americans do not have the kinds of current government-issued photo ID required by the most restrictive new identification laws passed this past year. The numbers are far worse for specific populations. For example, 18% of 18-24 year-old citizens and 18% of citizens 65 or older lack current government-issued photo IDs. Among African Americans, approximately one in four do not possess such ID. And according to another study, 78% of African-American men aged 18-24 in Milwaukee County, Wisconsin do not have a driver's license

Other independent empirical studies have come to the same conclusions. *[Weiser goes on to list the findings of a number of national and state surveys from 2001 to 2009.]* . . .

A number of the new photo ID laws are drafted in a way that makes it more difficult for voters of color and younger voters to qualify. For example, South Carolina, Texas, and Tennessee explicitly exclude state-issued student photo IDs from the list of acceptable identification, and Wisconsin included requirements that Wisconsin State University's student IDs did not meet (at least at the time of enactment). Texas and Tennessee, despite not allowing state student IDs, do allow the use of concealed-carry handgun permits to vote. This legislative choice disproportionately harms African Americans, who are under-represented among concealed-carry handgun permit holders and over-represented among students. For instance, African Americans make up 16.9% of the Texas public university student population, but received less than 7.7% of the state's concealed-carry permits in 2010.

Racial minorities will also frequently face greater obstacles to obtaining the newly required documentation. For example, acceptable forms of identification under the Texas law can be obtained at driver's license offices. Approximately one-third of Texas counties, however, do not have a driver's license office, and Latinos in these counties are significantly less likely to have common photo IDs. . . . Latino households are also less likely to have access to a vehicle, making it harder for Latinos to travel the distance to the closest driver's license office. . . .

In contrast to the claims of many photo ID supporters, photo ID laws risk depressing voter turnout. Indeed, the most rigorous empirical study to date, recently described in the leading journal of political science methodology, *Political Analysis*, concludes that the strictest forms of voter ID requirements reduce turnout among registered voters. And contrary to the claims of some, there is no evidence that photo ID laws increase turnout. At a time when Hispanic voting rates, as well as raw numbers, went up sharply up in neighboring states, Hispanic turnout in Georgia went up much less than in sister states without a photo ID requirement in effect. In fact, adjusting for growth in the voting-age Hispanic citizen population, the increase in Hispanic votes cast between 2006 and 2010 was over 250% greater in North Carolina than in Georgia. Similarly, the increase in black turnout in North Carolina was 129.7% greater than the increase in black turnout in Georgia between 2006 and 2010.

b. Photo ID Laws Do Not Improve Election Integrity

Photo ID laws also fail to meaningfully improve the security of our elections system. The only problem they have the potential to address is in-person impersonation fraud, and study after study confirms that problem to be exceedingly rare, and far rarer than the disenfranchisement caused by photo ID requirements . . .

For several years, the Brennan Center has studied claims of voter fraud in order to distinguish unfounded and exaggerated tales of fraud from reliable, verified claims of election misconduct. Our analytic method was published in a monograph entitled *The Truth about Voter Fraud*, which catalogs the recurrent methodological flaws that lead to allegations of voter fraud, and debunks baseless — though often repeated — reports of voter fraud. In our research we have found virtually no fraud of the type that a photo ID requirement could fix. To the contrary, allegations of voter fraud typically prove baseless upon inspection. A recent example occurred in South Carolina, where state election officials proved that what had appeared to be voting in the name of dead people was actually just mistakes in list matching and clerical errors.

There is little to no reliable evidence of any in-person impersonation fraud in the country. Again, this form of fraud is *the only* misconduct that photo ID laws address.

Other available studies also show that the incidence of in-person voter impersonation is extraordinarily rare. Between October 2002 and September 2005, as part of a high-priority national effort to investigate and enforce laws against voter fraud, the Department of Justice brought 38 cases; of those, only one conviction involved impersonation fraud. In a comprehensive examination of the 9,078,728 votes cast in Ohio's 2002 and 2004 general elections, a total of four were found to be fraudulent meriting legal action by the Board of Elections and County Prosecutors; there is no evidence that any of the four convictions could have been prevented by a photo ID law. A comprehensive analysis of the 2004 Washington gubernatorial election revealed 6 cases of possible double voting and 19 cases of alleged voting in the name of deceased individuals out of a total 2,812,675 ballots cast; the rate of ineligible voting that thus might have been remedied by ID requirements was 0.0009%. In an extensive study searching for voter fraud in all 50 states, Barnard political scientist Lorraine Minnite concluded that deliberate instances of voter fraud are extremely rare. . . .

c. The Impact of Proof of Citizenship Laws

Nationwide, at least 7% of voting-age Americans do not have ready access to proof of citizenship documentation, according to our 2006 study. Based on this, the Brennan Center estimates that well over half a million citizens may not have the necessary proof of citizenship documentation now required in Kansas and (in some cases) Tennessee, and that will be required in Alabama, to register to vote. . . .

d. The Impact of New Voter Registration Restrictions

New laws restricting voter registration drives will result in far less community-based voter registration activity, which will have disparate impacts on minority voters. . . .

e. The Impact of Early Voting Changes

Minority voters will also bear the brunt of new laws restricting early voting. In 2008, a large number of American-American churches in Florida and Ohio organized successful "souls to the polls" drives, whereby churchgoers were provided free rides to the polls for early voting on Sunday. In Florida, 33% of citizens who voted early on the Sunday before Election Day were African American, even though African Americans make up only 13% of the citizen voting age population. Additionally, 24% were Latino, even though Latinos make up only 16% of the citizen voting age population. Now, Florida has eliminated voting on the Sunday before the election, and Ohio has passed a law eliminating Sunday voting entirely.

f. The Impact of Laws Making It Harder to Restore Voting Rights

Actions to prevent the restoration of voting rights to previously incarcerated citizens will prevent tens and possibly hundreds of thousands from being able to vote and disproportionately hit minorities the hardest. . . .

III. The Role of the Department of Justice in Enforcing Federal Protections of the Right to Vote

The Department of Justice, through its Voting Rights Section, plays a critical role in the monitoring and enforcement of laws protecting the right to vote, including the seminal Voting Rights Act of 1965, the National Voter Registration Act of 1993 (NVRA or "Motor Voter" Law), the Help America Vote Act of 2002 (HAVA), and the Uniformed and Overseas Citizens Absentee Voting Act of 1986 (UOCAVA), as amended by the 2010 Military and Overseas Voter Empowerment Act (MOVE Act). . . .

a. Enforcement of Section 5 of the Voting Rights Act

The Voting Rights Act of 1965 is widely regarded as the most effective federal civil rights statute of the 20th Century, and was reauthorized by Congress in 2006 with overwhelming support. Under Section 5 of the Act, certain jurisdictions with a history of discriminatory voting practices must demonstrate—either to a three-judge federal court or the Department of Justice—that changes to their voting laws do not have a retrogressive impact on minority voters, a process known as preclearance. Under Section 5, these states bear the burden of demonstrating that their voting laws have neither the purpose nor effect of harming the state's minority voters. When jurisdictions submit voting changes to the Department of Justice for preclearance, the Department is obligated to assess the evidence submitted by those jurisdictions and to determine whether they have met their burden of showing that those changes have no discriminatory purpose and no discriminating effect. When jurisdictions file preclearance actions in federal court, the Department is the defendant in those actions.

Although the Department has considered thousands of requests for preclearance of voting changes over the past three and a half years, it has only considered three so far relating to the new laws restricting voting:

- In June of 2011, South Carolina sought preclearance from the Justice Department for its new voter ID law requiring voters to produce government-issued photo ID at the polls. The Department rejected the state's request, in part because the state's own data demonstrated that "minority registered voters were nearly 20% more likely to lack DMV-issued ID than white registered voters, and thus to be effectively disenfranchised by [the] new requirements."
- Similarly, the state of Texas submitted its new photo ID law to the Department of Justice in July 2011, seeking preclearance for the State's photo ID law. The Department objected to preclearance, among other reasons, because the state's own data showed that a Hispanic voter is between 46.5 and 120 percent more likely than a non-Hispanic voter to lack the main state-issued photo IDs.

- The state of Florida withdrew an administrative preclearance request from the Department of Justice, and filed a federal lawsuit in the District of Columbia in 2011 before the Department had issued an opinion on provisions of the state's new law that restricts early voting and voter registration. After reviewing all evidence provided by the state, the Department has taken the position in court papers that Florida has not met its burden of showing that recent restrictions on voting and voter registration were passed with neither the intent nor the effect of harming minority voters.

In each of these cases, which are now being considered by three-judge panels of the District of Columbia, the Department properly found that states have failed to meet their burden under the Voting Rights Act that the laws at issue do not harm minority voters. What is more, in none of these cases have the states at issue offered evidence of the existence of an actual problem these new legal restrictions were supposedly designed to address. . . .

b. Enforcement of the NVRA

While the Department of Justice has been actively enforcing several federal voting laws, there have been few actions to enforce the National Voter Registration Act—and Section 7 of the NVRA in particular. Section 7 is designed to increase the number of registered voters on the rolls by providing voter registration opportunities for individuals who access services at public assistance agencies. This law is a critical protection to ensure that millions of low-income citizens have opportunities to register to vote. Enforcement of Section 7 has been far too rare, especially considering the hugely successful outcomes of such enforcement. . . .

IV. Improving the Voter Registration System

Rather than simply rely on the Department of Justice's enforcement of the NVRA, Congress should work to pass new legislation to improve our voter registration system to make it more secure and accessible to all eligible voters. Congress has a role to set minimum standards for the states to follow in registering voters for federal elections. Modernizing our voter registration systems will not only make the voter rolls more complete and accurate and save money, it will also further curb the small potential for voter fraud.

Our current voter registration system is outmoded, costly, and rife with error. Despite technological advances, the system still relies largely on handwritten paper forms, and places the onus of registering on the voter rather than state officials. A recent study by the Pew Center on the States found that about 50 million eligible Americans are not captured by the current voter registration system and 1 in 8 voter registration records contains significant inaccuracies. . . .

A modernized voter registration system benefits voters, election officials, and the integrity of our voting systems. Our current registration system demands an enormous amount of time, money, and effort from local officials. Excessive clerical work also distracts from the planning and supervision necessary to ensure a sound Election Day. This overburdened registration process exacerbates other problems on Election Day, leading to long lines, chaotic polling locations, and overwhelmed volunteers. Voter registration modernization will free up resources and allow election officials to concentrate on important pre-election preparations to ensure elections run smoothly, rather than processing a surge of registration forms typically received a week or two before Election Day. Key reforms can make the system work better for election administrators and the voters they serve.

Source: Weiser, Wendy R. Testimony Delivered to the House Judiciary Committee's Subcommittee on the Constitution Regarding Restrictive Voting Laws and Oversight of the Department of Justice. April 18, 2012. Accessed June 25, 2019. https://www.govinfo.gov/content/pkg/CHRG-112hhrg73859/html/CHRG-112hhrg73859.htm.

Supreme Court Decision in *Shelby v. Holder* Strikes Down Key Sections of the Voting Rights Act, 2013

On June 25, 2013, the U.S. Supreme Court handed down perhaps the most consequential decision impacting voting and elections in America since the passage of the Voting Rights Act in 1965. In Shelby County v. Holder, *a slim 5–4 court majority reversed an appeals court ruling and struck down Section 4(b), which contained the coverage formula for Section 5 of the Act. Section 5 had required nine southern states with a proven history of discriminating against black voters to get preclearance, or approval from changing any of their election laws and procedures without first getting the approval of federal authorities. Without Section 4(b) in place, no formula existed for determining which states fall under Section 5 preclearance rules. So while Section 5 was still technically part of the Voting Rights Act legislation, the Shelby ruling essentially rendered it null and void.*

The court's decision was praised by white Southern lawmakers who said that they were sick of being punished for the sins of past generations and declared that they would now have greater flexibility to combat voter fraud and otherwise modernize their voting practices. Voting rights advocates, however, expressed horror at the decision and warned that it would spur a flood of new laws that would have the effect of disenfranchising minorities.

Within hours of the decision, the state of Texas (one of the nine states affected by Section 5) announced that it intended to impose a strict new voter ID law—one that supporters said would improve the integrity of elections but that critics described as a transparent move by the state's Republican party to suppress the vote of minorities who were more likely to support Democrats. The news out of Texas made it clear to both supporters and critics of the court's decision that in the wake of Shelby v. Holder, *the landscape of election law and voting rights had been significantly altered.*

Following are excerpts from the court's decision, the majority opinion penned by Chief Justice John Roberts, and a dissenting opinion written by Justice Ruth Bader Ginsburg.

Majority Decision

The Voting Rights Act of 1965 was enacted to address entrenched racial discrimination in voting, "an insidious and pervasive evil which had been perpetuated in certain parts of our country through unremitting and ingenious defiance of the Constitution." *South Carolina v. Katzenbach,* 383 U. S. 301, 309. Section 2 of the Act, which bans any "standard, practice, or procedure" that "results in a denial or abridgement of the right of any citizen . . . to vote on account of race or color," 42 U. S. C. §1973(a), applies nationwide, is permanent, and is not at issue in this case. Other sections apply only to some parts of the country. Section 4 of the Act provides the "coverage formula," defining the "covered jurisdictions" as States or political subdivisions that maintained tests or devices as prerequisites to voting, and had low voter registration or turnout, in the 1960s and early 1970s. §1973b(b). In those covered jurisdictions, §5 of the Act provides that no change in voting procedures can take effect until approved by specified federal authorities in Washington, D. C. §1973c(a). Such approval is known as "preclearance." The coverage formula and preclearance requirement were initially set to expire after five years, but the Act has been reauthorized several times. In 2006, the Act was reauthorized for an additional 25 years, but the coverage formula was not changed. Coverage still turned on whether a jurisdiction had a voting test in the 1960s or 1970s, and had low voter registration or turnout at that time. Shortly after the 2006 reauthorization, a Texas utility district sought to bail out from the Act's coverage and, in the alternative, challenged the Act's constitutionality. This Court resolved the challenge on statutory grounds, but expressed serious doubts about the Act's continued constitutionality.

Petitioner Shelby County, in the covered jurisdiction of Alabama, sued the Attorney General in Federal District Court in Washington, D. C., seeking a declaratory judgment that sections 4(b) and 5 are facially unconstitutional, as well as a permanent injunction against their enforcement. The District Court upheld the Act, finding that the evidence before Congress in 2006 was sufficient to justify reauthorizing §5 and continuing §4(b)'s coverage formula. The D. C. Circuit affirmed. After surveying the evidence in the record, that court accepted Congress's conclusion that §2 litigation remained inadequate in the covered jurisdictions to protect the rights of minority voters, that §5 was therefore still necessary, and that the coverage formula continued to pass constitutional muster.

Held: Section 4 of the Voting Rights Act is unconstitutional; its formula can no longer be used as a basis for subjecting jurisdictions to pre-clearance. In Northwest Austin, this Court noted that the Voting Rights Act "imposes current burdens and must be justified by current needs" and concluded that "a departure from the fundamental principle of equal sovereignty requires a showing that a statute's disparate geographic coverage is sufficiently related to the problem that it targets." 557 U. S., at 203. These basic principles guide review of the question presented here. State legislation may not contravene federal law. States retain broad autonomy, however, in structuring their governments and pursuing legislative objectives. Indeed, the Tenth Amendment reserves to the States all powers not specifically granted to the Federal Government, including "the power to regulate elections." *Gregory v. Ashcroft,* 501 U. S. 452, 461–462. There is also a "fundamental principle of equal sovereignty" among the States, which is highly pertinent in assessing disparate treatment of States. *Northwest*

Austin, supra, at 203. The Voting Rights Act sharply departs from these basic principles. It requires States to beseech the Federal Government for permission to implement laws that they would otherwise have the right to enact and execute on their own. And despite the tradition of equal sovereignty, the Act applies to only nine States (and additional counties).That is why, in 1966, this Court described the Act as "stringent" and "potent," *Katzenbach,* 383 U. S., at 308, 315, 337. The Court nonetheless upheld the Act, concluding that such an "uncommon exercise of congressional power" could be justified by "exceptional conditions." Id., at 334.

In 1966, these departures were justified by the "blight of racial discrimination in voting" that had "infected the electoral process in parts of our country for nearly a century," *Katzenbach,* 383 U. S., at 308. At the time, the coverage formula—the means of linking the exercise of the unprecedented authority with the problem that war-ranted it—made sense. The Act was limited to areas where Congress found "evidence of actual voting discrimination," and the covered jurisdictions shared two characteristics: "the use of tests and devices for voter registration, and a voting rate in the 1964 presidential election at least 12 points below the national average." Id., at 330. The Court explained that "[t]ests and devices are relevant to voting discrimination because of their long history as a tool for perpetrating the evil; a low voting rate is pertinent for the obvious reason that widespread disenfranchisement must inevitably affect the number of actual voters." Ibid. The Court therefore concluded that "the cover-age formula [was] rational in both practice and theory." Ibid. Nearly 50 years later, things have changed dramatically. Largely because of the Voting Rights Act, "[v]oter turnout and registration rates" in covered jurisdictions "now approach parity. Blatantly discriminatory evasions of federal decrees are rare. And minority candidates hold office at unprecedented levels." *Northwest Austin,* supra, at 202. The tests and devices that blocked ballot access have been forbidden nationwide for over 40 years. Yet the Act has not eased §5's restrictions or narrowed the scope of §4's coverage formula along the way. Instead those extraordinary and unprecedented features have been reauthorized as if nothing has changed, and they have grown even stronger . . . (b) Section 4's formula is unconstitutional in light of current conditions.

> In 1966, the coverage formula was "rational in both practice and theory." *Katzenbach,* supra, at 330. It looked to cause (discriminatory tests) and effect (low voter registration and turnout), and tailored the remedy (preclearance) to those jurisdictions exhibiting both. By 2009, however, the "coverage formula raise[d] serious constitutional questions." *Northwest Austin,* supra, at 204. Coverage today is based on decades-old data and eradicated practices. The formula captures States by reference to literacy tests and low voter registration and turnout in the 1960s and early 1970s. But such tests have been banned for over 40 years. And voter registration and turnout numbers in covered States have risen dramatically. In 1965, the States could be divided into those with a recent history of voting tests and low voter registration and turnout and those without those characteristics. Congress based its coverage formula on

that distinction. Today the Nation is no longer divided along those lines, yet the Voting Rights Act continues to treat it as if it were. . . .

The Government has a fallback argument—because the formula was relevant in 1965, its continued use is permissible so long as any discrimination remains in the States identified in 1965. . . . But history did not end in 1965. In assessing the "current need" for a preclearance system treating States differently from one another today, history since 1965 cannot be ignored. The Fifteenth Amendment is not designed to punish for the past; its purpose is to ensure a better future. To serve that purpose, Congress—if it is to divide the States—must identify those jurisdictions to be singled out on a basis that makes sense in light of current conditions. (3) Respondents also rely heavily on data from the record com-piled by Congress before reauthorizing the Act. Regardless of how one looks at that record, no one can fairly say that it shows anything approaching the "pervasive," "flagrant," "widespread," and "rampant" discrimination that clearly distinguished the covered jurisdictions from the rest of the Nation in 1965. *Katzenbach,* supra, at 308, 315, 331. But a more fundamental problem remains: Congress did not use that record to fashion a coverage formula grounded in current conditions. It instead reenacted a formula based on 40-year-old facts having no logical relation to the present day . . .

Majority Decision (Roberts)

. . . In 1966, we found [that] . . . the "blight of racial discrimination in voting" had "infected the electoral process in parts of our country for nearly a century." *Katzenbach,* 383 U. S., at 308. Several States had enacted a variety of requirements and tests "specifically designed to prevent" African-Americans from voting. *Id.*, at 310. Case-by-case litigation had proved inadequate to prevent such racial discrimination in voting, in part because States "merely switched to discriminatory devices not covered by the federal decrees," "enacted difficult new tests," or simply "defied and evaded court orders." *Id.*, at 314. Shortly before enactment of the Voting Rights Act, only 19.4 percent of African-Americans of voting age were registered to vote in Alabama, only 31.8 percent in Louisiana, and only 6.4 percent in Mississippi. *Id.*, at 313. Those figures were roughly 50 percentage points or more below the figures for whites. *Ibid.* In short, we concluded that "[u]nder the compulsion of these unique circumstances, Congress responded in a permissibly decisive manner [in passing the Civil Rights Act, including Section IV preclearance requirements]" *Id.,* at 334, 335. We also noted then and have emphasized since that this extra-ordinary legislation was intended to be temporary, set to expire after five years. *Id.*, at 333; *Northwest Austin,* supra, at 199. At the time, the coverage formula—the means of linking the exercise of the unprecedented authority with the problem that warranted it—made sense. We found that "Congress chose to limit its attention to the geographic areas where immediate action seemed necessary." *Katzenbach,* 383 U. S., at 328. . . . It accurately reflected those jurisdictions uniquely characterized by voting discrimination "on a pervasive scale," linking coverage to the devices used to effectuate discrimination and to the resulting disenfranchisement. *Id.*, at 308. The formula ensured that the "stringent remedies[were] aimed at areas where voting discrimination ha[d] been most flagrant." *Id.,* at 315.

Nearly 50 years later, things have changed dramatically. Shelby County contends that the preclearance requirement, even without regard to its disparate coverage, is now unconstitutional. Its arguments have a good deal of force. In the covered jurisdictions, "[v]oter turnout and registration rates now approach parity. Blatantly discriminatory evasions of federal decrees are rare. And minority candidates hold office at unprecedented levels." *Northwest Austin,* 557 U. S., at 202. The tests and devices that blocked access to the ballot have been forbidden nation-wide for over 40 years. Those conclusions are not ours alone. Congress said the same when it reauthorized the Act in 2006, writing that"[s]ignificant progress has been made in eliminating first generation barriers experienced by minority voters, including increased numbers of registered minority voters, minority voter turnout, and minority representation in Congress, State legislatures, and local elected offices." The House Report elaborated that "the number of African-Americans who are registered and who turn out to cast ballots has increased significantly over the last 40 years, particularly since 1982," and noted that "[i]n some circumstances, minorities register to vote and cast ballots at levels that surpass those of white voters." That Report also explained that there have been "significant increases in the number of African-Americans serving in elected offices"; more specifically, there has been approximately a 1,000 percent increase since 1965 in the number of African-American elected officials in the six States originally covered by the Voting Rights Act. . . .

The preclearance statistics are also illuminating. In the first decade after enactment of §5, the Attorney General objected to 14.2 percent of proposed voting changes. In the last decade before reenactment, the Attorney General objected to a mere 0.16 percent. There is no doubt that these improvements are in large part because of the Voting Rights Act. The Act has proved immensely successful at redressing racial discrimination and integrating the voting process. During the "Freedom Summer" of 1964, in Philadelphia, Mississippi, three men were murdered while working in the area to register African-American voters. On "Bloody Sunday" in 1965, in Selma, Alabama, police beat and used tear gas against hundreds marching in support of African-American enfranchisement. Today both of those towns are governed by African-American mayors. Problems remain in these States and others, but there is no denying that, due to the Voting Rights Act, our Nation has made great strides. Yet the Act has not eased the restrictions in §5 or narrowed the scope of the coverage formula in §4(b) along the way. Those extraordinary and unprecedented features were reauthorized—as if nothing had changed. In fact, the Act's unusual remedies have grown even stronger. When Congress reauthorized the Act in 2006, it did so for another 25 years on top of the previous 40—a far cry from the initial five-year period. Congress also expanded the prohibitions in §5. We had previously interpreted §5 to prohibit only those redistricting plans that would have the purpose or effect of worsening the position of minority groups. In 2006, Congress amended §5 to prohibit laws that could have favored such groups but did not do so because of a discriminatory purpose, even though we had stated that such broadening of §5 coverage would "exacerbate the substantial federalism costs that the preclearance procedure already exacts, perhaps to the extent of raising concerns about §5's constitutionality," In addition, Congress expanded §5 to prohibit any voting law "that has the purpose of or will have the effect of diminishing the ability of any citizens of the United States," on account of race, color, or language minority status, "to elect their preferred candidates of choice." In light of those two amendments, the bar that covered jurisdictions must clear has been raised even as the conditions justifying that requirement have dramatically improved. We have also previously highlighted the concern that "the preclearance requirements in one State [might] be unconstitutional in another." Nothing has happened since to alleviate this troubling concern about the current application of §5. Respondents do not deny that there have been improvements on the ground, but argue that much of this can be attributed to the deterrent effect of §5, which dissuades covered jurisdictions from engaging in discrimination that they would resume should §5 be struck down. Under this theory, however, §5 would be effectively immune from scrutiny; no matter how "clean" the record of covered jurisdictions, the argument could always be made that it was deterrence that accounted for the good behavior. . . .

In 1965, the States could be divided into two groups: those with a recent history of voting tests and low voter registration and turnout, and those without those characteristics. Congress based its coverage formula on that distinction. Today the Nation is no longer divided along those lines, yet the Voting Rights Act continues to treat it as if it were. . . .

There is no valid reason to insulate the coverage formula from review merely because it was previously enacted 40 years ago. If Congress had started from scratch in 2006, it plainly could not have enacted the present coverage formula. It would have been irrational for Congress to distinguish between States in such a fundamental way based on 40-year-old data, when today's statistics tell an entirely different story. And it would have been irrational to base coverage on the use of voting tests 40 years ago, when such tests have been illegal since that time. But that is exactly what Congress has done.

* * *

Striking down an Act of Congress "is the gravest and most delicate duty that this Court is called on to perform." *Blodgett v. Holden,* 275 U. S. 142, 148 (1927) (Holmes, J., concurring). We do not do so lightly. That is why, in 2009, we took care to avoid ruling on the constitutionality of the Voting Rights Act when asked to do so, and instead resolved the case then before us on statutory grounds. But in issuing that decision, we expressed our broader concerns about the constitutionality of the Act. Congress could have updated the coverage formula at that time, but did not do so. Its failure to act leaves us today with no choice but to declare §4(b) unconstitutional. The formula in that section can no longer be used as a basis for subjecting jurisdictions to preclearance. Our decision in no way affects the permanent, nation-wide ban on racial discrimination in voting found in §2. We issue no holding on §5 itself, only on the coverage formula. Congress may draft another formula based on current conditions. Such a formula is an initial prerequisite to a determination that exceptional conditions still exist justifying such an "extraordinary departure from the traditional course of relations between the States and the Federal Government." *Presley,* 502 U. S., at 500–501. Our country has changed, and while any racial discrimination in voting is too much, Congress must ensure that the legislation it passes to remedy that problem speaks to current conditions. The judgment of the Court of Appeals is reversed. It is so ordered.

Dissenting Opinion (Ginsburg)

In the Court's view, the very success of §5 of the Voting Rights Act demands its dormancy. Congress was of another mind. Recognizing that large progress has been made, Congress determined, based on a voluminous record, that the scourge of discrimination was not yet extirpated. The question this case presents is who decides whether, as currently operative, §5 remains justifiable, this Court, or a Congress charged with the obligation to enforce the post-Civil War Amendments "by appropriate legislation." With overwhelming support in both Houses, Congress concluded that, for two prime reasons, §5 should continue in force, unabated. First, continuance would facilitate completion of the impressive gains thus far made; and second, continuance would guard against backsliding. Those assessments were well within Congress' province to make and should elicit this Court's unstinting approbation. I "[V]oting discrimination still exists; no one doubts that." Ante, at 2. But the Court today terminates the remedy that proved to be best suited to block that discrimination. The Voting Rights Act of 1965 (VRA) has worked to combat voting discrimination where other remedies had been tried and failed. Particularly effective is the VRA's requirement of federal preclearance for all changes to voting laws in the regions of the country with the most aggravated records of rank discrimination against minority voting rights. . . .

The sad irony of today's decision lies in its utter failure to grasp why the VRA has proven effective. The Court appears to believe that the VRA's success in eliminating the specific devices extant in 1965 means that preclearance is no longer needed. With that belief, and the argument derived from it, history repeats itself. The same assumption—that the problem could be solved when particular methods of voting discrimination are identified and eliminated—was indulged and proved wrong repeatedly prior to the VRA's enactment. Unlike prior statutes, which singled out particular tests or devices, the VRA is grounded in Congress' recognition of the "variety and persistence" of measures designed to impair minority voting rights. *Katzenbach,* 383 U. S., at 311; supra, at 2. In truth, the evolution of voting discrimination into more subtle second-generation barriers is powerful evidence that a remedy as effective as preclearance remains vital to protect minority voting rights and prevent backsliding. Beyond question, the VRA is no ordinary legislation. It is extraordinary because Congress embarked on a mission long delayed and of extraordinary importance: to realize the purpose and promise of the Fifteenth Amendment. For a half century, a concerted effort has been made to end racial discrimination in voting. Thanks to the Voting Rights Act, progress once the subject of a dream has been achieved and continues to be made. The record supporting the 2006 reauthorization of the VRA is also extraordinary. It was described by the Chairman of the House Judiciary Committee as "one of the most extensive considerations of any piece of legislation that the United States Congress has dealt with in the 27½ years" he had served in the House. 152 Cong. Rec. H5143 (July 13, 2006) (statement of Rep. Sensenbrenner). . . .

After exhaustive evidence-gathering and deliberative process, Congress reauthorized the VRA, including the coverage provision, with overwhelming bipartisan support. It was the judgment of Congress that "40 years has not been a sufficient amount of time to eliminate the vestiges of discrimination following nearly 100 years of disregard for the dictates of the 15th amendment and to ensure that the right of all citizens to vote is protected as guaranteed by the Constitution." 2006 Reauthorization §2(b)(7), 120 Stat. 577. That determination of the body empowered to enforce the Civil War Amendments "by appropriate legislation" merits this Court's utmost respect. In my judgment, the Court errs egregiously by overriding Congress' decision.

* * *

For the reasons stated, I would affirm the judgment of the Court of Appeals.

Source: Supreme Court of the United States. *Shelby County, Alabama, v. Holder, Attorney General to the United States, et al.* Argued February 27, 2013. Decided June 25, 2013. Excerpts from Decision, Majority Opinion (Roberts), and Dissenting Opinion (Ginsburg). 570 U.S. 2 (2013). Accessed April 2, 2019. https://www.supremecourt.gov/opinions/12pdf/12-96_6k47.pdf.

Attorney General Holder Urges Re-Enfranchisement for Former Prisoners, 2014

On February 11, 2014, Obama administration Attorney General Eric Holder delivered a speech at Georgetown University Law Center in which he urged the restoration of full voting rights to people convicted of crimes who had "fulfilled their debt to society"—completed their sentence—and returned to their communities to work and raise their families. He urged states, each of which have their own, often dramatically different voting laws pertaining to convicted felons—both those currently serving time and those who have been released after doing their time—to pass legislation re-enfranchising former prisoners. According to a 2016 analysis by a nonprofit organization called the Sentencing Project, approximately 6.1 million Americans were barred from voting that year because of felony disenfranchisement laws. Many experts believe that these disenfranchisement laws disproportionately impact communities of color. In 2018 voters in Florida passed a ballot measure to restore voting rights to an estimated 1.4 million residents who had previously been unable to vote due to felony convictions (people convicted of murder or sexual offenses were not included in the measure), but as of spring 2019, state Republican lawmakers opposed to the measure were working to limit its application.

Following are excerpts from Holder's remarks.

Today, we gather in recognition of the fact that, although our laws and procedures must be continually updated, our commitment to the cause of justice must remain constant. From its earliest days, our Republic has been bound together by its extraordinary legal system, and by the enduring values that define it. These values—of equality, opportunity, and justice under law—were first codified in our founding documents. And they are put into action every day by leaders like you—and the talented men and women who learn, at great institutions like Georgetown, what it means to be a steward of the law—and an advocate for those whom it protects and empowers. . . .

Criminal justice reform is essentially not a partisan issue. It's about providing legal professionals and law enforcement leaders with the 21st-century solutions they need to address 21st-century challenges. It's about shaping a system that deters and punishes crime, keeps us safe, and ensures that those who pay their debts have the chance to become productive citizens. Most importantly, it's about answering fundamental questions—about fairness and equality—that determine who we are, and who we aspire to be, not only as a nation, but as a people—a people resolved to move forward together, and committed to implementing criminal justice policies that work for everyone in this country.

This is the challenge—and the extraordinary opportunity—that brings us together this morning. And it's the same challenge that drove me, roughly one year ago, to launch a targeted Justice Department review of our criminal justice system: to identify areas for improvement and make this system as efficient, as effective, and as just as possible.

Last August, I announced a new "Smart on Crime" initiative—based on the results of this review—that's already allowing the Justice Department to strengthen the federal system; to increase our emphasis on proven diversion, rehabilitation, and reentry programs; and to reduce unnecessary collateral consequences for those seeking to rejoin their communities. Among the key changes we're implementing is a modification of the Department's charging policies—to ensure that people who commit certain low-level, nonviolent federal drug crimes will face sentences appropriate to their individual conduct—rather than stringent mandatory minimums, which will now be reserved for the most serious criminals. . . .

As we work with Members of Congress to refine and pass this legislation, my colleagues and I are simultaneously moving forward with a range of other reforms. We're investing in evidence-based diversion programs—like drug treatment initiatives and veterans courts—that can serve as alternatives to incarceration in appropriate cases. We're working to target law enforcement resources to the areas where they're needed most. And we're partnering with state officials, agency leaders, and others—including members of the Federal Interagency Reentry Council, comprised of Cabinet Secretaries and leadership from throughout the Obama

Administration—to advance proven strategies to help formerly incarcerated people successfully rejoin their communities.

After all, at some point, 95 percent of all prisoners will be released. And just as we expect everyone who commits a crime to pay their societal debts, we also expect them to remain sober and crime-free upon their release. We expect them to get jobs and find housing. And we expect them to become productive, law-abiding members of society . . .

Yet formerly incarcerated people continue to face significant obstacles. They are frequently deprived of opportunities they need to rebuild their lives. And in far too many places, their rights—including the single most basic right of American citizenship—the right to vote—are either abridged or denied.

As the Leadership Conference Education Fund articulated very clearly in your recent report, "there is no rational reason to take away someone's voting rights for life just because they've committed a crime, especially after they've completed their sentence and made amends." On the contrary: there is evidence to suggest that former prisoners whose voting rights are restored are significantly less likely to return to the criminal justice system. As your report further notes, a study recently conducted by a parole commission in Florida found that, while the overall three-year recidivism rate stood at roughly 33 percent, the rate among those who were re-enfranchised after they'd served their time was just a third of that.

Unfortunately, the re-enfranchisement policy that contributed to this stunning result has been inexplicably and unwisely rolled back since that study was completed. And, in other states, officials have raised hurdles to be faced by those with past convictions seeking to regain their access to the ballot box. And that's why I believe that, today—starting here and now—it is time for criminal justice leaders to come together to address this issue. It is time to fundamentally reconsider laws that permanently disenfranchise people who are no longer under federal or state supervision.

These restrictions are not only unnecessary and unjust, they are also counterproductive. By perpetuating the stigma and isolation imposed on formerly incarcerated individuals, these laws increase the likelihood they will commit future crimes. They undermine the reentry process and defy the principles—of accountability and rehabilitation—that guide our criminal justice policies. And however well-intentioned current advocates of felony disenfranchisement may be—the reality is that these measures are, at best, profoundly outdated. At worst, these laws, with their disparate impact on minority communities, echo policies enacted during a deeply troubled period in America's past—a time of post-Civil War repression. And they have their roots in centuries-old conceptions of justice that were too often based on exclusion, animus, and fear.

The history of felony disenfranchisement dates to a time when these policies were employed not to improve public safety, but purely as punitive measures—intended to stigmatize, shame, and shut out a person who had been found guilty of a crime. Over the course of many decades—court by court, state by state—Americans broadly rejected the colonial-era notion that the commission of a crime should result in lifelong exclusion from society.

After Reconstruction, many Southern states enacted disenfranchisement schemes to specifically target African Americans and diminish the electoral strength of newly-freed populations. The resulting system of unequal enforcement—and discriminatory application of the law—led to a situation, in 1890, where ninety percent of the Southern prison population was black. And those swept up in this system too often had their rights rescinded, their dignity diminished, and the full measure of their citizenship revoked for the rest of their lives. They could not vote.

In the years since, thanks to the hard work, and the many sacrifices, of millions throughout our history, we've outlawed legal discrimination, ended "separate but equal," and confronted the evils of slavery and segregation. Particularly during the last half-century, we've brought about historic advances in the cause of civil rights. And we've secured critical protections like the Civil Rights Act of 1964 and the Voting Rights Act of 1965.

Yet—despite this remarkable, once-unimaginable progress—the vestiges, and the direct effects, of outdated practices remain all too real. In many states, felony disenfranchisement laws are still on the books. And the current scope of these policies is not only too significant to ignore—it is also too unjust to tolerate.

Across this country today, an estimated 5.8 million Americans—5.8 million of our fellow citizens—are prohibited from voting because of current or previous felony convictions. That's more than the individual populations of 31 U.S. states. And although well over a century has passed since post-Reconstruction states used these measures to strip African Americans of their most fundamental rights, the impact of felony disenfranchisement on modern communities of color remains both disproportionate and unacceptable.

Throughout America, 2.2 million black citizens—or nearly one in 13 African-American adults—are banned from voting because of these laws. In three states—Florida, Kentucky, and Virginia—that ratio climbs to one in five. These individuals and many others—of all races, backgrounds, and walks of life—are routinely denied the chance to participate in the most fundamental and important act of self-governance. They are prevented from exercising an essential right. And they are locked out from achieving complete rehabilitation and reentry—even after they've served the time, and paid the fines, that they owe.

Fortunately—despite unfortunate steps backward in a few jurisdictions, and thanks to the leadership of policymakers from both parties and criminal justice professionals like you—in recent years we have begun to see a trend in the right direction. Since 1997, a total of 23 states—including Nebraska, Nevada, Texas, and Washington State—have enacted meaningful reforms. In Virginia, just last year, former Governor McDonnell adopted a policy that began to automatically restore the voting rights of former prisoners with non-violent felony convictions.

These are positive developments. But many of these changes are incremental in nature. They stop well short of confronting this problem head-on. And although we can be encouraged by the promising indications we've seen, a great deal of work remains to be done. Given what is at stake, the time for incrementalism is clearly over.

Eleven states continue to restrict voting rights, to varying degrees, even after a person has served his or her prison sentence and is no longer on probation or parole—including the State of Florida, where approximately 10 percent of the entire population is disenfranchised as a result. In Mississippi, roughly 8 percent of the population cannot vote because of past involvement with the criminal justice system. In Iowa, action by the governor in 2011 caused the state to move from automatic restoration of rights—following the completion of a criminal sentence—to an arduous process that requires direct intervention by the governor himself in every individual case. It's no surprise that, two years after this change—of the 8,000 people who had completed their sentences during that governor's tenure—voting rights had been restored to fewer than 12.

That's moving backwards—not forward. It is unwise, it is unjust, and it is not in keeping with our democratic values. These laws deserve to be not only reconsidered, but repealed. And so today, I call upon state leaders and other elected officials across the country to pass clear and consistent reforms to restore the voting rights of all who have served their terms in prison or jail, completed their parole or probation, and paid their fines.

I call upon experts and legislators to stand together in overturning an unfortunate and outdated status quo.

And I call upon the American people—who overwhelmingly oppose felony disenfranchisement—to join us in bringing about the end of misguided policies that unjustly restrict what's been called the "most basic right" of American citizenship.

I applaud those who have already shown leadership in raising awareness and helping to address this issue. Later today, this conference will hear from Senator Rand Paul, who has been a leader on this matter. His vocal support for restoring voting rights for former inmates shows that this issue need not break down along partisan lines.

Bipartisan support will be critical going forward because, even in states where reforms are currently taking hold, we need to do even more. And we need to make sure these positive changes are expanded upon—and made permanent.

Virginia's progress has come through the executive power of its former governor, rather than the legislature—meaning that, without action by state lawmakers, these reforms can be reversed by any future executive with the stroke of a pen. More broadly, the inconsistent patchwork of laws affecting felony disenfranchisement varies so widely between states—and, in some places, between cities and counties—that even those who administer the laws are sometimes unfamiliar with how to apply them. The New York Times noted in 2012 that this kind of confusion means that many who are legally allowed to vote erroneously believe that their rights are restricted. And too often, those who do understand their rights are wrongfully turned away.

Today—together—we need to correct this injustice. As the evidence has shown, and as I pointed out in an amicus brief—filed more than a decade ago, in a case challenging Florida's disenfranchisement law—permanent exclusion from the civic community does not advance any objective of our criminal justice system. It has never been shown to prevent new crimes or deter future misconduct. And there's no indication that those who have completed their sentences are more likely to commit electoral crimes of any type—or even to vote against pro-law enforcement candidates.

What is clear—and abundantly so—is that these laws sever a formerly incarcerated person's most direct link to civic participation. They cause further alienation and disillusionment between these individuals and the communities that our Smart on Crime policies encourage them to rejoin. And particularly at a time when our prisons are overflowing—and many who are serving sentences for nonviolent drug crimes find themselves trapped in a vicious cycle of poverty and incarceration—it is counterproductive to exclude these individuals from the voting franchise once their involvement with the corrections system is at an end. It is contrary to the goals that bring us together today. And it is not consistent with the cherished ideals that once led Supreme Court Justice William Brennan to call disenfranchisement "the very antithesis of rehabilitation."

Whenever we tell citizens who have paid their debts and rejoined their communities that they are not entitled to take part in the democratic process, we fall short of the bedrock promise—of equal opportunity and equal justice—that has always served as the foundation of our legal system. So it's time to renew our commitment—here and now—to the notion that the free exercise of our fundamental rights should never be subject to politics, or geography, or the lingering effects of flawed and unjust policies.

After all, at its most basic level, this isn't just about fairness for those who are released from prison. It's about who we are as a nation. It's about confronting—with clear eyes, and in frank terms—disparities and divisions that are unworthy of the greatest justice system the world has ever known. It's about ensuring that we hold accountable those who do wrong—while preserving the values our nation has always held sacred. And it's about protecting the American people and strengthening our communities—while enabling all of our citizens, no matter who they are or where they're from, to make their voices heard.

Source: Holder, Eric. Remarks on Criminal Justice Reform at Georgetown University Law Center, February 11, 2014. United States Department of Justice, Justice News. Accessed April 15, 2019. https://www.justice.gov/opa/speech/attorney-general-eric-holder-delivers-remarkson-criminal-justice-reform-georgetown.

A Democratic Senator Calls for Strengthening the Voting Rights Act in Response to *Shelby County v. Holder*, 2014

In June 2013 a narrow 5–4 majority of the U.S. Supreme Court negated significant provisions of the historic 1965 Voting Rights Act, ruling in Shelby County v. Holder *that they were no longer necessary to protect voters in states with a history of racial discrimination at the ballot box. The decision stunned and angered voting rights advocates and civil rights leaders including Congressman John Lewis (D-Georgia), who called the decision a "dagger in the heart" of the Voting Rights Act: "I disagree with the court that the history of discrimination is somehow irrelevant today. The record clearly demonstrates numerous attempts to impede voting rights still exist, and it does not matter that those attempts are not as 'pervasive, widespread or rampant' as they were in 1965. One instance of discrimination is too much in a democracy."*

Many Democrats in the Senate condemned the decision as well, and vowed to introduce legislation to strengthen the Voting Rights Act. One year after the Shelby County v. Holder *decision came down, for example, Senator Patrick Leahy (D-Vermont) introduced a Voting Rights Amendment Act of 2014 designed to provide greater protection of voting rights, especially in regions of the country with a history of race-based voter suppression. Leahy's remarks introducing the legislation reflect many of the concerns expressed by critics of the court's* Shelby v. Holder *decision. However, Leahy and his fellow sponsors were never able to secure enough political support to get the proposed legislation through the Senate.*

One year ago today five justices on the Supreme Court disregarded extensive findings of Congress and gutted the Voting Rights Act. During oral argument, Justice Scalia foreshadowed the majority's view of the law when he asserted that Congress's support of the Voting Rights Act was based on the "perpetuation of racial entitlement." I could not disagree more with Justice Scalia. There is no right more fundamental to our existence as American citizens than the right to vote. Every eligible American is entitled to vote and no voter should have their vote denied, abridged, or infringed.

In the Shelby County decision, the justices made clear that Congress could update the Voting Rights Act based on current conditions. In response, I worked with Congressmen Sensenbrenner, Conyers, and Lewis to forge a bipartisan compromise to update and modernize the law. This bill was introduced six months ago on the eve of the weekend celebrating Dr. Martin Luther King's holiday. At the time, I was hopeful that Senate Republicans would join me in supporting this important bill. Despite repeated efforts, I am troubled to report that as of this hearing, not a single Senate Republican has stepped up to the plate. I thank my fellow Senate Democrats on this Committee, who have all joined as co-sponsors. I hope that my fellow Senate Republicans on Committee will do the same.

The House Republican leadership has shown a similar lack of willingness to act on this critical bill. Not only have House Republicans refused to vote on or markup the bill, but they refuse even to hold a hearing. This is unfortunate because the Voting Rights Act has never been a partisan issue. From its inception and through several reauthorizations, the Voting Rights Act has always been a bipartisan effort. In fact, when President George W. Bush signed the most recent reauthorization in 2006, the vote in the Senate was unanimous and the vote in the House was 390-33. Congress too often is gridlocked, but there is almost unanimous agreement on the principle that no American should be denied his or her right to vote or to participate in our democracy. I can only hope that Republicans will come to the table so we can work together as Americans to update and strengthen the foundation of this important law. It would be a travesty if the Voting Rights Act were to become partisan for the first time in our Nation's history.

The Voting Rights Amendment Act updates and strengthens the foundation of the original law to combat both current and future discrimination. It does so in a way that is based on current conditions and recent history.

Under the Voting Rights Amendment Act, all states and jurisdictions are eligible for Section 5 protections under a new coverage formula, which is based on repeated voting rights violations in the last 15 years. This coverage provision is based solely on a state's or local jurisdiction's recent voting rights record. Significantly, the 15-year period "rolls" or continuously moves to keep up with "current conditions," as the Supreme Court stated should be a basis for any coverage provision. If a state that is covered establishes a clean record moving forward, it will fall out of coverage. In addition, the existing bailout provision would still be available for states or jurisdictions that can establish that they had a clean record in a 10-year span. These provisions ensure that the coverage provision is not overinclusive because jurisdictions that have not repeatedly violated the voting rights of its constituents can come out from under preclearance requirements.

The bill would also improve the Voting Rights Act to allow our Federal courts to bail-in the worst actors for preclearance. Current law permits states or jurisdictions to be bailed in only for intentional voting rights violations, but to ensure that the worst discrimination in voting is captured, the bill would amend the Act to allow states or jurisdictions to be bailed in for discriminatory results-based violations, where the effect of a particular voting measure is to deny an individual his or her right to vote.

In recognition that voters need to be aware of changes in laws affecting their right to vote, the bill provides for greater transparency in elections. Sunlight is a great disinfectant, as Justice Brandeis once observed. And in this instance, the additional sunlight will protect voters from discrimination. The transparency provisions provide for public notice and information in three areas. The first part requires public notice of late breaking changes in Federal elections. The second part requires information on polling place resource allocation for Federal elections. And the third part requires information on changes to electoral districts, including demographic information, to deter racial gerrymandering, impermissible redistricting, and infringement on minority voters. The last part requires this information for Federal, state and local elections because impermissible conduct oftentimes occurs in state and local elections.

And finally, the bill revises the preliminary injunction standard for voting rights actions. The principle behind this part of the proposal is the recognition that when voting rights are at stake, obtaining relief after the election has already concluded is too late to vindicate the individuals' voting rights. We recognize that there will be cases where there is a special need for immediate, preliminary relief where the plaintiff can establish that the voting measure is likely to be discriminatory.

This proposal responds to the Supreme Court's Shelby County decision in order to ensure that all Americans are protected against racial discrimination in voting. And a year after the Shelby County decision, it is clear that voters need more protection from racial discrimination in voting. As we approach a national election, it is not hard to see that attempts to deny and infringe upon the right to vote are only increasing. Just last week, the Brennan Center for Justice released a report called "The State of Voting in 2014." According to this report, since 2010, 22 states have passed new voting restrictions that make it more difficult to vote. Of the 11 states with the highest African-American turnout in 2008, 7 of those states have new restrictions in place. Of the 12 states with the largest Hispanic growth from 2000 to 2010, 9 have passed laws making it harder to vote.

A separate report issued yesterday entitled "Shelby County: One Year Later," demonstrates how harmful election law changes have occurred because of the Court's decision.

In addition, the Leadership Conference on Civil and Human Rights released a report last week entitled "The Persistent Challenge of Voting Discrimination," which details nearly 150 voting rights violations since 2000. And each of these cases impact thousands and sometimes tens of thousands of voters. Racial discrimination in voting clearly remains a significant problem in our democracy. And the persistent refrain that the Federal government should not involve itself in local elections is clearly wrong, as the report demonstrates that the vast majority of voting violations takes place in local elections. I ask unanimous consent that these reports be included in the Record.

The statistics and evidence in these reports reaffirm Chief Justice Roberts's acknowledgment that "voting discrimination still exists; no one doubts that." Recognizing this, it is time for Congress to act.

There are some who argue that nothing more needs to be done because other provisions of the Voting Rights Act are still in effect. But these same individuals who praise the existence of the other sections of the Voting Rights Act are often the very same ones who are working to undermine and strike down this landmark law. The hypocrisy of some of these individuals gives me pause as to whether they are truly concerned with discrimination in voting, or whether their true goal is to see the Voting Rights Act removed from the books altogether.

Section 2 of the Voting Rights Act continues to be a critical component of the Act. It is a general anti-discrimination provision that prohibits voting practices that have the purpose or result of discriminating on the basis of race, color, or membership in a minority language group. Plaintiffs may bring a lawsuit in Federal court challenging the voting practice, but the burden is on the plaintiffs to establish that there is a purpose or effect of discrimination. While Section 2 provides one avenue for plaintiffs to pursue an attempt to stop voter discrimination, history shows us that Section 2, on its own, is insufficient to resolve all our voter discrimination problems. This was confirmed by the 2006 Report from the House Judiciary Committee, which stated that "failure to reauthorize the temporary provisions [Section 5 and its coverage formula], given the record established, would leave minority citizens with the inadequate remedy of a Section 2 action."

Not only is Section 2 on its face an insufficient protection, but there simply are not enough resources to prosecute all the instances of discrimination through litigation. Section 5 provides for an alternative administrative mechanism that helps resolve certain voting issues without having to go through long, protracted litigation. Litigation and the courts are not the only answer when trying to root out discrimination in voting. This is a principle that both Democrats and Republicans should be able to support.

Next week marks the 50th anniversary of the signing of the Civil Rights Act. Just as Congress came together five decades ago to enact the Civil Rights Act, Democrats and Republicans must work together now to renew and to strengthen the Voting Rights Act. I hope all Republicans will work with us to enact the meaningful protections in the Voting Rights Amendment Act.

Source: Leahy, Patrick. Statement of Senator Patrick Leahy, Chairman, Senate Judiciary Committee Hearing on the Voting Rights Amendment Act, S. 1945: Updating the Voting Rights Act in Response to *Shelby County v. Holder*, June 25, 2014. Accessed June 25, 2019. http://www.leahy.senate.gov/press/senate-judiciary-committee-holds-hearing-on-the-voting-rights-amendment-act-.

President Obama Accuses GOP of Restricting Ballot Access for Partisan Gain, 2014

In an April 11, 2014, appearance at the annual conference of the National Action Network (NAN) civil rights organization, Democratic President Barack Obama offered some of the most extensive and pointed criticisms of the modern Republican Party's record on voting rights of his entire presidency. In his remarks, Obama flatly accused GOP lawmakers and officials of violating the constitutional rights of voters of color for the sole purpose of making political gains. Following are pertinent excerpts from his NAN address:

Just as inequality feeds on injustice, opportunity requires justice. And justice requires the right to vote. Johnson—President Johnson, right after he signed the Civil Rights Act into law, told his advisers—some of whom were telling him, well, all right, just wait; you've done a big thing now; let's let the dust settle, don't stir folks up. He said, no, no, I can't wait. We've got to press forward and pass the Voting Rights Act. Johnson said: "About this there can and should be no argument. Every American citizen must have an equal right to vote."

Voting is a time when we all have an equal say: Black or White, rich or poor, man or woman. Doesn't matter. In the eyes of the law and in the eyes of our democracy, we're all supposed to have that equal right to cast our ballot to help determine the direction of our society.

The principle of one person, one vote is the single greatest tool we have to redress an unjust status quo. You would think there would not be an argument about this anymore. But the stark, simple truth is this: The right to vote is threatened today in a way that it has not been since the Voting Rights Act became law nearly five decades ago.

Across the country, Republicans have led efforts to pass laws making it harder, not easier, for people to vote. In some places, women could be turned away from polls just because they're registered under their maiden name, but their driver's license has their married name. Senior citizens who have been voting for decades may suddenly be told they can no longer vote until they can come up with the right ID.

In other places, folks may learn that without a document like a passport or a birth certificate, they can't register. About 60 percent of Americans don't have a passport. Just because you don't have the money to travel abroad doesn't mean you shouldn't be able to vote here at home. And just to be clear, I know where my birth certificate is, but a lot of people don't. [*Laughter*] A lot of people don't. I think it's still up on a website somewhere. [*Laughter*] You remember that? That was crazy. That was some crazy stuff. [*Laughter*] I hadn't thought about that in a while. [*Laughter*]

Now, I want to be clear: I am not against reasonable attempts to secure the ballot. We understand that there has to be rules in place. But I am against requiring an ID that millions of Americans don't have. That shouldn't suddenly prevent you from exercising your right to vote.

The first words put to paper in our American story tell us that all of us are created equal. And we understand that it took a long time to make sure that those words meant something. But 50 years ago, we put laws in place, because of enormous struggles, to vindicate that idea, to make our democracy truly mean something. And that makes it wrong to pass laws that make it harder for any eligible citizen to vote, especially because every citizen doesn't just have the right to vote, they have a responsibility to vote.

So yes, we're right to be on guard against voter fraud. Voter fraud would impinge on our democracy as well. We don't want folks voting that shouldn't be voting. We all agree on that. Let's stipulate to that, as the lawyers say.

But there's a reason why those who argue that harsh restrictions on voting are somehow necessary to fight voter fraud are having such a hard time proving any real, widespread voter fraud. So I just want to give you some statistics. One recent study found only 10 cases of alleged in-person voter impersonation in 12 years—10 cases. Another analysis found that out of 197 million votes cast for Federal elections between 2002 and 2005, only 40 voters—out of 197 million—were indicted for fraud. Now, for those of you who are math majors, as a percentage, that is 0.00002 percent. [*Laughter*] That's not a lot. So let's be clear: The real voter fraud is people who try to deny our rights by making bogus arguments about voter fraud.

And I have to say, there have been some—some of these officials who have been passing these laws have been more blunt. They said, this is going to be good for the Republican Party. Some of them have not been shy about saying that they're doing this for partisan reasons.

"It is wrong," President Johnson said, "deadly wrong, to deny any of your fellow Americans the right to vote in this country." It is wrong to change our election rules just because of politics. It is wrong to make citizens wait for 5, 6, 7 hours just to vote. It is wrong to make a senior citizen who no longer has a driver's license jump through hoops and have to pay money just to exercise the rights she has cherished for a lifetime. America did not stand up and did not march and did not sacrifice to gain the right to vote for themselves and for others only to see it denied to their kids and their grandchildren. We've got to pay attention to this.

Some of the folks from Chicago know—Crider knows—one of the first jobs I had out of law school was to lead a voter registration drive in my home State of

Illinois. We registered more than 150,000 new voters. And as an organizer, I got to help other citizens exercise their most cherished and fundamental rights. That mattered to me.

And as President, I'm not going to let attacks on these rights go unchallenged. We're not going to let voter suppression go unchallenged. So earlier this week, you heard from the Attorney General, and there's a reason the agency he runs is called the Department of Justice. They've taken on more than a hundred voting rights cases since 2009. They've defended the rights of everybody from African Americans to Spanish speakers, to soldiers serving overseas.

Earlier this year, a bipartisan commission I appointed chaired by my election lawyer and Mitt Romney's election lawyer came up with a series of modern—or commonsense reforms to modernize voter registration and to curb the potential for fraud in smart way and ensure that no one has to wait for more than half an hour to cast a ballot. States and local election boards should take up those recommendations. And with the 50th anniversary of Freedom Summer almost upon us, I urge Members of Congress to honor those who gave their lives so that others could exercise their rights and update the Voting Rights Act. Go ahead and get that done.

Do it because the right to vote is something cherished by every American. We should not be having an argument about this. There are a lot of things we can argue about, but the right to vote? I mean, what kind of political platform is that? [*Laughter*] Why would you make that a part of your agenda, preventing people from voting? How can you defend that? There are a whole bunch of folks out there who don't vote for me, didn't vote for me, don't like what I do. The idea that I would prevent them from voting and exercising their franchise makes no sense.

Black or White, man or woman, urban, rural, rich, poor, Native American, disabled, gay, straight, Republican or Democrat—voters who want to vote should be able to vote. Period. Full stop. Voting is not a Democratic issue, it's not a Republican issue. It's an issue of citizenship. It's what makes our democracy strong.

But it's a fact: This recent effort to restrict the vote has not been led by both parties, it's been led by the Republican Party. And in fairness, it's not just Democrats who are concerned. You had one Republican State legislator point out—and I'm quoting here—"Making it more difficult for people to vote is not a good sign for a party that wants to attract more people." [*Laughter*] That was a pretty—that's a good insight. [*Laughter*] Right? I want a competitive Republican Party, just like a competitive Democratic Party. That's how our democracy is supposed to work: the competition of ideas. But I don't want folks changing the rules to try to restrict people's access to the ballot.

And I think responsible people, regardless of your party affiliation, should agree with that. If your strategy depends on having fewer people show up to vote, that's not a sign of strength, that's a sign of weakness.

And not only is it ultimately bad politics. I believe ultimately it harms the entire country. If voting is denied to the many, we risk ending up stuck year after year with special interest policies that benefit a fortunate few. And injustice perpetuates inequality. But remember, just as injustice perpetuates inequality, justice opens up opportunity. And as infuriating as efforts to roll back hard-earned rights can be, the trajectory of our history has to give us hope. The story of America is a story of progress. No matter how often or how intensely that progress has been challenged, ultimately, this Nation has moved forward. As Dr. King said, "The arc of the moral universe is long, [but; White House correction.] it bends towards justice." We move forward on civil rights and we move forward on workers' rights, and we move forward on women's rights and disability rights and gay rights. We show that when ordinary citizens come together to participate in this democracy we love, justice will not be denied. So the single most important thing we can do to protect our right to vote is to vote.

So I'm going to make one last point here. We're going to have an Attorney General that looks at all the laws that are being passed. We're going to have civic organizations that are making sure that State laws and local laws are doing what they're supposed to do. We will fight back whenever we see unfairly the franchise being challenged. But the truth is that, for all these laws that are being put in place, the biggest problem we have is people giving up their own power, voluntarily not participating.

The number of people who voluntarily don't vote, who are eligible to vote, dwarfs whatever these laws are put in place might do in terms of diminishing the voting rolls.

So we can't treat these new barriers as an excuse not to participate. We can't use cynicism as an excuse not to participate. Sometimes, I hear people saying, well, we haven't gotten everything we needed. You know? We still have poverty. We still have problems. Of course. These things didn't happen overnight.

When I was down in Texas, everybody was celebrating the day that the civil rights law was finally passed. Remember, there were decades in which people sacrificed and worked hard. Change doesn't happen overnight, but it happens as long as we don't purposely give our power away. Every obstacle put in our path should remind us of the power we hold in our hands each time we pull that lever or fill in that oval or touch that screen. We just have to harness that power. We've got to create a national network committed to taking action. We can call it the National Action Network.

So I want you to go out there and redouble your efforts. Register more voters. Help more folks to get their rights. Get those souls to the polls. If they don't let you do it on Sunday, then do it on Tuesday instead. I know it's better going to the polls on Sunday because you go to church, you're getting a little meal. [*Laughter*] You got the bus waiting for you. I understand. But you can do it without that if you—if we have to.

We're at a time when we're marking many anniversaries. And it's interesting for me—I've been on this Earth 52 years, and so to see the progress we've made is to see my own life and the progression that's happened. You think about Brown v. Board of Education, and the Civil Rights Act, and the Voting Rights Act, and Freedom Summer. And with those anniversaries, we have new reason to remember those who made it possible for us to be here. Like the three civil rights workers in Mississippi—two White, one Black—who were murdered 50 years ago as they tried to help their fellow citizens register to vote. James Chaney and Andrew Goodman and Michael Schwerner believed so strongly that change was possible, they were willing to lay down their lives for it. The least you can do is take them up on the gift that they have given you. Go out there and vote. You can make a change. You do have the power. I've run my last election, but I need you to make sure that the changes that we started continue for decades to come.

Thank you, God bless you, and God bless America.

Source: Obama, Barack. Remarks at the National Action Network's 16th Annual Convention in New York City. April 11, 2014. Accessed April 3, 2019. https://obamawhitehouse.archives.gov/the-press-office/2014/04/11/remarks-president-national-action-networks-16th-annual-convention.

President Obama Urges Americans to Defend Voting Rights for All, 2015

In the wake of the U.S. Supreme Court's controversial decision in Shelby County v. Holder (2013) *to strike down foundational pillars of the landmark Voting Rights Act (VRA), Republican-controlled state governments in many parts of the country passed legislation placing new restrictions or requirements on voters, including curtailment of early voting options, new voter ID laws, more stringent voter registration requirements, and closures of polling places in ways that dramatically increase lines at other voting sites. Between the time of the Shelby County decision and the 2016 presidential election, in fact, fourteen states implemented new restrictions on voting. This development elicited expressions ranging from concern to outrage from Democrats, voting rights advocates, and even President Barack Obama. In the following weekly address Obama delivered on August 8, 2015, he used the fiftieth anniversary of the signing of the VRA to urge Americans to exercise their right to vote and combat efforts to roll back voting rights.*

Hi, everybody. The right to vote is one of the most fundamental rights of any democracy. Yet for too long, too many of our fellow citizens were denied that right, simply because of the color of their skin.

Fifty years ago this week, President Lyndon Johnson signed a law to change that. The Voting Rights Act broke down legal barriers that stood between millions of African Americans and their constitutional right to cast a ballot. It was and still is one of the greatest victories in our country's struggle for civil rights.

But it didn't happen overnight. Countless men and women marched and organized, sat in and stood up, for our most basic rights. For this they were called agitators and un-American; they were jailed, and they were beaten. Some were even killed. But in the end, they reaffirmed the idea at the very heart of America: that people who love this country can change it.

Our country is a better place because of all those heroes did for us. But as one of those heroes, Congressman John Lewis, reminded us in Selma this past March, "There is still work to be done." Fifty years after the Voting Rights Act, there are still too many barriers to vote and too many people trying to erect new ones. We've seen laws that roll back early voting, force people to jump through hoops to cast a ballot, or lead to legitimate voters being improperly purged from the rolls. Over the years, we've seen provisions specifically designed to make it harder for some of our fellow citizens to vote. In a democracy like ours, with a history like ours, that's a disgrace.

That's why, as we celebrate the 50th anniversary of the Voting Rights Act, I'm calling on Congress to pass new legislation to make sure every American has equal access to the polls. It's why I support the organizers getting folks registered in their communities. And it's why, no matter what party you support, my message to every American is simple: Get out there and vote, not just every 4 years, but every chance you get. Because your elected officials will only heed your voice if you make your voice heard.

The promise that all of us are created equal is written into our founding documents, but it's up to us to make that promise real. Together, let's do what Americans have always done: Let's keep marching forward, keep perfecting our Union, and keep building a better country for our kids.

Thanks, everybody. Have a great weekend.

Source: Obama, Barack. The President's Weekly Address, August 8, 2015. Accessed April 3, 2019. https://obamawhitehouse.archives.gov/the-press-office/2015/08/08/weekly-address-reaffirming-our-commitment-protecting-right-vote.

Oregon Burnishes Reputation as Electoral System Innovator with Motor Voter Law, 2015

In 1998 Oregon voters approved a ballot measure making the state the first one in the nation to fully embrace a vote-by-mail election system. The success of this innovation led a number of other states to expand their own vote-by-mail offerings. Less than twenty years after that historic first, Oregon became a voting trailblazer in another regard, establishing a system whereby Oregonians would be automatically registered to vote through the state's Department of Motor Vehicles (DMV). The new law automatically registered citizens to vote when they registered a car or secured a driver's license.

The new system, which was championed and signed into law by Democratic Governor Kate Brown, had an immediate impact. An estimated 390,000 Oregonians registered to vote through the DMV in the first two years after the law went into effect. Studies have found that it was particularly helpful to rural citizens, young voters, senior citizens, and people of color across the state, and that it has contributed to Oregon's reputation as the most voter-friendly state in the nation. "In Oregon," Brown pointedly told Politico *in 2019, "we actually want people to vote in our state."*

Following are Brown's remarks upon signing the Motor Voter law on March 16, 2015.

This is an extraordinarily unique and humbling opportunity. In my role as Secretary of State, I proposed a new way of registering to vote: New Motor Voter. It was my top priority, and I am thrilled that I am about to sign this into law as Governor.

Over thirty years ago, Del Reilly, the clerk of Linn County had a vision to make voting as convenient and accessible as possible by putting a ballot in the hands of every eligible Oregonian through vote by mail.

This bill will fully implement that goal by ensuring that virtually every eligible Oregonian will be able to have their voice be heard. Building on the federal Motor Voter Bill, this bill will modernize how the DMV and the SOS work to register citizens to vote. During the testimony on the bill, a legislator said to me, “It’s already so easy to register, why would we make it easier?”

My answer is that we have the tools to make voter registration more cost effective, more secure and more convenient for Oregonians, why wouldn’t we??

This New Motor Voter law will allow organizations to spend their resources educating and engaging voters rather spending enormous amounts of time and energy to do voter registration ensuring that our government is one that works for all of us.

Oregon is a true leader in accessibility to voting, I encourage every eligible Oregonian to participate in the process, and I challenge other states to examine their policies and find ways to ensure there are as few barriers as possible in the way of a citizen’s right to vote.

Your vote is your voice and every voice matters.

Under this proposal, more voices will be heard!

I want to thank the many individuals and groups who have worked so hard to not only pass this legislation but whose mission statement is to protect the right to vote, to educate voters and to engage voters.

Source: Brown, Kate. Remarks on Signing State Motor Voter Bill, March 16, 2015. State of Oregon: Office of Governor Kate Brown. Accessed April 22, 2019. https://www.oregon.gov/gov/media/Pages/speeches/NMV-031615.aspx.

Study Reveals Closures of Polling Places on “Massive Scale” in the Wake of *Shelby* Decision, 2016

The Leadership Conference Education Fund is a civil rights education and research program of the Leadership Conference on Civil and Human Rights, a coalition of more than two hundred national civil and human rights organizations across the United States. In 2016, the Leadership Conference Education Fund published a report documenting widespread polling-place closures in states with a history of disenfranchising voters of color after the Supreme Court struck down key elements of the 1965 Voting Rights Act. Following are excerpts from that report.

Introduction

In advance of the first presidential election in 50 years without the full protections of the Voting Rights Act (VRA), the nation has been subject to a resurgence of state and local measures to disenfranchise voters of color. It has been three years since the U.S. Supreme court handed down its shameful ruling in *Shelby County v. Holder,* which made Section 5 of the VRA inoperable and opened the door to racial discrimination at every juncture of the electoral process.

Voters and advocates have fought many of these proposals tooth and nail in courthouses, statehouses, and council chambers nationwide. At the same time, countless voting laws have changed without public notice or scrutiny because *Shelby* removed federal oversight and transparency requirements from states and jurisdictions previously covered by Section 5—areas of the country with the most pernicious and adaptive records of implementing scheme after scheme to deny or abridge access to the ballot. . . .

This report describes how some of these same jurisdictions are making voting more confusing and less accessible by engaging in massive reductions in the number of polling places.

Polling place closures are a particularly common and pernicious tactic for disenfranchising voters of color. Decisions to shutter or reduce voting locations are often made quietly and at the last minute, making pre-election intervention or litigation virtually impossible. These changes can place an undue burden on minority voters, who may be less likely to have access to public transportation or vehicles, given continuing disparities in socioeconomic resources. Once an election is conducted, there is no judicial remedy for the loss of votes that were never cast because a voter's usual polling place has disappeared.

There are many reasons to close polling places that have nothing to do with discrimination and this report is not an indictment against all polling place reductions. The enactment of early voting and voting by mail both make consolidating polling places an attractive option for election officials who must contend with tightening budgets and there are ways to ensure that reductions are done in concert with public participation and without disadvantaging communities. But prior to the *Shelby* decision there was a process to ensure that jurisdictions known to engage in voting discrimination weren't using budget cuts or voter modernization as cover to disenfranchise people of color . With Section 5 in place, jurisdictions would have to demonstrate that saving money by making changes to polling places did not disenfranchise voters of color. In a world without Section 5, that process—that protection for minority voters—has ceased.

Pre-*Shelby,* jurisdictions were required to give substantial notice to voters about any planned polling place closures. And they were required to consult with the minority community to ensure that any proposed voting change was not discriminatory.

Post-*Shelby,* voters have to rely on news reports and anecdotes from local advocates who attend city and county commission meetings or legislative sessions where these changes are contemplated to identify potentially discriminatory polling place location and precinct changes. In the vast majority of instances, closures have gone unnoticed, unreported, and unchallenged.

National Findings

In some states, there has been a widespread effort to close polling places since **Shelby.**

Our analysis finds that, since *Shelby,* hundreds of polling places have been closed in counties once covered by Section 5. Voters in these counties will have at least 868 fewer places to cast ballots in the 2016 presidential election than they did in past elections, a 16 percent reduction.

Out of the 381 counties in our study, 165 of them—43 percent—have reduced voting locations.

Some states have closed polling places on a massive scale. In Arizona, almost every county reduced polling places. In Louisiana, 61 percent of parishes reduced polling places. In our limited sample of Alabama counties, 67 percent closed polling places. In Texas, 53 percent of counties in our limited sample reduced voting locations. . . .

Our analysis does not take into account the myriad of other polling places changes that could impact voters, such as relocations within counties or to places that are less accessible or familiar to minority voters, or changes to hours of operation.

Without a concerted effort to document how these reductions are being conducted in each county—something that was unnecessary before *Shelby*—we do not have documented justification or outcomes in the vast majority of them.

Counties and states with known records of voting discrimination are closing polling places on a massive scale.

Without protections for voters, states and counties that are placing new restrictions on voting are also dramatically reducing the number of polling places.

- **Alabama**—Even with a limited sample of 18 Alabama counties, the trend of 12 counties reducing 66 polling places is cause for concern in the state.
- **Arizona**—By sheer numbers and scale, Arizona is the leading closer of polling places in the aftermath of *Shelby. Almost every county in the state reduced polling places in advance of the 2016 election* and almost every county closed polling places on a massive scale, resulting in 212 fewer polling places. Pima County has closed more voting locations than any county in our study and counties with a demonstrated record of discrimination, like Cochise County, have reduced polling places without any oversight.
- **Louisiana**—Since *Shelby,* 61 percent of Louisiana parishes have closed a total of 103 polling places since 2012. This includes parishes like Terrebonne, which is subject to pending litigation for discrimination against Black voters.
- **Mississippi**—About 34 percent of the 59 Mississippi counties surveyed have closed polling places since *Shelby,* resulting in at least 44 fewer

polling places for the 2016 election. Closures have happened in places like Lauderdale County where Meridian is the largest city. After Meridian voters elected their first Black mayor, the majority-White county election commission moved polling places out of Meridian's Black churches even though both the mayor and the pastor of one of the churches objected.

- **North Carolina**—Since *Shelby,* formerly covered counties in North Carolina have closed polling places even after significant opposition from minority communities and advocates. Pasquotank and Cleveland counties are the leaders for polling place reductions in the state even though both have established records of voting discrimination.
- **Texas**—Almost half of all counties in our sample closed polling places since *Shelby,* resulting in 403 fewer voting locations for the 2016 election than in past years. These closures come as the state's voter ID law has become a leading example of voting discrimination since *Shelby* and include reductions in counties like Medina, Caldwell, Nueces, and Galveston—each with established records of discrimination and recent violations of the Voting Rights Act.

When justification is given, counties cite a broad set of reasons to reduce polling places.

There are justifiable reasons to reduce polling places and consolidations can be executed equitably. But the loss of Section 5 means that there is no process to ensure that reductions are disclosed to the public, are conducted with the input of impacted communities, and do not discriminate against voters of color.

In many counties, there was no public notice or justification of closures. In counties where there was news coverage or public justification for consolidations, the vast majority cite the ability to save money.

Some counties, particularly in Arizona and Texas, have consolidated polling places as part of a move to a "supre-precinct" or "vote center" system for Election Day. Under this system, there are dramatically fewer polling places but voters from anywhere in a county can cast ballots at any of the remaining voting sites.

Some counties that have expanded voting options for residents cite the growth of voting by mail and early voting as reasons that fewer Election Day polling places are needed. In some instances, reducing polling places and converting to vote centers is justified as a possible means to increase voter turnout. Without Section 5, there are no protections for voters of color to ensure that when reductions are made for seemingly reasonable purposes, they do not disadvantage voters of color.

Some counties with unusually high polling place closures—like Jefferson parish, Louisiana, and Nueces, McLennan, and Galveston counties in Texas—purported to do so to comply with the Americans with Disabilities Act (ADA), which sets rules regarding the accessibility of polling places for voters with disabilities. Each of the above counties was either under investigation or in the middle of litigation regarding whether their polling sites complied with the ADA. These jurisdictions appear to have opted to close or consolidate inaccessible polling places rather than take steps to either move them or make the existing locations accessible. In interviews, disability rights organizations have roundly condemned the use of ADA compliance as an excuse for the unnecessary closure of polling places as a denial of voting access to all, including people with disabilities.

Notice, transparency, and advocacy make a difference.

When communities are notified about proposed reductions or consolidations of polling places, that notice can lead to advocacy that makes an impact on the final outcome. We've seen organized efforts across all states to prevent reductions or to advocate for equity through activism, community engagement with decision makers, and even advocacy for statewide transparency laws.

Advocacy and media attention directed at polling place closures in Maricopa county, Arizona, Daphne, Alabama, and in Georgia's Bibb and Hancock counties have all blunted or reversed the impact of shuttered voting locations in those counties. But these are the exceptions to the rule.

In South Carolina, a combination of a longstanding requirement that polling place changes be approved by multiple governance bodies, required mailing to inform all voters subject to polling place changes, a requirement that precinct level changes be approved by the general assembly, and a state law passed in the wake of *Shelby* that mandates the publication of local precinct changes in a state registry have provided a level of transparency and process on electoral changes unlike any other formerly covered state. . . .

Conclusion

Without oversight, transparency, and accountability, counties formerly covered by Section 5 closed hundreds of polling places in advance of the first presidential election in 50 years without a fully operable Voting Rights Act.

Because of the pervasive voting discrimination that has continued in many of these counties, these consolidations should have been subjected to review to ensure that they did not infringe on the rights of voters.

Texas, Arizona, and Louisiana—each with a nefarious and adaptive history of voting discrimination—have all made alarming reductions in polling places. And voters throughout North Carolina, Mississippi, and Alabama will face polling place reductions in 2016, all put in place without the transparency, notice, and consultation once required by Section 5. . . .

The only way these closures could be prevented or scrutinized to ensure fairness at the national level is to pass at least one of the two bipartisan Voting Rights Act restoration bills currently pending in Congress. Both bills require nationwide transparency for changes in precincts and polling places, which could give voters and advocates the tools they need to be informed about these changes and to engage in a responsible process to ensure that polling place closures, moves, and consolidations are considered with all voters in mind.

Source: Leadership Conference Education Fund. *The Great Poll Closure.* November 2016, pp. 1, 4–6, 14. Accessed April 3, 2019. http://civilrightsdocs.info/pdf/reports/2016/poll-closure-report-web.pdf. Used with permission of the Leadership Conference on Civil and Human Rights.

6

Open Partisan Warfare over Voting Rights: 2016 to Present

Although the environment surrounding elections, voting, and democracy in the United States has always featured political undercurrents, recent elections and the political environment in which they have occurred have dramatically increased the scrutiny under which elections are being conducted across America. As political parties and candidates strive to win elections, the rules that govern voting, registration, and representation continue to be tools utilized by political elites to determine who is eligible to participate and the rules that will facilitate or constrain that participation. While this approach may result in temporary wins and losses for political parties, for the public the manipulation of the election system from internal and external actors has profoundly negative consequences. Many observers fear that voting rules and regulations that are clearly being advanced for partisan advantage are eroding public faith in the integrity of American elections.

GROWING CONCERNS ABOUT AMERICAN ELECTIONS

After the 2000 presidential election, the environment in which elections occur changed dramatically. During the 2004 election, voters continued to experience challenges related to the administration of elections. Voters reported experiencing long lines, Direct Recording Electronic (DRE) voting machines not accurately recording voter preference, and poorly trained poll workers (Powell and Slevin, 2004). The challenges persisted into the 2008 and 2012 elections, as voters (especially in poor and communities with high percentages of minorities) continued to experience long lines on Election Day and last-minute changes and challenges to voter identification requirements. There were reports of voters waiting seven hours to vote, and research found that the wait times for African American voters were double those of white voters. In the wake of persistent reports of administrative irregularities on Election Day in 2012, President Obama through Executive Order established the President's Commission on Election Administration (PECA), also known as the Bauer-Ginsberg Commission. The goal of the commission was to generate recommendations to improve the voting system and experience for voters.

In addition to administrative challenges, there were also challenges to the legitimacy of elections and their outcomes. In both 2008 and 2012, the legitimacy of Obama's candidacy and presidency was challenged by political opponents who questioned his American citizenship (despite clear and abundant evidence that he had been born in the United States) and falsely asserted that his victory was the result of illegal voting by non-citizens who were not eligible to vote. Claims of voter fraud continued to be raised by Republican presidential nominee Donald Trump and other members of the party during the months leading up to the 2016 presidential election. In the months following the election, in which Trump defeated Democratic nominee Hillary Clinton in the electoral college despite losing the popular vote by more than 2.8 million votes, some questioned the legitimacy of Trump's win, raising concerns about reports that Russia and other international actors had interfered with the election in a variety of ways, including spreading falsehoods and propaganda in the form of "fake news" across American social media.

These concerns led to action on the part of the federal government to enhance the resources available to states and local jurisdictions for protecting their voting systems. In January 2017, the United States Department of Homeland Security identified the American electoral system as critical infrastructure. At the time of designation, then-DHS Secretary Jeh Johnson observed, "Given the vital role elections play in this country, it is clear that certain systems and assets of election infrastructure meet the definition of critical infrastructure, in fact and in law" (Election Assistance Commission). The sectors included in the critical infrastructure designation are considered "so vital to the United States that their incapacitation or destruction would have a debilitating effect on security, national economic security, national public health or safety, or any combination thereof" (United States Department of Homeland Security). The designation of the electoral system as critical infrastructure puts elections in the same category of importance for governance in the United States as the power grid, transportation, and water systems.

CLAIMS OF VOTER SUPPRESSION AND VOTER FRAUD

On May 11, 2017, Trump signed Executive Order 13799, which created the Presidential Advisory Commission on Election Integrity. The commission was tasked with reviewing claims of fraud, improper voter registration, and voter suppression. Shortly after the commission was created, Vice President Mike Pence was named chairman and former Kansas Secretary of State Kris Kobach was named vice chairman.

The commission and its mandate immediately encountered fierce resistance, however, from Democrats and some election experts who claimed that the commission had actually been formed to place a veneer of respectability over GOP efforts to suppress the vote of people who were more likely to vote the Democratic ticket. Critics claimed, for example, that the commission was not evenly bipartisan in its membership, unlike previous election and voting commissions such as the Commission on Federal Election Reform (Carter-Baker), the National Commission on Federal Election Reform (Carter-Ford), and the Presidential Commission on Election Administration (Bauer-Ginsberg). Critics also charged that Kobach's presence on the commission made its work automatically suspect. "This commission will have no integrity if its vice-chair is Kris Kobach," declared the American Civil Liberties Union (ACLU). "The ACLU has sued Kobach four times on voter suppression—and won every case. The problem we have in this country isn't voter fraud—it's voter suppression. And on that front, Kobach is Public Enemy #1" (ACLU, 2017).

One of the first acts of the commission was to request voter data and information from all fifty states. The information requested included registrants' full names, addresses, dates of birth, political parties, the last four digits of their social security numbers, a list of the elections they voted in since 2006, information on any felony convictions, information on whether they were registered to vote in other states, their military status, and whether they lived overseas.

After the request was issued, a majority of states and the District of Columbia refused to provide certain types of voter information due to concerns about voter privacy and the risk that confidential voter information might be made public (Stark and Hauck, 2017). By July 2017, seven lawsuits had been filed in relation to the commission. Plaintiffs in the lawsuits included the American Civil Liberties Union, the Lawyers' Committee for Civil Rights Under Law, the National Association for the Advancement of Colored People, and the Election Privacy Information Center. In addition to the lawsuits, there were also calls to defund the commission (Carney, 2017). In December 2018, the commission was ordered by Judge Colleen Kollar-Kotelly of the U.S. District Court for the District of Columbia to share information with Maine Secretary of State Matthew Dunpap (D), who claimed that Kobach had not been sharing documents or information with him or other members of the commission (Watkins, 2017). Two weeks after the order, on January 3, 2018, the Trump Administration disbanded the commission.

CONFLICTS OF INTEREST, FAULTY MACHINES, AND CALLS FOR VOTING REFORM

In the states, many chief election officials found themselves in the position of being responsible for the administration of the election that would decide if they would win the election in which they were running. In Georgia, accusations of voter suppression and disenfranchisement were at the center of race the between Brian Kemp (Republican) and Stacey Abrams (Democrat). Using his authority as the sitting Secretary of State, Kemp was accused of trying to disenfranchise voters by enforcing Georgia's exact-match voter-verification process. The process requires that a voter's name on their government-issued identification be an exact match to their name as listed on the voter-registration roll. As an example, a missing middle initial, accent mark, or hyphen could result in a voter's ability to vote being put on hold. During the 2018 early voting period, more than 53,000 voters were put on hold due to mismatched names; the majority of these were black voters. Civil rights groups filed suit, arguing that the law's requirements were tantamount to voter suppression efforts to disenfranchise minority voters. On Friday, November 2, just three days before the election, U.S. District Judge Eleanor Ross ruled in a separate matter that Georgia had to relax the restrictions that could prevent more than three thousand people who were flagged as noncitizens from voting.

Questions were also raised about the process used to remove voters from the voter-registration rolls. In Georgia and other states, the process for voter removal is triggered when a voter does not participate in an election. In Ohio, for example, the complete process for removal takes six years. When a voter misses an election, communication is sent from the elections office to the voter. If the voter does not participate or reply to any of the communication attempts over the six years, the voter is removed. The Supreme Court has ruled that this process, at least in Ohio, is in compliance with the 1993 National Voter Registration Act. Although the process for the removal of voters in Georgia is similar to other states, an American Public Media analysis found that under Kemp's administration, Georgia cancelled over 1.4 million voter registrations, including nearly 670,000 in 2017 alone. This rate surpasses that of most states (Caputo, Hing, and Kauffman, 2018).

Challenges and criticisms of the voting equipment used in some states also persisted. Straight party ticket voters in Texas who were using Direct Record Entry (DRE) machines to record their preferences claimed that the voting machines were changing their selections. After hearing the news, many wondered if the changing of votes on the machines was the result of maleficence and an intentional effort to change the outcome of the election. Others blamed the voting machine technology. Both parties, Republican and Democrat, warned their voters about the potential problem. Although perceived as malfeasance or a problem with the technology, according to Sam Taylor, spokesperson for the Secretary of State, "the changing of votes was the result of voters using the selection wheel before the ballot is finished rendering on the screen." Although reported as a widespread problem, the Secretary of State's Office reported that they had received fewer than twenty complaints about the issue. Hart InterCivic, the company that manufactures the machine, also responded to allegations that the machines were malfunctioning. In a statement released by Hart, "eSlate simply records the voter's inputs. It does not, and cannot, 'flip' or 'switch' votes." A spokesman also said that the company's voting devices comply with the state's election code and have been used "reliably across Texas" since 2002. "Most importantly, the eSlate displays all voter choices on a ballot summary page, once the voter has made all selections," the statement said. "This gives the voter the opportunity to verify that they have marked the intended choices before casting the ballot. If the voter has mismarked a choice or has changed their mind, they have the option of returning to any contest that needs to be changed." Although the state and Hart InterCivic released statements to counteract the narrative surrounding the perceived malfunctioning and provided guidance to ensure voters could effectively mark their preferences, the incident contributed to the narrative of growing doubt about the integrity of American elections (Samuels, 2018).

State election officials have also had to defend their state's practices from criticisms from members of Congress. Following the 2018 midterm election, Paul Ryan, former Speaker of the United States House of Representatives, characterized the rules that govern the counting of provisional and absentee ballots in California as "bizarre" after several competitive House races weren't called until weeks after the election. The election resulted in several seats flipping from the Republican Party to the Democratic Party. Compared to policies in other states, California allows absentee ballots to be counted if they are mailed by Election Day and arrive at the registrar by the Friday after the election. As was the case in 2018, this process can result in close races being called days or weeks after Election Day. California Secretary of State Alex Padilla defended the policies used in California to ensure that every ballot is counted properly.

> It is bizarre that Paul Ryan cannot grasp basic voting rights protections . . . It shouldn't defy logic that election officials are meticulous in counting every eligible ballot. California works to ensure every ballot is counted properly and every ballot is accounted for. In the most populous state in the nation—and the state with the largest number of registered voters—this takes time. (Padilla, 2018)

At the conclusion of the 2018 midterm election, the Democratic Party gained control of the United States House of Representatives. One of the first pieces of legislation passed in the House was House Resolution 1. The bill not only addresses voting rights but also campaign finance reform and lobbying. In the realm of voting rights, the bill authorizes national voter registration, makes Election Day a national holiday for federal elections, ends partisan gerrymandering in federal elections, stops the removal of voters from rolls due to the return of nonforwardable mail, enhances election security, and supports the recruiting and training for more poll workers before the 2020 election to reduce long lines at the polls. Republican Senate Majority Leader Mitch McConnell, however, announced that he had no intention of bringing the House's voting reform bill up for a vote in the Senate.

SOURCES

ACLU (American Civil Liberties Union). "Trump's Voting Commission Is a Sham." 2017. Accessed June 25, 2019. https://action.aclu.org/petition/sham-voting-commission.

Caputo, Angela, Geoff Hing, and Johnny Kauffman. "They Didn't Vote . . . Now They Can't." October 19, 2018. Accessed June 25, 2019. https://www.apmreports.org/story/2018/10/19/georgia-voter-purge.

Carney, Jordain. "Schumer: Dems will Try to Disband Trump Voter Fraud Panel in Must Pass Bill." *The Hill.* August 24, 2017. Accessed June 25, 2019. https://thehill.com/blogs/floor-action/senate/347793-schumer-dems-will-try-to-disband-trump-voter-fraud-panel-in-must.

Election Assistance Commission. Elections-Critical Infrastructure. Accessed June 25, 2019. https://www.eac.gov/election-officials/elections-critical-infrastructure/.

Levy, Pema. "New Documents Show Trump's Election Integrity Commission Was Preparing Report on Voter Fraud without Proof." August 3, 2018. Accessed June 25,

2019. https://www.motherjones.com/politics/2018/08/new-documents-show-trumps-election-integrity-commission-was-preparing-report-on-voter-fraud-without-proof/.

Padilla, Alex. "California Secretary of State Alex Padilla Response to Paul Ryan Comments on CA Elections." California Secretary of State's Office press release. November 29, 2018. Accessed June 25, 2019. https://www.sos.ca.gov/administration/news-releases-and-advisories/2018-news-releases-and-advisories/california-secretary-state-alex-padilla-response-paul-ryan-comments-ca-elections/.

Powell, Michael, and Peter Slevin. "Several Factors Contributed to Lost Voters in Ohio." *Washington Post.* December 15, 2004. Accessed June 25, 2019. https://www.washingtonpost.com/archive/politics/2004/12/15/several-factors-contributed-to-lost-voters-in-ohio/73aefa72-c8e5-4657-9e85-5ec8b2451202/?noredirect=on&utm_term=.711bd31682b6.

Presidential Commision on Election Administration. *The American Voting Experince: Report and Recommendation of The Presidential Commission On Election Administration.* 2014. Retrieved from https://www.supportthevoter.gov/files/2014/01/Amer-Voting-Exper-final-draft-01-09-14-508.pdf.

Samuels, Alex. "Here's How to Avoid Problems with Straight-Ticket Voting in Texas." *Texas Tribune.* October 26, 2018. Accessed June 25, 2019. https://www.texastribune.org/2018/10/26/texas-voting-machines-2018-straight-ticket-midterm-elections/.

Stark, Liz, and Grace Hauck. "Forty-Four States and DC have Refused to Give Certain Voter Information to Trump Commission." CNN Politics. July 5, 2017. Accessed June 25, 2019. https://www.cnn.com/2017/07/03/politics/kris-kobach-letter-voter-fraud-commission-information/index.html.

United States Department of Homeland Security. "Critical Infrastructure Sectors." Accessed June 25, 2019. https://www.npr.org/2018/10/22/659591998/6-takeaways-from-georgias-use-it-or-lose-it-voter-purge-investigation.

Watkins, Eli. "Judge Sides with Dem Member Suing Trump Voting Commission." CNN Politics. December 25, 2017. Accessed June 25, 2019. https://www.cnn.com/2017/12/24/politics/matthew-dunlap-voter-fraud-commission/index.html.

PRIMARY DOCUMENTS

President Trump and Vice President Pence Tout Election Integrity Commission, 2017

In November 2016, Republican presidential nominee Donald Trump's electoral college victory over Democratic nominee Hillary Clinton vaulted him to the White House, even though he actually lost the popular vote to Clinton by about three million votes. Trump responded to this perceived shadow over his victory by claiming, without evidence, that Clinton's popular vote tally included millions of illegal votes. Many of Trump's supporters seized on this claim, which reflected a fairly common GOP conviction that voter fraud—usually benefiting Democrats—had become a serious problem in U.S. politics.

On May 11, 2017, Trump signed an executive order creating a bipartisan Presidential Advisory Commission on Election Integrity. This commission, chaired by Vice President Mike Pence, was charged with examining federal election processes for the purposes of identifying cases of real or potential voting fraud. But Trump's own unsubstantiated claims about voter fraud, as well as the presence on the commission of individuals such as Kansas Secretary of State Kris Kobach, a high-profile supporter of voting restrictions who, critics alleged, was one of the nation's most shameless promoters of unfounded myths about voter fraud, led many voting-rights groups and Democrats to view the commission with skepticism. As journalist Vann R. Newkirk II wrote in U.S. News and World Report, from its first days of operation, the commission was "dogged by allegations that its true purpose [was] not eliminating voter fraud, but instigating voter suppression."

When the commission held its first public meeting on July 19, 2017, in Washington, DC, both President Trump and Vice President Pence reported that it was making great progress in gathering pertinent information from state election officials. Trump and Pence also emphasized that the commission included election officials from the Democratic Party, and they asserted that the only goal of the commission was to make U.S. elections more secure from fraud and error. Excerpts from the public remarks that Trump and Pence delivered at that meeting are reprinted below.

But these assurances did not mollify the critics. The "voter fraud" commission was beset with legal challenges from voter rights groups such as the NAACP Legal Defense and Education Fund, MALDEF (Mexican American Legal Defense and Educational Fund), and the Brennan Center for Justice. In addition, public skepticism about the true intent of the commission remained strong, in part because many state election officials—including some Republicans—refused the commission's requests for information on voters, citing privacy considerations.

On January 3, 2018, Trump issued an executive order abruptly disbanding the commission that he had created only one year earlier. "Many mostly Democrat States refused to hand over data from the 2016 Election to the Commission On Voter Fraud," Trump asserted later that same day on Twitter. "They fought hard that the Commission not see their records or methods because they know that many people are voting illegally." An official White House statement offered a similar perspective: "Despite substantial evidence of voter fraud, many states have refused to provide the Presidential Advisory Commission on Election Integrity with basic information relevant to its inquiry. Rather than engage in endless legal battles at taxpayer expense, today President Donald J. Trump signed an executive order to dissolve the Commission, and he has asked the Department of Homeland Security to review its initial findings and determine next courses of action."

Critics of the commission, however, celebrated its sudden collapse. "The commission's entire purpose was to legitimize voter suppression," Vanita Gupta, the former head of the Justice Department's Civil Rights Division, told the New York Times. *"The abrupt abandonment of the commission makes clear that it had become a thoroughly discredited body that could not find evidence of mass voter fraud."*

THE VICE PRESIDENT: Well, good morning. Please be seated. On behalf of the First Family, welcome to the White House. And welcome to the inaugural meeting of the Presidential Advisory Commission on Election Integrity.

Just over two months ago, on May the 11th, President Trump signed an executive order to create a commission to, in his words, help to "promote fair and honest federal elections" — the foundation of our democracy.

Election integrity matters to every American. President Calvin Coolidge reminded us, in his words, that the "whole system of American government rests on the ballot box." And President Reagan declared that the "right to vote is the crown jewel of American liberties."

By establishing this commission, President Trump is taking action to ensure that the ballot box remains inviolate, and that the crown jewel shines brighter than ever before.

At the President's direction, I'll have the honor to serve as chairman of this commission. And it's a privilege to convene this first meeting today. President Trump knows that the integrity of our electoral system transcends party lines, and I'm grateful this commission has brought together a distinguished group of bipartisan election experts and public officials from federal, state, and the local level. And together, this bipartisan group will perform a truly non-partisan service to the American people.

I'd especially like to recognize our vice-chairman, who you'll hear more from after the President's remarks, a man whose long service has established him as a national leader on election integrity, Kansas Secretary of State Kris Kobach. I also, as a point of personal privilege, would like to express my thanks and appreciation to Indian's Secretary of State, Connie Lawson, who joins us as a part of this panel.

President Trump knows that the principle of "one person, one vote" is foundational to the American system of democracy. This commission has been charged to study the registration and voting processes used in federal elections. The commission will identify the laws, rules, policies, activities, strategies, and practices that will enhance the American people's confidence in the integrity of our electoral system. We'll also explore the vulnerabilities in our system that could lead to improper voter registration and even improper voting.

This commission, let me be clear—this commission has no preconceived notions or preordained results. We're fact-finders. And in the days ahead, we will gather the relevant facts and data, and at the conclusion of our work, we will present the President with a report of our findings.

I'm confident this commission will have a healthy and robust debate, but the President and I expect nothing less, because respectful debate is also a hallmark of our democracy. And I know that we'll find many areas of common ground, as well. . . .

This President knows that the success of our democracy depends on the American people's confidence in this electoral system. And the President and I are both confident that this bipartisan commission will make the strongest democracy in the history of the world even stronger.

And so with gratitude for his commitment to fair and honest elections, it is my high honor and distinct privilege to introduce to all of you the 45th President of the United States of America, President Donald Trump.

THE PRESIDENT: Thank you very much. Please, be seated. Mr. Vice President, distinguished guests, and members of the media: I'm honored to welcome you here today as the bipartisan Presidential Advisory Commission on Election Integrity prepares to conduct its first official meeting. Very, very important.

This commission is tasked with the sacred duty of upholding the integrity of the ballot box and the principle of "one citizen, one vote." Every time voter fraud occurs, it cancels out the vote of a lawful citizen and undermines democracy. Can't let that happen. Any form of illegal or fraudulent voting, whether by noncitizens or the deceased, and any form of voter suppression or intimidation must be stopped.

I'm pleased that more than 30 states have already agreed to share the information with the commission and the other states. That information will be forthcoming. If any state does not want to share this information, one has to wonder what they're worried about. And I asked the Vice President, I asked the commission: What are they worried about? There's something. There always is.

This issue is very important to me because, throughout the campaign and even after it, people would come up to me and express their concerns about voter inconsistencies and irregularities, which they saw. In some cases, having to do with very large numbers of people in certain states. All public officials have a profound responsibility to protect the integrity of the vote. We have no choice. If we want to make America great again, we have to protect the integrity of the vote and our voters.

This is not a Democrat or a Republican issue, it's an American issue. It's about the concern of so many Americans that improper voting has taken place and canceling out the votes of lawful American citizens. That is why President Theodore Roosevelt once said, it is the affair of every honest voter, wherever born, to see that no fraudulent voting is allowed anywhere.

I want to thank Vice President Pence for chairing the commission. I also want to thank Kansas Secretary of State Kris Kobach for serving as vice-chair. It's going to be a lot of work. They're going to work very hard over a fairly short period of time. And I want to thank you both very much—Kris, Mike.

This is a bipartisan panel consisting of both Republican and Democratic leaders and experts on voter integrity. I'd like to personally thank each of our panel members for serving. Really do appreciate it.

In addition to the chair and vice-chair, this distinguished bipartisan panel includes: Indiana Secretary of State Connie Lawson—thank you; New Hampshire Secretary of State, Bill Gardner—thank you; Maine Secretary of State, Matthew Dunlap; former Ohio Secretary of State, Ken Blackwell; Election Assistance Commissioner, Christy McCormick; former Arkansas State Representative, David Dunn—thank you, David; Wood County West Virginia Clerk, Mark Rhoades; Heritage Foundation Senior Legal Fellow and Manager of the Election Law Reform Initiative—a real expert—Hans von Spakovsky; President and General Counsel of the Public Interest Legal Foundation—great group—J. Christian Adams; and Jefferson County, Alabama Probate Judge, Alan King. Thank you. Thank you very much.

Each of you has been entrusted with a great responsibility of helping to advance the cause of fair, honest, and lawful elections. Your work will help protect our democracy. This will be a very transparent process. It's going to be very open for everybody to see. You will approach this important task with a very open mind and with no conclusions already drawn. You will fairly and objectively follow the facts wherever they may lead.

I look forward to the findings and recommendations your report will produce, and I share your report as soon as I can and as soon as possible with the American people so the full truth will be known and exposed, if necessary, in the light of day. We call on every state to give its full support and total cooperation in this effort. Most of them have really done brilliantly, and we appreciate it. And the rest, all of that information will be forthcoming.

Source: Remarks by President Trump and Vice President Pence at the Presidential Advisory Commission on Election Integrity Meeting, July 19, 2017. Accessed April 4, 2019. https://www.whitehouse.gov/briefings-statements/remarks-president-trump-vice-president-pence-presidential-advisory-commission-election-integrity-meeting/.

A Legal Battle over the Voting Rights of American Citizens in U.S. Territories, 2017–2018

When the Uniformed and Overseas Citizens Absentee Voting Act (UOCAVA) became law in 1986, it mandated that states allow absentee voting by citizens in federal elections when they relocate outside the United States. In a strange quirk, however, the statute—which had been crafted in large part to make it easier for military personnel to vote by absentee ballot—mandated that states permit citizens residing in the Northern Mariana Islands to vote absentee but made no such provision for U.S. citizens living in four other U.S. territories: American Samoa, Guam, Puerto Rico, and the U.S. Virgin Islands.

*In 2015, several Illinois residents who had taken up residence in the latter territories filed a lawsuit (*Segovia v. United States*) in which they asserted that by giving residents of the Northern Mariana Islands voting rights but not doing the same for citizens in other territories, the UOCAVA in effect discriminated against certain territorial residents in violation of the Fifth Amendment. The plaintiffs argued that the law should be changed so that absentee voting rights were extended to American citizens residing in every U.S. territory. "If I had moved to any U.S. territory except Guam, Puerto Rico, or the U.S. Virgin Islands, or even to a foreign country, I could still vote for President today," declared lead plaintiff Luis Segovia, a U.S. Army veteran who served two tours in Afghanistan and one in Iraq. "This kind of discrimination isn't just morally wrong, it's unconstitutional. My right to vote should not depend on my Zip-code." But the Seventh Circuit Court of Appeals ruled against the plaintiffs in* Segovia v. United States, *arguing that they did not have legal standing to challenge the law, and a year later the U.S. Supreme Court declined to hear the appeal.*

Following are two documents reflecting the views of the Trump administration and Segovia's supporters, respectively. The first excerpt is from a letter written by U.S. Department of Justice attorney Carleen M. Zubrzycki in which she urges the court to heed a ruling it had made in another 2017 case, Sessions v. Morales-Santana. *In that case, the court had resolved an "equal protection discrimination" issue by reducing the legal rights of the previously favored constituents rather than lifting the rights of those that had been the victims of discrimination. The Trump administration's Department of Justice, in other words, wanted the court to reduce the voting rights of American citizens living in any U.S. territory rather than strengthen voting rights across the territories. The second document is an excerpt from a legal brief filed by legal scholars in support of Segovia and the other plaintiffs.*

September 11, 2017

Gino J. Agnello
Office of the Clerk
United States Court of Appeals for the Seventh Circuit
Everett McKinley Dirksen United States Courthouse
219 S. Dearborn Street
Room 2722
Chicago, IL 60604

Re: *Segovia v. United States, et al.*, No. 16-4240 (7th Cir.)
(scheduled for oral argument September 15, 2017)

Dear Mr. Agnello:

Pursuant to FRAP 28(j), we write to notify the Court of *Sessions v. Morales-Santana,* 137 S. Ct. 1678 (June 12, 2017), which held that the proper remedy for an equal protection violation consisting of favorable treatment for a discrete group was to eliminate the favorable treatment for that group, rather than expanding more favorable treatment to everyone.

In *Morales-Santana,* the Supreme Court held that a provision of the Immigration and Nationality Act (INA) extending citizenship to certain children with one U.S. citizen parent violated equal protection principles because it provided more lenient rules for unwed U.S. citizen mothers than for unwed U.S. citizen fathers.

The Supreme Court unanimously held that the proper remedy for this equal protection violation was to eliminate the favorable treatment of mothers, rather than expanding the rights of fathers. The Court stressed that "the appropriate remedy is a mandate of equal treatment, a result that can be accomplished by withdrawal of benefits from the favored class as well as by extension of benefits to the excluded class." . . . Which of these approaches to take "is governed by the legislature's intent, as revealed by the statute at hand." . . . Looking to the text and structure of the INA, the Court concluded that Congress would have preferred to eliminate the "discriminatory exception" favoring mothers . . .

Here, plaintiffs contend that a statute expressly defining "the United States" to include Puerto Rico, America Samoa, the U.S. Virgin Islands, and Guam as part of the United States violates equal protection because the statute does not mention the Northern Mariana Islands (CNMI) (which became a Territory after the statute was enacted). Under the logic of *Morales-Santana,* if that were an equal protection violation, the proper remedy would be to treat CNMI like the four major territories that Congress expressly addressed in the statute.

Sincerely,

Carleen M. Zubrzycki
Attorney

INTRODUCTION AND SUMMARY OF ARGUMENT

Puerto Rico, Guam, the U.S. Virgin Islands, American Samoa, and the Northern Mariana Islands are U.S. territories organized under the Constitution's Territories Clause. The Federal Uniformed and Overseas Citizens Absentee Voting Act (UOCAVA), and the Illinois Military Overseas Voter Empowerment Act (Illinois MOVE Act), each extend the right to vote in Illinois federal elections to Illinois residents who move to the Northern Mariana Islands and a number of smaller, mostly uninhabited U.S. possessions. The Illinois MOVE Act further extends voting rights in Illinois federal elections to ex-Illinoisans in American Samoa. Former Illinoisans lose the right to vote in Illinois federal elections if they move to Puerto Rico, Guam, or the U.S. Virgin Islands.

The Seventh Circuit held that this distinction does not violate the Fourteenth Amendment's Equal Protection Clause because "the residents of the territories have no fundamental right to vote in federal elections." *Segovia v. United States,* 880 F. 3d 384, 390 (7th Cir. 2018). In reaching this conclusion, the Seventh Circuit erroneously upheld a law disenfranchising some and not other identically situated citizens (ex-residents of Illinois living in U.S. territories) based solely on their current territory of residence.

Only one aspect of the present case distinguishes it from a run-of-the-mill malapportionment or disenfranchisement case like those this Court has decided in the past. Illinois and Congress could have chosen to exclude all ex-Illinois residents from federal elections in the state. . . . Instead, by statute, Illinois and Congress elected to expand the franchise to encompass some ex-residents now residing in U.S. Territories and not others.

Amici urge the Court to take this case to make clear to the courts below that this distinction is irrelevant. Once a state legislature or Congress extends the right to vote to one group of people, they cannot deprive another identically situated group of people of the right to cast a vote purely based on geography.

This case is an appropriate vehicle to resolve several enduring circuit splits over the origins and operation of the right to vote. Because the Seventh Circuit applied the wrong standard of scrutiny to a plainly stated disenfranchisement claim, the Court can readily reverse and remand for consideration of remedy—while making it clear that the "fundamental political right, because preservative of all rights," *Yick Wo v. Hopkins,* 118 U.S. 356, 370 (1886), is no less fundamental when the citizens in question acquire their right to vote by a state or federal statute.

Sources: Letter from Carleen M. Zubrzycki, U.S. Department of Justice, Civil Division, to 7th Circuit, U.S. Court of Appeals. September 11, 2017. Accessed March 28, 2019. https://www.scribd.com/document/359009585/Trump-DOJ-Letter-Remedy-is-to-Level-Down-Voting-Rights; Brief of Voting Rights Scholars as *Amicus Curiae* Supporting Petitioners, "Introduction and Summary of Argument." 2018. *Luis Segovia et al, v. United States of America, et al., on Appeal from the United States Court of Appeals for the Seventh Circuit.* Accessed March 28, 2019. https://www.scribd.com/document/379987132/Segovia-v-United-States-Voting-Rights-Scholars-Amicus-Brief.

Civil Rights Legend John Lewis Decries Voter Suppression in America, 2018

On August 6, 2018, the fifty-third anniversary of the signing of the landmark Voting Rights Act, Representative John Lewis of Georgia's Fifth District marked the occasion by issuing a bleak assessment of the state of contemporary voting rights in the United States. Lewis, who was also one of the leading figures in the civil rights movement that spurred the passage of the 1965 Voting Rights Act, charged that voter suppression—especially against people of color—had become an elemental threat to American democracy. Following is the full text of Lewis's statement.

Today, on the 53rd anniversary of the signing of the Voting Rights Act (VRA) by President Lyndon Johnson, we celebrate a milestone in American history. With the stroke of a pen, millions of Americans were ushered into the democratic process. In 1964 in Holmes County, Mississippi, there were only twelve black registered voters. By 1965, there were 28,500, and by 1984 there were 406,000. There were only a handful of minority elected officials anywhere in the country before the VRA was signed. Today there are thousands. Millions of Latino, Asian, Native American, and language minorities can now vote in America, and many now serve as elected officials because of this one law.

Though an increase in voter registration is frequently used to demonstrate the VRA's impact, increasing the voter rolls was not the central purpose of the legislation. It was intended to stop state-sponsored terrorism, intimidation, and unjust, humiliating practices—literacy tests, poll taxes, and even lynching—which led people of color to fear registering and voting on Election Day. Even Chief Justice Roberts admitted in his fateful opinion in the *Shelby v. Holder* decision that voting discrimination still runs rampant in America. Yet the Supreme Court put politics before the facts and gutted the VRA anyway.

Since the *Shelby* decision, voter discrimination is on the rise. Thousands of people of color are being systematically denied access to the ballot box, many of whom have voted all their lives. In a recent Brennan Center for Justice Report, it focused on the purging of voter rolls, just one of several voter suppression tactics now in use. Brennan called purging "a growing threat" to voting rights and discovered that in 2016 more than 200,000 names had been improperly deleted from voter rolls in Brooklyn, and 7,700 in Arkansas. Thousands of citizens were wrongfully denied the right to vote in the last election. Between 2014 and 2016, Brennan found almost 4 million names were "purged" from the voting rolls.

As the election of 2016 proves, just a few thousand votes can change the future of our nation. There are forces that want to drain public resources and put them in the pockets of private interests, want to serve only the rich, and disregard the will of the people. Your vote has the power to stop those strategies, and that is why it is at risk.

There are two immediate answers to this problem. Americans must vote in this election like never before. And Congress must also act to restore the VRA to its original strength. Several bipartisan proposals have already been drafted. Congress should make our democracy a priority and take action on these proposals before the election of 2018, but especially before the election of 2020. The vote is the most powerful non-violent tool we have for change in a democratic society. The power of people to have a voice in their own future must be protected at all costs.

Source: Lewis, John. "Rep. John Lewis on the Regression of Voting Rights in America." Press release. August 6, 2018. Accessed April 2, 2019. https://johnlewis.house.gov/media-center/press-releases/rep-john-lewis-regression-voting-rights-america.

Federal Judge Strikes Down New Hampshire's "Signature-Mismatch" Voting Law, 2018

Some of the election laws and voting restrictions that states have passed in the 2010s in the name of combating voter fraud have withstood judicial scrutiny and been allowed to stand. Perhaps the most notable of these court decisions was the U.S. Supreme Court's October 2014 decision to overturn a lower court ruling that had struck down a Texas voter ID law as unconstitutional. The court's unsigned decision made the ID law, regarded by supporter and opponent alike as the most restrictive one in the country, the law of the land in Texas. But other voting restrictions passed by states during this time were tossed out without ceremony by the courts. One such law was a New Hampshire statute that had been passed regarding absentee ballots. It required that voting "moderators" confirm that the voter signature on those ballots "matched" the signature of the voter already on file. If the moderators—none of whom underwent any formal training in handwriting analysis—determined that the signatures did not match, they were authorized to throw the ballots away.

This law was challenged by several New Hampshire voters whose absentee ballots were rejected in the 2016 election. They not only charged that their constitutional rights had been violated by the law, which they characterized as unfair and capricious, they also noted that in 2016 all 275 rejected absentee ballots came from only 26 percent of New Hampshire's 318 polling sites—a fact that the plaintiffs asserted showed that the law was being enforced arbitrarily and inconsistently.

On August 14, 2018, U.S. District Judge Landya McCafferty sided with the plaintiffs in the case, Saucedo v. Gardner. *Following are excerpts from her decision.*

ORDER

This case concerns New Hampshire's signature-match requirement for absentee ballots. The act of signing one's name is often viewed as a rote task, a mechanical exercise yielding a fixed signature. A person's signature, however, may vary for a variety of reasons, both intentional and unintentional. Unintentional factors include age, physical and mental condition, disability, medication, stress, accidents, and inherent differences in a person's neuromuscular coordination and stance. Variations are more prevalent in people who are elderly, disabled, or who speak English as a second language. For the most part, signature variations are of little consequence in a person's life.

But in the context of absentee voting, these variations become profoundly consequential. The signature-match requirement in RSA 659-50, III requires every local election moderator to compare the signature on a voter's absentee-ballot application to the signature on an affidavit that the voter sends with the absentee ballot. If the signature on the affidavit does not appear "to be executed by the same person who signed the application," the moderator must reject the voter's ballot." . . . The purpose of the requirement is to ensure that the same person executes both the absentee-ballot application and the affidavit. In recent elections, however, the signature-match requirement has disenfranchised hundreds of absentee voters.

. . . This signature-matching process is fundamentally flawed. Not only is the disenfranchised voter given not right to participate in this process, but the voter is not even given notice that her ballot has been rejected due to a signature mismatch. Moreover, moderators receive no training in handwriting analysis or signature comparison; no statute, regulation, or guidance from the States provides functional standards to distinguish the natural variations of one writer from other variations that suggest two different writers; and the moderator's assessment is final, without any review or appeal.

Plaintiffs Mary Saucedo, Maureen P. Heard and Thomas Fitzpatrick are among the 275 absentee voters whose ballots were rejected in the 2016 General Election as a result of RSA 659:50, III. They bring suit against defendants William M. Gardner (New Hampshire's Secretary of State), and the New Hampshire Secretary of State's Office, alleging constitutional claims under 42 U.S.C. Section 1983, and a claim under the Americans with Disabilities Act ("ADA"). . . .

Taken as a whole, and in light of the fundamental importance of the right to vote, the current process for rejecting voters due to a signature mismatch fails to guarantee basic fairness. The infirmity with the statute begins with vesting moderators with sole, unreviewable discretion to reject ballots due to a signature mismatch. Such discretion becomes constitutionally intolerable once other factors are taken into account: the natural variations in voters' signatures combined with the absence of training and functional standards on handwriting analysis, and the lack of any review process or compliance measures. And there is an easy fix—an existing procedure that, with minor refinement, could reduce the risk that qualified voters are wrongly disenfranchised and bolster the State's interests in preventing voter fraud and safeguarding voter confidence in elections.

Therefore, in light of the undisputed, material facts in the record, plaintiffs are entitled to summary judgment on their procedural due process claim. The court grants plaintiffs' requires for declaratory relief insofar as RSA 659:50, III is unconstitutional under the Fourteenth Amendment of the United States Constitution. . . .

The court [also] concludes that plaintiffs have demonstrated an entitlement to permanent injunctive relief. . . . The court enjoins defendants from enforcing RSA 659:50, III. Although the enforcement of the provision falls primarily on local election officials, i.e., nonparties, the court is confident that the Secretary of State will take appropriate steps to ensure that this injunction is enforced. . . .

Source: U.S. District Court for the District of New Hampshire. "Order," *Mary Saucedo, et al. v. William Gardner, Secretary of State of the State of New Hampshire, et al.* August 14, 2018, pp. 1–3, 44–45. Accessed June 25, 2019. www.nhd.uscourts.gov/sites/default/files/opinions/18/18NH160.pdf.

President Trump's National Security Team Warns of "Pervasive" Russian Election Meddling, 2018

In the wake of widespread evidence of Russian efforts to influence the 2016 U.S. presidential election, voting rights advocates urged the Trump administration to take decisive steps to make sure that all American voters would have their voices heard in future elections. The administration's efforts to reassure the public that American elections would be protected from foreign interference, however, were complicated by public statements by Trump himself ridiculing the notion that Russian President Vladimir Putin and/or Russian intelligence organizations had influenced the 2016 election in any way. Trump's remarks flatly contradicted reports such as a January 2017 Intelligence Community Assessment (ICA) produced by the Central Intelligence Agency (CIA), National Security Agency (NSA), and Federal Bureau of Investigation (FBI), which stated that "Russian activities in the run-up to the 2016 presidential election represented a significant escalation in a long history of Russian attempts to interfere in U.S. domestic politics. . . . We assess Russian President Vladimir Putin ordered an influence campaign in 2016 aimed at the U.S. presidential election. Russia's goals were to undermine public faith in the U.S. democratic process, denigrate Secretary Clinton, and harm her electability and potential presidency. We further assess Putin and the Russian Government developed a clear preference for President-elect Trump."

Criticism of the Trump administration for not taking the issue of election integrity seriously reached new heights in July 2018, when Trump declared at a joint press conference in Helsinki, Finland, with Putin that he believed the Russian president's denials that he or his government had meddled in any American elections. Two weeks later, the White House arranged a press conference with the administration's top intelligence officials on the issue of election security. During the press briefing, Director of National Intelligence Dan Coats, FBI Director Christopher Wray, Secretary of Homeland Security Kirstjen Nielsen, Director of the National Security Agency General Paul Nakasone, and National Security Advisor Ambassador John Bolton all asserted that President Trump was deeply invested in protecting the integrity of American elections. But they also refuted him by stating that Russia had clearly interfered in the 2016 presidential election—and showed every sign of wanting to influence and disrupt future U.S. elections. The following are excerpts from that press briefing, which was led by White House Press Secretary Sarah Huckabee Sanders.

Hours after the press conference concluded, Trump attended a campaign rally in Pennsylvania in which he complained that his relationship with Putin was "being hindered by the Russian hoax." As NBC News journalists Jonathan Allen and Lauren Egan noted, Trump's rally statements presented a jarring contrast to the press briefing earlier in the day: "The two events created a split-screen effect: America's intelligence experts warning voters that Russia is trying to undermine democracy while Trump tells them it's all political chicanery."

SANDERS: Good afternoon. Since the beginning of his administration, President Trump has implemented a whole-of-government approach to safeguard our nation's elections. The President has made it clear that his administration will not tolerate foreign interference in our elections from any nation-state or other dangerous actor.

Last year, the President signed an executive order to strengthen and review the cybersecurity of our nation and its critical infrastructure. Last week, the President chaired a meeting of his National Security Council to address ongoing threats. He asked the officials standing next to me to brief the American people on the work being done to protect the integrity of our elections.

Efforts are underway to provide cybersecurity assistance to state and local authorities, and actions to investigate, prosecute, and hold accountable those who illegally attempt to interfere in our political and electoral process.

To address these matters further, I want to welcome Director of National Intelligence Dan Coats, FBI Director Christopher Wray, Secretary of Homeland Security Kirstjen Nielsen, Director of the National Security Agency General Paul Nakasone, and National Security Advisor Ambassador John Bolton to make some comments and take questions on this topic. . . .

DIRECTOR COATS: Well, as Director of National Intelligence, I would like the American people to know that the intelligence community and all of its agencies are postured to identify threats of all kinds against the United States. The President has specifically directed us to make the matter of election meddling and securing our election process a top priority. And we have done that, and are doing that, and will continue to do so.

We have incorporated the lessons learned from the 2016 election, and implemented a broad spectrum of actions to share more information across the federal government, as well as with state and local governments, and also with the public and the private sector. The intelligence community continues to be concerned about the threats of upcoming U.S. elections, both the midterms and the presidential elections of 2020.

In regards to Russian involvement in the midterm elections, we continue to see a pervasive messaging campaign by Russia to try to weaken and divide the United States. These efforts are not exclusive to this election or future elections, but certainly cover issues relevant to the election.

We also know the Russians tried to hack into and steal information from candidates and government officials alike. We are aware that Russia is not the only country that has an interest in trying to influence our domestic political environment. We know there are others who have the capability and may be considering influence activities. As such, we will continue to monitor and warn of any such efforts.

I am committed to making sure that the intelligence community is working together in integrating across organizations and missions, and seeking greater transparency with the public. The ODNI has instituted a broad spectrum of actions covering collection, analysis, reporting, education, and partnerships all designed to provide the best threat assessments to federal, state, and local officials, as well as to the public and private sector when necessary.

For example, my office leads the interagency working group—now meeting weekly, as a push towards November—with the Department of Justice, FBI, Department of Homeland Security, the CIA, and NSA inclusive of regional, cyber, and counterintelligence experts, all focused on ensuring election security and integration of our efforts.

The intelligence community's focus right now is persistent support to the FBI, to the Department of Homeland Security, and other agencies in their election responsibilities. And my office is ensuring these organizations receive timely and proactive intelligence community support.

SECRETARY NIELSEN: Well, good afternoon. Thank you all for joining us. I want to start by briefly mentioning that, on Tuesday, DHS hosted the first national cybersecurity summit. This brought together government, industry leaders, and academia to discuss opportunities to join forces to counter threats to our nation's critical infrastructure. . . .

Across every critical infrastructure sector, from energy to financial services, to transportation, to communication, and so many others, a single attack can have widespread and cascading consequences. I look forward to working with the nation's leading minds in the digital realm as we stand up the National Risk Management Center.

But it's not just risk to our prosperity, privacy, and infrastructure we have to worry about, and that's why we're here today. Our democracy itself is in the crosshairs. Free and fair elections are the cornerstone of our democracy, and it has become clear that they are the target of our adversaries, who seek, as the DNI just said, to sow discord and undermine our way of life.

I fully share the intelligence community and the ODNI's assessments of past efforts and those today to interfere with our election and of the current threat. Our adversaries have shown they have the willingness and capability to interfere in our elections.

DHS has and continues to work closely with state and local election officials throughout the country by offering a range of services to help identify weaknesses in their election systems. Whether it's offering no-cost, voluntary technical assistance or sharing best practices for securing online voter registration databases, or providing technical advice on ransomware and destructive malware, our department stands ready to provide tailored support based on each jurisdiction's unique needs. This is yet another example where one size does not fit all.

I am pleased to inform you that, to date, all 50 states, the District of Columbia, and over 900 local governments have partnered with DHS in order to bolster the resilience of the nation's election infrastructure. Various states also have organic capabilities, and are engaging with the private sector and academia to improve the security of elections.

Election infrastructure is not a destination. It requires aggressive and ongoing vigilance. Everyone must play their role to ensure that every vote is counted, and is counted correctly—all of us up here today, members of Congress, state and local election officials, and the public. . . .

DIRECTOR WRAY: Good afternoon, everybody. Last fall, after I—shortly after I became Director, I stood up a new foreign influence taskforce at the FBI, which was designed to identify and counteract the full range of malign foreign influence operations targeting our democratic institutions and our values. . . .

So just a few examples of some of the things we've seen over the past: targeting U.S. officials and other U.S. persons through traditional intelligence tradecraft;

criminal efforts to suppress voting and provide illegal campaign financing; cyber-attacks against voting infrastructure, along with computer intrusions targeting elected officials and others; and a whole slew of other kinds of influence, like both overtly and covertly manipulating news stories, spreading disinformation, leveraging economic resources, and escalating divisive issues.

But it's important to understand this is not just an election cycle threat. Our adversaries are trying to undermine our country on a persistent and regular basis, whether it's election season or not.

There's a clear distinction between, on the one hand, activities that threaten the security and integrity of our election systems, and, on the other hand, the broader threat of influence operations designed to manipulate and influence our voters and their opinions.

With our partners, we're trying to counteract both threats. We have three pillars to our operational strategy. The first pillar is our investigations and our operations. . . . The second . . . is focused on information sharing and intelligence sharing. We're working closely with our partners in the intelligence community and in the federal government, as well as with our state and local partners, to establish a common operating picture. . . .

The third pillar of our approach is based on our strong relationships with the private sector. Technology companies have a frontline responsibility to secure their own networks, products, and platforms. But we're doing our part by providing actionable intelligence to better enable them to address abuse of their platforms by foreign actors. . . .

The reality is, it's going to take all of us working together to hold the field, because this threat is not going away. As I have said consistently: Russia attempted to interfere with the last election, and continues to engage in malign influence operations to this day.

Q. Thank you, Sarah. Director Coats, if I could direct a question to you?

DIRECTOR COATS: Sure.

Q. Let me take you back, if I could, to Helsinki. The President seemed to indicate that he may believe Vladimir Putin, when he says he doesn't—didn't have any influence in the 2016 election. What is your belief about the Russian government involvement in meddling in 2016? And if, as you say, Russia continues to try to influence our electoral process, does that mean that nothing much came of the meeting with Putin? Or is it other-than-government actors who are involved here?

DIRECTOR COATS: Well, in relationship to the 2016 election—of course, none of us were in office at that particular time—but both the President, the Vice President, and I think everyone on this stage has acknowledged the fact that the ICA was a correct assessment of what happened in 2016.

We have subsequently made the determination to make this a top priority, that it doesn't happen again. And we're throwing everything at it. And we will have and will be discussing that here today.

Relative to my discussions with the President on whatever issue it is, those—I do not go public with that. I don't think that's the right—the proper thing to do. So our focus here today is simply to tell the American people: We acknowledge the threat, it is real, it is continuing, and we're doing everything we can to have a legitimate election that the American people can have trust in.

In addition to that, it goes beyond the elections. It goes to Russia's intent to undermine our democratic values, drive a wedge between our allies, and do a number of other nefarious things. And we are looking at that also.

Today we are here to talk about the elections coming up and what we're doing in ensuring the American people we're going to have a legitimate—

Q. If I could just clarify, because both you and Director Wray said that Russia continues to try and meddle in our elections—

DIRECTOR COATS: They do.

Q. —and influence voters. Are we talking about rogue Russian individuals or are we talking about the Kremlin?

DIRECTOR COATS: I'm thinking you can—both. And even add to that. Russia has used numerous ways in which they want to influence through media—social media, through bots, through actors that they hire through proxies. All of the above and potentially more. I can't go into any deep, deep details on what is classified. But it is pervasive. It is ongoing with the intent to achieve their intent, and that is drive a wedge and undermine our democratic values.

SANDERS: Toluse.

Q. Thank you. I have a question for Director Wray. Thank you. Special Counsel Robert Mueller has indicted more than 20 Russian officials based on work by the FBI for meddling in the 2016 elections.

Now the President has tweeted that that investigation by the Special Counsel is a hoax and should be shut down. I know you've said that you don't believe it is a hoax. But why would the American people believe what you're saying about the FBI when the President says that the investigation by the Special Counsel is a hoax, and when the Press Secretary, yesterday, said that there was a lot of corruption within the FBI? Do you have any response to those statements coming from the White House?

DIRECTOR WRAY: Well, I can assure the American people that the men and women of the FBI, starting from the Director all the way on down, are going to follow our oaths and do our jobs.

SANDERS: Saagar.

Q. Thank you, Sarah. I have a question for Director Coats. Director Coats, how would you characterize the current efforts—Russian efforts—to meddle in the 2018 election relative to 2016? Is it more intense? Do you see those efforts focused on a particular party? And, in general, is the pace of those operations in any way relative to 2014, 2012? Or is it more intense?

DIRECTOR COATS: Relative to what we have seen for the midterm elections, it is not the kind of robust campaign that we assessed in the 2016 election. We know that, through decades, Russia has tried to use its propaganda and methods to sow discord in America. However, they stepped up their game big time in 2016. We have not seen that kind of robust effort from them so far.

As I mentioned publicly sometime—just a few weeks ago, we're only one keyboard click away from finding out something that we don't—haven't seen up to this particular point in time. But right now, we have not seen that.

Q. To follow up sir, do you see it directed to any particular party? In its current 2018 efforts, is there any particular party that is benefitting from current 2018 Russian efforts?

DIRECTOR COATS: What we see is the Russians are looking for every opportunity, regardless of party, regardless of whether or not it applies to the election, to continue their pervasive efforts to undermine our fundamental values.

SANDERS: Jeff. Go ahead.

Q. Thank you, Sarah. Also for Director Coats. In the run-up to the—

DIRECTOR COATS: I'm trying to get off here. (Laughter.)

Q. —and perhaps Ambassador Bolton could weigh in this as well. But in the run-up to the Helsinki Summit, U.S. officials, ambassadors to NATO, ambassadors to Russia said that the President would raise the issue of malign activity with President Putin. But he didn't discuss that, at least, at the press conference.

You're saying, today, that the President has directed you to make the issue of election meddling a priority. How do you explain the disconnect between what you are saying—his advisors—and what the President has said about this issue?

DIRECTOR COATS: I'm not in a position to either understand fully or talk about what happened at Helsinki. I'll turn it over to the National Security Director, here, to address that question.

AMBASSADOR BOLTON: The issue was discussed. And, in fact, President Putin said—I thought at the press conference, but certainly in the expanded bilateral meeting when the two leaders got together with their senior advisors—President Putin said the first issue that President Trump raised was election meddling.

Q. I guess the question is, at the press conference, the President didn't highlight any of the malign activities that you have and that his advisors have. And so, should Americans believe that he is listening to your advice, or that he is going his own way when he's having meetings like he did with the President of Russia?

AMBASSADOR BOLTON: I think the President has made it abundantly clear to everybody who has responsibility in this area that he cares deeply about it and that he expects them to do their jobs to their fullest ability and that he supports them fully. . . .

SANDERS: Mike Shear.

Q. This, I guess, would be for maybe Secretary Nielsen or Mr. Wray. These meddling campaigns seem to fall into two broad categories: the, sort of, information campaigns, which challenge the information upon which American use to make their determinations, and then the more physical interferences into the machinery of voting; the tabulation of voting, the voter roles, the machinery that the states run.

Can you guys describe what you're seeing specifically in the run-up to this coming election? In both of those areas, do you worry more about one than the other? Do you have—are there specific threats that maybe you can't even talk about but that you can say there have been specific threats in both of those categories? And how should Americans process that where we're going to go to the polls in a few months? Should people be confident that when they pull the lever, they're secure?

DIRECTOR WRAY: Well, I think we've said this fairly consistently, that in the context of 2018, we are not yet seeing the same kind of efforts to specifically target election infrastructure—voter registration databases, in particular.

What we are seeing are the malign influence operations—in effect, information warfare that we talked about. And that didn't really—that's a 24/7, 365 days-a-year phenomenon that doesn't turn, necessarily, on whether or not we're in the middle of an election season or not.

But, as Director Coats said, any moment is just a moment before, you know, the dial can be turned up one, much as we saw in 2016. Again, not in terms of affecting the vote count, but in terms of potential penetration of voter registration databases or something like that. And that, in turn, can be a vehicle for them to try to sow discord or undermine confidence. And we have to make sure we're pushing back on it, which is what we're doing. . . .

Source: Press Briefing by Press Secretary Sarah Sanders and National Security Officials. August 2, 2018. Accessed April 4, 2019. https://www.whitehouse.gov/briefings-statements/press-briefing-press-secretary-sarah-sanders-national-security-officials-08022018/.

House Speaker Pelosi Urges the Passage of Sweeping Expansion of Voting Rights, 2019

In the November 2018 midterm elections, the Democratic Party made major gains in the U.S. House of Representatives and recaptured majority control for the first time since 2010. Eager to send a message about their political and legislative priorities, Democratic Speaker of the House Nancy Pelosi (CA-12), Democracy Reform Task Force Chair John Sarbanes (MD-3), and other members of the House party leadership rushed to pass a bill containing an ambitious set of reforms designed to expand voting rights and reduce the influence of big money in politics. House Bill 1 (HB1) included provisions mandating Election Day registration, automatic voter registration, two weeks of early voting, protections against "purges" of voter rolls, enfranchisement for ex-felons, the establishment of independent commissions to draw congressional maps for elections (thus ending partisan gerrymandering), and adoption of paper ballots in every state in the union. It even included provisions making Election Day a federal holiday and another requiring presidential candidates to publicly release their tax returns.

All 234 Democratic members of the House voted for HB1, popularly known as the For The People Act, ensuring fairly easy passage on March 8, 2019. By contrast, all 193 Republicans voted against the bill, citing potential First Amendment infringements on campaign spending and excessive federal interference in election laws that have traditionally resided primarily with states. "This new Democrat Socialist majority wants the federal government to interfere in our free and fair elections," charged House Republican Leader Kevin McCarthy (CA-23). "This bill today . . . is a massive federal government takeover that would undermine the integrity of our elections." Similar sentiments were expressed by

Republican Senator Mitch McConnell, the head of the GOP-controlled Senate. He said that he had no intention of allowing the For the People Act to come up for a vote in the upper chamber.

Following are remarks that Pelosi made in advance of the House vote on the For The People Act.

I want to salute our colleague from Maryland, Congressman John Sarbanes, for being a relentless and persistent advocate for honoring the Constitution of the United States and giving people confidence their voice and their vote count as much as anyone's in this country.

That's what H.R. 1 is about: giving people confidence that we can do what we say without the influence of big, dark, special interest money weighing in on the process.

Our Constitution, Mr. Speaker, as you know, begins, 'We the People'—a beautiful statement of purpose for our nation. 'We the People.' They envisioned—our Founders—envisioned a government that would work for the people—serving the people's interests, fighting for their aspirations, hopes and dreams.

We have a responsibility to honor that vision of our Founders. Honoring our oath of office to uphold the Constitution of the United States. Honoring the sacrifice of our men and women in uniform for the sacrifices that they make for our freedom and freedom throughout the world. And worthy of the aspirations of our children.

We can only do this if we have a government that is committed to transparency, to as much bipartisanship as possible and to being unifying for our country.

In the election, the American people voted for just that. They voted for a Congress that would restore transparency, bipartisanship and unity—be unifying in Washington, D.C., so that the government would be, again I can't say it enough, work for the people.

On day one, reflecting the priorities of our just outstanding Freshman Class, our new Democratic Majority honored the people's trust by introducing H.R. 1, the For the People Act.

Again, let me salute John Sarbanes, the Chair of our Democracy Reform Task Force, who is the godfather of this bill.

Today, we are proud to be bringing this transformative legislation to the Floor of the House: H.R. 1. And it is H.R. 1 because it is of primary importance, restores the people's faith that government will work for the people and not the special interests.

We are ending the dominance of big, dark, special interest money in politics. We are ensuring clean, fair elections with Congressman John Lewis, our hero, with his Voter Empowerment Act to increase access to the ballot box.

Democrats or Republicans, or people who don't—or Independent, people who do not register as a party, should want everyone to be able to vote without obstacles. This legislation will remove obstacles to participation, whether they're obstacles of closing polling places in certain neighborhoods, obstacles of reducing hours that those polling places are open, reducing the number of days for early voting and the rest; it will reduce those obstacles.

We also are protecting the sacred right to vote through Congresswoman Terri Sewell's H.R. 4, which is an offspring of this legislation: the Voting Rights Advancement Act, to secure, again, and restore the Voting Rights Act. It is part of H.R. 1, but it will be taken up separately because of the need to establish the constitutional basis in an ironclad way as we go forward.

And, I'm so pleased, Madam Chair, and I thank you and the House Administration—your committee—reinstating the House Administration Subcommittee on Elections led by Congresswoman Marcia Fudge, which began its out-of-Washington hearings in Brownsville, Texas.

I was just in Texas. People were delighted that your subcommittee came there—that Congresswoman, Chairwoman Fudge's committee came there to hear the stories of voter suppression that exist throughout the country. Especially among people who may have a last name that may sound foreign to some and questionable therefore, to them, but who are American citizens eligible to vote.

And we are cleaning up corruption and ensuring that public officials again work for the people's interests. You can't say it enough. We must pass this legislation so we can break the grip of special interests.

You know we talk about obstacles to participation and suppression of the vote, and we talk about what we talked about earlier, whether it's voting—number of polling places, number of hours, number of days, degree of identification that's required in some areas or more so than in others, different surnames and the rest—but, one of the biggest suppressors of the vote is the suffocation of the airwaves by big, dark, special interest money.

There are some people in this country, I hope none of them in this body, but there are some people in this country who think that the only way to win an election is to suppress the vote—one way or another. And, by bombarding and suffocating the airwaves with information that is not factual, by disrupting elections by putting out messages in the social media that are misleading, these—the resources that make all of this possible are as much a voter suppressor than anything you can name.

So that is why, when we put forth our For the People agenda: one, lower the cost of health care costs by reducing the cost of prescription drugs. Secondly, to increase paychecks. Lower health care costs, bigger paychecks by building the infrastructure of America in a green way.

People have confidence that we could do that because H.R. 1, which was essential to our For the People agenda, would, again, diminish the role of big, special interest money and increasing the voice of every person in our country, including increase the impact of small donor participation in elections.

When we put power back in the hands of the American people, as this legislation does, we can make much more progress on hard issues facing our nation. And the American people know that.

It removes a great deal of skepticism that they have in politics and government. It instills confidence that their voice will be heard, that their cause will be addressed, and that their interest will be served. Again, lowering health care costs by reducing the cost of prescription drugs, people's voices will be heard—a big issue in the election. Increasing paychecks by building infrastructure of America, in a bold, green, modern way. Safeguarding consumer protections, workers' rights, the rights of the LGBTQ community and addressing the concerns of our beautiful Dreamers—in legislation that we'll take up, launch next week.

Protecting clean air, clean water, confronting the climate crisis, and so much more. That has been, and let me add—a bill that we passed last week, which was historic in the House, finally passing a bill for commonsense background checks for gun violence prevention. Again, defying the big money in that arena.

There should be nothing partisan or political about empowering the American people and making sure that government works for them.

Our Founders provided a vision for our country. They wrote a Constitution making us the freest people in the world, a model for the rest of the world. That enabled people—thank God they made it amendable, so that we could expand power and voting rights and the rest.

And what's exciting about this Congress, which has over 100 women in it for the first time, is that in the course of this Congress, we will be celebrating the 100th anniversary of women having the right to vote. But the right to vote must be accompanied by removing obstacles to that participation. And that is what we are doing today.

And how do we answer our Founders, if one day we are meeting them in the next life? How do we say to them, I did everything in my power to suppress the vote? Or do we say, honoring your vision, we removed every obstacle for those who are legitimately eligible to vote to do so, and to have their vote counted as cast.

To honor the oath we take and to honor the people's trust, I strongly urge a bipartisan vote for this bill: For the People.

Source: Pelosi, Nancy. "Pelosi Floor Speech Advocating for H.R. 1, The For The People Act." Office of Nancy Pelosi, Speaker of the House, March 6, 2019. Accessed April 23, 2019. https://www.speaker.gov/newsroom/3619-2/.

Senate Majority Leader McConnell Uses North Carolina Election Fraud to Attack Democrats, 2019

In the weeks following the November 2018 midterm elections, it was discovered that the campaign for North Carolina's Ninth Congressional District waged by Republican winner Mark Harris had engaged in serious absentee ballot fraud. Harris was never sworn in, and when the state board of elections announced that it would hold a new election to fill the ninth district seat, Harris declined to run again.

The scandal was widely seen as a public-relations black eye for Republicans. But on February 26, 2019, Republican Senate Majority Leader Mitch McConnell delivered a floor speech in which he claimed that the unfolding events in North Carolina actually illustrated the pressing need for new voting safeguards and regulations supported by Republicans—and which Democrats almost unanimously opposed. He indicated that the fraud in North Carolina never would have occurred if Democrats weren't so opposed to voter ID laws and other "election security" measures. Following are excerpts from McConnell's floor speech.

Democrats responded angrily to McConnell's remarks, describing his speech as cynical and dishonest political spin. They emphasized that elections experts agreed that the voter ID laws championed by McConnell and other Republicans would have not prevented the absentee ballot fraud in North Carolina. They also accused the majority leader of knowingly conflating voter fraud—which is when a voter casts a vote illegally—with election fraud (when a legitimate vote cast by a legal voter has been changed or otherwise manipulated). In the days following McConnell's speech, several news organizations including the Associated Press and PolitiFact released "fact checks" that described several of McConnell's claims as false or misleading.

Madam President, on a final matter, anyone who has been attentive to the news these past few days has learned about the complete debacle that unfolded in last November's election for North Carolina's Ninth Congressional District. Soon after election day, allegations of illegal ballot harvesting and vote tampering clouded a close result. The wrongdoing seemed to have benefited the Republican candidate over the Democratic. Just last week, we saw the State Board of Elections unanimously call for a new election.

For years and years, every Republican who dared to call for commonsense safeguards for Americans' ballots was demonized by Democrats and their allies. We were hit with leftwing talking points that insisted that voter fraud was not real—it never happens, they said—that fraud just didn't happen and that modest efforts to ensure that voters are who they say they are and are voting in the proper places were really some sinister, rightwing plot to prevent people from voting.

As you might expect, now that an incident of very real voter fraud has become national news and the Republican candidate seems to have benefited, these longstanding Democratic talking points have been really quiet. We haven't heard much lately from the Democrats about how fraud never happens. They have gone silent. Now some are singing a different tune. There is a new interest in ensuring the sanctity of American elections.

I have been focused for decades on protecting the integrity of elections, so I would like to welcome my friends on the left to their new realization. They have just discovered that this subject really matters, but I have yet to see any evidence that they are actually interested in cleaning up the conditions that lead to messes like this one in North Carolina.

At the root of the North Carolina debacle is a practice that is known as ballot harvesting. Essentially, it is a means by which campaign representatives can collect absentee ballots on the premise of delivering them to a polling place or an election office. That is what ballot harvesting is. So think about it. Who in American politics keeps long lists of potential voters? Who mobilizes networks of people to go door-to-door? Who funds and stands up to these kinds of canvassing organizations? Who does those things?

I am sorry to say that there are not huge teams of politically neutral Eagle Scouts who rove the country and hope to use ballot harvesting to politely make voters' lives more convenient. This is not an Eagle Scout activity. The folks who really lick their lips at the prospect of mass ballot harvesting are political operatives, of course—political operatives, interest groups, and one-sided political machines. This is why many jurisdictions, including in North Carolina, have outlawed the practice altogether. I will say that again. Many jurisdictions, including in North Carolina, have outlawed this practice altogether.

Ballot harvesting threatens to change the nature of our representative democracy. Forget about persuading people and spurring them to turn out to the polls; this practice makes elections a kind of scavenger hunt to see which side's operatives can return to headquarters with the most ballots in the trunks of their cars, and once those operatives take ahold of these ballots, the voters have no way to keep tabs on whether they were ever delivered.

Of course, a system that invites political operatives to be rewarded for turning up ballots will open the door to misbehavior. Remember, it is illegal in North Carolina and in most States for the obvious reason, but I have noted with interest that the Democrats' new focus on this practice has yet to extend to California. I wonder why. Well, in California, it is legal. It is a common practice in California. California allows anyone—not just family members but anyone—to show up at polling places on election day with ballots that are not theirs. Welcome to California.

Reports suggest that Orange County alone saw—listen to this—250,000 absentee ballots dropped off on election day last year. The county's registrar told the newspaper that some individuals dropped off hundreds of other people's ballots. We have no way to know if those ballots were sealed or if the people had even voted when they were harvested. The only evidence we have that the voter cast his or her ballot is the signature.

This past election cycle turned out favorably for California Democrats, amazingly enough. These late-arriving ballots seemed to help turn several races their way. Maybe this helps explain why: When House GOP leaders expressed concern over ballot harvesting in California, the State's Democratic secretary of state mocked their concern by saying: "What they call strange and bizarre we call democracy." Now ballot harvesting has thrown out an election result in the U.S. House of Representatives—legal in California, illegal in North Carolina.

Maybe that helps explain why, as it stands, the Democrat Politician Protection Act—Speaker Pelosi's massive new Federal takeover of the way States and communities run their elections—contains no effort whatsoever to crack down on ballot harvesting. It is not in there. Instead, it contains provision after provision that would erode the protections that are supposed to ensure votes reflect the voices of the voters whose names are on the envelopes.

It contains provision after provision that would erode the protections that are supposed to ensure that votes reflect the voice of the voter whose name is on the envelope.

Provision after provision would erode commonsense protections and bring the guardrails down. So would a serious reform bill aimed to take away States' abilities to impose meaningful ID or signature requirements for voters. Would someone concerned about restoring democracy dismiss signature verification as an obstacle to be removed? I don't think so.

Perhaps these facts signal that Democrats see a political advantage in eroding commonsense protections and would rather keep that advantage than make episodes like the North Carolina mess less likely to happen in the future.

An example of real-live voter fraud is staring the country right in the face right now in North Carolina. Yet Democrats choose at this moment to propose a sprawling Federal takeover of election law that would erode the integrity of our elections even further.

So that, I think, pretty well underscores what the priorities of today's Democrat Party is.

Source: McConnell, Mitch. "Voter Fraud." *Congressional Record* [Senate], 165, no. 35, (February 26, 2019): S1447–S1448. Accessed April 23, 2019. https://www.govinfo.gov/content/pkg/CREC-2019-02-26/html/CREC-2019-02-26-pt1-PgS1447-7.htm.

Texas Voter Eligibility Investigation Halted by District Judge, 2019

On January 25, 2019, Texas Secretary of State David Whitley issued a dramatic announcement that his office had discovered that approximately 95,000 non-U.S. citizens living in Texas had matching voting registrations with the state—and that about 58,000 of them had apparently illegally voted in one or more Texas elections (non-American citizens are not eligible to vote in U.S. elections). Whitley vowed to investigate these apparent lawbreakers and refer them to the appropriate authorities for legal action. "Integrity and efficiency of elections in Texas require accuracy of our state's voter rolls," declared Whitley, "and my office is committed to using all available tools under the law to maintain an accurate list of registered voters. Our agency has provided extensive training opportunities to county voter registrars so that they can properly perform list-maintenance activities in accordance with federal and state law, which affords every registered voter the chance to submit proof of eligibility. . . . Eligible Texas voters . . . should not have their voices muted by those who abuse the system."

Texas Attorney General Ken Paxton, President Donald Trump, and numerous conservative media figures treated Whitley's announcement as proof of their claims that voter fraud was rampant across the country and that GOP-led calls for new voting restrictions were based on legitimate concerns about election integrity. But voting rights advocates and many elections experts said that Whitley's findings were deeply flawed. "Whitley compiled his purge list by using Department of Public Safety records to identify individuals who presented documents indicating that they were noncitizens when they obtained or renewed a driver's license," wrote journalist Mark Joseph Stern, who covers legal issues for Slate. "It cross-referenced that list with the voter rolls, and voilà, found 95,000 names that appeared on both. What Whitley did not consider is the fact that more than 50,000 Texans are naturalized each year—and when they gain citizenship, they do not have to inform the Department of Public Safety. Thus, it's overwhelmingly likely that a huge number of people Whitley flagged have become U.S. citizens and are lawful voters" (Stern, "Texas Retracts Claim of Mass Voter Fraud Touted by Trump," Slate, *April 26, 2019).*

One month after Whitley's widely publicized announcement, a district judge shut down the state's purge of voter rolls. On February 27, 2019, District Judge Fred Biery issued a ruling in which he stated that "the evidence has shown . . . that there is no widespread voter fraud" in Texas. He added that while he found Whitley's actions to be a "good faith effort" to protect the integrity of the state's voter rolls, as a result of the state's investigation, "perfectly legal naturalized Americans were burdened with what the court finds to be ham-handed and threatening correspondence from the state which did not politely ask for information but rather exemplifies the power of government to strike fear and anxiety and to intimidate the least powerful among us." Following are excerpts from Biery's court order.

Two months after this ruling, on April 26, 2019, Whitley quietly withdrew his advisory and halted the voter purge his office had begun as part of a settlement with voter rights groups that had filed suit against him and the state of Texas.

Before the Court are a number of preliminary issues related to protecting the integrity of the election process and ensuring the Equal Protection of the laws for all Texans. There is unanimity among the parties, counsel and the Court that non-American are ineligible to vote.

The evidence has shown in a hearing before this Court that there is no widespread voter fraud. The challenge is how to ferret the infinitesimal needles out of the haystack of 15 million Texas voters. The Secretary of State through his dedicated employees, beginning in February 2018, made a good faith effort to transition from a passive process of finding ineligible voters through the jury selection system in each county to a proactive process using tens of thousands of Department of Public Safety driver license records matched with voter registration records. Notwithstanding good intentions, the road to a solution was inherently paved with flawed results, meaning perfectly legal naturalized Americans were burdened with what the Court finds to be ham-handed and threatening correspondence from the state which did not politely ask for information but rather exemplifies the power of government to strike fear and anxiety and to intimidate the last powerful among us. No Native born Americans were subjected to such treatment. . . . Out of 98,000 new American voters on the list, thus far approximately 80 have been identified as ineligible to vote. Almost immediately upon sending the list, the government had an "oops" moment, realizing that 25,000 names should not have been included. It appears this is a solution looking for a problem. Indeed, Secretary of State Whitley has accepted responsibility and apologized for the failure to seek confirmation of the accuracy, appropriateness, competency and due diligence of the process before the rollout. Though promising more transparency, the Secretary has resisted plaintiffs' legal concerns as opposed to entering into an agreed solution precluding further fear and intimidation. . . .

While the Court awaits proposed findings of fact and conclusions of law regarding the preliminary injunction issues, the Court is prepared to address some issues.

Defendants Whitley and Paxton have moved to dismiss, alleging the Court has no jurisdiction and plaintiffs have failed to state a claim. To the extent defendants rely upon state statutes in support of the jurisdictional motion, the Court holds that the United States Constitution trumps state law in appropriate circumstances, this being one. Moreover, given the highly credible evidence presented by the plaintiffs, the Court finds overwhelmingly that claims for relief have been properly stated. Accordingly, defendants' motion to dismiss is DENIED.

Plaintiffs have also sued Attorney General Paxton, whose only involvement shown thus far is a press release, which the Court finds arguably vituperative in tone but nevertheless states the Attorney General's authority and, therefore, without further proof is within his First Amendment right to free speech. Clearly, this statement is not yelling fire in a crowded theater and therefore not subject to being censured. While the Court would prefer that political rhetoric be neutralized to more civil discourse, Article III of the Constitution bestows no power on the federal judiciary to make wishes come true. Accordingly, plaintiffs' request for relief regarding the press release is DENIED.

The court awaits final advice from the individual counties which are parties concerning whether they will agree to pause the process, particularly not sending any notice of examination letters without prior approval of the Court. Local officials can continue to find out if in fact someone is registered who is not a citizen, so long as it is done without communicating directly with any particular individual on the list. In addition, local officials are ORDERED not to remove any person from the current voter registration list until authorized by this Court. As to the first rollout of 98,000, the Secretary of State is ORDERED to tell other counties which are not parties to this litigation, or party counties which will not agree to a pause, not to send any notice of examination letters nor remove voters from registration without prior approval of the Court with a conclusive showing that the person is ineligible to vote.

With reference to the new lists being prepared based on contemporaneous applications for driver licenses and applications to register to vote, the Secretary of State may proceed with the monthly rollouts. However, the Secretary of State is affirmatively ORDERED to advise and direct local voting officials not to send notice of examination letters nor remove voters from registration without prior approval of the Court.

The Court further finds and concludes the Secretary of State, though perhaps unintentionally, created this mess. As Robert Fulghum taught in *All I Really Need to Know I Learned in Kindergarten,* "always put things back where we found them and clean[] up our own messes." . . .

IT IS SO ORDERED.

Source: United States District Court for the Western District of Texas, San Antonio Division. "Order." *Texas League of United Latin American Citizens et al, v. David*

Whitley, in his Official Capacity as Secretary of State for the State of Texas; et al. Civil Action no. SA-19-CA-074-FB. February 27, 2019. Accessed May 6, 2019. https://texascivilrightsproject.org/wp-content/uploads/2019/02/Voter-Purge-MTD-Order.pdf.

Voting Controversies in Georgia Governor's Race Prompts Investigations, Reforms, and New Controversies, 2019

The election for governor in 2018 in the state of Georgia was perhaps the most heated and controversial gubernatorial contest in the entire nation. The contest, which pitted Democratic candidate Stacey Abrams, a liberal black woman, against Republican nominee Brian Kemp, a conservative white man who also served as supervisor of Georgia's elections as the state's sitting secretary of state. In the months leading up to the November 2018 election, Abrams and her supporters repeatedly highlighted the state's removal of hundreds of thousands of citizens from voting rolls for being infrequent voters, as well as other voting restrictions that they said had a disproportionate impact on traditional Democratic voting constituencies. Critics also bitterly criticized Kemp for refusing to step down as secretary of state—or at least recuse himself from all oversight of an election in which he was competing—once he won the Republican nomination for governor. They charged that this decision was a shocking conflict of interest that would diminish public faith in the integrity of the election. Kemp and his supporters, meanwhile, asserted that he was fully capable of carrying out his secretary of state duties in an impartial manner. They also defended the various voter restrictions that Kemp had implemented as necessary steps to combat voter fraud, although they did not cite any actual instances of voter fraud that the state had uncovered.

Election Day in Georgia did nothing to assuage doubts about whether everyone with a legitimate vote had their vote counted. As the day dragged on, reports proliferated of missing votes, problems with absentee ballots, and extremely long lines at polling places in majority black communities, even as large numbers of working voting machines sat idle in warehouses. The furor surrounding these problems was further intensified by the fact that the race between Abrams and Kemp was a very close one. Kemp was eventually declared the winner, but only after narrowly avoiding a mandatory statewide manual recount.

In the months following the election, Abrams pointedly refused to concede, announced her intention to advocate for voting rights across the country, and called Kemp "an architect of voter suppression." For his part, Kemp insisted that he had acted legally throughout the campaign, and Republicans characterized Democratic complaints about the 2018 election as sour grapes.

Nonetheless, after Kemp assumed office in January 2019, he and Republicans in the state legislature quietly set about crafting legislation designed to blunt some of the criticisms—expressed not only in Georgia but around the country—of the state's electoral system. A number of the reforms addressed complaints raised by Democrats about voter registration and eligibility rules and polling place closures and relocations, but the law that was eventually passed by the GOP-controlled legislature and signed by Kemp on April 2, 2019, also authorized Georgia to switch to electronic touchscreen machines statewide. These machines print out paper reproductions of the filled-out ballots, but critics say that such systems are particularly vulnerable to cyberattacks and manipulation—and more expensive than a true paper ballot voting system, despite the assertions of Brad Raffensperger, Kemp's successor as secretary of state.

At the same time that this election reform bill wound its way through the Georgia General Assembly, Democratic leaders of the U.S. House of Representatives announced their intention to investigate the controversies that swirled around the 2018 election. On March 6, 2019, the chairs of the House Committee on Oversight and Reform and the Subcommittee on Civil Rights and Civil Liberties sent letters to Kemp and Raffensperger demanding a wide range of documents related to reported voting problems experienced by Georgians in the 2018 election. They set a deadline of March 20 for delivery of those documents, which was not met by Kemp or Raffensperger. But as of late April 2019, the leaders of the House investigation said that Georgia officials had assured them that they would cooperate fully with the inquiry.

Following are two documents related to the 2018 election in Georgia and its aftermath. The first is the letter of inquiry that was sent to Governor Kemp by the House Subcommittee on Civil Rights and Civil Liberties. The second is a press release from the office of Secretary of State Raffensperger extolling the election reform bill that the state's GOP-led legislature crafted in the wake of the tumultuous 2018 election.

Letter from Elijah E. Cummings, Chairman, Committee on Oversight and Reform, and Jamie Raskin, Subcommittee on Civil Rights and Civil Liberties, to Georgia Governor Brian P. Kemp

Dear Governor Kemp:

The Committee on Oversight and Reform is investigating recent reports of serious problems with voter registration, voter access, and other matters affecting the ability of people in Georgia to exercise their right to vote. The Committee is particularly concerned by reports that Georgians faced unprecedented challenges with registering to vote and significant barriers to casting their votes during your tenure as Secretary of State and during the 2018 election.

For example, under your leadership, the Secretary of State's Office reportedly cancelled voter registrations for more than 1.4 million Georgians, including 670,000 in 2017 alone. In 2018, 53,000 Georgians, most of them minorities, who tried to register had their applications placed on hold by your office.

In addition, county and state officials have closed more than 200 polling places across Georgia since 2012. Officials reportedly considered closing nearly all polling sites in one majority African American county, although they ultimately relented after public scrutiny. In other counties with significant minority populations, voters waited for hours to cast their ballots, even though hundreds of available voting machines sat unused in government warehouses. In addition, a recent report found an unusually high number of "undervotes" for Lieutenant Governor among African American voters in the 2018 general election.

For these reasons, please provide the following documents by March 20, 2019, for the time period from January 1, 2017, through the present:

1. All communications related to any voter roll purges, list maintenance activity, or other government actions to remove voters from the rolls or cancel registrations pursuant to Georgia's "use it or lose it" law, O.C.G.A. Section 21-2-234, including the voter roll purge conducted in July 2017, which reportedly resulted in more than 500,000 people being removed from Georgia's voter rolls for inactivity;
2. All communications related to the placement of voter registration applications on hold or in pending status under the Secretary of State's "exact match" policy interpretation of the Georgia voter registration statute, O.C.G.A. Section 21-2-22-.1.6, or any other efforts to delay or deny approval of voter registrations in advance of the 2018 elections;
3. All documents related to closing, moving, or consolidating polling sites, including:
   a. Any consideration of the close of polling sites in Randolph County or other locations in Georgia;
   b. Any consideration of using the Americans with Disabilities Act as a basis for closing polling sites or limiting polling site hours; and
   c. Any communications with or regarding consultants hired by state or local officials in connection with this issue;
4. All documents related to the sequestration of voting machines, or other actions that prevented voting machines from being used on Election Day, including the sequestration of voting machines in Cobb, DeKalb, Fulton, or other counties;
5. All documents related to undervotes or drop-offs in voting rates in any state or federal races in the 2018 general election, including with respect to the Lieutenant governor race or other races;
6. All documents related to your ethical or legal obligations or possible conflicts of interest while simultaneously running for Governor and overseeing the state's elections as Georgia's Secretary of State; and
7. All documents related to the allegation by the Georgia Secretary of State's Office on November 3, 2018, that there had been a failed attempt to hack the state's voter registration system, and that the Secretary of State's Office had opened an investigation into the Democratic Party of Georgia.

For purposes of this request, please produce responsive communications involving:

- You, during your terms as Secretary of State, Governor, and time in between;

- Officials in the Georgia Governor's Office;
- Senior officials or managers at the Georgia Secretary of State's Office, including anyone in the Secretary's leadership team, Election Division management, or others;
- Georgia county election officials;
- Federal officials or officials from other states;
- Anyone affiliated with your gubernatorial campaign or any other campaign in the 2018 election;
- Anyone affiliated with a local, state, or federal political party;
- Anyone affiliated with a group that made political expenditures in the 2018 election;
- Employees of any election equipment vendors, including Election Systems & Software (ES&S); or
- Anyone affiliated with any other outside group.

The Committee on Oversight and Reform is the principal oversight committee of the House of Representatives and has broad authority to investigate "any matter" at "any time" under House Rule X. The Committee has examined state voting and elections issues on numerous occasions, including multiple hearings in the 115th Congress on federal and state election security efforts. In addition, the Subcommittee on Civil Rights and Civil Liberties has oversight jurisdiction over voting rights issues under Committee Rules. . . .

Thank you for your attention to this matter.

Sincerely,

Elijah E. Cummings
Chairman
House Committee on Oversight and Reform

Jamie Raskin
Chairman
Subcommittee on Civil Rights and Civil Liberties

Georgia House Passes Bipartisan Bill for More Secure, Accessible, and Transparent Elections (Press Release)

Republican leaders in the House of Representatives took the first step in bringing Georgia's voters a more secure, accessible, and transparent election system. House Bill 316 (HB 316), which passed yesterday with bipartisan support, would update Georgia's aging voting machines and introduce new reforms to expand access and ease of voting for registered, eligible voters.

"HB 316 is a bipartisan bill which prioritizes the interests of our communities and represents a victory for the common-sense solutions which are supported overwhelmingly by Georgia's voters and elections officials," said Secretary of State Brad Raffensperger. "Chairman Fleming and Members of the House should be applauded for responding to partisan rhetoric and accusations with a real plan for progress."

The bill provides for touchscreen-marked paper ballots and will transition our state to a deliberately-designed election system with a paper ballot, so that voters can rest assured with physical proof that their choice has been counted at the ballot box. The bill also introduces new measures to keep voters on the rolls longer and to cut back on human error in the voter registration process—bringing new voters into the fold and keeping more Georgians eligible to vote.

"HB 316 is the next step in a long line of voter-centric reforms that have enabled better elections for our voters, and I am proud to lead efforts to keep Georgia moving on a bright path forward," said Chairman Barry Fleming. "This legislation will guarantee ballot access for every eligible voter while protecting election integrity and prioritizing transparency—while also keeping more hard-earned money in our taxpayers' pockets."

HB 316 has been transmitted to the Georgia Senate for consideration.

Sources: Committee on Oversight and Reform, U.S. House of Representatives. "Chairmen Seek Documents from Georgia Governor and Secretary of State on Reports of Voter Suppression." March 6, 2019. Accessed April 23, 2019. https://oversight.house.gov/news/press-releases/chairmen-seek-documents-from-georgia-governor-and-secretary-of-state-on-reports; Office of Georgia Secretary of State Brad Raffensperger. "Georgia House Passes Bipartisan Bill for More Secure, Accessible, and Transparent Elections." February 27, 2019. Accessed April 23, 2019. http://sos.ga.gov/index.php/elections/georgia_house_passes_bipartisan_bill_for_more_secure_accessible_and_transparent_elections.

Index

About the Editor

Bridgett A. King, PhD, is an assistant professor and director of the Master of Public Administration Program at Auburn University. She teaches graduate and undergraduate courses in state institutions and policy, public policy, and diversity in public administration. Her research focuses on political participation, voter disenfranchisement, and citizen perceptions of the electoral system. Formerly a voting rights researcher in the Democracy Program at the Brennan Center for Justice at New York University, she contributes regularly to the Election Center Certified Election/Registration Administrator Program (CERA) and is an affiliated researcher with the Public Affairs Research Council of Alabama (PARCA).